CISTERCIAN STUDIES SERIES: NUMBER ONE HUNDRED SEVENTY-NINE

THE
CISTERCIAN ABBEYS
OF BRITAIN

Far from the Concourse of Men

edited by

David Robinson

with contributions by

Janet Burton, Nicola Coldstream, Glyn Coppack,
Richard Fawcett and David Robinson

Cistercian Publications

Kalamazoo, Michigan - Spencer, Massachusetts

Design by Icon Design
Printed in Indonesia

Published by B. T. Batsford Ltd
583 Fulham Road, London, SW6 5BY
Published in the United States by
Cistercian Publications, WMU Station, Kalamazoo, Michigan

ISBN 0 87907 779 4

Front Cover

A detail of early thirteenth-century capitals in the east processional doorway at
Valle Crucis Abbey in Wales
(Photograph by Paul Highnam for Cadw: Welsh Historic Monuments).

Back Cover and Above

A fifteenth-century painting of St Bernard of Clairvaux (d. 1153), depicted as the founder of abbeys.
Bernard's name dominates the early history of the Cistercian order
(By courtesy of Musée des Beaux-Arts, Dijon).

CONTENTS

PREFACE

Nine hundred years ago, a group of twenty-one dissenting monks, headed by their abbot, Robert (d. 1110), quit the prosperous Burgundian abbey of Molesme and went in search of a new location where they might follow a life of true austerity and perfect solitude. In tradition, on 21 March 1098 (the feast of St Benedict), the rather bedraggled group of companions settled in a heavily wooded area south of the great ducal city of Dijon. It was a place which was to be remembered and graphically described as one 'of horror — a vast wilderness'. And it was here that the brothers began to cut down the thickets and to erect the temporary wooden buildings of what they called simply the *Novum Monasterium*, the 'New Monastery'. Unaware of it, they had sown the seeds of the Cistercian adventure.

The fledgling community had one very simple and clear objective. 'You should know', wrote Hugh of Lyons to Pope Paschal II (1099–1118), 'that they come from a place which is called the New Monastery. They migrated to that place ... in order to lead a stricter and more consecrated life according to the Rule of blessed Benedict'. Indeed, such was the uncompromising approach to this most celebrated of monastic codes, it meant for an especially harsh early regime at the house. More than once, poverty pushed Robert of Molesme's experiment close to extinction. The turning point came early during the abbacy of Stephen Harding (1109–34), with recruitment and growth undoubtedly transformed following the arrival of the charismatic Bernard 'of Clairvaux' at the gates of the New Monastery in 1112–13.

Eventually, as Janet Burton explains in her account of the adventure, the New Monastery was soon to be given the name Cîteaux, and it was the Latin form — *Cistercium* — which gave identity to the emerging Cistercian order. Commonly known as the 'White Monks' (after the colour of their habits), as they began to disperse across Europe, the fame of the Cistercians grew enormously. 'The story spread everywhere', a thirteenth-century chronicler was moved to record, 'that men of outstanding holiness and perfect religion had come from a far land ... soon they grew into a great company'. By the time of St Bernard's death in 1153, almost 340 Cistercian abbeys had been founded, and the total was eventually to rise to more than 700. In many ways, they might be considered pioneers of the European ideal. In all, their achievement was staggering, quite without parallel in western monasticism, and one of the most remarkable phenomena in the life of the medieval church.

It is perhaps the architectural legacy left to us by the White Monks which provides the most tangible evidence of their extraordinary and intensely personal form of religious life. As Nicola Coldstream reminds us, Cistercian monasteries were built to last. Their remains continue to grace some of the most beautiful valleys in Britain. And, given that so many sites are in State care, in concert with the nonacentenary itself, colleagues at Cadw: Welsh Historic Monuments, English Heritage, and Historic Scotland, felt it was very much this architectural legacy which should be celebrated through the publication of a full gazetteer of all eighty-six British abbeys. Even in ruins, several of the larger churches rank among the very finest monastic remains to be seen anywhere in Europe. Taken as a whole, the British corpus of Cistercian buildings stands second to none.

The idea of producing a book to coincide with the 1998 anniversary first emerged a few years ago. Not surprisingly, the coordination of its production has involved drawing together many diverse strands, incurring numerous debts of gratitude along the way. To begin with, at Cadw: Welsh Historic Monuments, Tom Cassidy, Andrew Hood, and Richard Avent gave the support which allowed the project to get off the ground, and they have since provided great encouragement along the way. David Breeze, at Historic Scotland, and Valerie Horsler, at English Heritage, were also enormously helpful. At Batsford, it was the enthusiasm of Monica Kendall which did so much in the early stages to ensure the success of the venture. More recently, Naomi Roth has been extremely patient as deadlines have come and gone.

Meanwhile, a host of museums and other bodies, as well as many friends and colleagues, have provided illustrations, information on particular sites, or have simply been agreeably helpful. In this respect, I should especially like to thank Sally Abrahams, Grenville Astill, Michael Aston, Graham Brown, Stuart Harrison, Cathy Houghton, John Kenyon, Bill Klemperer, Richard Morris, John Newman, Andrew Pye, Malcolm Thurlby, and the brothers at Buckfast Abbey. Unless they are otherwise credited, all other illustrations are from the photographic libraries at Cadw: Welsh Historic Monuments, English Heritage and Historic Scotland.

Nicola Coldstream would like to thank Peter Fergusson, Stuart Harrison and Glyn Coppack for so generously allowing her to read parts of their important study on Rievaulx before publication. Her discussion of the thirteenth-century building is based on Peter Fergusson's work, and all the ideas about Cistercian shrines and their significance for the presbytery of Rievaulx are his. Any errors are hers. Peter Fergusson has, in addition, over many hours of discussion, helped to clarify many of the issues raised in the architecture chapter. Of course, as the content of gazetteer entries confirms, everyone who studies Cistercian architecture in Britain is deeply in Professor Fergusson's debt.

Two other colleagues at Cadw: Welsh Historic Monuments, Christine Kenyon and Angela Piccini, have helped in a variety of ways during the production of the book. The whole layout is so much the better for they having looked at it with critical eyes. I should also like to mention three other highly creative people whose contributions have so enhanced the appearance and value of the work. Paul Highnam has taken many of the handsome new photographs of both English and Welsh sites; Pete Lawrence has done wonders in so many aspects of the production of the maps and plans; and Androulla Webb has brought everything together in the most striking of designs.

Finally, I would like to offer warm thanks to my four co-authors for the great enthusiasm they brought to the project, and for the good cheer with which they met the tight deadlines.

Cardiff   David M. Robinson
21 March 1998

THE CISTERCIAN ADVENTURE

by
Janet Burton

The beginnings of monastic life lay in the deserts of Egypt and Palestine in the third and fourth centuries AD, as men and women fled the concerns of society to follow a life of solitude and prayer. Some lived alone, as hermits; others banded together to form small groups, allowing a measure of communal support in their spiritual endeavours. Both these ideals — of solitary and communal monasticism — spread to the West, where monasteries, communities in which men and women drawn to a life of prayer and worship could pursue their spiritual vocation in retreat from society, came to be a familiar part of the landscape of medieval Europe.

During the first centuries of monasticism in the West, there was a variety of patterns of life which monks and nuns could follow. However, from the ninth century, for the vast majority of houses, the basis of observance was the *Rule of St Benedict*, a blueprint for the everyday life and government of a religious community compiled by Benedict of Nursia, probably between AD 535 and 550, for his monastery at Monte Cassino. The 'little rule for beginners', as Benedict himself called it, laid down a carefully regulated yet demanding lifestyle. The monastic day was constructed around eight offices of corporate worship (known as the *Opus Dei*, or 'Work of God'), which began with the Night Office at around 2.00 a.m. The services were punctuated by periods of reading and meditation (*lectio divina*) and manual labour. These activities melded together: meditation led to private prayer; and work, whether domestic, craft, or agricultural, was at one and the same time a token of humility, an act of worship, and an economic necessity. Even eating had a spiritual significance, and meals were taken without conversation, and to the accompaniment of suitable reading.

However, the concept of the monastic life was not static. By the eleventh century, emphasis was being placed more on the liturgical function of monks; those who remained 'in the world' perceived monastic communities as 'powerhouses of prayer' in which monks as spiritual soldiers interceded and fought against the devil for the souls of humankind. More time was therefore spent at the *Opus Dei*, and work was squeezed out of the daily routine. Moreover, social attitudes had changed, and many saw manual labour as the preserve of peasants, and unsuitable for monks, whose vocation was prayer. These developments can best be seen in the most successful of all monasteries in the tenth and eleventh centuries, Cluny (Saône-et-Loire), which spread its customs, its own particular concept of the monastic life, to its hundreds of affiliated monasteries throughout Europe. At Cluny the services expanded in number and length until they filled virtually the whole day, leaving little time for other activities beyond the tasks necessary for the management of a large corporation. The phrase which became associated with Cluny was 'the beauty of

Above: *A thirteenth-century fresco of St Benedict of Nursia at Subiaco in Italy. The saint is depicted holding a copy of his* Rule, *probably written between AD 535 and 550. It was the* Rule of St Benedict *which provided the supreme guide for the Cistercian way of life (Scala, Florence).*

Left: *A fifteenth-century manuscript illustration depicting St Bernard preaching to his monks in the chapter house at Clairvaux. In many ways, Bernard was the driving force behind the expansion of the Cistercian order in the second quarter of the twelfth century (Musée Condé, Chantilly, Ms. 71, f. 36).*

holiness', the enrichment of worship by elaborate chanting, fine vestments, rich ornaments and splendid buildings.

The late eleventh and twelfth centuries, a period of intellectual ferment, religious renewal and economic prosperity, brought with them both reaction to contemporary practices and an explosion of new forms of monastic life. There were many catalysts for growth and reform. Among the most powerful were the desire to return to primitive monasticism, and an emphasis on the eremitical, or solitary aspect of monasticism. Of all these experiments, the Cistercian was the most spectacular and the most successful.

THE FOUNDATION OF CÎTEAUX

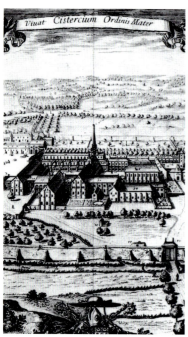

The origins of the Cistercian order are to be traced to the foundation of Cîteaux, on the edge of the Côte d'Or in Burgundy, in 1098. This engraving by P. Brissard shows the abbey about 1674. Cîteaux was suppressed in 1790, and was subsequently destroyed (Bibliothèque Nationale, Paris).

The origins of the Cistercian order are to be found in the events of 1098 at a prosperous monastery in Burgundy named Molesme, which had been founded some twenty years earlier by its abbot, Robert (d. 1110). Robert was a restless man, constantly searching for a more satisfying spiritual life. In 1098, he led a group of monks from Molesme to found another monastery at Cîteaux, just fourteen miles (22.5km) south of the important ecclesiastical centre of Dijon (Côte-d'Or). What happened to provoke that secession is recorded in two narrative sources, the *Exordium Parvum* ('The Little Beginning'), and the shorter *Exordium Cistercii* ('The Origin of Cîteaux').[1] The dating of these narratives has posed considerable problems for historians. At the core of each, however, seems to be an account — no longer extant — of the foundation of Cîteaux compiled around 1119, which was later worked into the *Exordium Cistercii* (possibly at Clairvaux in 1123 or 1124), and into the *Exordium Parvum* possibly around 1150.[2] It is important to remember, therefore, that what these accounts present are retrospective reconstructions, reworkings of how a primitive *Exordium* may have documented the origins of Cîteaux. Even this earliest hypothetical source would itself have been a later view of events, seen from twenty years after the foundation. The two surviving documents differ somewhat in their emphases. The *Exordium Cistercii* suggests that Robert's discomfort was caused by the wealth and prosperity which Molesme had achieved, and by the feeling that 'possessions and virtue do not usually sit well together'. The *Exordium Parvum* stresses that Robert and his companions were dissatisfied with the failure of the community of Molesme to observe the *Rule of St Benedict*. These two explanations are not incompatible, and they reflect motives that gave rise to other monastic movements of the period, such as the orders of Tiron and Savigny in northern France, or the congregations of Vallombrosa and Camaldoli within Tuscany in Italy, and, perhaps most famous of all, La Grande Chartreuse (Isère) in the French Alps, fountain of the Carthusian order. These, too, were inspired both by a desire to return to more primitive monastic observances (those of the desert monks, and the *Rule of St Benedict*, stripped of the accretions which it had acquired in the centuries since its composition), and a desire to follow a life of poverty, a distaste for the wealth and landed possessions enjoyed by successful Benedictine monasteries.

Fuelled by this twin impulse, Robert and the twenty or twenty-one monks who left Molesme with him settled in the diocese of Chalons-sur-Saône, at a location described by the *Exordium Cistercii* as 'a place of horror, a vast wilderness' — imagery which evoked the deserts of the East, and was to become a feature of Cistercian writings. That Robert enjoyed support for this enterprise did not, of

1   Lekai 1977; Bouton and Van Damme 1985; Matarraso 1993
2   Auberger 1986; Holdsworth 1986a

itself, guarantee that the 'New Monastery' as it was first known, would prosper, and indeed the community encountered difficulties. The monks who had remained at Molesme, deprived not only of their abbot but also of their senior brothers, petitioned the pope for Robert's return. Robert was forced to agree, and the former prior of Molesme, Alberic, became abbot of Cîteaux (1099–1109) in his place. On his death, Alberic was succeeded by an Englishman, Stephen Harding (1109–34), another monk of Molesme whose career, which began in the monastery of Sherborne in Dorset, was that of a man searching for a more satisfying spiritual experience. After many years, it was at Cîteaux that he was to find fulfilment.

Life in the new monastery was difficult. Although the local lord, the duke of Burgundy, gave assistance in constructing buildings, the austere lifestyle of the monks did not initially prove attractive to recruits, nor to those benefactors on whose endowments monasteries generally relied. The turning point appears to have come early in the abbacy of Stephen Harding. Grants of land were received, and recruits began to arrive, so that by 1113 numbers had grown sufficiently for a second monastery, La Ferté (Saône-et-Loire), to be founded. In 1113, too, there arrived at Cîteaux the man who was to become perhaps the most famous Cistercian of all, a young nobleman named Bernard of Fontaines. Bernard brought with him to Cîteaux a string of relatives and friends whom his own enthusiasm had persuaded to renounce the world. The growing number of novices led to further foundations: Pontigny (Yonne) in 1114; and Morimond (Haute-Marne) and Clairvaux (Aube) in 1115. Bernard himself was founding abbot of Clairvaux, and was to remain in that office until his death in 1153.

Accordingly, fifteen years after the monks left Molesme for their 'desert', Cîteaux began to acquire a family. This was not unprecedented. Cluny, for instance, had gathered to itself a great monastic empire of dependent priories throughout Europe. What was revolutionary about the Cistercians, however, was that they developed into an order with a constitution. This was the work, even the genius, of Stephen Harding.

It was in 1119 that Stephen presented to Pope Calixtus II the *Carta Caritatis*, 'The Charter of Love', which was in effect the constitution of the order. By this time the Cistercian family had spread to the third generation. Clairvaux had founded Trois Fontaines (Marne) in 1118, and Fontenay (Côte-d'Or) in 1119; Morimond sent monks to Bellevaux (Haute-Saône, 1119) and Pontigny to Bouras (1119). Stephen was determined that the young family should not drift apart, but be held together by the bonds of love and a common observance. The *Carta* is uncompromising about the need for uniformity:

Therefore we will and command that everyone should observe the Rule of St Benedict *in all matters just as it is observed in the New Monastery. No-one is to add any other interpretation to a reading of the holy rule, but understand it and hold to it as our ancestors, the holy fathers, the monks of the New Monastery, understood and held to it, and as we do today.*

Stephen did not stop at an expression of uniformity, but put in place two quite novel devices for ensuring the unity of the order. These were the annual General Chapter, and the process of annual visitation. Quite when the first Chapter was held is uncertain — it may have been in 1115 when the third and fourth daughter houses

Founded in 1114, Pontigny was the second daughter house of Cîteaux. The abbey church survives (David Robinson).

St Bernard was the founding abbot of Clairvaux in 1115. Traces of the abbey structures survive amid the later buildings which now serve as a prison (David Robinson).

STEPHEN HARDING AND THE FORMATION OF THE CISTERCIAN ORDER

In this manuscript illumination of 1111 from Cîteaux, a monk (possibly Stephen Harding) lies at the feet of an angel (Bibliothèque Municipale, Dijon, Ms. 170, f. 6v).

St Stephen Harding (d. 1134) in a manuscript illustration of about 1125. The saint is portrayed holding a representation of his abbey church (Bibliothèque Municipale, Dijon, Ms. 130, f. 104).

THE DEVELOPMENT OF A CISTERCIAN PHILOSOPHY

had been founded — but after 1119 it was regularized, and all abbots were required to present themselves at Cîteaux once a year at a date which came to be established as the feast of the Exaltation of the Holy Cross (14 September). The initial purpose was to provide a regular opportunity for the renewal of the ties of love and mutual support which Stephen saw as the basis of the Cistercian life. In time, however, the Chapter became the forum for the development of legislation, and the disciplinary body of the order. Visitation was the second means of strengthening the bond between Cistercian houses. Once a year the abbot of each mother house was obliged to visit all daughter houses founded from his abbey to ensure that all was well. Cîteaux itself was not exempt, but visited by the abbots of its four eldest daughters. In time the phenomenal growth of the Cistercian order and its wide geographical dispersal made attendance by all abbots at the Chapter, and the visitation of all daughter houses each year, impossible, so that modifications had to be made. However, the result of the far-sightedness of Stephen and his contemporaries was the most cohesive monastic congregation ever, and perhaps the first true monastic order.

The Cistercian expansion continued unabated after 1119, as Cîteaux and its four eldest daughters sent out more colonies; and the families spread into yet another generation. In 1120 the order began to disperse beyond the confines of its Burgundian heartland. La Ferté sent colonies to Tigletio (1120) in the diocese of Genoa, and Locedio (1124) in the diocese of Vercelli; while Morimond established daughters in Germany at Camp (1123) and Ebrach (1127) and a granddaughter, via Bellevaux, at Lucelle in Alsace (1124). The Cistercian order was on its way to becoming a truly international organization.

In 1098, and in the years which followed, it might have seemed that the Cistercians did not differ markedly from other contemporary reform movements. However, in the next three decades they developed a philosophy, or ideology, by which they distinguished themselves from other monks. The hallmark of Cistercian monastic observance, as articulated in the *Carta Caritatis* and the *Exordium Parvum*, was a literal observance of the *Rule of St Benedict*. These insisted that their monks follow the guidelines provided by the *Rule* about food and drink, taking two simple meals a day (one in winter). Their clothing was to be plain and inexpensive, and furs and fine linen were forbidden. They pruned the liturgy, thus allowing manual labour to be restored to the timetable.

All this speaks of a desire for a strict interpretation of the *Rule*; but in their search for a pure form of monastic life the Cistercians sometimes went beyond the *Rule*, and placed their own interpretations and constructions on it. Moreover, the Cistercian desire for uniformity meant that, as they developed new ideas about observances and practices, they could not leave their implementation to chance. The General Chapter therefore became the governing body of the order, passing statutes (*statuta*) which could be added to the growing corpus of regulations. These first seem to have been brought together in around 1150,[3] and the sequence of legislation is therefore not entirely clear. We have to see the first half of the twelfth century as a period of evolution. A Cistercian philosophy, or identity, was not created in 1098, or even in 1119, but developed over the years, sometimes in response to changing circumstances.

3 Auberger 1986; Holdsworth 1986a
4 Lekai 1977; Bouton and Van Damme 1985

It was probably from the very beginning of Cistercian expansion, however, that the monks rejected the urban locations common among Benedictine houses. Cîteaux itself was founded in a 'desert', and the Cistercians insisted that their monasteries be founded 'not in towns or around fortified places or in villages, but in places far from the concourse of men'.[4] Further regulations concerning new foundations were drawn up. Each was to be established with a minimum of twelve monks and an abbot; certain buildings were to be in place before a site was occupied; each house was to be provided with the same books; and all monasteries were to be dedicated to the Blessed Virgin Mary, the 'Queen of Heaven and Earth'.

Under Stephen Harding a puritanical attitude towards the furnishing of monastic churches developed. Although Stephen appears to have enjoyed the beauty of manuscript illumination, he was firm in his belief that church furnishings, and the ornaments and vestments to be used in services, were to be plain. An early statute reads: 'Every ornament, vessel and utensil of the monastery must be without gold, silver or precious stones, except the chalice and the communion reed. We are allowed to have these two things made of silver or of gold-plate, but never of pure gold'. Stephen brought to Cistercian philosophy an austerity which characterized their early buildings.

In the matter of recruitment, the Cistercians introduced an important modification of the *Rule*. Benedict had made provision for both adult entrants to the monastic life, and oblates — children placed by their parents in a monastery to receive their education and later take vows. The Cistercians set their faces against this, and insisted that the monastic vocation be a matter of personal volition. They therefore brought to an end the practice of child oblates, and placed a minimum age

A Cistercian monk illustrated in an English thirteenth-century chronicle which records the foundation of Cîteaux in 1098 (British Library, Cotton Nero Ms. D II, f. 108r).

This thirteenth-century English manuscript illustration depicts events of early Cistercian history. On the left, Stephen Harding commissions a group of monks to found new abbeys. On the right, the abbots of Le Ferté, Clairvaux (St Bernard), Pontigny, and Morimond are shown with their churches. The group of working monks at the centre reminds us of the importance of manual labour in the early Cistercian ideal (Cambridge University Library, Ms. Mm. 5. 31, f. 113r).

(fifteen) on novices. This provides a clue to their distinctive interpretation of the *Rule of St Benedict*. They concentrated not just on externals, but on the very concept of being a monk. Cistercian writings stress the individual monk and his goal. The monastic community was still of extreme importance, but as the context for individual growth, and less as a corps of soldiers fighting humanity's spiritual and penitential battles. The community was the leaven for the growth of the individual.[5]

The Cistercians also came to be distinctive in their attitude towards economic matters, and recent years have witnessed much debate among historians about the development of their ideas in this area.[6] As the section of society entrusted with praying for the welfare of humankind, monks were customarily supported by donations of land and other economic assets from the laity. As a result, by the eleventh century, many monasteries had become wealthy institutions. They were landowners and landlords in town and countryside, and thus a part of the economic framework of society. They were patrons of parish churches, which they might appropriate to their own use. Those which were town-based were closely linked to the urban economy. The Cistercians deliberately rejected such contact with society, not only by physically placing themselves 'far from the concourse of men', and by limiting the use of Cistercian monasteries as places of hospitality. They extended the ideal of seclusion also by rejecting the types of economic asset which would bring them into contact with secular society. For example, they early came to shun the possession of churches and the revenues these might bring with them, including tithes; and they would not accept assets such as ovens and mills which others would

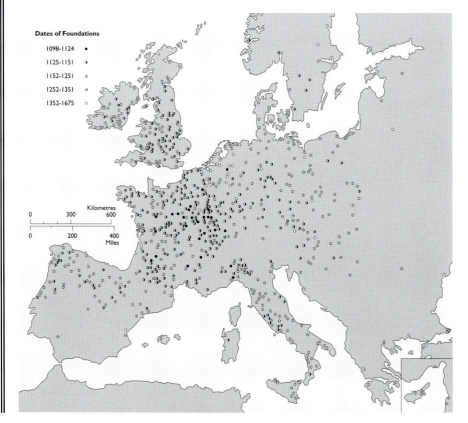

Dates of Foundations

1098–1124	●
1125–1151	○
1152–1251	◉
1252–1351	◎
1352–1675	○

5   Newman 1996
6   Auberger 1986; Berman 1986; Berman 1992; Bouchard 1988; Bouchard 1991

be forced to pay to use. The reason for these rejections was an unwillingness to profit from revenues which should have supported others — tithes were meant for the parish priest and for the poor and not for monks. They further refused manors, a traditional form of landholding which entitled the lord to the unpaid labour of peasants. Instead, they developed an economy based on the direct exploitation of land.

By the mid-twelfth century a distinctive attitude towards economic matters had become a plank of Cistercian ideology, not only in their insistence on land as the only form of endowment which they were prepared to accept, but in the way in which they managed their estates through granges, or outlying farms, and the way in which these were staffed. The challenge which had faced the Cistercians was how to exploit their estates effectively, and yet preserve their seclusion from society in order to fulfil their spiritual role without distraction; their answer was the *conversi*. In traditional monastic usage a *conversus* (plural *conversi*) was one who had come to the monastic life as an adult. The Cistercian *conversi*, however, were not monks, but lay men who were taken into the monastery to work, rather than to pray. Although not monks, they were regarded as full members of Cistercian communities, and took vows as monks did. They made a lifelong commitment to their house and to the order. The Cistercians were the first order to exploit this new type of 'quasi-monk' effectively, and, in their development of the *conversi*, opened the monastic vocation to a class of society to whom it had hitherto been largely denied. In a time of rising population and shortages of land, the security of life within a Cistercian abbey must have been an appealing prospect.

The early history of the Cistercian order is dominated by the name of St Bernard. In some measure this is because of the way in which the Cistercians themselves represented their own past. Bernard was recognized in his own day as a major figure, and it is not therefore surprising that Cistercian writings accorded him a prominent role in the history of the order. Texts such as the *Vita Prima*, the earliest life of Bernard, consciously elevated his status; it is still not certain, for instance, whether Bernard — as the *Vita Prima* suggests — came to Cîteaux in 1112 (and was therefore responsible for the initial expansion of the order) or in 1113, when numbers had already grown sufficiently for the first daughter house to be founded. Nevertheless, his importance in developing and defining a Cistercian identity was significant. This definition grew, in part, out of controversy. By the early 1120s the Cistercians had emerged as rivals to traditional monasticism. They were attracting recruits, and probably patrons, from other houses, and by their very stance against what was current practice they appeared critical of Cluny. They themselves claimed to be the upholders of the true monastic tradition, but they were open to the accusations of 'novelty' and arrogance. An early example of the turmoil into which Cîteaux had thrown the monastic world comes from Bernard's own family. His nephew, Robert, took vows as a Cistercian monk, but was later persuaded by the prior of Cluny that his parents had promised him as a youth to Cluny, and that this vow took precedence over Robert's own. He therefore left the Cistercian life for the Cluniac. In a long letter written in an attempt to persuade Robert to return, Bernard set Cistercian and Cluniac practices side by side, and concluded that Cistercian austerity rather than Cluniac indulgence and softness, was the way to Heaven.

Two monks shown splitting a log in a Cîteaux manuscript completed in 1111 (Bibliothèque Municipale, Dijon, Ms. 170, f. 59r).

ST BERNARD AND THE DEVELOPMENT OF CISTERCIAN IDENTITY

An early thirteenth-century manuscript illustration of St Bernard writing, inspired by the hand of God. Two pupils or novices are shown at his feet (Bodleian Library, Oxford, Ms. Laud Misc. 385, f. 41v).

Right: *Founded by Bishop William Giffard of Winchester in 1128, Waverley Abbey was the earliest Cistercian plantation in Britain.*

'Arise, soldier of Christ, I say arise. Shake off the dust and return to the battle. You will fight more gloriously after your flight, and you will conquer more gloriously', he wrote.[7]

The differences between Cîteaux and Cluny led to a 'war of polemic' in which both parties produced tracts which justified their way of life. One of the earliest was Bernard's *Apologia* (1125),[8] in which he roundly condemned abuses in the monastic life: excesses in clothing, and food and drink, which he associated with Cluny. He railed at monks who dressed in habits made from fine fabrics, whose meals comprised several elaborately prepared courses, and who drank wine excessively and for pleasure rather than in moderation. He also condemned — in a monastic context — the use of gold and silver, unnecessarily large churches, and images in church and cloister which would distract the monk from his worship and contemplation. Although plainness in church decoration and ornament had become a feature of Cistercian practice under Stephen Harding, it was the *Apologia* that articulated and defined the austerity in architecture so characteristic of the White Monks. Superfluity in size and decoration was to be strictly avoided.

St Bernard was an eloquent writer and speaker and a charismatic figure. He was an important factor in the development of Cistercian thought. Moreover, as a figure of European stature, he also did much to raise the profile of the order. He corresponded with popes, kings and bishops, preached the Second Crusade (1147) and launched the military order of Knights Templar. He intervened in ecclesiastical matters throughout Europe, and in 1145 his pupil, Bernard Paganelli, as Eugenius III (1145–53), became the first Cistercian to rise to the office of pope. In many ways the period between the death of Stephen Harding in 1134 and that of Bernard in 1153 saw the hub or focus of the order pass from Cîteaux to Clairvaux. In 1153 the roll call of Cistercian houses stood at around 340, of which as many as 183 derived from the family of Clairvaux. By 1200 there were to be more than 500 abbeys, and the eventual total stood at upwards of 700.

THE FIRST CISTERCIAN FOUNDATIONS IN BRITAIN 1128–32

In 1128 the Cistercians made their first landfall in Britain, when a colony from l'Aumône (Loir-et-Cher), invited by Bishop William Giffard of Winchester (1107–29), settled at Waverley. The new abbey was twenty-sixth in line from Cîteaux. There were numerous routes through which knowledge of religious movements spread, and family and political contacts must have been important. It is not surprising, therefore, that when, three years later, a kinsman of Giffard, Walter fitz Richard de Clare (d. 1138), decided to make a Cistercian foundation he too should turn to l'Aumône. On 9 May 1131 the second British and first Welsh Cistercian settlement was made at Tintern, just a few miles from Walter's castle of Chepstow.

The foundation of a Cistercian house could not happen overnight. The founder had to ensure that rudimentary buildings were in place; and, in order to avoid giving offence, the Cistercians were careful to gain the permission of the local bishop before making a settlement within his diocese. It is this 'prehistory' of Cistercian foundations which is most often hidden from view. Just occasionally, however, we have a glimpse of events. It was St Bernard's Clairvaux which was the mainspring of Cistercian expansion in Britain. In 1131, a group of monks from Clairvaux presented themselves at the court of the English king, Henry I (1100–35). With them

7 Leclercq, Talbot and Rochais 1957–77; James 1953

8 Leclercq, Talbot and Rochais 1957–77; Leclercq and Casey 1970

they carried a letter from Bernard, in which he informed the king — obliquely it is true — that he intended that the monks should found a Cistercian monastery on English soil. The plan is couched in the military imagery often applied to monasticism and so beloved of Bernard: the monks from Bernard's army, the soldiers of Christ, were to reconnoitre, report back to their abbot, and seize the plunder which rightfully belonged to the Lord. That 'plunder' was the site of the abbey of Rievaulx.

Bernard was known to Henry I; the two had met in January 1131, and this may indeed have provided Bernard with the opportunity to launch what he would undoubtedly have thought of in terms of a military campaign to spread the Cistercian message. However, others must have been involved. At Clairvaux were a number of men from the north of England, among them William, Bernard's secretary, and founding abbot of Rievaulx (1132–45); and Bernard was in correspondence with Henry Murdac (d. 1153), a master in the schools of York, later to be a monk of Clairvaux and abbot of Fountains. The north of England was, therefore, not unknown territory to Bernard. Moreover, the archbishop of York, Thurstan (1114–40), had since 1119 been fully aware of Cîteaux and its growing family. Finally, crucial to the enterprise was Walter Espec (d. 1154), a baron closely associated with Henry I's government in the north of England, who provided land for the new abbey, a classic Cistercian site set in the deep valley of the river Rye on the edge of the North Yorkshire Moors, no more than three miles (4.8km) from Espec's castle at Helmsley. Rievaulx Abbey, one of the premier Cistercian abbeys in England, dated its foundation to 5 March 1132, at the beginning of a remarkable twenty-year period of Cistercian expansion in Britain.

The foundations of Rievaulx and Fountains are inextricably linked. In origins, however, they could not have been more different. Rievaulx was a 'textbook' foundation, with the site having been inspected and approved in advance of colonization. Fountains was born of schism at the Benedictine abbey of St Mary, York, in circumstances which invited comparison with Cîteaux itself. Hugh of Kirkstall, who in the early thirteenth century chronicled the history of Fountains, was in no doubt as to what had occasioned the trouble at St Mary's which led to the departure of a number of monks; and it is through his account, part of which derived from an elderly eye-witness, Serlo, that the story unfolds.[9] When the band of Cistercian monks sent by Bernard from Clairvaux, *en route* for Rievaulx, stopped in York, their purity, austerity and holiness crystalized discontent which already existed there, discontent which focused on the wealth and prosperity of St Mary's. It was as if the Cistercian way of life offered the answer for which the restless York monks had been searching. Their departure was not planned, but when Archbishop Thurstan, whom they had called to assist them, attempted to visit St Mary's on 9 October 1132 he was confronted by the aged abbot, horrified at the 'novelty' of the reform that was proposed and backed by leading Benedictines from other parts of Yorkshire. In the ensuing fracas, Prior Richard and twelve monks were hustled out of the chapter house, and forced to take refuge in Thurstan's household. In December, the archbishop provided them with a site, a piece of land in the valley of the river Skell three miles (4.8km) from his manor of Ripon. It was not, as planned foundations would have been, provided with temporary buildings, and the monks had to shelter beneath the rocks and the branches of an elm tree. In spring 1133 they determined on adoption of the Cistercian way of life, and, through the intermediary

Founded from St Bernard's Clairvaux in 1132, Rievaulx was one of the premier Cistercian abbeys of England and was the fount of the White Monk colonization in Scotland.

of William of Rievaulx, requested Bernard to accept them into the family of Clairvaux. Bernard sent one of his monks, Geoffrey d'Ainai, to instruct the new community in the Cistercian way of life: 'on his advice they built the monastic offices and learnt to sing the chant and say the psalms as the old man taught them. They embraced his orders with reverence, and like wax accepts the impress of the seal so they received the form of the Cistercian way of life'. Just as Cîteaux had struggled to survive, so too, as Hugh tells it, did the monks of Fountains. In despair they asked Bernard for help and he offered them a grange of Clairvaux to convert into an abbey. The transfer was not necessary, however, as they acquired local benefactors and influential recruits. Fountains prospered, and within a few years was in a position to send out its own daughter house to Louth Park (1137), the first of eight.

Such is the story woven by Hugh of Kirkstall from the oral and written sources available to him, and how far his account of the origins of Fountains is modelled, consciously or unconsciously, on the beginnings of Cîteaux, we cannot know. However, what binds together the stories of Rievaulx and Fountains — between them the fount of thirteen daughters and sixteen houses of the third generation — is the remarkable reputation for holiness, simplicity and austerity which the Cistercians had acquired as early as 1132, and which won them both the recruits and the patrons which they needed to survive and flourish, and which gave strength to the Cistercian organization. St Bernard was able to plan the mission from Clairvaux to Britain, and direct it from afar, using his connections with princes and churchmen to foster the new foundations. Cistercian involvement in its own expansion was active, not passive. Cistercian success owed as much to the international network which the order had built up as to the appeal of its spirituality.

The English houses largely derived from the three mother houses of Waverley, Rievaulx and Fountains. The exceptions were few: Tintern sent forth a daughter house to Kingswood (1139) and a second to Tintern Parva in Ireland (1201–03); Boxley (1143/46), a daughter house of Clairvaux, sent out a single colony to Robertsbridge (1176); Dore Abbey (1147) was the only British daughter house of Morimond, though in turn it established colonies at Grace Dieu (1226) and Vale Royal (1274). The factors which influenced Cistercian foundations are manifold, and not always easily identifiable. Sometimes the choice of mother house was determined by geographical proximity. However, personal connections were also important. The Cistercians attracted the patronage of the highest nobility and clergy of England, many of whom were closely connected by marriage or political and tenurial relationships. When Robert, earl of Leicester (d. 1168) founded a Cistercian house at Garendon in 1133 he drew monks from Waverley. Within a few years his brother, Waleran, count of Meulan and earl of Worcester (d. 1166), and his steward, Ernald de Bosco, had turned to Garendon for monks to establish their own houses at Bordesley (1138) and Biddlesden (1147). Bordesley became the mother of Stoneleigh, founded as a hermitage on its first site at Red Moor by King Stephen (1135–54); of Merevale, founded by Robert de Ferrers, earl of Derby (d. 1159); and of Flaxley, founded by Roger, earl of Hereford (d. 1155). The names of the founders read like a roll-call of royalty and aristocracy.

The family of Rievaulx, as we shall see, looked mainly to the north, but its first

Fountains was born out of a dispute among the community at the Benedictine abbey of St Mary's in York in 1132. A dissident group of monks broke away from the house, and was eventually settled in the valley of the river Skell by Archbishop Thurstan.

DISPERSAL IN ENGLAND

9 Walbran 1863–1918

aint bernard chapelain de la
vierge marie descendy de la mai
son des roix de bourgongne et

colony, established in 1136, was Warden, which Rievaulx's founder, Walter Espec, planted on his family estates in Bedfordshire. Warden spawned three colonies, at Sawtry (1147), Sibton (1150), and Tilty (1153). In addition Rievaulx established daughters at Revesby in Lincolnshire (1143) and Rufford in Nottinghamshire (1146). The expansion of the Fountains family took place within a fairly tight chronological span (1137–51); geographically, the English daughters and granddaughters lay in the eastern part of the country (Northumberland, Lincolnshire, Bedfordshire, Yorkshire), but Fountains was one of only two British Cistercian houses to send a colony overseas, to Norway: it founded a daughter house at Lysa, near Bergen (1146), and its daughter house Kirkstead established Hovedö, near Oslo (1147).

In 1152 the Cistercian General Chapter clearly felt that the order had expanded to the limits which its organization could sustain. It therefore forbade the establishment of any new Cistercian house. This was ineffective, although in England the main expansion was over by that date. Some twenty-eight monasteries had been founded since 1132. How are we to explain the remarkable Cistercian success? First, there can be no doubt of the appeal of Cistercian spirituality; the austerity, poverty, simplicity and seclusion described by William of Malmesbury and Orderic Vitalis proved to have a powerful attraction for recruits and patrons alike. Second, the expansion coincided with a troubled period in England, the dispute between King Stephen and his cousin, the 'Empress' Matilda (d. 1167), which brought warfare to some parts of the country, and disorder and breakdown of government in others. In such a climate of uncertainty monasticism flourished. Fighting men, concerned at their prospects for salvation, might compensate for the violent acts they had perpetrated by founding or endowing a religious house. Sometimes they swelled the ranks of recruits, as they often took the habit towards the end of life. In other instances members of the nobility seized lands from rivals, and gave legitimacy to their claims by founding a monastery on them. The Cistercians caught the tide of popularity at precisely the right time to benefit from bad consciences and tenurial uncertainty.

Although part of the attraction of the Cistercians was their seclusion and isolation, their involvement in a high profile dispute may have served to raise their own image. Although these two concepts may seem to be contradictory, they are not. The Cistercian concern for the right order of society and moral regeneration of the clergy who had responsibility for the souls of humanity, meant that they saw it as their duty to intervene in ecclesiastical affairs through the network of friendships and contacts which they had built up.[10] From 1143 the northern Cistercians opposed the newly elected archbishop of York, William fitz Herbert (1143–47 and 1153–54), siding with those who accused him of simony (having bought his office), intrusion (being put into office by the king's officials) and immorality. The intervention of the abbots of Rievaulx and Fountains and a barrage of letters from St Bernard demanding William's removal, kept the affair in the public eye, and pressure was maintained until the Cistercian pope, Eugenius III, deposed William in 1147. His successor was a Cistercian, Henry Murdac, a Yorkshireman who had entered the monastic life at Clairvaux, had been founding abbot of Vauclair, and was sent in 1143–44 by Bernard to Fountains where he was elected abbot. To observers, the Cistercians stood for a wave of ecclesiastical reform and high standards, rooting out the old practices and ushering in a new era. Opponents of

10 Newman 1996

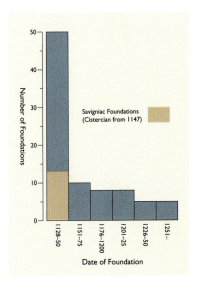

Graph showing the rate of growth of Cistercian abbeys in Britain.

Much of the expansion of the Cistercian order in Britain took place within the reign of King Stephen (1135–54). The king is depicted in this thirteenth-century manuscript illustration (British Library, Royal Ms. 14 C VII, f. 8v).

King Stephen, such as William de Roumare (d. 1161) and Ranulf 'de Gernon' (d. 1153), founders of Revesby, may also have rejoiced at the Cistercians' disposal of the archbishop of York whom the king had approved, and those aspiring to the foundation of a monastery would have found the Cistercians an attractive choice in more ways than one.

If 1132 was an *annus mirabilis* for the Cistercian order, with the foundation of both Rievaulx and Fountains and a massive expansion in Europe, then so too was 1147, the official foundation date of Biddlesden, Bruern, Dore, Kirkstall, Margam, Roche, Sawley, Sawtry, and Vaudey (Merevale was founded only a year later in 1148). And 1147 was the year of the Second Crusade, preached by St Bernard. Firm evidence to link Cistercian expansion with the crusade is lacking, but we can say that at the very least St Bernard's call to arms would have highlighted the order once again, and it may also have suggested that if a man felt unable to go on crusade, the foundation of a Cistercian house might be an appropriate substitution. Indeed, in 1151, William 'le Gros', count of Aumâle (d. 1179) — who had still not taken steps to fulfil a vow he had made to go to the Holy Land — was persuaded by the monk of Fountains who was supervising the construction of Aumâle's abbey of Vaudey, that the foundation of a second house (Meaux) would be more than adequate recompense.

There was also a rhythm of expansion dictated by the growth of the mother houses.[11] A house like Rievaulx, attractive to recruits, could continue to grow, placing pressure on the economic resources of the house, or it could relieve that pressure by sending out a colony. There was a degree of Cistercian initiative — as seen at Meaux — in the expansion, an element of deliberate colonization. In order to grow, the Cistercians needed to find patrons, men and women who could provide them with a site, and sufficient land to support the initial community. Their desire for rural sites and uncultivated lands might mean that the cost of foundation of a Cistercian house would be considerably less than, for instance, a Benedictine abbey or Cluniac priory. This could only have enhanced their attraction. Moreover, founders might hope to benefit from the successful agricultural practices of the White Monks.

THE ORDER OF SAVIGNY AND ITS BRITISH HOUSES

Not all the abbeys which were members of this great order were founded as Cistercian houses. Some were existing abbeys or priories which, attracted by the spirituality of the White Monks, sought incorporation into the order. An early example was the ancient Benedictine abbey of Cadouin (Dordogne) which, in 1119, had surrendered its independence to become a daughter house of Pontigny. The greatest boost to the order, and to the Norman and British families in particular, came in 1147 when the order of Savigny (Manche) placed itself under the Cistercian wing. Savigny was another of the new orders of the period which sprang from a desire for a purer, more austere life. Its influence spread, and by 1147 it comprised a congregation on both sides of the channel. The organization of the order, however, clearly fell well below Cistercian standards. The system of filiation appeared to work less well than it should, and there was tension between houses, for instance between Savigny and Furness, the premier Savigniac house in England, concerning jurisdiction over Byland, and between Byland and Calder.[12] It was both admiration for the White Monks and the difficulties which he encountered in governing his own

11 Holdsworth 1994
12 Burton 1991
13 Powicke 1950
14 Powicke 1950

flock that led Abbot Serlo of Savigny to seek the union; and approval was given at the General Chapter of 1147. For some English houses, such as Byland, where Cistercian austerities in economic measures were evidently already practised, the transition was doubtless a painless one. Elsewhere local Cistercians helped to ease the path: the abbot of Revesby was sent to Swineshead 'to illuminate it with the Cistercian way of life'.[13] Furness, perhaps seeing a threat that its independence would be curbed, held out against the union, but was overruled, and at the time of the merger eleven English and two Welsh houses were added to the Cistercian order.

Cistercian expansion north of the border derived almost entirely from Rievaulx, and had at its origins a personal connection. One of the most famous British Cistercians is Ailred, abbot of Rievaulx (1147–67). From his biography, written immediately after his death by Walter Daniel, a monk of Rievaulx, we learn of Ailred's background, and how he came to enter the monastic life.[14] He derived from a venerable family, the hereditary married priests of Hexham in Northumberland; his grandfather was removed by Archbishop Thomas II of York (1109–14) to make way for the Augustinian canons whom he installed in the church in 1113–14. Ailred, probably educated at Hexham and then at Durham, then found a trusted place at the court of David I (1124–53) of Scotland. He had always had a monastic vocation, and a visit to Rievaulx in 1134 sealed his wishes. Although Walter Daniel doubtless romanticized the story of Ailred's 'conversion' the main lines seem clear enough. Ailred was on David's official business in York with Archbishop Thurstan, and this completed, he stayed the night with Walter Espec at his castle of Helmsley. He had heard about the White Monks newly settled nearby, and the following day paid them a visit. He was welcomed warmly, decided to join the community, and within a few years became novice master. In 1143 he became founding abbot of Revesby, but in 1147 returned to rule the mother house.

After Ailred's entry into Rievaulx, it was only a matter of time before his former patron, David I, determined on a Cistercian foundation. David was a cultured man, interested in new ecclesiastical movements, who had already founded abbeys of Tironensian monks and priories of Augustinian canons. By 1134, probably because of the presence of Ailred there, David had become a patron of the monks of Rievaulx, and in 1136 — only four years after its foundation — he drew a colony to found a daughter house of Melrose. In 1142 he collaborated with Fergus, lord of Galloway, in a second house at Dundrennan. The presence of Ailred at Rievaulx must have eased negotiations, and ties were strengthened further when David's stepson, Waldef, who had left the Scottish court to enter an Augustinian priory in Yorkshire, became a Cistercian. Not without some misgivings did he opt for the rigours of the White Monks, but he persisted and in 1148 he returned to Scotland to become abbot of David's foundation at Melrose. Under the sponsorship of the Scottish royal house, foundations in the third and fourth generations were sent out, as far north as Deer and Kinloss. More so than in England, the Cistercian expansion in Scotland derived its strength from the support of the royal house.

Admiration for the White Monks and a desire to share in this great spiritual adventure certainly prompted David to sponsor these Scottish foundations. But the expansion was not without its political dimensions. In 1136, David had declared his support for his niece, the 'Empress' Matilda, and her claim to the throne of England,

EXPANSION IN SCOTLAND

Ailred, abbot of Rievaulx (1147-67), depicted in a twelfth-century manuscript illustration (Bibliothèque Municipale, Douai, Ms. 392, f. 3r).

which had been snatched the year before by Stephen of Blois. With this as justification, David invaded the north, seized Northumberland and Cumbria, and was only prevented from extending Scottish influence further south into Durham and Yorkshire when defeated at the battle of the Standard (1138). Nevertheless, he did not surrender his ambition to redraw the English–Scottish border further to the south; and the cultivation of ecclesiastical links may have been an integral part of this plan. In 1150 David and his son Henry (d. 1152) cemented the Scottish hold on conquered Cumbria by the foundation of an abbey at Holmcultram, deriving from Melrose.

THE CISTERCIANS IN WALES

Rhys ap Gruffudd (d. 1197), prince of the Welsh kingship of Deheubarth, was a munificent patron of the White Monks in south-west Wales. He especially 'loved and cherished' Strata Florida. This fourteenth-century tomb-effigy of Rhys lies in St Davids Cathedral.

By 1140 the geography of monasticism in Wales was quite different from that in England.[15] There were none of the great, independent, Benedictine abbeys which were to be found in England, and few of the houses of Augustinian canons so fashionable there. The Welsh monasteries were Benedictine cells or priories, planted by the Norman conquerors as dependencies of English, Norman or French houses. Like the castles and boroughs which they often nestled beside, they were symbols of foreign domination and conquest, and few of the native Welsh would either give them material support or enter them as monks. Tintern, and the two Savigniac houses, Neath (1130) in the south and Basingwerk (1131) in the north, were founded by Marcher lords, and endowed by them and their followers. They had no native Welsh dimension, nothing to attract Welsh patronage.

In 1140 it must have looked as if this pattern would continue, for Whitland Abbey was founded from Clairvaux by Bernard, bishop of St Davids (1115–48), who had been a close associate of King Henry I. The first successful colonization in the heart of Welsh Wales came in 1164 with the foundation of Strata Florida by Robert fitz Stephen, constable of Cardigan Castle. However, the defining moment in the history of Strata Florida, and indeed in the history of the Welsh Cistercians, came the following year when, in a turnabout of political fortunes, Rhys ap Gruffudd (d. 1197), prince of Deheubarth, overran Ceredigion, and assumed the patronage of Strata Florida; he also became a generous benefactor of Whitland. To Rhys and other Welshmen it was clear that there need be no English dimension to the Cistercians. The mother house of the order lay in Burgundy, and the filiation of Whitland was via another Burgundian house, Clairvaux. The Cistercians could be supported and endowed, and the spiritual benefits of monastic patronage enjoyed, without compromising political loyalties. Moreover the austerity of the Cistercians and the eremitical aspects of their life, made them natural heirs of the *clas* churches destroyed by the Normans in an attempt to introduce into the conquered areas of Wales an ecclesiastical system and structure with which they were familiar.

There are no documentary traces of Rhys's patronage of Strata Florida until 1184, when he issued a charter to the abbey which 'since its inception [he had] loved and cherished', confirming the wide pastures, arable and mountain land he had granted; shortly afterwards he provided a new site, allowing the monks to move from *yr hen fynachlog* (the old monastery) to a more congenial spot a mile and a half (2.4km) away, where the ruins can now be seen. However, the survival of the monastery and the dispersal of daughter houses suggests that in 1165 Rhys took an immediate interest in its fortunes. The Cistercian expansion in Wales now blossomed. Whitland sent further colonies to Strata Marcella, near Welshpool, in

15 Cowley 1977

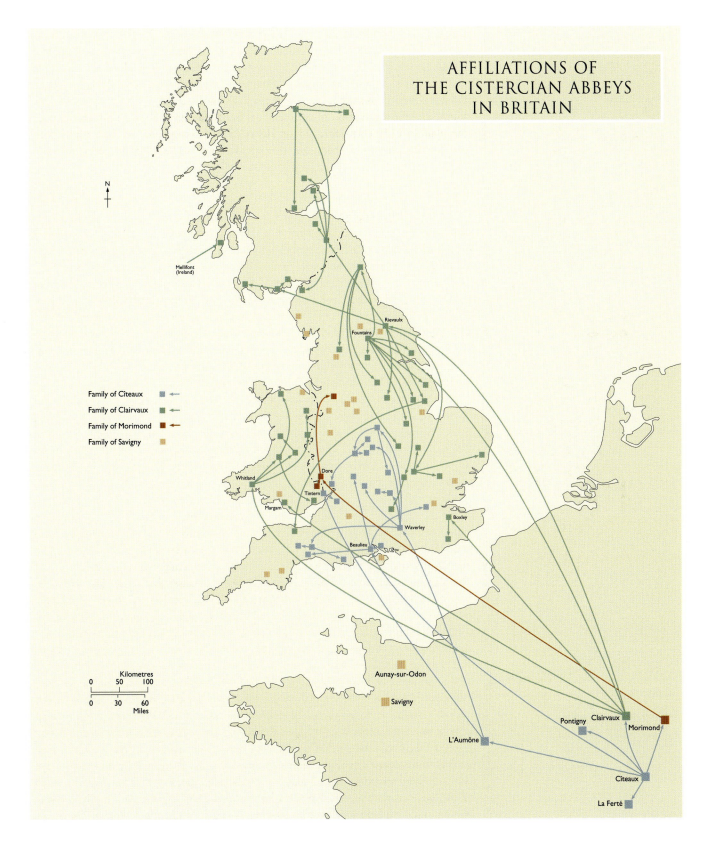

AFFILIATIONS OF THE CISTERCIAN ABBEYS IN BRITAIN

Family of Cîteaux
Family of Clairvaux
Family of Morimond
Family of Savigny

Mellifont (Ireland)

Rievaulx

Fountains

Whitland

Dore

Tintern

Margam

Boxley

Waverley

Beaulieu

Kilometres
0   50   100

0   30   60
Miles

Aunay-sur-Odon

Savigny

Pontigny   Clairvaux

Morimond

L'Aumône

Cîteaux

La Ferté

Like many Cistercian patrons, the Welsh prince, Llywelyn ab Iorwerth, spent his last hours in the habit of a monk. Llywelyn died at Aberconwy in 1240 and was buried in the abbey church (Corpus Christi College, Cambridge, Ms. 16, f. 133).

ROYAL ABBEYS

After a dispute with the Cistercians, King John (1199–1216) eventually chose to establish the abbey of Beaulieu in 1203–04. It was the only British house directly colonized by Cîteaux. John is shown hunting in this fourteenth-century manuscript illustration (British Library, Cotton Claudius Ms. D II, f. 116).

16 Hockey 1976; Holdsworth 1992

1170 at the invitation of Owain Cyfeiliog (Owain ap Gruffudd, d. 1197), prince of Powys, and to Cwmhir (1176), where the house was erected on land granted by Cadwallon ap Madog (d. 1179), prince of Ceri and Maelienydd. Strata Florida planted colonies in the south at Llantarnam (1179), founded by Hywel ap Iorwerth (d. 1211), lord of Caerleon, and in the north at Aberconwy (1186), fostered and endowed by Llywelyn ab Iorwerth (Llywelyn Fawr, d. 1240), prince of Gwynedd. Aberconwy became the burial place of several of the princes of Gwynedd who aspired to be princes of all Wales, and after the final defeat of Welsh independence in 1282–83 the abbey was destroyed and removed to Maenan to make way for the English king's castle and walled town at Conwy.

Throughout their existence, the Welsh Cistercians maintained strong links with the native Welsh dynasties. They received their members as monks, often clothing them in the Cistercian habit as death approached; they provided them with their burial place; they celebrated their deeds in their annals; and they fostered Welsh culture by their patronage of poets and copying of Welsh texts. They were an integral part of Welsh society and Welsh political aspirations. It was the Cistercian house of Cwmhir which gave a final resting place to Llywelyn ap Gruffudd, the last native prince of Wales, in 1282. However, there was a price to pay for their loyalty. In 1212, King John (1199–1216) ordered the destruction of Strata Florida which, he claimed, 'harbours our enemies'. Moreover, the Welsh abbeys and their possessions at large were liable to be attacked in times of tension between the Welsh and the English. Many houses suffered badly in the wars of the 1270s and 1280s, and received compensation from the English Crown.

In 1152 the Cistercian General Chapter attempted to halt the growing tide of foundations. In Wales, however, the main period of expansion came after 1152, and in Scotland foundations continued unabated. In England the pace slowed, but the order enjoyed a brief though significant resurgence in the early part of the thirteenth century, which owed its origins to a man who is, at first sight, an unlikely source: King John.[16] Early relations between the king and the order were soured by John's need for money. In 1200 he attempted to extend a tax imposed in the previous year to the Cistercians; they, however, claimed that they could not pay without consulting the General Chapter. With Hubert Walter, archbishop of Canterbury (1193–1205), acting as intermediary they offered 1,000 marks (£666) as a voluntary payment. Their gesture was refused, and, in retaliation for what he saw as their lack of cooperation, John ordered that all their livestock within the royal forests be confiscated. Representatives of the order went to Lincoln to plead with the king; he agreed to a reconciliation and gestures of good will were made by both sides. The Cistercians received John into the confraternity of the order, and the king offered to establish an abbey. The site which he chose at Faringdon was inspected and approved by the abbot of La Ferté, and it was occupied by monks from Cîteaux in 1203. By 1204, however, the site had been abandoned — site changes are recorded at over a third of the Cistercian abbeys in Britain — and the monks removed to Beaulieu in the New Forest.

Royal patronage allowed Beaulieu to flourish, and John's son, Henry III (1216–72), contributed generously towards the costs of construction. As numbers grew, colonies were possible. Netley was planned towards the end of his life by Peter des Roches, bishop of Winchester (1205–38). It was left to his executors to complete the project (1239), though eventually Henry III assumed the patronage of the house. Hailes (1246) was another royal foundation, by Richard of Cornwall (d. 1272), Henry III's brother; he and his wife were buried there, and their son, Edmund (d. 1300), rebuilt Hailes after a fire in 1271, and donated the relic, the phial of Holy Blood, which transformed the abbey into a pilgrimage centre. Edward I (1272–1307) laid the foundations for Vale Royal Abbey (1277), to which in 1281 he transferred the monks he had previously established at Darnhall (1274). The final Cistercian house was — in contrast to the spirit of the early Cistercians — an urban house, St Mary Graces on Tower Hill in London (1350), founded by King Edward III (1327–77).

THE CISTERCIANS AND OXFORD

Despite the presence in the Cistercian order of men of high intellectual calibre, and the prolific literary activity of men such as St Bernard and Ailred of Rievaulx, the order did not place a high priority on study for its own sake. It sought to fulfil the daily obligations of each monk, laid down by the *Rule*, to devote a portion of the day to reading and meditation, but it did not wish to see study assume too important a part of the monastic day. This remained a characteristic of Cistercian observance, although a change in attitude can be seen with the advent of Stephen of Lexington, a master at Oxford, who became successively a monk of Quarr, and abbot of Stanley (1223), Savigny (1229) and Clairvaux (1243). Stephen set up the first Cistercian house of study, St Bernard's in Paris, in 1247, marking the

---

TWO VIEWS OF THE CISTERCIANS FROM THE OUTSIDE

How did the non-Cistercian world perceive or identify the White Monks by the 1120s and 1130s? Two accounts will help us approach an answer to that question. The first is from an Englishman, William, monk-librarian of the Benedictine abbey of Malmesbury, who could write (about 1124) — even before the Cistercians reached Britain — that their way of life was seen by many as 'the surest road to Heaven', and that the Cistercians were 'a model for all monks, a mirror for the diligent, a spur to the indolent'.[1] William's account quite understandably stresses the role of the Englishman Stephen Harding in the creation and success of the order. However, his portrait of Cistercian practice shows that by the 1120s the Cistercian monks had a reputation for being abstemious in their dress, and adhering to the *Rule of St Benedict* so strictly 'that they think no jot or tittle of it should be disregarded'. In accordance with the *Rule* they performed manual labour at stated hours, and shared their simple meals as laid down by Benedict. Much of William's account of the Cistercians is taken up with how Stephen adopted austerity in church furnishings, and rejected gold and silver — common in Cluniac houses — for their monasteries; they 'loved pure minds more than glittering vestments'.

Our other witness is Orderic Vitalis, English-born monk of the Norman Benedictine house of St Evroult, whose essay on the origins of the Cistercian order can be dated to around 1135.[2] Orderic noted that the Cistercians were distinguished by their use of undyed garments in contrast to the usual black — it was this that led them to become known as the White Monks. They were strict in their keeping of the regulations on silence and manual labour, and were distinguished by their austerity and seclusion from the world. For Orderic, however, it seems to have been the location of their monasteries which fascinated:

They have built monasteries with their own hands in lonely, wooded places and have thoughtfully provided them with holy names, such as Maison-Dieu, Clairvaux, Bonmont, and l'Aumône and others of the like, so that the name alone invites all who hear to hasten and discover for themselves how great the blessedness must be which is described by so rare a name.

It is striking testimony to the discipline and cohesiveness of the Cistercians that by the 1130s a non-Cistercian could say of them, that 'by the great good they do they shine out in the world like lanterns burning in a dark place'.

1 Stubbs 1887–89
2 Chibnall 1973

entry of the Cistercians into the universities. In 1281 an English house was established by Edmund, earl of Cornwall, at Rewley, dependent on Thame, to allow for study at Oxford, and in 1292 the General Chapter ordered every English monastery to send one student for every twenty monks. The Oxford house did not prosper, however, as abbots seemed to have been reluctant both to allow monks to leave the stability of the cloister, and to bear the cost of their study. By 1344 the General Chapter was having to fine the English houses for not complying with its demands. The monks complained about the remoteness of Rewley and the lack of books, and in 1437 Archbishop Henry Chichele (1414–43) was persuaded to found St Bernard's (now St John's) as the Oxford Cistercian college.

SITES AND DEPOPULATION

Gerald of Wales (d. 1223), at first a great admirer of the White Monks, was to become one of their most fierce critics. Gerald is portrayed in this thirteenth-century manuscript illumination (Cambridge University Library, Ms. Ff. 1. 27, f. 1v).

Give the Cluniacs today a tract of land covered with marvellous buildings, endow them with ample revenues and enrich the place with vast possessions: before you can turn round it will be all ruined and reduced to poverty. On the other hand, settle the Cistercians in some barren retreat which is hidden away in an overgrown forest: a year or two later you will find splendid churches there and fine monastic buildings, with a great amount of property and all the wealth you can imagine.[17]

Gerald of Wales (d. 1223), who within a few years of writing this was to become a fierce critic of the White Monks, was not alone in his admiration for their successful colonizing efforts. Their own statutes enjoined them to seek sites 'far from the concourse of men', and in Britain by and large they did so, settling in remote spots and underpopulated areas. Sometimes, however, solitude proved difficult to find: Britain was a well-settled land by the 1130s, and moreover the sites and endowments which some founders offered were already occupied. On occasion, therefore, in order to achieve seclusion, villages were depopulated, and their inhabitants relocated.[18] This is documented at Revesby, where the villagers of three settlements were offered alternative lands by the founder. The site chosen by Adam, monk of Fountains, for a daughter house at Meaux, was already occupied, and similar depopulation took place. Throughout the Middle Ages the abbey of Valle Crucis was known by the alternative name of Llanegwestl, the settlement which it displaced in 1201. It was instances such as these which fed the story of Cistercian avarice, with accusations voiced by men like Walter Map, archdeacon of Oxford (d. 1209/10), that if the Cistercians could not find a desert they created it: 'they make a solitude that they may be solitaries'.[19] The picture is not, however, entirely negative, for some displaced peasants were given land elsewhere; others joined the community as lay brothers, swelling the numbers of monastic workers.

By the late twelfth century, charges of avarice were not uncommon, though some, like Gerald, admitted that the Cistercians put their wealth to good use in the care of the sick and the feeding of the poor. It was the remarkable economic success of the White Monks which led to such stories. There is an inherent irony in the way in which an order of monks, wedded to the ideals of poverty and austerity, became some of the most successful economic managers in the Middle Ages. How could this happen?

17 Thorpe 1994
18 Donkin 1978
19 James, Brooke and Mynors 1983

Research has shown that the Cistercian ideas on the most desirable economic basis on which their abbeys should operate may have emerged slowly. The order, although committed to an austere way of life, did not shun economic activity. On the contrary, even the earliest monks recognized that they had to support themselves economically. Moreover, many Cistercian abbeys came to be sizeable communities: Rievaulx under Ailred allegedly contained 140 monks, as well as 500 lay brothers and hired workers. Food and clothing needed to be provided; buildings had to be constructed, furnished and repaired. All this could not happen without some economic activity. What characterized the Cistercians was less their 'taming of the wilderness' — the traditional view of the White Monks — than their development of a landbased economy which owed nothing to the prevailing manorial structure, which brought houses of other orders and congregations into contact with tenants and villagers. Cistercian economic success was due to their ability to consolidate their lands around granges, which were carefully differentiated from the estates of their neighbours.

Through grant, purchase, and exchange, they came to control wide acres of pasture, forest and arable. They were active in assarting, the clearance of lands — marsh, moor and forest — for cultivation, though less in Britain than on the frontiers of eastern Europe. The consolidation of lands in turn allowed for efficient use of resources, and the development of specialized economic activity. They were aided by the concession, granted in 1132 by Pope Innocent II (1130–43), that they

THE CISTERCIAN GRANGE

During the early Middle Ages, the success of the Cistercian grange was based on the availability of a devout army of lay brothers to work the land. This famous work scene from a Cîteaux manuscript completed in 1111 shows a monk reaping corn (Bibliothèque Municipale, Dijon, Ms. 170, f. 75v).

VI CON TRA

The barn at Great Coxwell (Oxfordshire) was situated on one of Beaulieu Abbey's most significant properties. This magnificent late thirteenth- or early fourteenth-century structure serves as a reminder of many hundreds of such barns which once existed on Cistercian granges throughout Britain (RCHME, Crown Copyright).

should be exempt from the payment of tithes (the tenths of produce due to the parish church) on lands which they cultivated themselves, although in 1215 this was restricted to *novalia*, lands newly brought into cultivation. Some granges were largely arable, with the *grangia*, or granary, lying at the centre of the complex; others were pastoral, while yet more could support mixed economic activity. Where resources existed granges could develop specialized industrial activities. Fountains' grange of Bradley, for example, was a centre for pottery production; at a grange in the west of Yorkshire the monks engaged in iron mining.

Above all it was with the keeping of sheep and the production of wool that the Cistercian name was most closely linked, as the Yorkshire chronicler William of Newburgh realized when, in the 1190s, he remarked that wool was 'the chief part of their substance'.[20] The very location of many of their abbeys, from the hills of Scotland to the moors of north Yorkshire, the Lincolnshire wolds and the Welsh mountains, meant that the type of land they were likely to receive was upland and moorland suitable for the keeping of sheep. They were not the first monastic sheep farmers, but they turned it into an art form. Their flocks were concentrated on their granges; they could be gathered for shearing on the sheep-stations (*bercarie*) placed at convenient locations, and the wool brought together in the great wool sheds which, along with the granaries for the storage of arable produce, lay at the heart of the grange complex. The Cistercians pioneered the use of manure; they graded fleeces and sold them according to quality rather than as mixed wool; and they paid attention to the problems of breeding and disease.

CISTERCIAN WOMEN

When the first Cistercians left Molesme they had no intention of founding an order; even further from their minds was that their way of life might appeal to women as well as men. Yet, almost as soon as Cîteaux and its family began to prosper, the Cistercians found that they had female adherents. The nunnery of Jully (1113) may have been intended to accommodate the women whose menfolk had entered Cîteaux, women 'widowed' by their husbands' decision to become Cistercians. Certainly the first prioress was Elizabeth, the wife of Guy, who had become a monk with his more famous brother, St Bernard, and in 1128 Elizabeth was succeeded by Bernard's sister Humbelina. In 1124 some nuns left Jully in order to live a stricter life, and established a nunnery at Tart, just a few miles from Cîteaux. Any links were informal, however, and until 1213 there was no place for women within the organization of the order.

This did not mean that women did not share the religious fervour inspired by the White Monks. Soon there appeared convents of women which claimed to be following Cistercian customs, and some apparently received official recognition. Pope Alexander III, for example, in issuing documents for three English nunneries, described them as following Cistercian institutes. The dilemma for the White Monks was that theirs was a masculine order which made no provision for supervision of female houses; moreover women were not allowed into Cistercian monasteries or granges. Accordingly these 'Cistercian' nunneries were not recognized by the order. We do not know on what basis they claimed Cistercian identity — was it austerity in dress, food, and architecture, or a conformity to Cistercian economic practices?

There was a clear divergence between the official line of the order — that there was no such thing as a Cistercian nun — and the attitude of women and their patrons, who evidently did not share this opinion. Local Cistercian men may have been willing to establish informal links: Rhys ap Gruffudd founded a Cistercian nunnery at Llanllyr, which was associated with the male house of Strata Florida, and Llanllugan was similarly associated with Strata Marcella. In the early thirteenth century, pressure from women forced Cistercian men to recognize female houses, though they were strictly controlled. In England two nunneries were founded as Cistercian abbeys, Marham (Norfolk) and Tarrant (Dorset). However, those nunneries formally recognized by the order were vastly outnumbered by the priories which were 'unofficially' Cistercian, claiming Cistercian privileges and following an austere way of life.

By the end of the twelfth century, the Cistercians were in control of vast flocks of sheep all over Britain, and we can discern a growing efficiency not just in the production of wool — and that from their own flocks was supplemented by purchases and by tithes which some abbeys came to possess — but also in the disposal of wool not required by the community.[21] The earliest indications that the Cistercians were engaged in trading comes with the securing of privileges to travel, and exemptions on toll. Some, like the monks of Rievaulx, enjoyed freedom of movement for themselves and their goods from within a few years of the foundation, and King David I granted similar privileges to all the Scottish Cistercian houses. At first, trade may have been local, or through middlemen. But by the thirteenth century Cistercian houses were securing trading concessions from the counts of Flanders, and licences from the English king to trade overseas, both with Flanders and the great merchant houses of Italy.

A list, datable to the 1260s, gives the names of 102 abbeys and priories trading in wool with Flanders; many of these were Cistercian houses, and the house recorded with the greatest value of wool for sale was the Welsh Cistercian abbey of Neath. The *Pratica della Mercatura* of the Italian merchant Francesco Balducci Pegolotti, which has been dated to between 1281 and 1296, lists sixty-five British religious houses trading with Flemish and Italian merchants. Eighty-five per cent of these were Cistercian houses, and Fountains was recorded as the chief exporter with seventy-six sacks of wool for export. Second was Rievaulx (sixty sacks) and in third place, rivalling the ancient Benedictine Cathedral Priory of Christ Church, Canterbury with fifty sacks, was the Yorkshire Cistercian abbey of Jervaulx. To translate sacks into the number of fleeces they contained, and to place a value on them is a hazardous business, but a figure of 10,000 sheep producing forty-five sacks of wool has been suggested.[22] This suggests that Fountains had available, for this one market, the wool of nearly 17,000 sheep. For all the difficulties of interpreting these raw figures — and bearing in mind that other abbeys with lower figures may have been trading elsewhere or through middlemen — this demonstrates the dominance of the Cistercians in the wool trade, although by the following century others had emulated their practices, and the Cistercian share in the market was falling.

Even by the late twelfth century Cistercian economic practices were beginning to be transformed. The factors which led to change are complex, though a general problem which the order encountered concerned the *conversi*. From the late twelfth century, there were instances of rebellion. The circumstances varied, but a common thread was growing dissatisfaction among the *conversi* with their second-class status within Cistercian communities as well as the austere conditions under which they lived and worked. Discontent was manifest particularly on granges, where instances of drunkenness and disobedience led the General Chapter to place a ban on beer drinking. Problems with the *conversi* may have been one of the factors which led to a redefinition of Cistercian attitudes towards the leasing of estates. Although it initially required abbeys to cultivate land directly, the General Chapter came to allow the leasing of land for rent. At first (1208), this was intended to apply to lands which lay at a great distance from the house — accepting such lands meant that the monks could not conform to the regulation which demanded that granges

THE CISTERCIANS AND TRADE

THE DECLINE OF THE CONVERSI AND ECONOMIC CHANGE

20 Howlett 1884–90
21 Donkin 1978; Graves 1957
22 Knowles 1948–59

be no more than a day's journey from the abbey. Later it was stated that land which senior monks deemed 'less useful' might be leased.[23]

In Britain, the major economic changes came with the beginnings of the decline in the numbers of lay brothers in the thirteenth century, and the devastation of the Black Death of 1348–49; with a fall in the working population, labour came to be in demand, and *conversi* could hope for increased wages and better conditions outside the monastery. The Black Death therefore hastened an existing decline among the *conversi*, and one of the unique planks of the Cistercian economy all but disappeared. The difficulties were exacerbated by political conditions: in Wales by the damage sustained by some houses in the wars of the 1270s and 1280s, and again during the rebellion of Owain Glyn Dŵr in the early fifteenth century; and in the north of England by Scottish incursions after the English defeat at Bannockburn (1314). This led to the widespread leasing of granges, and a reliance on money rents. The Scottish houses also suffered damage in the wars of the fourteenth and early sixteenth centuries, exacerbating financial difficulties.

In the later Middle Ages many houses fell into debt. This arose for a number of reasons, among them ambitious building campaigns, acquisition of lands, and speculation in the selling of wool. Some abbeys, prominent in wool production, began the practice of pledging, or selling the commodity in advance. In 1181 the General Chapter attempted to prevent wool sales for more than one year in advance, but the practice persisted. As long as yields were sustained there was little to fear. However, when, as in 1280, there was an epidemic of disease such as sheep-scab, production fell drastically and deficit followed. In 1280 Rievaulx was on the point of bankruptcy and the king took it into his own custody, appointing an administrator to take charge of its affairs. The debt of Fountains Abbey soared from £900, owed to the Jews of York, in 1274, to £6,373 in 1291, when the king was forced to intervene.[24] Meaux Abbey had debts of £3,678 in 1280, of which £2,500 was owed to merchants and moneylenders. These are, naturally, only snapshots in the long history of Cistercian life in Britain, but they demonstrate both that the White Monks could not resist prevailing economic trends, and that they had, by the later Middle Ages, lost the distinctive economic outlook which had characterized them in earlier centuries. However, many recovered from the severe difficulties of the thirteenth and fourteenth centuries, and by the time of the *Valor Ecclesiasticus*, the great survey of religious houses commissioned in 1535, were in a healthy economic situation.

THE CISTERCIANS FROM THE THIRTEENTH TO THE SIXTEENTH CENTURIES

The records which would allow us to assess the strength of links between the British Cistercians and the order as a whole are sporadic. There are some indications that strong ties were maintained. The General Chapter continued to dispatch visitors and appoint local abbots to settle disputes. It disciplined those who failed to attend, and did its best to address the problems posed by the *conversi*. It maintained the regulations of the order: for instance in 1246 the prior and cellarer of Beaulieu were deposed for having allowed a woman — Queen Eleanor — to stay in the monastery for three weeks, and for serving meat to lay people visiting, both on the occasion of the dedication of the abbey.[25] However, travel to and from Cîteaux was time-consuming and expensive — for the abbot of Aberconwy in north Wales the journey took over a month. Moreover, even from the twelfth century,

there were tensions between the position of the British Cistercian abbeys as local houses, with royal and aristocratic patrons, and their role as members of an international order. In 1166 King Henry II (1154–89) threatened the English Cistercians if the abbey of Pontigny continued to give refuge to the exiled archbishop of Canterbury, Thomas Becket (d. 1170). In 1208, when Pope Innocent III (1198–1216) placed England under an interdict, the Cistercians claimed to be exempt; in retaliation King John confiscated their possessions, excepting only his own abbey of Beaulieu, and Margam, which twice a year gave him hospitality on his journeys to Ireland.

Later still, attendance at the General Chapter was made more difficult by the French wars of Edward I. In 1298 he banned abbots from attending, and this restriction was repeated on several occasions in the following century. Edward's objections, it would appear, were mainly financial. It had become the custom for the General Chapter to be supported by financial contributions from its abbeys, and the king feared that the money raised in Britain and taken to the Chapter might fall into French hands. The ban may have induced some feelings of relief from a burdensome duty, but the attempts of the abbots of Waverley, Tintern and Quarr to hold a 'provincial chapter' in 1342 were overruled by the General Chapter, clearly determined not to see its authority undermined. However during the Great Schism it did indeed become the practice for meetings of English abbots to take place to deal with matters of discipline and to make decisions about local matters; this was sanctioned by the General Chapter in 1433 and became an accepted part of the government of the order. Governmental ties may have been loosening, but this did not mean the end of the bonds of affection and loyalty which are evident both in the letters sent by the Cistercian abbots to Cîteaux, and in the contribution of money and objects to the mother house of the order.[26]

THE END OF MONASTIC LIFE IN BRITAIN

By the sixteenth century the religious orders were coming under increasing attack. Although it is impossible to generalize about popular attitudes, there were certainly those who felt that the spiritual drive, or fervour, had gone out of the monastic life. In some cases indifference became hostility, as accusations of immorality were made. In England and Wales, what hastened the demise of a way of life was, on the one hand, the claim by Henry VIII (1509–47) to supreme authority over the church and, on the other, his need for money. By the 1530s the signs were ominous. An early victim was Abbot Edward Kirby of Rievaulx, who in 1533 questioned the king's assumption of authority in the Church of England. Kirby was deposed by the king's commissioners, and the abbot of Fountains, William Thirsk, who had refused to condemn Kirby, was forced to resign three years later.[27] In 1535 the assault became more general, and as a preliminary to suppression Henry VIII's commissioners made a systematic valuation of church property throughout the English and Welsh dioceses, the *Valor Ecclesiasticus*. Further commissioners then conducted visitations of all abbeys and priories, and noted the number of religious in each, and the quality of religious life practised there. This provided the ammunition for closure.

In 1536 an Act of Parliament ordered the suppression of monasteries valued at less than £200 per annum, masking the financial motive behind a moral façade ('Forasmuch as manifest sin ... is daily used and committed among the little and small abbeys ...'). Those religious who requested to leave the monastic life were granted a pension; others were transferred to larger establishments. It was not only the religious who felt threatened by the changes that were in the air. In the north, local uprisings, known collectively as the Pilgrimage of Grace, though disparate in many of their aims, agreed on one demand: the restoration of the dissolved smaller houses. Numerous Cistercians as well as members of other orders were dragged, willingly or unwillingly, into the rebels' plans. At Kirkstead the monks were forced to join the Lincolnshire rebels on their march — or see their abbey burnt. Sawley Abbey was restored and became a centre of dissident activity. Many paid the price of their association with rebellion. Abbot Adam Sedbar of Jervaulx, who claimed he had been dragged from his monastery to join the rebels, and Abbot William Thirsk, deposed from office at Fountains and then resident at Jervaulx, were executed at Tyburn. The abbots of Sawley and Whalley were condemned to hang at Lancaster. Richard Harrison of Kirkstead was another victim. The abbey of Jervaulx suffered a particularly cruel fate. As well as Sedbar, a monk named George Lazenby was executed (August 1535), and another died in prison. The abbey was forfeited, and the remaining monks turned out without pensions.

The greater houses, spared in 1536 — and those 'lesser houses', like Neath, Strata Florida and Whitland, which had bought exemption from suppression — were not to survive much longer. By 1540 the voluntary surrender of all the religious houses in England and Wales had been obtained, their sites and estates granted, rented, or sold to new owners, and their inhabitants pensioned off.

As a prelude to the dissolution, in 1535 Henry VIII's commissioners made a systematic valuation of church property throughout the English and Welsh dioceses. The resulting document is known as the Valor Ecclesiasticus. *This image of the king comes from the opening folio of the survey (Public Record Office, E 344/22).*

This map showing the valuation of Cistercian houses of England and Wales is based on the great survey of 1535. The Scottish houses cannot easily be compared with the relative values recorded in the English and Welsh dioceses.

   As in England and Wales, members of the monastic orders in Scotland had faced criticism for laxity of observance and immorality, and the situation was compounded by the Scottish system of commendation, by which some abbeys were headed by lay commendators appointed by the king. These often had their own, rather than the communities', interests at heart, as at Melrose, where in 1556 the commendator was alleged to have kept the abbey so short of funds that the church was not in a state to be used. The end of monastic life came in 1560 when the Scottish Parliament took the decision to deny the authority of the papacy. After 1560 the functions of monastic men and women ceased, but many continued for some time to live within their convent walls and enjoy their revenues until their abbeys were transformed into secular lordships. In this way the Scottish religious were more fortunate than their English and Welsh counterparts.

   The Cistercian adventure in Britain had lasted just over four hundred years. In that time the order had become interwoven in the fabric of society. In their heyday, during the twelfth century, the reputation of the White Monks was at its zenith, and its houses formed part of the greatest international ecclesiastical organization ever seen. Cistercian abbeys were patronized by kings, bishops and aristocracy, and yet they touched the lives of town dweller and peasant through their recruitment of novices from their locality, and as traders, landlords and estate managers. Their legacy is still with us, in the remains of their agricultural practices, in their manuscripts, and above all in their buildings which still grace the landscape.

26 Talbot 1967
27 Woodward 1966

THE MARK OF ETERNITY
THE CISTERCIANS AS BUILDERS

by
Nicola Coldstream

THE CISTERCIANS AND ARCHITECTURE

Despite their now ruinous condition, Cistercian monasteries were built to last. Often of fine ashlar masonry, so tempting to later builders, the remains that grace some of the most beautiful valleys in Britain still arouse in visitors the same emotions that inspired Wordsworth at Tintern. Yet the history of Cistercian architecture is traditionally presented as a reflection of the order's spiritual decline. The early excavators of Cistercian abbeys helped to establish an image of simple, plain beginnings in the twelfth century, followed by a change to new designs and lavish decoration that were largely indistinguishable from medieval architecture in general. Later Cistercian architecture reinforced the impression given by their way of life, of betrayed ideals and infringement of the rules. Evidence in such buildings as Rievaulx, Fountains, Tintern and Melrose supported it, as did late nineteenth- and early twentieth-century attitudes, which saw cycles of growth, maturity and decline in history, in architecture and in monasticism. The Cistercians were not the only reformed religious order of the late eleventh century: the Augustinian canons had emerged following papal initiatives some thirty years earlier; the Carthusians first took root in the 1080s; and independent Augustinian congregations — such as the Premonstratensians — were to follow in the next century. All were later to lose their moral pre-eminence to the new orders of mendicant friars, who preached holy poverty in towns rather than in rural seclusion. In the late Middle Ages, all the religious orders acquired a reputation for laxity. Yet only the Cistercians and their architecture somehow seem to provoke these censorious outbursts.

We may question whether it is legitimate to use architecture as an indicator of moral health; and whether to moralize or condemn is even justified. Since the 1970s, research in many disciplines has produced a more complicated picture of Cistercian development. Discoveries in building chronology have changed the accepted evolutionary pattern, and we know more about the stylistic connections between Cistercian churches and those outside the order. These suggest that a reappraisal of the Cistercians and their architecture is long overdue.

Owing to some well-publicized texts, such as St Bernard's *Apologia*, written in the 1120s, and some equally well-known buildings, we have formed a clear picture of Cistercian architectural requirements. The early sources on which the *Exordium Parvum* was to be based say that buildings should be simple, neutral and without colour. The surviving mid-twelfth-century church at Fontenay (Côte-d'Or) in Burgundy, together with the many Cistercian ruins all over Europe, including what is left of the naves at Rievaulx and Margam, seem to bear out this opinion and set

Left: Detail of early thirteenth-century capitals in the east processional doorway in the abbey church at Valle Crucis.

Below: The twelfth-century cloister alleys at Fontenay in Burgundy, an abbey frequently cited as representing the essence of Cistercian architecture (Peter Humphries).

Bottom: The Cistercian church at Staffarda (Piedmont) in Italy (David Robinson).

the standard from which the Cistercians are deemed to have slipped. But this interpretation oversimplifies cause and effect. These early writings appeared in the context of the very first generation of Cistercian buildings; compared to such structures, the later Fontenay and Rievaulx are statements of unimaginable grandeur.

The Cistercians tried to control building through both visitations to individual abbeys, and through prescriptive instructions issued from the General Chapter; but we actually know very little about their thinking on architecture. The General Chapter had much to say on liturgical vessels and furnishings, yet there is only one statute concerning architecture: that of 1157, which prohibits stone bell towers. The church built at Meaux in the 1160s was pulled down because it was deemed inappropriate, and in the 1190s Vaucelles (Nord) in north-east France was criticized on the same grounds. But by this time Cistercian architecture was already varied; and some scholars suggest that individual abbots could personally influence aspects of their buildings. In truth, we cannot usefully even guess how Meaux and Vaucelles may have transgressed.

Our difficulty lies less in architecture as such than in our interpretation of architectural decoration. The Cistercians deplored figure sculpture because imagery distracted the meditating monk from his search for spiritual union with God. As the order was founded at the exact time that Romanesque sculpture was beginning to flourish, imagery was a problem from the beginning, and as early as 1109 sculpture was forbidden in Cistercian churches. But between the late eleventh century and the early sixteenth, there were radical changes in patterns of religious practice. St Bernard, whose mysticism was stimulated from within, had recognized that religious imagery was necessary to help the laity to see God; but the later-medieval world was more intensely visual than he could have imagined. The individual was now more responsible for his own salvation, and contemporary piety, encouraged by visionary mystics, demanded that people expiate their sins by entering imaginatively into the sufferings of Christ and the saints, through contemplating an appropriate image. A Cistercian monk of the fifteenth century would have spent a childhood surrounded by and spiritually involved with religious imagery. Churches were full of carved and painted figures, many of them built into the fabric as statues, corbels and vault bosses.

It is not, however, figure sculpture that presents us with a problem. It was kept out of Cistercian churches until late in their history. It is the other forms of architectural enrichment — foliage capitals, unstructural colonnettes, wall arcading, rose windows and window tracery — that we also categorize as decoration and were prominent in Cistercian churches from the mid-twelfth century onwards. The Cistercians were enthusiasts for rose windows by the 1140s, and shortly afterwards developed elaborate designs for piers with moulded profiles or applied detached shafts. Such features offer alternative interpretations: either that the Cistercians abandoned their ideals within a generation, or that modern presumptions about the 'ideals' are too strict, and that such things did not infringe the rules, because they were seen not as decoration but as extensions of the architecture.

We may reach a clearer understanding by asking what the architectural enrichment was for. Above all, a church is the house of God, the setting for the mass and the Divine Office, the *Opus Dei* — the monks' cycle of daily prayer. In a sense it becomes an offering to God. The Cistercians had honoured God in the luminosity

Figure sculpture was far from uncommon in Cistercian churches during the later Middle Ages. This late thirteenth- or early fourteenth-century detail on a roof boss from Dore Abbey shows a monk kneeling before his abbot, or possibly a bishop.

even of their early buildings, for they greatly espoused the medieval equation of light with God, and arranged their church windows accordingly. As architecture developed in the twelfth and thirteenth centuries, style increasingly reflected the building's function and significance, and the widely held belief that as an offering to God it should be appropriately adorned. The introduction of colour, in wall plaster, painted abstract decorations on columns and windows, and in tiled floors, was another aspect of this belief. If Cistercian churches are understood, like all churches, as offerings to God and the saints, the urge to embellish begins to make sense. From the thirteenth century there was much more, both portable furnishings such as altarpieces, and architectural sculpture. The *pulpitum* screens that blocked off the monks' choir to the west were occasionally as magnificent as any found in secular churches: remains of the Tintern *pulpitum* have been identified, likewise a possible rood screen and shrine at Dore; and others probably await discovery. Benefactors invaded the churches with monumental tombs and effigies. If we think about late-medieval Cistercians in this context, the measure of their resistance to the decorated interior is impressive.

This history of Cistercian architecture may be seen in four broad phases: the very early years, with the first buildings, in timber then stone between the early twelfth century and about 1130; the rapid expansion of the order and the first great churches in the 1130s; the second half of the twelfth century, with an expanded liturgy and the development of altar spaces; and the period after about 1190. Britain was colonized from 1128, at the turn of the first and second phases, when the movement had existed for a whole generation, and was becoming institutionalized. Already by the 1150s the strong Burgundian architectural influence was giving way to more local styles; gradually we see Cistercian buildings as part of general developments in British architecture, with definable regional variations. Yet running through their architectural history is a restraint that sets them apart.

Archaeology has traditionally played a large part in the story of Cistercian architecture, and site studies, involving both excavation and the analysis of loose stones, are essential tools in enriching our understanding. In this chapter, however, we shall look primarily at the standing remains. Not all Cistercian churches were as architecturally magnificent as Fountains, Rievaulx or Tintern, and some have all but vanished. Some vanished buildings — for example Meaux and Coupar Angus — were evidently of great architectural interest. So we should be aware that, however consistent the story may seem, there are large gaps in the evidence.

In due course, benefactors were to invade Cistercian churches with their tombs and effigies. This drawing shows an early fourteenth-century effigy from Fountains. It most likely covered the tomb of Henry Percy, lord of Alnwick (d. 1315).

Most of the abbeys as they survive today represent several stages in their architectural evolution: at Rievaulx, for example, we see a twelfth-century nave, a thirteenth-century presbytery, and monastic ranges dating down to the fifteenth century, built of stone and arranged round a cloister. The very first Cistercian buildings were quite different. None survives above ground, but we know from excavation and documentary evidence that they were timber-framed and grouped together without a cloister. It is as if, in their anxiety to return to St Benedict's precepts, the founders of the movement rejected current Benedictine planning.[1]

The regulation laid down in one of the earliest Cistercian prescriptive chapters, dating perhaps to 1113, states: 'No abbot shall be sent to a new place without at

THE FIRST WOODEN BUILDINGS

I   Schaefer 1982

The names of several early abbot-builders are known from England. In this manuscript illumination of the late twelfth-century, monks are portrayed building with angelic help (British Library, Additional Ms. 39943, f. 39).

least twelve monks ... and without the prior construction of such places as an oratory, a refectory, a dormitory, a guest house, and a gatekeeper's cell, so that the monks may immediately serve God and live in religious discipline'. It is very precise, providing exactly for the needs and obligations of the monks: a viable group, obligations to prayer and hospitality, the need for food, sleep and protection from the world. Beyond listing the necessary buildings, it says nothing about their style or arrangement.

Chroniclers liked to record that the monks put up the first buildings with their own hands, but usually the patron had them built, on advice from the mother house. The monks' quarters provided by Count William of Aumâle at Meaux were so acceptable that when more space was needed Abbot Adam (1150–60) built a larger version of the same design. While the monks and lay brothers may have worked as unskilled labour, and monks are recorded as builders through the thirteenth century, lay professionals were hired from the beginning.

In Britain, however, advisers were also present.[2] Geoffrey d'Ainai (d. 1140), sent from Clairvaux to Fountains, instructed the fledgling convent on Cistercian practice. As the order expanded, he may well have trained the next generation of abbot-builders — Robert of Newminster (d. 1159), Adam of Meaux and Alexander of Kirkstall (d. 1182). It was recorded that the abbeys of Newminster, Woburn and Kirkstall were built 'after the manner of our order', which suggests that there was a clear idea of what was, or was not, required even for the temporary buildings. Geoffrey d'Ainai seems to have been a joint master mason at the new Clairvaux from 1135, but whether he, Adam or other abbot-builders were genuine architects or only administrators is uncertain.

The timber buildings were simple and cheap to build, being replaced in stone often within a few years, probably when the monastery was judged to be viable: at Cîteaux a small stone church had replaced the wooden oratory by 1106. But they had wider connotations, perhaps recalling the wooden buildings at Molesme, with its church of interlaced branches. This would be in keeping with the medieval stress on origins and memory. St Bernard himself was said to be nostalgic for the wooden church at Clairvaux, which he could see from his room in the new stone monastery. But the wooden buildings were also symbolic: at Bordesley, where the first monastic buildings were taken down, the precious timbers were used to cover the monks' graves. They seem to have symbolized the earliest days of the order, their resemblance to hermits' cells emphasizing the close relation to contemporary eremitical movements in Burgundy.

Right: The churches at Cîteaux and Clairvaux have long disappeared, and the earliest surviving example in the Cistercian cradle-lands is now Fontenay, built in 1139–47 (David Robinson).

The second timber church at Clairvaux, built soon after 1115, is described as square, with an aisle surrounding a taller central space and, under the same, continuous roof, an adjoining refectory with the dormitory above it. In Britain, apart from the Bordesley timbers, surviving remains of wooden buildings have been excavated at Fountains and also at Sawley. At Fountains, postholes below the south transept of the present church indicate two buildings, one perhaps a small, rectangular church, the other a domestic building, possibly two-storeyed. If the interpretation is correct, the first buildings at Fountains may have been related to those of the mother house at Clairvaux. But even if they were, this disposition was not followed when Fountains established its daughter house at Meaux. The later medieval Meaux chronicle (*Chronica Monasterii de Melsa*) describes a timber-framed building for the lay brothers and, for the monks, a two-storey structure with

2 Fergusson 1983; Fergusson 1984b

EARLY STONE CHURCHES

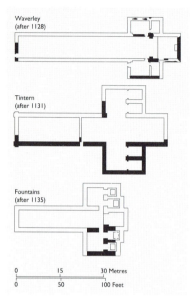

Waverley
(after 1128)

Tintern
(after 1131)

Fountains
(after 1135)

0   15   30 Metres
0   50   100 Feet

Comparative ground plans of early Cistercian churches in Britain.

THE BERNARDINE PLAN

the dormitory on the ground floor and the chapel above. Moreover, from the excavated evidence, it appears that the development of the early buildings at Sawley may well have been very similar to the documented pattern known at Meaux.

Unfortunately, the appearance of the early stone Cistercian churches is equally vague: at Cîteaux and Pontigny they seem to have been small and rectangular. They provide no real context for the first stone churches in Britain.

The part-excavated fragments of Waverley and Tintern, built in the early 1130s, with Fountains I following after 1135, suggest that by this time, although no Burgundian precedent survives, the British Cistercians favoured a distinctive type of church. Indeed, the earliest stone church now traced at Rievaulx (Rievaulx I) seems to have been of similar design; Sawley, too, was set out along these lines; and Lysa (a daughter of Fountains situated in Norway) is another example of the plan. In essence, the design comprised an aisleless nave, a rectangular chancel, and short transept arms, all probably lower than the nave in height. At Fountains the rectangular sanctuary and chapels were built apparently to a stepped plan. There was no crossing — at Waverley the transepts were effectively walled off from the main vessel, but at Tintern and Fountains they were perhaps more open to it. The Tintern nave has been reconstructed with a wooden roof, but the chancel, the transepts and their chapels may have had barrel vaults. At Waverley, however, it may have been only the transept chapels which were vaulted.

These churches would have contrasted markedly with their Anglo-Norman contemporaries. An Anglo-Norman church of any pretension has aisles, a marked crossing with at least a low lantern tower, and, although not fully vaulted, would have been articulated with much surface decoration in the form of wall arcading, and carved capitals, corbels and doorways. Yet these small, plain churches were not peculiar to the Cistercians; the other reformed orders — the Augustinians and Premonstratensians — also built them. At this stage, then, there was no distinctively Cistercian style, rather a desire for architecture appropriate to the reform movement as a whole. The Cistercians had now begun to build for permanence.

In 1135, while these first stone Cistercian churches were going up in Britain, a monumental stone church was built at Clairvaux. Brother Geoffrey d'Ainai and a mason named Archardus laid out an eleven-bay aisled nave, transepts with square-ended chapels on their east and west sides, and a rectangular, projecting sanctuary. This church — known as Clairvaux II — has disappeared, and the best surviving example of such a plan is at Fontenay in Burgundy, built in 1139–47. The pointed barrel vault over the nave runs continuously through to the presbytery, with no marked crossing. The presbytery and transepts are both lower than the nave. The transept chapels are vaulted by pointed barrels; in the nave, the aisle bays are differentiated into separate chapels by barrel vaults set at right-angles to the main vessel. Decoration is confined to plain foliage capitals, but the interior is suffused in soft light that enters through the aisle windows and those of the presbytery and east gable.

The high altar stood in the sanctuary, and the monks' choir ran westwards through the unsegregated crossing into the second or third bay of the nave. The monks' choir was closed off by the *pulpitum* screen, with the rood screen beyond it. Filling the nave west of the rood screen was the lay brothers' choir: the length of the nave reflected the increase in the number of lay brothers. It was the provision for the lay brothers that differentiated Cistercian church layouts. Traces of the stone screens that separated the choirs from the aisles survive in many churches in Britain, notably at Buildwas, Byland, Fountains, Strata Florida and Tintern.

This church type characterizes Cistercian churches throughout Europe, and we find examples of the plan being built down to the late Middle Ages. The plan provokes instant recognition. Because it was devised in St Bernard's lifetime, was built at Clairvaux and diffused throughout the order, it has since the 1950s been called 'Bernardine'. Whether Bernard had anything to do with it is unknown, but it is on the Bernardine plan that all modern ideas of Cistercian uniformity are based.

Different elevations were built on the Bernardine plan, but to the Cistercians the important aspect was the disposition of liturgical space, and a ground plan can easily be passed over great distances in a simple drawing. Whatever the elevation, the liturgical spaces were the same in all Bernardine churches.

The Bernardine plan is not important for its supposed associations with the wishes of the saint. The building of monumental aisled stone churches, together with the adoption of the traditional Benedictine monastic plan of buildings around a cloister, signifies that in the 1130s the burgeoning Cistercian movement left its eremitical origins behind, however regretfully, and became an institution. The wooden buildings of the 1150s at Meaux show that such ideals lingered in temporary quarters; but by the thirteenth century there is little sign of them in the record. From the 1130s, the Cistercians joined the monastic establishment. The next generation of churches in Britain was to bear this out.

Abbot Henry Murdac's works at Fountains from 1144 — the addition of aisles to the church and the layout of a cloister — presaged the change. The first great churches to survive were built at Rievaulx and Fountains after 1147, and at Kirkstall from 1152. In Scotland the destroyed first church of Melrose was evidently closely based on its mother house at Rievaulx. It is through the survivors that we can trace the initial adoption of Burgundian Romanesque forms followed by increasingly local details and the onset of early Gothic modes. These churches, requiring professional skills in the geometry of setting out and stone cutting, were built by lay masons; but Rievaulx at any rate seems to have been built with direct knowledge of Burgundy. This knowledge could have come with special advisers, like Geoffrey d'Ainai in the previous decade; but it could equally have come with Abbot Ailred (1147–67) himself.

All three churches — Rievaulx II, Fountains II and Kirkstall — have the Bernardine plan. The narrow nave aisles at Rievaulx and Fountains suggest that the source of their plans was not Clairvaux itself, but Vauclair (Aisne) in Picardy, the home of Henry Murdac and his successor Abbot Richard III (1150–70) before they came to Fountains. Rievaulx survives least well. Much of its elevation has to be inferred from other buildings. But if the inferences are correct, Rievaulx adopted the style favoured by the Cistercians of the Burgundian heartland: their local Romanesque in a plain, reduced form, as exemplified at Fontenay.

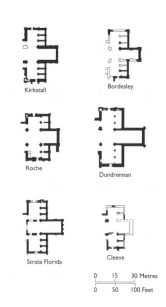

Comparative plans (examples only) showing the east ends of British Cistercian churches of Bernardine form.

THE FIRST GREAT CHURCHES

The elevation of Rievaulx has been reconstructed with two storeys — a pointed arcade and round-headed clerestory windows, the exterior articulated by string-courses, as on the surviving transepts. The aisles were vaulted with pointed barrel vaults set at right-angles to the main vessel, which was probably roofed in wood. There was no marked crossing, and the transepts and presbytery probably joined the nave at equal height. The square piers were plain except for chamfers on the inner angles. A galilee porch stood at the west. The galilee, the pointed arches, the transverse barrels and the chamfered piers are all strongly Burgundian and without parallel in Anglo-Norman Romanesque. Rievaulx differs from Fontenay in its wooden roof and the equal height of all parts. Clairmont (Mayenne) in western

THE MONASTIC BUILDINGS

Once the Cistercians had adopted the normal Benedictine arrangement of buildings round a cloister in the 1130s, they followed convention except for two changes to allow for their specific requirements. The west range, which normally contained the abbot's living quarters as well as storage, was given over to the lay brothers, and the abbot was accommodated elsewhere. The other change was to the alignment of the refectory.

In Benedictine abbeys the refectory lay on an east–west axis parallel to the south walk of the cloister. From the 1150s the Cistercians built their refectories on a north–south alignment at right-angles to the cloister walk. In established abbeys the refectory was realigned when the claustral buildings were renewed. Although a few smaller houses kept the former arrangement, the new alignment was adopted throughout the Cistercian filiation, and so characteristic is it that you can always recognize a Cistercian monastery from its ground-plan alone.

The reason for the change was that it made space for the warming house and the kitchen to be placed either side of the refectory off the south walk. The monastic kitchen was often placed at a slight distance, to lessen the risk of fire. But the *Rule of St Benedict* did not allow a monk to leave the cloister, and the chance of a fire was evidently less important to the Cistercians than the literal interpretation of the *Rule*. The monks could now reach the kitchen without leaving the cloister.[1]

The east range, with the chapter house on the ground floor and the dormitory above, was conventionally planned, and, as in other monasteries, the monks entered the church at night via the stair leading from the dormitory directly into the transept. Traces of the night stairs, or the door opening on the first floor, survive in many abbey churches. In a Cistercian abbey the chapter house was often more flamboyantly decorated than the church, with finer mouldings and, later, figure sculpture on the vault bosses. The late medieval chapter houses at Valle Crucis and Balmerino have elaborate tracery. The chapter house was the most important building after the church. The monks assembled there daily for readings of the *Rule*, for confessions, to discuss monastery business, and commemorate former monks and benefactors. The chapter house was also the burial place of the abbots. It was usually square or rectangular, with a vestibule where the lay brothers could sit. But the chapter house built at Rievaulx in Ailred's time was a two-storey, apsed structure which, it is suggested, was modelled on the great burial basilicas of early Christian Rome, thus emphasizing the necrological function of the building.[2]

The Rievaulx chapter house has been associated with Ailred's influence. That abbots imposed their personalities on building programmes quite early on has been argued also for Dore, where the chapter house was built probably under Abbot Adam I shortly after 1200.[3] The Dore chapter house is a twelve-sided polygon. Although polygonal chapter houses were soon to be adopted widely in Britain, Dore was among the earliest. It was possibly modelled on the early twelfth-century circular chapter house of Worcester and was preceded by the chapter house at Margam: Dore and Margam (and the later Whalley) have the only known polygonal chapter houses in Cistercian architecture. All three chapter houses — Rievaulx, Dore and Margam — were allowed to remain standing, even though they were built in the period when Cistercians are known to have been particularly anxious about appropriate buildings. These chapter houses again raise the question of how we should understand the Cistercians' building policy.

The almost complete collapse of a truly communal life by the late fifteenth century is best seen in the monastic buildings, for that was where most building effort was dedicated. Many were the alterations: dormitories were divided into separate rooms, abbots' houses were enlarged, at Cleeve the refectory was rebuilt to resemble a secular hall. It is in these changes rather than the churches that we find the most convincing physical evidence of the loss of the original monastic ideal. But no religious order was able to maintain the religious dedication of its forebears.

1 Fergusson 1986
2 Fergusson and Harrison 1994
3 Hillaby 1988–90

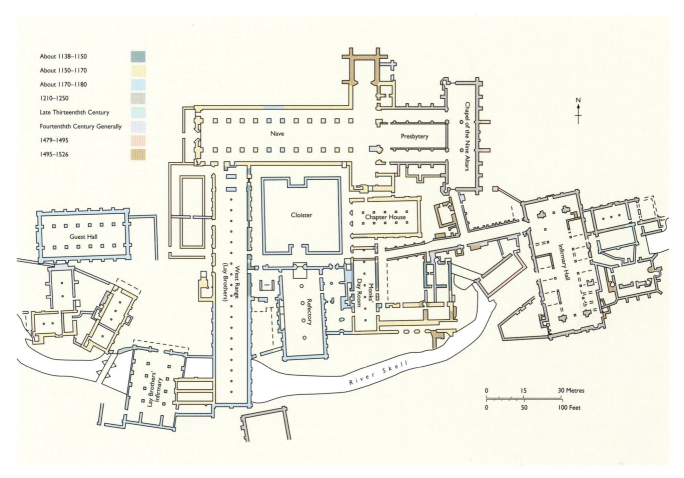

About 1138–1150
About 1150–1170
About 1170–1180
1210–1250
Late Thirteenthth Century
Fourtenthth Century Generally
1479–1495
1495–1526

Guest Hall

Nave

Presbytery

Chapel of the Nine Altars

Cloister

Chapter House

West Range (Lay Brothers)

Refectory

Monks' Day Room

Infirmary Hall

Lay Brothers' Infirmary

River Skell

N

0   15   30 Metres
0   50   100 Feet

France gives an idea of its likely appearance. Both may derive from the almost unknown great church at Cîteaux, which was built in the 1140s.

At Fountains, where more survives, the Burgundian Romanesque of Rievaulx lingered. It may be seen in the surviving transept chapels with their pointed barrel vaults and solid dividing walls, in the aisles vaulted with transverse barrels, and in the galilee porch. The nave, however, has details that are not Burgundian: the cylindrical piers, with moulded bases and scalloped capitals; the attached shafts facing the aisles, carrying the junction of the arcade and barrel vaults; the transept arches, moulded in two chamfered orders — already more articulation than Rievaulx — and the three orders in the nave arcade. The clerestory is deeper, the string-courses more prominent.

The general articulation of surfaces, as well as individual elements, is Anglo-Norman, and represents a move away from the strong Burgundian influence at Rievaulx. Its significance can perhaps be overstated. If Rievaulx is seen as the standard, a statement of Cistercian ideals, any introduction of decorative detail can be interpreted as a weakening of resolve. But as we saw earlier, we may be in danger of imposing on the Cistercians a set of attitudes that we think they should hold. What is remarkable about these mid-twelfth-century abbey churches is not that they took on more local characteristics, but that the builders of Rievaulx apparently managed to import a style that was so alien to contemporary Yorkshire. Given the

The ground plan of Fountains illustrates the mature layout of a Cistercian abbey church and monastic buildings.

The church at Clairmont in western France gives an idea of the likely appearance of the early church at Rievaulx, and also that at Margam (David Robinson).

43

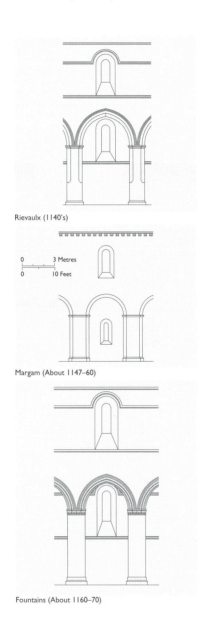

Rievaulx (1140's)

0   3 Metres

0   10 Feet

Margam (About 1147–60)

Fountains (About 1160–70)

THE BEGINNINGS OF GOTHIC

3 Harrison 1995
4 Fergusson 1984b; Wilson 1986

conditions of twelfth-century life, the degree of consistency and control that the Burgundian influence represents is extraordinary. That it did not last is of no consequence: the wonder is that it appeared at all.

Kirkstall, too, has greater articulation. Kirkstall is the sole early Cistercian great church in the north, with its twelfth-century east end standing to full height — a design, like Fountains, of transept chapels with pointed barrel vaults and solid dividing walls, but with applied shafts and soffit rolls at the entrance arches. Kirkstall's building programme overlapped that of Fountains, and they have elements in common, including a rose window, even if of quite different patterns and construction techniques.[3]

Segregated crossings, with high arches to the nave, sanctuary and transepts, and supporting low towers, were built or inserted into Cistercian churches from the 1140s. The surviving crossings at Fountains (dating from the 1160s), at Kirkstall and at Buildwas show that their towers conformed to the requirement to rise one storey only above the roofs. Although stone bell towers were forbidden in 1157, a bell tower can be freestanding, and this statute need not relate to crossing towers. By adopting the segregated crossing, the Cistercians were joining other orders and the secular church in divorcing liturgical arrangement from architectural design, for the monks' choir now ran across the newly opened spaces. But the extra light and spaciousness of a crossing and lantern tower, as well as building fashion, may have persuaded them.

The real innovations at Kirkstall appear in the nave. The aisles have rib vaults. Like the crossing, they create an open, spacious effect, a reduction of solidity seen also in the piers. The piers are 'moulded', that is, composed of coursed masonry with an undulating outline. In the western bays they resemble groups of separate shafts. This type of pier is known as 'fasciculated' or 'bundled'. While the rib vaults have English precedents at the cathedrals of Durham and Lincoln, the fasciculated pier derives from north-east France. Its use spread rapidly to England, appearing not only at Kirkstall but at Furness, Byland and Roche, and in the east guest house of Fountains. Outside the Cistercian milieu, it was used in the crypt of York Minster and at Ripon Minster. All these buildings in one way or another show awareness of the newly emerging forms of French Gothic architecture. This was to be the main influence on the next generation of Cistercian buildings, which would at the same time show closer links to non-Cistercian churches.

In the second half of the twelfth century the building boom in northern Europe gathered pace. The architectural ideas that had been developing in France since the 1130s spread to England in piecemeal fashion, from different centres, and to several buildings. In the south, the first coherent Gothic design was Canterbury Cathedral in the 1170s. There ribbed vaults, large windows, and wall-passages lightened the mass of masonry, and applied decorative colonnettes linked the vaults and elevation into visual unity.

The introduction of Gothic to the north has become synonymous with the Cistercians. But in practice the situation was more complicated. By then, Cistercian building was becoming closely related to church building in general, and we can no longer treat Cistercian architecture as a separate phenomenon. The abbots who came and went between northern England and the General Chapter in Burgundy travelled through the areas of most active building — Flanders, Picardy and Champagne — and undoubtedly brought architectural ideas with them. But Cistercian abbots were not the only people involved. Although in the north the Cistercians had set the pace by providing most of the building work, the other orders and the secular church were soon to catch up. As masons were employed at different sites, it was inevitable that ideas would circulate without discrimination. Architecturally, the picture is not so much confused as incoherent, with different design solutions offered at different buildings. Any building project involved the wishes of the patrons, the creativity and experience of the masons, and the response of either to other buildings. In an individual case, the relative importance of any one of these can only be guessed at.

The extent and nature of the Cistercian contribution to northern Gothic architecture is debated, owing partly to chronological uncertainties and partly to unresolved difficulties in defining the nature of Gothic. In so far as Gothic uses the same language of arches and vaults, it can be seen as a continuation of Romanesque by other means. But the vocabulary is assembled in different ways, with new techniques of geometry and construction. In Britain, which never willingly shed the squat solidity of Romanesque, Gothic can easily become a matter of surface ornament, the interplay of pointed arches, multiple shafts, and rib vaults. Paradoxically, as we have seen at Kirkstall, the new lessons of light, open spatial organization were learned early; yet by largely ignoring the French apsidal east end, and adopting square-ended plans, the British created very different spaces. If the French sources of the early Gothic Cistercian churches — Furness, Roche and Byland — have been identified correctly, their builders were taking ideas almost at random. The result, while superficially Gothic, is not particularly French.

Nor is it exclusively Cistercian. The Cistercians were not trying to subvert or overthrow traditional monasticism and monastic architecture, but to return to what they saw as the true way. For this they selected appropriate building designs from the common stock. They actually chose the new, lighter massing and sharper mouldings for some conventual buildings, such as chapter houses, while still preferring the heavy Romanesque for their churches. This poses several intriguing and as yet unanswered questions, but it also shows that they were making considered choices.

The architects of Furness and Roche flirted with new forms and spatial expansion.[4] The transept chapels are rib vaulted, as at Kirkstall, and not divided by solid walls. Mouldings and details suggest that they were both influenced by churches in Picardy and the Aisne valley, but drew on different buildings. Furness and Roche combine the Bernardine plan with a three-storey elevation, the first in English Cistercian architecture. At Furness the middle storey was cosmetic, neither a gallery nor a wall-passage but a series of twin-arched openings into the aisle roof space; it did, however, articulate the wall surface. The nave arcade had piers of alternating pattern — cylindrical and fasciculated — and the rib vaulting in the aisles included a wall-rib around the window: this helped in construction to support the wooden centering of the vault, and remained to add elegance to the join of the vault and the wall.

At Furness the details do not add up to a coherent design, and although individually they were to enter the vocabulary of Gothic architecture, the isolation of Furness prevented it from influencing any churches beyond one or two relatively

Left: Comparative bay elevations at the early churches of Rievaulx, Margam and Fountains.

Kirkstall is the sole early Cistercian great church to survive in the north of Britain. The nave had bundled piers, and there were rib vaults in the aisles (Malcolm Thurlby).

The church at Roche combines the Bernardine plan with a three-storey elevation.

local monasteries such as Holmcultram and Calder. The influence of Roche was equally limited.

Roche is much less homogeneous than it looks, and structurally is less 'Gothic' than its appearance suggests, which illustrates the gap between our perception of architectural style and the thought processes of twelfth-century masons. It was rib vaulted throughout, with the bays marked by emphatic vertical shafts. This makes it look rather 'Gothic', yet although the vaults were cut by French rather than English methods, the heavy, unbuttressed walls of its eastern parts are the antithesis of the light, thin walls that characterize French early Gothic buildings, and there are no wall ribs. The middle storey — twin blind arches in each bay — is visually more emphatic than at Furness, but it is not a true gallery.

Roche did not inspire copies. It probably influenced the three-storey, vaulted church at Kirkstead, relatively nearby, and the proportions and middle storey of the remodelled south transept of Dundrennan in south-west Scotland. Excavations at Newminster, Roche's mother house, produced comparable details. But in the 1170s it was Byland that was generating architectural excitement.

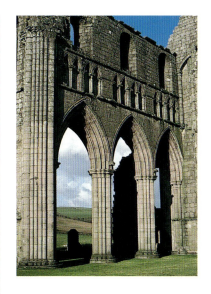

BYLAND AND JERVAULX NEW DESIGNS, NEW SPACES

Byland, begun about 1170, was built to a new, large scale, and to a new plan. Like Furness, it was a former Savigniac house and had had to change its site no fewer than three times. This may have contributed to loosening ties; but, for whatever reason, the design of its elevation is as unexpected as its plan, being comparable to none of its Cistercian contemporaries. Byland's sources are from outside the order.

Byland was not Bernardine, but was aisled throughout, with chapels on both the east and west aisles of the transept, and three aisled bays in the presbytery. The aisles continued around the high eastern terminal wall as a single-storey ambulatory providing space for five extra altars. There are precedents for this arrangement in southern England and possibly at York Minster, but Byland seems to be the first British Cistercian church to adopt it. It provides much increased space for altars at the east. How such altars were used in the daily rituals of the monastery is not yet clear, but the expansion of their earlier simple sanctuaries into great churches surrounded by chapels reflected a developed liturgy; no one went to the expense of enlarging a building for the sake of showing off. Any monk who was an ordained priest was obliged to say mass every so often; and the Cistercians were now so popular with patrons and benefactors that there was great demand for prayers and petitions on behalf of the laity. By 1200 such prayers were part of the monks' established routines. Clairvaux had been the first Cistercian house to expand its east end, the so-called Clairvaux III, with an apse, ambulatory and nine chapels, that was built after St Bernard's death in 1153. Pontigny followed with a similar plan; by 1193 Cîteaux and Morimond had the Byland type of rectilinear variant, with a row of eastern chapels. Thus, by the end of the century, the principal mother houses of the order had all abandoned the Bernardine plan. Byland appears to anticipate Cîteaux, but relative chronologies need to be clarified.

Like Furness and Roche, Byland had a three-storey elevation, but there the comparison ends. The elevation is both structurally and decoratively logical, a coherent design that betrays none of the signs of random selection that beset Furness, or the contradictions between appearance and structure that we find at

Above: *Aspects in the design of the south transept at Dundrennan in Scotland may have been influenced by the 1170s work at Roche (Malcolm Thurlby).*

Left: *Byland was the Cistercian building generating the greatest excitement in the north of England in the 1170s. The church was not Bernardine in form, but was aisled throughout. This superb aerial view shows the church and monastic buildings from the west (Skyscan Balloon Photography).*

The south transept chapels at Byland Abbey.

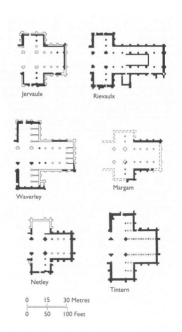

Comparative plans (examples only) of British Cistercian churches with aisled presbyteries.

Roche. It had fasciculated piers, a false gallery and a wall-passage at clerestory level. In the end wall of the transept, a second passage substituted for the gallery. The bay divisions were punctuated by vertical shafts rising from the spandrels of the arcade to the ceiling, which was probably a wooden barrel vault. The mouldings — including the arcade arches and the rib vaults of the aisles — were slender and sharp. Wall-ribs in the aisles added to the impression of rich linearity. In the two upper storeys wall-arcading framed the openings and pulled the whole composition together, while the lavish use of arches and shafts reduced the visual mass.

Certain details of construction, the double passage in the transept, and the general reduction of wall mass, presuppose knowledge of north-eastern French architecture, the abundant shaft work suggesting the area around Valenciennes (Nord). But Byland is not French. The clerestory passage and framing arches continued an Anglo-Norman design in updated form, as did the coating of the structure in architectural ornament. Compared to Roche, there was less vertical emphasis.

Byland is the first Cistercian church to look familiarly English. Burgundian Romanesque has been left behind, early Gothic French ideas have been absorbed into local practices. Byland is related to an architectural network that includes Ripon Minster — which shares the Byland design and disputes priority — the lost choir of York Minster and St Andrews Cathedral, as well as Premonstratensian, Benedictine and later Cistercian houses in the north. The great western rose, which had twenty-four spokes in its outer wheel, helped to establish the tradition of rose windows that persisted in the north until the late thirteenth century. Even the changes to the style of the Byland capitals, from waterleaf to volute to moulded, have exact parallels over a wide area. The decoration of shaft-rings and nailhead on the west front of Byland, which was built in the 1190s, has reflections at the Tironensian Arbroath Abbey and Benedictine Tynemouth. It appears also on parts of Rievaulx and Jervaulx. The remodelled north transept of Dundrennan adopted such details of Byland as heavily fasciculated piers and wall shafts rising from the spandrels of the arcade.

The Byland plan reappeared at Dore and later at Waverley, Meaux and possibly Newbattle, but the most popular plan for thirteenth-century churches proved to be that of Jervaulx, built in the 1190s. There a four-bay, aisled presbytery ended at a full height, flat east wall, giving a rectangular, box-like profile with no projecting chapels or ambulatory. This design is almost uniquely English. It had been built during the twelfth century at several churches over an area stretching from Kent and Hampshire in the south to Northumberland on the Scottish borders. It was, therefore, without regional connections, but it was very rare outside England. From the thirteenth century, the rectangular presbytery became the most popular form of eastern arm in British churches. It was extremely adaptable, as it could have as many bays as required, and the different liturgical spaces could be marked out at floor level by screens. Examples of rectangular aisled presbyteries built for the Cistercians included those at Aberconwy II (Maenan), Fountains, Hailes I, Margam, Neath, Netley, Rievaulx, Stanley and Whalley.

From Byland and Jervaulx onwards, then, we should see Cistercian architecture not as a distinct phenomenon, but in the context of British architecture as a whole. But before turning to developments in the thirteenth century, we need to look at what was happening further south.

The twelfth-century work in Wales and the west midlands was, on the whole, simpler and of a smaller scale than that in Yorkshire. Most of the Welsh houses were affiliated to Clairvaux, through Whitland, although Margam, too, was founded directly from St Bernard's Clairvaux. It seems likely that Whitland, Margam, Strata Florida, and probably Strata Marcella, were intended to have the Bernardine plan, at first with an unsegregated crossing. But eventually in both Wales and the west country the crossing tower became a standard feature. In the early thirteenth century, Strata Marcella's daughter house at Valle Crucis was to retain the Bernardine plan.

Elevation designs in this region followed the same pattern as the north. A 'Burgundian' phase quickly gave way to the influence of local styles. Margam, begun in the 1150s, and perhaps also Whitland, belong to the group that includes the nave of Rievaulx. The restored remains of the nave at Margam have a plain clerestory above essentially rectangular piers, barely articulated. It is just possible that the north transept chapels of Dore were originally roofed with barrel vaults.

But this was not to last long. As they are seen now, Strata Florida, Buildwas and Dore all have rib vaults in their transept chapels. Buildwas is an almost exact contemporary of Margam, but it already shows its regional connections. The two-storey nave elevation at Buildwas is squat and thick, with round arches and cylindrical piers that follow a west country tradition going back to the eleventh century. At Dore and Strata Florida, both begun later, regional connections are even more emphatic. The nave at Dore was similar to Buildwas, with cylindrical piers, but the clerestory windows were intended to sit high under the vault. Despite earlier suggestions, it seems the clerestory did not have an integrated triforium. Such an arrangement was common in west country great churches of the period, as in the nave of St Davids Cathedral, but at Dore there were probably deeply sloping sills.[5] It is, nevertheless, tempting to link Dore with St Davids, as both churches show a liking for variety in ornament, as does Strata Florida. Strata Florida is a building closely related to St Davids that also has features in common with Dore. But the designers of Dore drew more widely for ideas. The foliage of both Dore and Buildwas has parallels at such buildings as Wells Cathedral and Glastonbury Abbey. The surprisingly 'Gothic' vertical shafts in the reworked transepts at Dore seem to be derived from the Benedictine abbey at Gloucester (now the cathedral), or perhaps the lost church of the Augustinian abbey at Keynsham, near Bristol.

The Dore transepts did not, however, anticipate the design of the presbytery, which was extended soon after 1186 and took on much of the new Cistercian decorative idiom. It belongs to the new outlook of the thirteenth century.

From the thirteenth century onwards there was a new grandeur and spaciousness in architecture, which Cistercian buildings shared. They could adapt easily into the current preference for architectural enrichment with mouldings and applied shafts, and for the moulded capitals and bases that were the alternative to the exuberant stiff-leaf foliage. In the first half of the thirteenth century, in particular, architecture in Britain evolved along its own lines. There was insular disregard of the French taste for great height: churches were lower than their French counterparts, and height was suggested only in steeply pointed arches and tall lancet windows. Although many buildings kept the Anglo-Norman thick wall structure,

WALES AND THE WEST COUNTRY

The east end of Strata Florida, thought to have been under construction in the 1180s, and closely related to St Davids Cathedral.

The transepts and crossing at Dore were first raised in the 1170s. This view looks north across the transepts, with the presbytery to the right.

THE THIRTEENTH CENTURY A NEW OUTLOOK

5   Harrison and Thurlby 1997

One of several Cistercian churches founded in Scotland after 1200, Culross was built on the, by then, rather conservative Bernardine plan.

A stone effigy of Dervorguilla, founder of Sweetheart, bearing the embalmed heart of her beloved husband, John Balliol. It is to be seen at the abbey in south-west Scotland.

Right: Begun soon after 1186, the presbytery and surrounding chevet at Dore presage the new Cistercian outlook of the early thirteenth century. The tower was raised over the south transept chapels after the suppression.

which maintains the same thickness at every level, a few did have the French technique of thin upper walls supported by flying buttresses, a technique that was used in some Cistercian churches. Cistercian buildings both reflected and contributed to the architecture of their own regions. Sometimes a detail appeared first in a Cistercian church to be used later elsewhere, sometimes the other way round. As masons did not work exclusively for any one patron, experiment and innovation were a matter of luck and chronology.

Yet the Cistercians followed their own approach to building. They generally favoured stone-vaulted interiors with two storeys, three-storey elevations being rare. A significant theme in their architecture is their focus on the Cistercian movement itself. From about 1200, their buildings show awareness of the Cistercian past and their increasing distance in time from their beginnings. They used architecture to stay in touch, not with their eleventh-century origins, but with their years of youthful confidence in the 1130s and 1140s. The early tradition was kept alive by the retention of two characteristically Burgundian Romanesque features: the galilee porch, and the Bernardine plan. Both persisted longest in Scotland, Wales and the borders, where the abbeys were apt to be poorer and more isolated from developments at the heart of the movement. This cannot be the sole explanation, however, as some of the houses concerned were wealthy and several were royal foundations. The galilee did nearly go out of fashion, but galilees were built at Hailes, Sweetheart, Neath and Newminster, and in the fourteenth century a porch was added to the west front of Tintern. Of the eleven abbeys within the modern borders of Scotland no fewer than six — Glenluce, Sweetheart, Balmerino, Culross, Deer and Melrose — were built on the Bernardine plan, that at Melrose as late as 1385. A few later Bernardine plans appeared in England; and in Wales at Basingwerk and, as noted, also at Valle Crucis.

The Cistercians also showed awareness of their own past in the veneration of their founders and holy men. Relics and shrines had been important forms of commemoration throughout Christian history, but in these years there was a more intense focus on cults and the benefits that pilgrimage could bring. Although the physical evidence of Cistercian shrines is scanty, it is now becoming clear that they were relatively common. Clairvaux had been rebuilt in anticipation of Bernard's canonization, and other Cistercian houses had cults of individual abbots who were never formally canonized. At Rievaulx, the source of Cistercian colonization of the north, both William and Ailred were venerated, William at his shrine in the chapter house, Ailred — from an unknown date — in the presbytery of the church.

At Fountains there are remains of a broad, elevated structure behind the high altar that was almost certainly a shrine platform. We know nothing about a cult there, but elsewhere the Cistercians admitted saints and relics from outside the order: Edmund of Abingdon (d. 1240) at Pontigny, the relic of the Holy Blood of Christ at Hailes, and the Holy Cross at Dore. Sweetheart Abbey was named for the heart of John Balliol (d. 1268), buried there in the tomb of his widow, the abbey's founder, Dervorguilla (d. 1289). If Rievaulx is a shrine to the Cistercian past, and Hailes and Dore to the universal Church, Sweetheart celebrates divine and human love in a fusion of the mundane and the divine that is typical of late medieval spirituality. The three latter shrines legitimized the collection of relics, and the relic list compiled at Rievaulx in the sixteenth century, which is both lengthy and varied, probably typifies the situation elsewhere. Relics demanded appropriate settings. The

enlarged, luminous and gracefully moulded spaces of the new generation of Cistercian churches underscore the meaning and significance of the buildings themselves: at Rievaulx, it has been suggested, the splendour of the presbytery honours the cult of Ailred. This is entirely consonant with general developments in religious life, and would have been seen not as a decline in ideals but as an appropriate response to a changed but equally heartfelt ideal.

THE EARLY THIRTEENTH CENTURY IN THE NORTH

With the loss of the monumental early thirteenth-century church at Meaux, Cistercian building in the north at this time is represented by the new presbyteries of Fountains and Rievaulx. In style they show strong local connections while preserving specific Cistercian content; and some structural features — although mediated through English buildings — are undoubtedly French.

According to the *Narratio de Fundatione*, compiled in the early thirteenth century, the presbytery at Fountains was rebuilt because the old one was too dark and cramped. The new one, begun about 1205, is an aisled rectangle of seven bays, the two easternmost opening into a lofty transept with space for altars along the east wall. The Chapel of the Nine Altars was not built until the 1230s, and its only imitator was at Durham Cathedral about ten years later. At Durham the Chapel of the Nine Altars was devised in relation to the shrine of St Cuthbert behind the high altar. No cult is mentioned in the *Narratio*, but the evidence of Durham implies a

The new seven-bay presbytery at Rievaulx was probably under construction in the 1220s.

Stylistically, Rievaulx compares best with a scattered group of non-Cistercian churches in the north of England, including Benedictine Whitby seen here.

similar role for the Nine Altars of Fountains, although in neither place do we know how the altars were intended to function. The number of altars is the same as in the chevet of Clairvaux III, but this may be a coincidence.

To keep the proportion of its twelfth-century nave, Fountains had a two-storey elevation. The piers were of alternating fasciculated designs, and decorative colonnettes and shafts were deployed in the triple arches fronting the clerestory passage, the aisle wall arcading, and the arches flanking the aisle windows. The surfaces were ornate and linear, the wall-passages and slim piers contributed to a light, spacious interior.

The piers and the triple arcading, as well as some of the construction techniques, are so close to Beverley Minster that the two buildings may have had the same architect, though Fountains has a greatly reduced version of the design.[6] Most unusually, in both churches the vaults spring from part way up the clerestory: in most English churches the vaults spring from the clerestory sill, or even from below it. The high springing level pushes the vault well clear of the clerestory and adds to the impression of height and lightness. At both Fountains and Beverley the upper wall is thin and propped by steeply-pitched flying buttresses; the vault is not self-supporting, but oversails that of the aisle. This French Gothic technique was known in England — it had been used in the nave of Roche and at Canterbury Cathedral — but it was rare. The architect probably learned it at St Hugh's choir in Lincoln Cathedral, which had been built in the 1190s. In its walling system and flying buttresses, then, Fountains looked southwards.

Although it was in construction probably in the 1220s, when Fountains was still unfinished, if Rievaulx looked to Fountains at all, it was for the steep pitch of its flying buttresses. Rievaulx is different in every way: where the east wall of Fountains ended in what was to be the last of the great Cistercian rose windows, Rievaulx's eastern aspect opens in tiers of heavily moulded lancets. The elevation is a self-supporting thick wall structure of three storeys. Within the three-storey format, the presbytery and reworked transepts of Rievaulx present several different designs, both in the heavily moulded piers and arches, and in variations of the gallery openings. The shafts supporting the vault springers rise from different levels, and some end in elegant foliate corbels. The clerestory also has different designs, adapted for a wooden roof in the transept and for stone vaults in the presbytery: there the clerestory passage is fronted by triple arches, as at Fountains, but at Rievaulx the flanking arches are narrow and pushed to the sides, allowing the windows to be framed in a wide arch.

The earlier presbytery designs of the Augustinian priory of Hexham and the Benedictine abbey at Whitby share aspects of the Rievaulx scheme, including details of the elevation and the tiered lancets on the east wall. Stylistically, Rievaulx compares best with a scattered group of churches in the north that includes the abbeys of Kirkham (Augustinian) and Whitby, the transepts of York Minster, and Glasgow Cathedral. Thus, where Fountains seems to look southwards to the late twelfth-century French influences at Lincoln, Rievaulx looks mostly northwards, to an area of settled designs of the 1220s and 1230s, where French influence has been absorbed into English structures.

Uniquely at Rievaulx, the monks moved their choir into the new presbytery. At Fountains, despite the remarks in the *Narratio*, the monks' choir stayed in its traditional place in the crossing and nave, leaving the presbytery for the high altar.

The early Gothic presbytery at Fountains was begun in 1203, with the Chapel of the Nine Altars, seen here, completed in the 1230s.

6 Wilson 1991

Most Cistercian choirs seem to have moved eastward, if ever, only in the later Middle Ages after the loss of the lay brothers. We must therefore presume that the new eastern spaces were intended for the liturgy at the new altars. But at Rievaulx there may have been another purpose: there the great compositions of windows, the moulded and foliate decoration and the stone vault together composed an interior that was rich and luminous even by the standards of the time. The evidence suggests that just as Clairvaux III was built for St Bernard, at Rievaulx the presbytery was built as a setting for Ailred's shrine; and we can postulate that the monks moved near to the presence of their saint.

THE EARLY THIRTEENTH CENTURY IN THE SOUTH AND WEST

With the exception perhaps of Dore, before the late thirteenth century the south has no surviving buildings to compare with the grandeur of the northern abbeys or their state of preservation. If they have not vanished altogether, buildings are fragmentary. Many — such as Flaxley, Forde and Netley — were partly incorporated into later mansions; others had their stone robbed for use elsewhere.

We have all but lost what were probably the two great buildings of the first decade of the century: the new eastern arm of Waverley; and Beaulieu, which was founded in 1203–04. Waverley was an aisled rectangle with projecting chapels, like Byland, or perhaps in this instance Cîteaux III, which had been dedicated in 1193. Beaulieu, on the other hand, had an ambulatory with six or seven radiating chapels within the perimeter wall — a copy of Clairvaux III and Pontigny.

Apart from King Stephen's interest in several Savigniac foundations, Beaulieu might be seen as the first major royal Cistercian foundation in England. As such, it heralded the new pattern of patronage. Whereas in the twelfth century the leading Cistercian benefactors were drawn from the baronage, from 1200 several of the main patrons were members of the royal family. Beaulieu's patronage was reflected in its grand scale, and also perhaps in its plan. Beaulieu was founded not from Clairvaux but from Cîteaux, and the plan may have come through the Norman abbey of Bonport (Eure), which was also a royal foundation. There is evidence that in Britain ambulatory and radiating chapel plans are particularly associated with royal foundations. Such a plan was chosen in the mid-thirteenth century by Henry III for the Benedictine abbey of Westminster. It was adopted for the royal abbeys of Hailes and Vale Royal in the 1270s; and the only non-royal Cistercian abbey with this plan is Croxden.

Whatever the source of Beaulieu's plan, that of its superstructure is much clearer. Although the walls were very plain, it has richly detailed piers, with thin, coursed shafts alternating with shafts *en délit* — that is, monoliths cut against the grain of the stone bed — all grouped round a circular core. These piers and the mouldings in the later building phases associate Beaulieu with the great southern cathedrals of Chichester, Salisbury, Winchester, Wells and Canterbury, whose bishops were close allies of the king. Beaulieu should be read as a strong statement of high status architecture. With the loss of Waverley, the scant remains of Beaulieu now constitute almost the sole evidence of such work in Cistercian building in the south.

Beaulieu's version of the plan remained unique in England. Her daughter house at Netley has some similar mouldings, although they are all in common use in the south. But other features may be taken directly from Beaulieu. Both churches had

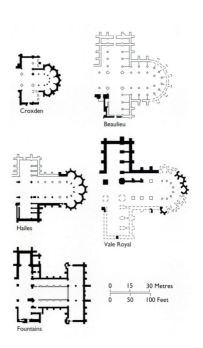

Ground plans of the east ends of British Cistercian churches with radiating chapels. Fountains is included for comparative purposes.

Right: *The great eastern transept at Fountains, known from its inception as the Chapel of the Nine Altars, was a truly remarkable feature. The central gable was originally filled by an elaborate rose window, with three lancets below.*

Croxden

Beaulieu

Hailes

Vale Royal

0   15   30 Metres
0   50   100 Feet

Fountains

The principal elevations at Netley were designed with two storeys masquerading as three.

WALES AND THE WEST

One of the aisle windows (restored) in the extended thirteenth-century presbytery at Margam.

twin lancet windows in each aisle bay, and the nave aisle walls are recessed behind plain arches. The window embrasures are framed by arches with colonnettes, Purbeck marble shafts at Beaulieu, coursed masonry at Netley.

The main elevation at Beaulieu is unknown, but Netley may possibly reflect it. Netley has two storeys masquerading as three. The upper storey is fronted by a wide arch, behind which is set a wall-passage at sill level and clerestory windows raised up into the head of the arch to clear the lean-to roof of the aisle. This gives the effect of a combined clerestory and triforium passage. There is a whole history of two-storey elevations in Gothic architecture. Two storeys were the natural choice for second rank churches, and clusters appear in different places at different times. The relations between one group and another, if any, are not clear. From now on, except at Rievaulx and Croxden, the Cistercians seem to have favoured them. The development and chronology of the open arch fronting a clerestory, with or without a passage, is difficult to establish owing to losses. A starting point for the wide arch may have been the clerestory of Rievaulx; the Netley design was used again at Tintern and Neath, and also at Melrose.

At first sight the evidence from Wales and the west looks as scant and ruinous as in the south. Yet, owing to the protracted building programmes at many houses as well as new foundations, the early thirteenth century was an energetic building period. The remains may be sparse, but there is enough to show the variety and exuberance of design and decoration. Conditions in this region were similar to those elsewhere. While church plans and elevations were of accepted Cistercian types, mouldings, piers and other details were in the style of other local buildings. Architectural ideas were exchanged between masons and patrons over a wide area from Margam in Glamorgan to Croxden in Staffordshire and Strata Florida and Valle Crucis in the heart of native Wales.

In almost every instance the stylistic influences are English. This is true even of Valle Crucis and Cwmhir, which were both Welsh princely foundations, Cwmhir in its day being one of the largest Cistercian churches in the country; but the style of both is related as much to work in England as in Wales. Strata Florida is perhaps something of an exception. The hood moulding of its west door ends in a triskelion motif that comes direct from long-standing native tradition. The doorway, with an original six orders of continuous roll mouldings — without capitals or bases — bound at frequent intervals by shaft rings, is a unique design. It manages, without figure sculpture, to achieve the richest effect, an effect that once continued on the interior of the building, where deceptively plain lancet windows and rubble walls were composed of contrasting coloured stones, embellished with painted ornament.

The presbytery of Dore, begun after 1186, already anticipates thirteenth-century developments. It interprets the plan of Byland on a small scale, and may also, like Byland, have had a wooden vault. It is richly ornamented with copious mouldings around doors and windows, including continuous roll mouldings, and forms of stiff-leaf foliage. The details are closely related to work at major sites in the west country, including Worcester Cathedral. Some features at Dore have parallels in the surviving arches of the nave of Cwmhir, now in Llanidloes parish church. We find the same story at Valle Crucis, and in the new choir of Margam. These buildings, both begun in the early thirteenth century, are in the architectural milieu of the west midlands. The fragmentary remains of Margam show close parallels with the Benedictine abbeys at Glastonbury and Pershore, and with Worcester Cathedral, especially the clustered piers with water-holding bases and alternately detached and coursed shafts. Valle Crucis seems to have been modified and finished in the second half of the thirteenth century, after an undocumented fire that has left traces on the stonework. It has rubble walls, but fine ashlar was used for its doors, piers and windows. Although Margam had chosen an aisled, rectangular choir, its contemporary, Valle Crucis, was Bernardine, like its mother house at Strata Marcella. Like Strata Marcella it has fasciculated piers and very fine, sharply cut mouldings, including the continuous roll moulding that had appeared at, for example, Dore and Worcester Cathedral. The continuous moulding is also found in the thirteenth-century chapter house vestibule and refectory of St Werburgh's, Chester. Very tall lancets similar to those of Valle Crucis appear in the chapter house of Chester and the transept of Lichfield Cathedral. The dates of all these buildings are too uncertain to establish priority, but the details can place Valle Crucis in a credible architectural context.

Croxden, too, belongs in this general grouping.[7] It has foliage designs in common with Lichfield, the very tall lancet windows and, like Valle Crucis, fasciculated piers. But not everything at Croxden can be explained by its immediate locality. Its elevation seems to have had three storeys, with a false gallery and a clerestory set into a thin upper wall. This is the last surviving Cistercian three-storey elevation in Britain, and is much less explicable than Rievaulx. The presbytery of Rievaulx was a great church, with the connotations of a shrine and built at the centre of northern monasticism. None of this applies to Croxden. The ground plan is even more puzzling. The wholly conventional nave and transept led to an eastern arm with an ambulatory and five radiating chapels. As we have seen, in Britain radiating chapel plans were associated with royal foundations. Croxden was not a royal foundation, but its nearest analogy is Mortemer (Eure) in Normandy, which attracted the patronage of Henry II, of whom Croxden's founder was an enthusiastic supporter. Perhaps the patrons of Croxden wanted to flaunt their royal connections, and, contrary to earlier Cistercian designs, decided to enhance the ambulatory plan with a three-storey elevation.

Between 1244 and 1251, King Henry III took over the patronage of Netley, and although his interest lapsed, his patronage left a very significant architectural feature: a large east window filled with tracery.

The four lights, in two pairs under containing arches, were surmounted by a large oculus, like the earliest patterned tracery, at Westminster Abbey and at Binham Priory in Norfolk. From the mid-thirteenth century, tracery, and ways of using it for windows and surface ornament, were to become one of the main interests of architects across Europe. Patterns evolved very rapidly: at Netley itself the remains of tracery in the later west window suggest a free flowing design more typical of the early fourteenth century.

Tracery may have come to Cistercian notice through the royal connection, for similar windows were made for Hailes, which was founded in 1246 by Henry III's brother, Richard, earl of Cornwall. Its original eastern arm was an aisled rectangle; the elevation may have been three-storey, and vaulted; and decorative details were

The remains of the north transept and its chapels at Valle Crucis. The tall lancets are similar to those in the chapter house at the cathedral church in Chester.

THE LATER THIRTEENTH CENTURY

7 Hoey 1993; Thurlby 1993

done in contrasting blue lias stone. Then, in 1270, Edmund of Cornwall presented the abbey with a phial of the Holy Blood of Christ. This was a new type of cult for the Cistercians. Unlike Rievaulx, which concerned the order's own pieties, the Holy Blood of Hailes was universal. It positively invited pilgrimage. The eastern arm was extended into an apse, ambulatory and five radiating chapels, probably using Westminster Abbey as a model.

At about the same time, Dervorguilla, widow of John Balliol, had founded the New Abbey in south-west Scotland, named Sweetheart by the monks when she was buried there with her husband's heart. At Sweetheart the Bernardine plan, a galilee porch and small wheel windows in the gables evoke the early years of the Cistercian movement, and the flat, squat elevation is a curious compromise between the archaic and the new. The arcade with its fasciculated piers and the low clerestory with an arcaded passage are divided by a strip of blank wall. A low crossing tower barely rose above roof level. But for all its simplicity, the masons took trouble with the elaborate mouldings and with the window tracery. All the main axes end in large windows. Not all the tracery survives, but it is clearly related to late thirteenth-century work in Lincolnshire and Yorkshire, where masons were exploring new tracery designs with enthusiasm.

Such patterns, based on circles cusped to make quatrefoil and cinquefoil shapes, were used also in the west front of Valle Crucis after the fire. The three two-light windows that fill the façade can be read as a traditional composition of lancets in developed form. Each pair of lights is topped by a small cusped circle. The west front has been compared to the Swiss church of Meudon in the former county of Savoy, and it may be associated with the Savoyard masons who were working on Edward I's castles in north Wales. If so, Valle Crucis would date from about 1280. This is contemporary with Edward's new abbey at Vale Royal in Cheshire, but we cannot connect the two buildings as the first church of Vale Royal is almost completely unknown.

In the late thirteenth century and into the fourteenth, south Wales was as active a building centre as the north. Its workshops, including those at Cistercian abbeys, were in close touch with work in London and the south-east, and later at such south-western centres as Wells and Bristol. At a time of rapid development in mouldings and tracery designs, Cistercian buildings were among the leaders, exchanging, and in some instances apparently innovating, designs and motifs. At Tintern and Neath for example, there is a type of door moulding known as a dying moulding, where the moulding has no base, but dies into the plinth, which anticipates a similar feature at the Augustinian abbey of Bristol (now the cathedral) by several years.[8]

Tintern is one of the best-preserved of all Cistercian churches. Built over the last thirty years of the thirteenth century, it combines a restrained two-storey elevation with great decorative richness. The fasciculated columns and window arches were embellished by shaftwork, most of which, except for the coursed shafts in the later phases, has gone. The elevation was further enriched by its astonishing windows. The tracery designs broadly followed changes in fashion in the leading centres of eastern England. Thus the east window resembles work at Lincoln Cathedral in the 1260s, but the intersecting lines and lobed shapes in the west window are very close to London tracery of the 1280s, reflecting the dominance of London at the very end of the century before regional designs emerged. The same types of pointed, fine

For all the simplicity seen in the plan at Sweetheart, the masons took trouble with elaborate mouldings and handsome window tracery.

Left: Tintern is one of the best-preserved of all Cistercian churches in Britain. The intersecting lines and lobed shapes of the west window are very close to the design of London tracery of the 1280s.

8 Morris 1997

tracery pattern appear in the galilee at Neath, picked out in white Sutton stone against the dark rubble sandstone background.

All but a trace of Tintern's painted decorative scheme has also disappeared; but the frilly cusping on the cloister door survives, as does the west door, with its rosette diaper pattern. Rosette diaper has connotations of sacred metalwork; here it is clearly a setting for the statue — presumably of the Virgin — that stood in the centre. Tintern's decorative elaboration culminated in the *pulpitum* screen of the later 1320s, with its deep ogee (S-curved) arches, ballflower ornament and miniature buttresses. This work of micro-architecture was as fine as its equivalents in non-Cistercian churches, and its style reveals the strong network of links between the great building centres of south-west England and south Wales in the 1320s. In these years, the era of the so-called Decorated style, a church interior could be actually defined by its sculptured decoration, and Cistercians were not immune. Imagery was now both a background and focus to veneration and prayer. Although the fine earlier figured bosses discovered at Hailes almost certainly came from the claustral buildings, those at Dore were the keystones of the vault built over the nave probably in the later thirteenth century, or perhaps the early fourteenth. They certainly infringe the twelfth-century rules against sculptured images, but their subject-matter — Christ in Majesty, the Virgin and Child, abbots and monks — was central to Cistercian devotion.

THE LAST YEARS

The earliest phase of the new church at Melrose included most of the presbytery, seen here from the south-west, and the outer walls of the transepts. These areas are very English in style.

By the mid-fourteenth century, the disappearance of the lay brothers caused a contraction of the monastic liturgical spaces, and naves seem gradually to have been divided into separate chapels for lay burials and prayer. The last Cistercian abbey to be founded, Edward III's St Mary Graces, had to be fitted awkwardly into its urban site in east London. Only two major church buildings were undertaken in the last two centuries before the Reformation: Vale Royal and Melrose. They show that, for the first time since the thirteenth century, architects were looking towards continental Europe.

Neither was the first church on the site, but rebuilding was intended to be comprehensive. At Vale Royal, a more modest church was planned to replace its collapsed predecessor. Of the choir initiated in 1359, only a very rough foundation survives. It appears to be that of an apse, ambulatory and seven radiating chapels alternating with six quadrangular spaces, which amounted to thirteen chapels in all. This bears no relation to any previous Cistercian plan, even those with radiating chapels. Suggested sources are Toledo Cathedral in Spain, which has a similar plan but no obvious link through people or circumstances; a lost French intermediary; or influence from Germany. The meagre evidence at Vale Royal itself offers no certain solution.

Melrose, however, provides evidence aplenty. It contrasts a Bernardine plan and two-storey elevation with a superstructure that is alive with sculpture and tracery. The plan, with chapels *en echelon*, may be based on the original church, but that they chose a Bernardine plan in the 1380s says something about the strength of the Cistercian tradition. The church was never finished, and in the absence of lay brothers we must assume that the elaborate nave was intended for the laity.

The earliest phase, the presbytery and parts of the transepts, is English in style, drawing inspiration from the grid pattern of horizontals and verticals in early

Perpendicular work. The immediate sources seem to lie in eastern England: the exterior decoration and tabernacle work resembles Howden in Yorkshire and the Lady Chapel of Ely Cathedral; the window tracery is akin to St Mary's church in Beverley, which is close to Howden. The later phases, however, draw on continental Europe. The row of chapels in the south aisle of the nave, with their fine traceried windows, were purpose built. Such chapels are commonplace in European architecture, for example at Eberbach in Germany, but in English churches they were normally contrived from existing spaces. The tracery in the south transept and nave of Melrose is curvilinear — based on ogee forms — and inspired by patterns from Germany, the Low Countries and northern France. Not only had curvilinear tracery in England been superseded by the straighter lines of Perpendicular, but continental curvilinear tracery uses the motifs differently, as, for instance, in the large mouchette wheels in the nave chapel windows, where dagger shapes pursue one another in a circle. Although the continental motifs may have been introduced by the Paris-born mason John Morow, who probably worked at Melrose about 1400, the links seem to be stronger in the last period, after his departure.

However 'Cistercian' the plan and elevation of Melrose may be, the richness of its decoration makes it indistinguishable from contemporary non-Cistercian churches. To foliage capitals and architectural ornament were added figured corbels and statuary. Unlike the figured work at Dore, the saints Peter, Paul and Andrew have no obvious relevance to Cistercian tradition. The arms of Abbot Hunter (1441–71) in the south transept vault follow the developing fashion for patrons to 'sign' their work with arms or rebuses.

At Fountains in the late fifteenth century Abbot John Darnton (1479–95) placed a carved image of himself beside a window that he had repaired. His successor, Marmaduke Huby (1495–1526), included his arms among the decoration of his new tower at Fountains. From the early fourteenth century at Culross, Cistercian crossing towers had become more prominent; Kirkstall was successfully heightened in the early sixteenth century, but at both Fountains and Furness such attempts had ended in trouble, and new towers were built at the west end (Furness) and off the north transept (Fountains). Huby's tower was pure self-aggrandizement, of both himself and the abbey. It proclaimed Fountains' high status among the Cistercian houses, and the importance of Huby himself.

In the last years before the Reformation the laity had invaded the church for worship, burial and the perpetual prayers that accompanied the late medieval death ritual. Churches were finely furnished: Melrose with choir stalls from Bruges, Furness with elaborate Perpendicular sedilia, Rievaulx with screens and panel paintings, to say nothing of Ailred's silver burial casket. It had always been easier for the poorer abbeys to keep strictly to Cistercian precepts. The thirteenth-century buildings at Fountains and Rievaulx — or the richly decorated chapel that survives at Kirkstead — are the product of houses that could afford this level of building. By the fifteenth century the religious outlook and expectations of clergy and laity alike had changed completely from conditions in the twelfth. Yet we should also recognize Cistercian efforts to maintain some distance from their contemporaries. Their architecture remained plain in comparison to that of other monastic orders, and even Melrose kept to tradition in planning if in little else. If Cistercian churches show anything, they show that the Cistercians kept a sense of identity to the last. If they had not, this book could not have been written.

This elaborate Perpendicular sedilia was inserted into the south wall of the presbytery at Furness shortly before the dissolution.

Abbot Marmaduke Huby's tower at Fountains was built in the early years of the sixteenth century by way of pure self-aggrandizement.

A GAZETTEER OF THE CISTERCIAN ABBEYS IN BRITAIN

by

Glyn Coppack,
Richard Fawcett,
and David Robinson

There were eighty-six 'permanent' Cistercian foundations in Britain, of which sixty-two lay in England, thirteen in Wales, and eleven in Scotland. Apart from the principal group, it is important to bear in mind that more than thirty communities changed site — at least once — before settling on a final location. By and large, little survives at any of the 'temporary' sites, and here they are considered within the context of the appropriate foundation narrative.

The gazetteer entries are arranged in alphabetical order, with no distinction made between countries. In the main, the content focuses upon the archaeological and architectural remains of the abbey buildings. The space devoted to any particular site is almost inevitably a reflection of the scale and importance of its known structures, and is by no means related to the fullness of the abbey's history. In all cases — to a greater or lesser degree — the buildings are placed within a broad historical framework.

Each entry is accompanied by a set of marginal notes. These begin with the dates of foundation and dissolution. The foundation itself was often a long-drawn-out process, spread over several years, especially when it involved a site change. In terms of the dissolution, in England and Wales the dates are comparatively clear-cut, falling between 1536 and 1540. But in Scotland, although religious life came to an end in 1560, the process of suppression was more gradual.

Following a brief description of the site location, and of the extent of the surviving remains, the marginal notes then list: the current county or appropriate local authority; the medieval diocese in which the abbey was situated; and a six-figure national grid reference. At the end of each entry, there is a marginal list of the most appropriate works for further reading. The full details can be found in the bibliography. Ground plans have been assembled for a total of sixty-six of the abbeys. The degree of completeness and accuracy of these vary considerably, depending on the quality of investigation at the site to date. All of the plans have been prepared to a uniform scale.

In terms of accessibility, the information is offered by way of guidance only. Those ruins maintained on behalf of the State — by Cadw, English Heritage, and Historic Scotland — are open to visitors on a regular basis. Many other sites are in the care of bodies such as the National Trust, or they are in some other way buildings or properties with regular times for public access. Elsewhere, it becomes far more difficult to summarize the precise current position. If in doubt, permission should be sought in advance of seeking to view the remains.

Left: Founded in 1131 by the royal justiciar, Walter Espec (d. 1154), Rievaulx Abbey in North Yorkshire is among the most celebrated Cistercian sites of Britain.

Map showing the locations of the Cistercian abbeys of Britain.

ABERCONWY ABBEY

1186–1537

Aberconwy I is represented by the parish church of St Mary in the centre of Conwy. Traces of the Cistercian church survive, especially in the west front. The site of Maenan Abbey (Aberconwy II) is located in the Conwy valley, about 7 miles (11.3km) to the south. Nothing of significance remains visible. A house of 1848–52 occupies the site, and is now converted to a hotel.

(Aberconwy I)	(Aberconwy II)
Conwy	Conwy
Bangor	St Asaph
SH 781776	SH 790657

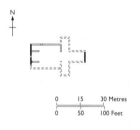

N

| 0 | 15 | 30 Metres |
| 0 | 50 | 100 Feet |

Aberconwy I

Several features of the abbey of Aberconwy I are to be seen in the west front of St Mary's church, Conwy.

Aberconwy was the first of the two Cistercian abbeys established in north-west Wales under the patronage of the princes of Gwynedd, with the founding colony arriving from Strata Florida in 1186. The monks were initially settled in a remote location on the mountainous fringe of Snowdonia (at Rhedynog-felen to the south of Caernarfon), though they were soon to discover that this had been a poorly judged siting. After several years of unbearable hardship, and certainly no later than 1192, the community moved to a more suitable location near the mouth of the river Conwy. Here, through a charter of 1198, the monks were given the especial protection and support of Prince Llywelyn ab Iorwerth (d. 1240). Within a generation of its uncertain beginnings, the abbey of Aberconwy had accumulated an estate of almost 40,000 acres (16,194ha). It mattered little that much of this land was mountain pasture; for the time being at least, the endowments were more than sufficient to meet the community's needs.

Now represented by St Mary's parish church, the site chosen for the abbey (Aberconwy I) was a comparatively flat area of land close to the tidal shore of the river. The cloister buildings lay on the north side of the complex, and apparently spread beyond the bounds of the present churchyard. Although several distinct elements of the Cistercian structure can be traced in the later fabric of St Mary's, different views have been expressed on the way they should be interpreted. On the one hand, it is just possible to reconstruct the ghost of an entire conventual church within the surviving layout, even if this would have been small and of somewhat unusual plan. Alternatively, the full 135 feet (41.1m) of St Mary's — from east to west — may represent no more than the length of the monastic nave. Much of the lower part of the west front, including the three simple lancet windows, is clearly Cistercian work. The west doorway, its arch springing from capitals enriched with stiff-leaf foliage, is also of the monastic period. It is, nevertheless, something of a later confection; the arch itself may have been derived from the former chapter house entrance. At the opposite end of the church, the base of the east chancel wall could well be part of the original building.

Aberconwy Abbey was to grow in the affections of the princes of Gwynedd. Indeed, its abbots were to serve as their advisors and emissaries, whilst the monastic church was to act as the mausoleum for the greatest of their dynasty. It was here, in April 1240, that Prince Llywelyn himself was laid to rest, having spent his last hours in the habit of a monk.

Just over five years later, in 1245–46, the abbey appears to have been sacked by English troops during a punitive royal campaign in Wales. Its lands, too, were ravaged and despoiled. Barely had the fortunes of the community been revived when Aberconwy was confronted by a phase of disruption of far greater proportions. In the spring of 1283, during his final conquest of Gwynedd, King Edward I determined upon building a castle and walled town at the mouth of the Conwy. There could be no room for sentiment. It would be necessary to uproot the Cistercian abbey, removing the monks without delay to a new site at Maenan (Aberconwy II). In March, the precinct was immediately pressed into royal use, and in due course the former conventual church was rebuilt to serve the English burgesses of the infant borough.

From the outset, it seems that the king regarded Maenan as a new royal foundation, to which the earlier abbey of the princes was to be united. Towards the end of March, Edward was present to see the inauguration of the new works; and he was at Maenan once again in October, probably for a ceremony of dedication. Shortly afterwards, the monks were to receive a payment of £100 by way of compensation for damages sustained during the war. The king also gave the abbey a set of glass windows, which — together with their ironwork — had probably been made at Chester. He further arranged for various other endowments to be assigned to the construction programme.

It is unfortunate that so very little else is known about the progress of the building works. Nor is it clear if any royal masons were involved in the early stages. Limited excavations were carried out on the site in 1968, and some details of the church were recovered. Even if the length of the nave could not be determined, the tentative plan based on this work suggests a structure of broadly similar form to that at Netley, and also to the near contemporary churches at

Tintern and Neath. From the architectural fragments recovered at Maenan, it would appear that building continued well into the fourteenth century.

In the late fifteenth and early sixteenth centuries, several abbots were praised by the native bards for their work as builders, and for having restored the fortunes of the house. But when it came to the time of the great survey of 1535, the abbey's annual income was assessed at a moderate £162. Despite the efforts of Abbot Richard ap Robert to save Aberconwy from early suppression, it had been dissolved by March 1537. In the destruction that followed, some of the materials were employed for the repair of the justice's hall in the borough of Caernarfon. In addition, a number of decorative features — including a set of pleasing windows which may have been derived from the abbey cloister — were to be used by John Wynn ap Maredudd (d. 1559) in his house at Gwydir.

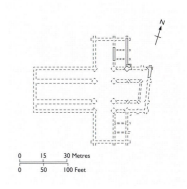

Aberconwy II

Brown, Colvin and Taylor 1963, 337–41
Butler 1964
Butler and Evans 1980
Hays 1963
Hughes 1895
RCAHMW 1956, 39–46

BALMERINO ABBEY

Balmerino, also known as St Edward's Abbey, was founded by the dowager Queen Ermengarde and her son, King Alexander II (1214–49), probably with the intention that it should be the queen's burial place. Ermengarde may have been planning the foundation as early as 1225, and in 1229 the new community was sent from Melrose, though there may have been a small colony there as early as 1227.

The abbey's site is on the north coast of Fife, overlooking the Firth of Tay, and it was presumably the location of the water supply which led to the cloister being set north of the church. The church had a rectangular presbytery, transepts with two-bay eastern chapel aisles, and a nave with a single aisle along the south side. A

lack of correspondence between the piers of the south aisle arcade and the wall shafts of the north nave wall, together with the fact that the single aisle is on the side away from the cloister, point to the aisle being a secondary addition. If that were the case, the original plan of the abbey church would have been strikingly similar to that of the other Fife house of the order, at Culross. The most complete remains of the church are in the north transept, where it adjoins the east claustral range, though there are also remains of the lower walls along the north nave wall and the west front. The plan of the rest of the church is known from excavations carried out in 1896, and the positions of walls and piers are now marked by turf mounds.

1227/29–1560

Balmerino Abbey is in the village of the same name, close to the southern shore of the Firth of Tay, about five miles (8km) west of the Tay road bridge. It is north of the A914, but can only be reached along small country roads. The fragmentary remains are cared for by the National Trust for Scotland, and are readily accessible.

Fife
St Andrews

NO 358246

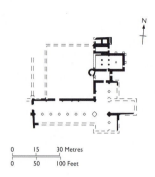

Campbell 1899, 71–305

Gifford 1988, 94–96

Knowles and St Joseph 1952, 72–73

MacGibbon and Ross 1896–97, **2**, 505–17

RCAHMCS 1933, 33–37

Turnbull 1841

The east claustral range survives more completely than the church because it was adapted as a residence after the Reformation, though it is now roofless. Next to the transept is the sacristy, and beyond the chapter house are the parlour and the undercroft of the latrine; all of these are barrel vaulted. The chapter house, however, was lavishly rebuilt in the later Middle Ages. Within the body of the range there is a rib-vaulted vestibule of three bays by two carried on octagonal piers, while the chapter house itself was entirely beyond the range and rose to a greater height, with four bays of tierceron vaulting around a central pier. This tierceron vault-

ing was destroyed when new floors were inserted after the Reformation. Nothing survives of the other claustral ranges, though to the north of the cloister is the south face of a barn, and to the north-east is part of another building of unknown use.

The abbey's closeness to the Tay led to its being attacked by the English in 1547, though there still seem to have been at least sixteen monks soon afterwards. After the Reformation, the commendatorship of the abbey changed hands on a number of occasions, but in 1603 the estates were erected into a temporal lordship for Sir James Elphinstone, who was to take the title Lord Balmerino.

BASINGWERK ABBEY

1131–1536/37

Situated at Greenfield near Holywell, off the B5121, Basingwerk Abbey is in the care of Cadw: Welsh Historic Monuments. The surviving remains include fragments of the church, the east range and the monks' refectory. The site is accessible at all reasonable times.

Flintshire

St Asaph

SJ 195774

The poet Tudor Aled (d. 1526) was fulsome in his praise of Basingwerk, and of its 'lovely situation on a haven within sight of the waters and the beauty of the country'. The abbey had been founded some four centuries earlier, probably in 1131, by Ranulf 'de Gernon', earl of Chester (1129–53). It was to be colonized with monks from the then highly fashionable Norman abbey of Savigny. At first, it

seems likely that the fledgling community was accommodated within the defences of a Norman fortification known as Hên Blas. In 1157, however, Basingwerk was placed under the supervision of Buildwas Abbey, and in the same year King Henry II granted the now Cistercian community a charter which virtually amounted to its refoundation. The move of three miles (4.8km) to the Greenfield site probably took place about this time; King Henry's charter referred to the 'chapel of Basingwerk in which the monks first dwelt'.

The abbey's border position meant that, over the twelfth and thirteenth centuries, the monks looked as much to the patronage of the Welsh princes as they did to the kings and nobility of England. Grants of land and property came from both sides. It was Henry II, for example, who gave the manor of Glossop in Derbyshire, which was to prove Basingwerk's single most profitable asset. And in 1240, Prince Dafydd ap Llywelyn (d. 1246) granted the monks Holywell church, together with the pilgrimage chapel and well-shrine of St Winifred.

At the permanent site, the earliest phase of stone building is probably represented by several sections of coarse rubble walling, to be seen in parts of the chapter house and the adjacent east range. It is difficult to be precise, but these areas may date to the third quarter of the twelfth century. A stone church of the period could lie somewhere beneath the later cloister, though exploratory trenches dug in 1937 failed to locate any trace.

On the basis of stylistic evidence, a major programme of reconstruction was initiated in the early years of the thirteenth

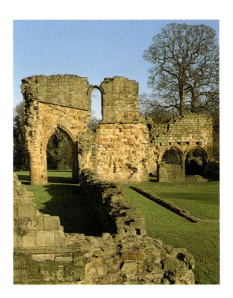

century. Work began with a comparatively small church, its plan still typical of the Bernardine ideals of half a century before. The short, square-ended presbytery is lost, but there are vestiges of the transepts, each with two small eastern chapels. Post-dissolution sources record the presence of three bells at Basingwerk, though from the surviving evidence of the crossing piers, it seems unlikely that there could have been a central tower of any great scale. The nave was arranged in seven narrow bays, the arcades apparently supported on octagonal piers.

The chapter house was rebuilt in much the same period, with its stone-vaulted extension entered by way of a pair of round-headed arches springing from a central octagonal column. Next to this, the day room, together with the monks' dormitory above, were also refashioned as part of the same programme. A little later, about the middle of the thirteenth century, a new refectory was constructed on the preferred Cistercian alignment at right-angles to the cloister. With its lancet windows, framed with hood and jamb mouldings, and with traces of the reader's pulpit, the refectory remains the most imposing structure surviving at Basingwerk. In the later fourteenth century, the cloister garth was to be surrounded with new arcades, and towards the end of the Middle Ages the southern end of the east range was modified, probably to form a domestic apartment.

One of the last abbots, Thomas Pennant (1481–1522), did much to transform the later fortunes of his house. Tudor Aled described him as a man 'with a fine taste for minstrelsy and a generous patron of the bards'. In 1535, Basingwerk's annual income was assessed at about £150, at which time there were probably no more than two or three monks at the house. Within two years, it had been dissolved, its choir stalls removed to the church of St Mary on the Hill, Chester, and some of the lead from its roofs taken for repairs at nearby Holt Castle.

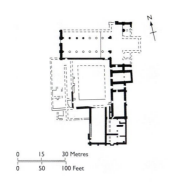

A now-blocked doorway in the thirteenth-century refectory at Basingwerk originally gave access to a short, arcaded passage, which in turn led to the reader's pulpit.

Left: *The most significant surviving feature of the church at Basingwerk is the west wall of the south transept. The round-headed arches of the thirteenth-century chapter house can also be seen to the right of this view.*

Hodkinson 1905
Knowles and St Joseph 1952, 108–09
Robinson 1996b
Williams 1981a

BEAULIEU ABBEY

1203/04–1538

Beaulieu is situated on the B3054, about 12 miles (19.3km) south-west of Southampton. The remains of the abbey, including the outline of the church, the west range, and the monastic refectory, lie in the grounds of the National Motor Museum and are accessible at regular opening times. The refectory serves as the parish church.

Hampshire
Winchester

SU 388026

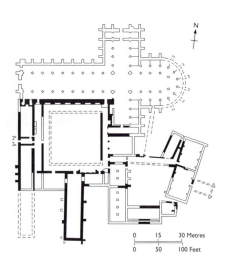

0   15   30 Metres
0   50   100 Feet

Having quarrelled with the Cistercians early in his reign, in a remarkable turnabout King John (1199–1216) decided to establish an abbey of their order by way of atonement for his misdeeds. The mediator in the difficult process of reconciliation was Hubert Walter, archbishop of Canterbury (1193–1205), a steadfast supporter of the White Monks who had been received into their confraternity in 1195. In return for his new-found generosity, the king sought the same privilege accorded to the archbishop: namely to become the object of prayers in every Cistercian monastery throughout the entire order. Good to his word, in 1203 John brought a community of monks to Faringdon in Berkshire (now Oxfordshire). A year later, the house was transferred to the site of a royal hunting lodge in the New Forest. Significantly, the scribes who drew up the king's earliest charter were particularly careful to call the abbey *Bellus Locus Regis*, Royal Beaulieu.

John was clearly determined to ensure that his new foundation would be of the greatest significance. Indeed, Beaulieu was immediately set apart as the only Cistercian abbey in Britain to be occupied by monks sent directly from Cîteaux. The king's initial endowments to the community were centred around the temporary site at Faringdon. His gifts in the New Forest were supplemented by those of his son, King Henry III (1216–72). Meanwhile, the monks had been busily engaged in purchasing parcels of land in a number of areas, notably along the river Avon. But such enterprise could never outweigh the importance of the royal donations, which by the end of the thirteenth century were probably accounting for well over three-quarters of the community's total income. It was royal connections, too, which led to the foundation of Beaulieu's daughter houses at Netley in 1239, Hailes in 1246, and St Mary Graces in London in 1350. In addition, a non-royal daughter was established at Newenham in 1247.

Although the estimates vary, John's provision of finance for the construction of the abbey was undoubtedly generous. The first record of payment dates to the time of the foundation, and in the course of the next ten years the king contributed at least £2,000 to the building fund. Thereafter, Henry III sought to complete his father's scheme, allocating revenues totalling £100 a year, and making several gifts of timber. In 1232, for example, he gave ten oaks for rafters in the church, and over the following decade at least ninety more oaks were sent to Beaulieu from the royal forests. One of the last such gifts was intended to provide the wood for the lay brothers' choir stalls. As normal, the work of construction appears to have begun with the presbytery and crossing, and by 1227 — when the monks 'entered their new church with great joy' — these areas were probably complete. The stylistic details suggest that much progress had also been made with the monastic buildings by the 1220s, particularly those in the east range. But the church was not finished until 1246. In June of that year it was dedicated by the bishop of Winchester, in the presence of King Henry and Queen Eleanor, surrounded by an assembly of great nobles. The king's brother, Richard of Cornwall (d. 1272), himself engaged in the preparations for the foundation of Hailes, was also present at the ceremony.

Today, apart from the south wall of the nave, the abbey church has almost entirely disappeared, and the principal remains are those of the west range, the monks' refectory, and fragments of the chapter house. Having been partially explored towards the end of the nineteenth century, the site was further excavated over a period of several years beginning in 1900. It was at this time that the outlines of the major buildings were marked out in gravel. More recently, the architectural details have been the subject of a further important study.

The plan of the church comprised a nine-bay aisled nave, developed transepts, and a three-bay extended presbytery with a semicircular apse. Beyond the presbytery aisle, there were probably eleven radiating chapels. The overall length of the church was 336 feet (102m), and aside from the later scheme at Vale Royal it was to prove the largest Cistercian building in the country. The design of the radiating chapels at the east end was ultimately derived from developments at Clairvaux, though the idea was possibly introduced to England via Bonport in Normandy, a house which had been founded in 1190 by John's brother, King Richard (d. 1199). In contrast, the layout of the Beaulieu transepts bore an uncanny resemblance to the pattern at Cîteaux. The north transept, with aisles on both the west and east sides, and with a galilee porch on the north side, must have been especially reminiscent of the Burgundian mother house. In the nave, although the aisle windows were very plain, the piers were richly detailed with alternating coursed and detached shafts grouped around a circular core. The design suggests that the Beaulieu arcades bore some resemblance to important early Gothic schemes in a number of cathedrals and greater churches of the south and west of England.

The monastic buildings lay to the south of the church, and of the east range the most prominent survival is the triple-arched chapter house façade. Further east, beyond the range, the foundations of the infirmary complex are set out in the turf. South of the cloister, the monks' refectory has been used as the parish church since the sixteenth century. Inside, although much

restored, the most notable feature is the handsome little arcaded stairway leading to the reader's pulpit. The heads of the three lancet windows at the southern end are decorated with dogtooth ornament. The west range, again much restored, also survives in a very complete state.

The walled precinct of the abbey fronted the tidal Beaulieu river, and covered a total area of about 58 acres (23.5ha). The only entrance was apparently on the river side, where the small outer gatehouse can still be seen. There was a mill alongside it. The arrangements within the inner or the great gatehouse included a porch and a fine hall on the ground floor, with two parallel chapels above.

In the great survey of 1535, Beaulieu's annual income was assessed at £326. The house survived until April 1538, when it was surrendered to the king's visitors by Abbot Thomas Stevens. A few months later, the manor of Beaulieu, an estate of some 8,500 acres (3,441ha), was granted to Thomas Wriothesley, later earl of Southampton (1547–50). The abbey church and many of the monastic buildings were pulled down, but it would seem that the inner gatehouse was early converted to provide domestic accommodation, and was to become known as Palace House. The conversion of the monks' refectory to the parish church probably took place within a year or two of the dissolution.

An aerial view of Beaulieu Abbey from the south-east. To the left is the former monks' refectory, now the parish church, with the low foundations of the abbey church appearing to the right (Lord Montagu of Beaulieu).

The processional doorway, which led from the east cloister walk into the abbey church, is one of the marked features of the ruins at Beaulieu (Lord Montagu of Beaulieu).

Hinton 1977
Hockey 1976
Holdsworth 1992
Hope and Brakspear 1906
Jansen 1984
Knowles and St Joseph 1952, 138–39
VCH Hampshire 1903, 140–46; 1911, 652–54

BIDDLESDEN ABBEY

1147–1538

The site of Biddlesden Abbey is about 4 miles (6.5km) north-east of Brackley, south of the A43. Nothing remains visible of the abbey buildings, and the site is now occupied by an eighteenth-century private house, Biddlesden Park.

Buckinghamshire
Lincoln

SP 633397

Fergusson 1984a, 111–12
Pevsner and Williamson 1994, 178–79
RCHME 1913, 63
Roundell 1858, 275–87; 1863, 33–38
VCH Buckinghamshire 1905, 365–69; 1927, 153–57

There were mixed motives behind the foundation of Biddlesden in 1147. Its founder was Ernald de Bosco, the steward of Robert de Beaumont, earl of Leicester (d. 1168), and its first monks came from the earl's own foundation of Garendon in Leicestershire. Apart from reasons of pure piety, however, it seems that one reason for Ernald's munificence was that he feared the land with which the abbey was initially endowed was likely to be taken back from him. Certainly there are records of lengthy litigation before the abbey obtained confirmation of its endowments.

Little is known of the abbey's history. One item of note is that the third recorded abbot, William Wibert, who had earlier been deposed as cellarer in 1192 because of misdemeanours, subsequently ran foul of Gerald of Wales (d. 1223) after becoming abbot. Gerald reported him to the abbots of Garendon and Cîteaux, result-ing in his deposition as abbot in 1198. The abbey was never a large one, having a net income of £125 in about 1535, at which time there were eleven monks.

Nothing remains visible of the abbey buildings apart from some *ex situ* fragments, though it can be assumed that the first generation of permanent structures was erected in the decades following the foundation. There may have been some rebuilding of the eastern parts of the church in the early thirteenth century, since in 1237 King Henry III granted wood for choir stalls. At the dissolution in 1538 the abbey was bought by Sir Robert Peckham, who incorporated parts of the monastic buildings within a house and who commenced demolition of the church. In about 1731 virtually everything which still remained was demolished by the owner at that time, Henry Sayer, in advance of building the new house of Biddlesden Park.

BINDON ABBEY

1171/72–1539

Bindon Abbey is situated off the A352, some 4 miles (6.4km) west of Wareham, and about half a mile (0.8km) east of the village of Wool. The ruins, which are in private ownership, include the low outer walls of the church, together with various traces of the monastic buildings, particularly those of the east range.

Dorset
Salisbury

SY 853868

The monks who were sent out from Forde Abbey to colonize a new foundation which had been proposed by William de Glastonia were first settled at Little Bindon. Apart from anything else, this coastal site — on the east side of Lulworth cove — proved physically just too demanding. A second patron fortunately stepped in, and it was through Roger de Newburgh's endowments that the community moved, in 1172, to the more suitable location at Bindon.

In addition to the site of the abbey, Roger and his wife Matilda gave the monks a clutch of lands and privileges in the surrounding area. Bindon's estates were to lay, for example, in Bovington, Chaldon, Nottington, and Pulham; the monks also possessed the manor of Bexington, the mill at Lulworth, and several properties within the borough of Dorchester. In 1280, the abbey was granted the right to hold a weekly market and a three-day annual fair at Wool.

As laid out, the Bindon buildings were clearly steeped in the traditions of the Bernardine model, with the church positioned on the north side of the cloister

ranges. It is difficult to be certain about the pace or progress of construction, but from the few surviving details it seems that almost everything was raised over the late twelfth and early thirteenth centuries. In 1213, whilst staying at Bindon, King John granted the monks fifty oaks and allowed them thirty cartloads of lead for roofing the monastery. His son, Henry III, gave another fifty oaks in 1235. This later gift was said to be specifically for 'rebuilding' the church, though from the ground plan alone there is no obvious trace of an extensive remodelling.

It was in the east end of the church, in particular, that the Bindon masons clung most closely to Bernardine characteristics. Here, a short square-ended presbytery projected from deep transepts, each with two vaulted chapels separated by solid walls. West of the crossing, the nave was arranged in eight aisled bays. The features of its elevation are now lost, but are partially recorded in an engraving of 1733, at which time the six west bays of the north arcade remained standing. The engraving depicts what appear to be rounded piers, with moulded capitals, supporting slightly pointed arches. A prominent string-course articulates the division between the arcade and the upper stage of the elevation. The clerestory windows are shown as single lancets, each one set over the apex of the arch below. There are also indications of vault springers. From this evidence, the Bindon nave was perhaps not unlike the marginally earlier example at Buildwas, or that in the almost contemporary church at Cleeve, both of which featured traditional west country cylindrical piers. This said, it must be noted that the extant base in the south arcade seems to bear the impression of an octagonal pier.

Among the other features of interest at Bindon, perhaps one of the most significant is the elaborate *pulpitum* screen which separated the choir from the west bays of the nave. Whatever the nature of its original arrangements, they were to be embellished in the first half of the fourteenth century. Elsewhere, in terms of the surviving monastic buildings, the chapter house and the dormitory undercroft can be readily identified. In the chapter house, which may date to the later 1170s, the vault ribs sprang from responds recessed into the lateral walls, a pattern which is also to be seen in the mother house at Forde.

During the later Middle Ages, the Bindon community was to suffer a succession of troubles, beginning in 1296 with the abbot being accused of causing the death of two monks. Worse was to follow. Such was the position in 1329, the abbey was said to be 'grievously burdened with debt for want of good rule'. In 1535, Bindon's income was given at £147, and it was scheduled for closure in the following year. Abbot John Norman paid the vast sum of £300 to avoid suppression, holding on until March 1539 when he and the seven remaining monks finally surrendered the house to the king's visitors.

Examples of thirteenth-century tile designs from the refectory at Bindon Abbey.

Bohs 1949
Fergusson 1984a, 112–13
Hills 1872
RCHME 1970, 404–06
VCH Dorset 1908, 82–86

BORDESLEY ABBEY

1138–1538

The ruins of Bordesley Abbey lie just east of the
A441 in Needle Lane, Waterside, in Redditch.
There is a visitor centre, and the abbey site is
freely accessible to the general public with the
eastern parts of the church conserved for display.

Worcestershire
Worcester

SP 046687

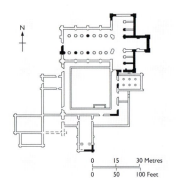

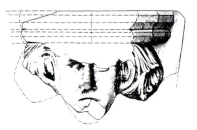

*Fragment of a probable thirteenth-century
corbel bracket, carved with a man's head,
found during excavations at Bordesley
(After Rahtz and Hirst 1976).*

*Following excavation, the crossing, the east
end, and the south transept at Bordesley have
been consolidated for display. The church
was begun in the 1150s (David Robinson).*

Bordesley Abbey was founded in 1138 by Waleran, count of Meulan and earl of Worcester (d. 1166). It was the first daughter house of Garendon, which had been founded by Waleran's twin brother, Earl Robert of Leicester. The site chosen was the valley of the river Arrow, at the junction of a stream called the Red Ditch. The site was carefully chosen to make the maximum use of available water, and the precinct of 89 acres (36ha) which had been developed by the early thirteenth century is remarkable for the evidence of water management it still demonstrates. Bordesley was suppressed in 1538 and was leased to Thomas Evans. Demolition began even before the site was leased. In 1542, the site was granted to Lord Windsor, whose family, the earls of Plymouth, owned it through to the present century. It is now owned by the Borough of Redditch and is being developed as a public park.

The abbey was first excavated by James Woodward in 1864, his work demonstrating the good degree of survival of the buried buildings. Since 1969, however, the site of the church has been further excavated by Philip Rahtz, Susan Wright, Susan Hirst, and David Walsh; the *capella ante portas* has been investigated by Mark Newman; and an industrial mill set within the precinct has been thoroughly examined by Grenville Astill. The results of this more recent work have revolutionized our knowledge of the site and its development.

The choice of a wet valley bottom for building the permanent structures meant that the community was forced to repair and refloor the abbey church on a regular basis. The excavations have uncovered evidence for frequent changes in liturgical practice, so often unrecorded on other sites. The first permanent church was begun in the early 1150s and the eastern parts were completed rapidly. The plan was Bernardine, with a small, square-ended presbytery, deep transepts with three square eastern chapels, and an aisled nave. The evidence suggests that a crossing tower may not have been planned at the outset, but one was almost certainly built, perhaps in a modification of an earlier

design as at Fountains or Buildwas.

By the end of the twelfth century, the crossing area of the church and presbytery had become unstable and required substantial strengthening. The eastern bays of the nave arcade were walled up (providing a backing to new choir stalls) and a new arch inserted into the opening into the south nave aisle from the transept, shoring up the south-west crossing pier. Clasping buttresses were added to the east wall of the presbytery. The crossing continued to give problems, and in the third quarter of the thirteenth century the western piers were largely rebuilt, suggesting a heightening of the lantern tower at that point. Whatever the intention, the work was not entirely successful, and in about 1300 the southern crossing arch was underbuilt to support it. Shortly before 1300, there was a catastrophic collapse of the north-west crossing pier which must have brought down a part of the tower. The western crossing piers were again rebuilt on massive foundations. Although this seems to have solved the problem, the north-east pier had to be rebuilt at the close of the fourteenth century. It was at this time that the western bays of the nave were reconstructed and new windows

inserted in the eastern bays of the clerestory. Chapels were inserted within the aisles, and the lay brothers' choir removed.

The cloister lay to the south of the church, and adopted the standard developed Cistercian plan. Only a small area at the north-east corner has been examined, and it is clear that the open cloister arcades were replaced by an enclosed structure with elaborate Perpendicular windows at the end of the fourteenth century. The cloister buildings can still be identified from their earthworks, with the inner court to the west, and outer court to the south and east. At the east end of the precinct, a twelfth-century watermill has been identified and excavated. Exceptionally, this was an industrial mill, with a waterwheel powering the bellows of a forge and driving trip hammers to make small objects such as nails, tenterhooks (for hanging cloth to dry), knives, tools, and arrowheads.

The great gate of the abbey, and its *capella ante portas*, lay to the west of the abbey church. The chapel, which survived in use as a church until 1805, was originally built in the early thirteenth century and was substantially rebuilt at the end of the century.

A grotesque corbel head, dated to about 1400, found during excavations in the north aisle at Bordesley Abbey. A divided tongue protrudes from the mouth, though its meaning is not entirely clear (Grenville Astill, Bordesley Abbey Project).

Astill 1993
Fergusson 1984a, 113–14
Hirst, Walsh and Wright 1983
Rahtz and Hirst 1976
Walsh 1979
Woodward 1866

BOXLEY ABBEY

Boxley was founded by William of Ypres, a son of the count of Flanders, in 1143 or 1146; it was a daughter house of Clairvaux. Little remains of its main buildings, other than a few fragments spread around the heavily relandscaped gardens of the brick-built house which stands over the site of the south-west corner of the conventual buildings. The basic layout of the abbey, however, was re-established through excavation in 1972–73.

The church was characteristically Bernardine in plan, having a rectangular presbytery, transepts with three chapels on the east side of each arm, and an aisled nave which was probably eight bays long. It seems possible the church was built in the time of the second head of the house, Thomas, who became abbot in 1152 or 1153, and who had earlier been a monk at Fontenay. A round-headed doorway at the west end of the south nave aisle is the sole significant visible feature from the church.

1143/46–1538

The site of Boxley Abbey is about 2 miles (3.2km) north of Maidstone, between the A229 and A249. Its fragmentary remains are within the grounds of the eighteenth-century private house which takes its name from the abbey, and they are not accessible to the public.

Kent
Canterbury

TQ 761588

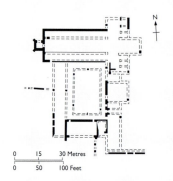

0 15 30 Metres
0 50 100 Feet

N

Fergusson 1984a, 114–15
Newman 1969, 149
Tester 1973
VCH Kent 1962, 153–55

Excavation has suggested that the only subsequent structural addition to the church was a small later medieval western tower, which was considerably less narrow than the nave.

Rather unusually, the cloister — which was south of the church — was of rectangular rather than square plan, being longer from north to south than from east to west. In the east claustral range, the square chapter house, which may have been covered by nine bays of vaulting carried on four piers, was separated from the transept by the sacristy. South of the chapter house were the parlour and slype and a long undercroft with the drain at its south end. The refectory, in the south range, ran parallel with the cloister, and had a warming house to its east. The best preserved medieval structure on the site is a barn to the south-west of the main complex, with a length of nearly 185 feet (57m); this appears to be of thirteenth-century date albeit with an eighteenth-century roof. There are also remains of stretches of boundary walls defining a precinct of about 17 acres (6.9ha).

One of the abbey's claims to fame was that it possessed a miraculous relic of the Holy Cross set in a crucifix, known as the Rood of Grace; and pilgrims' badges have been found which relate to this relic. At the dissolution in 1538 it was found that the eye movements of the Christ figure were operated by monks pulling wires, though it is likely that this 'exposure' was carefully staged as a warning to the credulous. Following the dissolution the abbot and nine monks were granted pensions, and a house was built on the site for the Wyatt family.

BRUERN ABBEY

1147–1536

The site of Bruern Abbey is off the A361, about 5 miles (8km) south-west of Chipping Norton and a mile (1.6km) west of Lyneham. There are no visible remains and the site, which is not accessible to the public, is occupied by the eighteenth-century private house which takes its name from the abbey.

Oxfordshire
Lincoln

SP 265203

Fergusson 1984a, 115
Sherwood and Pevsner 1974, 499–500
VCH Oxfordshire 1907, 79–81; 1972, 238–39

Bruern was founded in 1147 by Nicholas Basset, who was a joint sheriff in eleven counties, and the first monks were brought from Waverley. Nothing is known of the abbey's buildings, though extensions were evidently being made to the church around the second quarter of the thirteenth century. In 1232 King Henry III (1216–72) gave timber for building work taking place at that time. In 1250 altars were dedicated to the Virgin and St Edmund, which suggests the additions were nearing completion. However, the abbey may have overreached itself in this work, because in 1291 it was said to be deeply in debt. Further problems are indicated in 1366, when Abbot John de Dunster complained that the abbey's endowments could support no more than six monks at the time that he was requesting indulgences for those who contributed to works of repair. There was probably the usual measure of exaggeration in this. By 1535 there were still fifteen monks, though the net income of £124 at that time shows it to have been one of the less wealthy Cistercian houses.

Shortly before the dissolution, in 1532, Abbot Macy was found to have purchased his office from Cardinal Wolsey with the promise of 250 marks and 280 of the abbey's best oak trees. His attempts to recoup his expenditure from the abbey's income led to a rebellion by the monks, and he was deposed after a visitation by two of his brother abbots. The abbey was dissolved in October 1536 and its buildings were progressively destroyed, leaving little trace of its existence. The present house on the site was built for the Cope family in about 1720.

BUCKFAST ABBEY

In terms of its changing circumstance and fortune, Buckfast has a quite exceptional monastic history. Indeed, it stands apart from all the other Cistercian abbeys of Britain. To begin with, in 1018, more than a century before the arrival of the White Monks in England, a local nobleman had chosen this location in the valley of the river Dart for the foundation of a Benedictine monastery. Alas, little is known of the subsequent history of the Saxon house, though its holdings in Domesday Book (1086) included manors scattered around the north, east, and south sides of Dartmoor. Never particularly robust, it seems likely that by the early twelfth century the spiritual life of the community was in decline.

The languishing Benedictine abbey probably came to the attention of King Stephen (1135–54) when, in the summer of 1136, he had cause to journey to Exeter. In any case, it was in that year that he assumed responsibility for the house, choosing to grant all of its possessions to the Norman abbey of Savigny. Stephen was already an important benefactor of the Savigniac congregation, and the transfer was by no means out of step with his earlier patronage. Thereafter, the invigorated Buckfast community was to follow the customs of the French mother house until, in 1147, the entire Savigniac group — on both sides of the Channel — was placed under the wing of the Cistercian order.

Buckfast thus entered the third phase in its long history, emerging as one of the richest Cistercian abbeys in the south of England. Interestingly, its wealth owed less to further endowments than to the improved exploitation of those estates held by the original Saxon monastery. This said, Kingsbridge was undoubtedly among the more significant later acquisitions. The monks had rights to hold a weekly market and an annual fair here, and they were to foster the creation of a small borough to encourage trade. All in all, with the dissolution looming, in 1535 Buckfast's annual income was assessed at the comparatively large sum of £466.

The abbey was surrendered in February 1539, and a year later the manor of Buckfast and the site of the abbey were sold to Sir Thomas Dennys. The church and monastic buildings were part demolished, and gradually fell into further ruin. In 1800, the 'old walls' were acquired by Samuel Berry. He levelled what remained of the abbey church, and by about 1806 he had built a romantic castellated Gothic mansion on the west side of the cloister.

1136–1539

The abbey lies near the village of Buckfastleigh, just off the A38, and about 6 miles (9.7km) north-west of Totnes. Since 1882, Buckfast has been occupied by a community of Benedictine monks, now part of the English Benedictine Congregation. New buildings were raised over the site of the medieval originals, largely between 1907 and 1937. The abbey church and areas of the precinct are open to visitors at all reasonable times.

Devon
Exeter

SX 742674

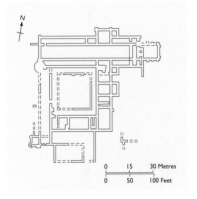

The ruins at Buckfast Abbey as depicted by Samuel and Nathaniel Buck in 1734 (Buckfast Abbey).

This thirteenth-century metalwork fitting is decorated with Limoges enamel, and was recovered in excavations at Buckfast (Buckfast Abbey).

In 1882 Buckfast entered the fourth phase in its monastic history, when the house was purchased by an exiled group of Benedictine monks from La Pierre-qui-Vire in France. Plans were set in hand to restore the abbey, and within two years the monks themselves — under some guidance — had laid bare the foundations of much of the medieval layout of the church and cloister ranges. Interpreting the results of this work is not altogether a straightforward task, though it seems reasonable to suggest that the initial stone monastery was raised by the Cistercian community in the middle years of the twelfth century. Thereafter, the aisled nave may well have remained largely unaltered, but the east end was almost certainly extended sometime between the late twelfth and the mid-thirteenth century. Such a rebuilding may be inferred from the single chapel seen in each transept. As at Dore, for example, the inner pair of chapels was doubtless sacrificed to form the aisles for the new presbytery. The square chapel recovered at the east end was probably a fourteenth-century addition to the church, and may have been the Lady Chapel noted in a documentary source.

The excavations and observations made in the 1880s also suggest that a consider-able amount of rebuilding was undertaken in the fifteenth century, including areas of the cloister, and possibly the chapter house. One survival from this later period is the so-called abbot's tower, which was located at the southern end of the west range. It must have formed part of the abbot's private lodgings, and comprises a three-storey block containing fine chambers.

Having exposed the outline of Cistercian Buckfast, the Benedictine community decided to rebuild the abbey as far as possible on the medieval foundations. Following a design by Frederick A. Walters, construction began in 1907. The church was consecrated in 1932, and the tower finally completed in 1937. The building work itself was undertaken by a small group of monks, normally just four, and never more than six. It was a remarkable achievement.

In more recent years, there have been excavations on precinct structures to the west of the abbey church. The most notable discovery is the partial survival of a massive fourteenth-century guest hall and later service block. The hall adjoined a boundary wall, with gates to the north and south, probably determining the limits of the inner court. East of the church, the entire precinct was bounded by the river Dart.

Brown 1988
Clutterbuck 1994
Fergusson 1984a, 115–16
Knowles and St Joseph 1952, 36–8
Rowe 1878, 53–137
Rowe 1884
Stéphan 1970
Walters 1923

BUCKLAND ABBEY

1278–1539

Buckland is situated about 7 miles (6.4km) north of Plymouth, and just over a mile (1.6km) off the A386. The most prominent survival is the abbey church, converted into a mansion following the dissolution. Presented in association with the City of Plymouth Museums and Art Gallery, Buckland is in the care of the National Trust.

Devon
Exeter

SX 487667

Hidden away in the wooded valley of the Tavy, beside a small tributary stream, Buckland was founded by Amicia de Redvers, the dowager countess of Devon and one of the greatest ladies of her day. In no small part, the abbey was to serve as a memorial to the members of Amicia's family, particularly her husband, Baldwin de Redvers, who had died in 1245, and her son who had been murdered in 1262. Amicia had taken the earliest steps in the process of foundation in 1273, partitioning the necessary lands in readiness, and arranging for a colony of monks to be sent out from Quarr on the Isle of Wight. That she should choose Quarr as the mother house causes no surprise, since it had been founded by the first Baldwin de Redvers (d. 1155) to be earl of Devon. So it was, that in April 1278, Abbot Robert and his seven monks finally arrived at Buckland from the Isle of Wight.

The endowment given by Amicia to the new community was especially lavish. The manors of Buckland, Bickleigh and Walkhampton, along with the large and valuable outlying estate at Cullompton in east Devon, amounted to over 20,000 acres (8,097ha). But these lands were far from the unencumbered and unpopulated areas of waste traditionally associated with the early Cistercians. From the first, the Buckland monks moved into a well settled and manorialized landscape, inheriting all the consequent feudal responsibilities for tenants and serfs. Nevertheless, grange centres were established, and lay brothers were quite definitely to feature in their management over the initial decades of the abbey's history.

A moderately wealthy house, in 1535 Buckland's income was assessed at almost £242. Having survived the first round of suppression closures, it was finally surrendered by Abbot John Toker and twelve monks in February 1539. Within two years Buckland had been purchased by Sir Richard Grenville (d. 1550) for just over £233. It was Grenville's grandson, another Richard (d. 1591), who by 1576 had probably completed the conversion of the abbey church into a Tudor mansion. Four years later, Buckland was acquired by Sir

Francis Drake (d. 1596) for the very hefty sum of £3,400. Drake's heirs continued to hold the house until the present century, gradually making various changes to suit the needs of the family. Extensive modifications were introduced in 1796–1801, and a fairly major programme of restoration was carried out after 1915. Disaster struck in 1938 when a serious fire damaged much of the former monastic nave. Subsequently, Buckland was to see a further round of sympathetic restoration and refurbishment.

In the Tudor conversions at Buckland, almost the entire abbey church was retained. From the details of the fabric, it seems clear that the original building was raised in a more or less continuous programme over the late thirteenth and early fourteenth centuries. Compared to those churches at all but the very poorest of houses, it was a markedly simple structure which may well have been designed in a deliberately restrained fashion. Unusually for this late period, both the nave and the presbytery were built without aisles, and together they reached no more than 125 feet (38m) in total length. There were two small eastern chapels to each of the transepts, and the crossing tower was also

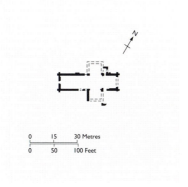

| 0 | 15 | 30 Metres |
| 0 | 50 | 100 Feet |

Following the dissolution of Buckland in 1539, by 1576 the abbey church had been converted to a Tudor mansion. This view is from the south, with the squat tower situated over the former monastic crossing (National Trust Photographic Library/George Wright).

Buckland was founded by the dowager countess of Devon, Amicia de Redvers. On this vault keystone at the site, the crowned head is thought to be a likeness of the countess (National Trust Photographic Library/Nick Carter).

Copeland 1953
Gaskell Brown 1995
Knowles and St Joseph 1952, 146–47
Mauchline, Hart-Davis and Meller 1996
Rowe 1878, 8–52

1135–1536

The abbey site is in Buildwas, on the west side of the B4378, 2 miles (3.2km) from Ironbridge. The extensive ruins of the church and monastic buildings are in the care of English Heritage and are open to the public.

Shropshire
Coventry and Lichfield

SJ 642004

Right: Buildwas is among the best-preserved twelfth-century Cistercian churches in Britain. This view looks through the western crossing arch towards two bays of the north nave arcade.

of comparatively modest proportions.

In the creation of Grenville's house, and in its subsequent modifications, the major loss has been that of the transepts. The south transept was removed in the Tudor programme so that light might be allowed to flood into the new great hall. At the same time, a large service wing was added to the south side of the presbytery. Such is the effect of the plaster ceiling and panelling, it is now difficult to appreciate that the hall itself stands at the very centre of the former monastic church. The arrangements are clearer on the top floor (in the Four Lives Gallery), where the four great transverse arches of the crossing are exposed. Here the most notable detail is the large fragment of cusped Geometric window tracery sitting just outside the apex of the east arch. Another of the more significant monastic survivals is to be seen back at ground-floor level, where the inner chapel of the north transept retains its stone vault. On the south side of the house, reset above a doorway, there is a vault keystone bearing a carved stone head.

Traditionally, this crowned face with outsize ears is thought to be a likeness of Amicia de Redvers.

The cloister lay to the northern side of the abbey church. Although little survives above ground, there are clear traces of the north range buildings within a current boundary wall. Beyond this, a structure known as Tower Cottage is likely to represent the abbot's accommodation. Buckland also retains two very important examples of the buildings associated with its precinct demesne farm. The most prominent of these is a truly magnificent barn which stands very close to the east side of the former church. Almost 160 feet (48.8m) long and 32 feet (9.8m) wide, it may have been constructed as early as the fourteenth century, though it has a superb arch-braced timber roof of fifteenth-century form. The second of the farm buildings is currently known as the Guesthouse, and now provides visitor facilities. Recently excavated, it was probably built in the fourteenth or fifteenth century and initially served as stabling.

BUILDWAS ABBEY

A Savigniac community from Furness was settled in the valley of the river Severn at Buildwas in 1135 by Roger de Clinton, bishop of Coventry (1129–48). Along with all other houses of that congregation, it became Cistercian in 1147, and new buildings were erected. The transformation of the site from Savigniac to Cistercian was achieved at the time of Abbot Ranulf, between 1155 and 1187. Although Buildwas did not have any daughter houses, it was given responsibility for Basingwerk in 1157 and St Mary's, Dublin, in 1166. The abbey was suppressed in 1536, the abbot's house being retained and extended as a private

residence. The church was converted to use as a barn, and the east range of the cloister retained as farm buildings. The greater part of the precinct has survived, and is defined by earthworks, with good evidence of water management, mills, and fishponds. The site of the church and cloister ranges was taken into State care in 1925 and the substantial ruins conserved for public display.

The church at Buildwas, complete to roof height but for the nave aisle walls, is among the best preserved twelfth-century examples of a Cistercian church in Britain. Built between 1150 and 1190, it comprises a short, square presbytery with a rib vault,

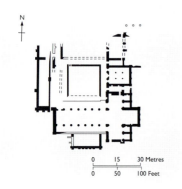

The twelfth-century rib vault in the chapter house at Buildwas was supported on four tall piers, alternately round and octagonal.

English Heritage 1993
Fergusson 1984a, 91–4, 116–17
Hills 1860
Knowles and St Joseph 1952, 106–07
Potter 1847
VCH Shropshire 1973, 50–59

transepts with two eastern chapels which were barrel vaulted, a crossing with a low tower (which was an addition to the original design), and a nave of seven bays. Two bays west of the crossing, there is a pronounced building break in the south nave arcade. This suggests a pause in building before the remainder of the nave was built to house the lay brothers' choir in the 1180s, though the north aisle had been completed earlier to enclose the south side of the cloister. Clear traces of the walls between the piers that backed the stalls of the choir monks and the lay brothers remain, though the walls themselves have been removed. An unusual feature of the church was the vaulted crypt below the north transept, entered by way of the cloister. There is also no west door in the church, the only access to the nave being from the west range into the north aisle. Around 1200, the presbytery was remodelled; its two tiers of eastern windows were combined and sedilia inserted into the south wall. In the fourteenth century, a large chapel was built on to the south side of the nave, apparently as a chantry for the Burnell family.

The cloister was positioned on the north side of the church to take advantage of drainage towards the river Severn. Here, the east range is broadly contemporary with the building of the north transept. The first floor was occupied as the monks' dormitory, with the base of the night door surviving in the transept wall. At ground-floor level, immediately to the north of the transept, was the library and sacristy, originally divided by a timber partition and still covered by a rib vault. To the north of these was the chapter house, which extended one bay beyond the range and which retains its rib vault supported on four tall piers, alternately round and octagonal. North of the chapter house was the parlour, and entered from this by a now blocked door at its east end was the monks' day room. This was of three bays, with an open arcade of three pointed arches in its east wall. To the east

View of the crossing tower and nave at Buildwas, seen from the north-west corner of the cloister.

of the arcade was an enclosed yard, later the infirmary cloister, and to the north of the day room lay the ground floor of the monks' latrines. The north side of the yard was closed by the infirmary, of which part of an early thirteenth-century arcade survives. The east side of the yard was closed by a substantial abbot's house which remains in private use.

The north range of the cloister comprised an east–west refectory, of which only the south wall is currently visible, though its north wall can be traced as an earthwork. It appears to be contemporary with the east range and must date to the 1160s or 1170s. At its east end there was a passage through the range, but there is no trace of a kitchen at the west end and this must have been outside the cloister. The west range was separated from the rest of the cloister by an enclosed lane. The southern end of the range itself was terraced into the rising ground on which the church stands. The range seems to predate the church and other cloister buildings, and it may have been a survival from the Savigniac layout. It was arranged on three floors, though only the basement survives. In the third quarter of the twelfth century, the west range was extended to the north to provide a refectory for the lay brothers; it was also widened slightly to the east.

BYLAND ABBEY

The early history of Byland Abbey is a clear reminder that monastic foundations were often far from trouble-free. It was in 1134 that the Savigniac house at Furness sent a colony of thirteen monks northwards to Calder in Cumberland. Some four years later, following a devastating Scottish raid, the community returned to Furness. But it seems the monks were refused entry, in part at least because their abbot, Gerald, would not resign his rank. They chose instead to set out for York, intending to seek the help of Archbishop Thurstan (1114–40). On the journey eastwards, the sorry troop was advised to ask for the assistance of Gundreda d'Aubigny at Thirsk. With the agreement of her son, Roger de Mowbray, she first settled the monks at Hood. From here, in 1143, they were obliged to move to a better site in the vill of Byland, but this in turn proved to be too close to Rievaulx: each house could hear the other's bells at all times of day and night. Then, in 1147 — the year in which the entire Savigny family was absorbed into the Cistercian order — the monks moved once again, this time travelling west across the moors to Stocking. Although they apparently built a stone church and other structures, Stocking must soon have been regarded as a temporary location. In the meantime, yet another site was being drained and prepared at Byland, and building work was already underway. At last, in 1177, the community moved to its permanent location.

Byland was to prosper, becoming one of the wealthy sheep-ranching abbeys of the north of England. In 1535, its assessed income was given at £238. The house was suppressed in 1539, and a year later was granted to Sir William Pickering (who also acquired Valle Crucis in Wales). It eventually passed to the Wombwell family, whose members still own it. The ruins were placed in State guardianship in 1921, and were cleared of fallen debris under the supervision of Charles Peers in the early 1920s as they were conserved for public display. The whole of the precinct, originally walled, survives as impressive earthworks.

Building work seems to have begun with the west claustral range as early as the

1134/77–1539

The abbey is in the village of Byland, on an unclassified road 2 miles (3.2km) south of the A170, between Thirsk and Helmsley. The extensive remains of the church and monastic buildings are in the care of English Heritage and are open to the public.

North Yorkshire
York

SE 549789

Reconstruction of the late twelfth-century rose window tracery from the west front at Byland (Stuart Harrison).

The foundation of Byland Abbey was a long-drawn-out process, involving several changes of site. Having initially settled at Calder in Lancashire in 1134, the monks finally moved to their permanent Yorkshire location in 1177.

1150s. This suggests that the lay brothers were settled at Byland soon after the site had been cleared and made ready, doubtless to assist with the construction itself. Contemporary with the building of the west range was the laying out of a large church, indicating the intention of building a cloister 145 feet (44m) square. Only the south wall of the nave, and west and south walls of the adjacent transept survive from this church, and it is uncertain how much of it was built. Between 1160 and 1165, the east and south ranges of the cloister were laid out to the standard Cistercian plan. South of the south transept was the library and sacristy. Next to these lay the chapter house, which was rib vaulted from four piers and projected one bay beyond the range to the east. To the south of the chapter house was the parlour, again rib vaulted, and then a passage through the range that led into the ground floor of the monks' latrine block. Next there was the day stair to the dormitory, still in its early Cistercian location, and then a door into the monks' day room of six double bays covered with a groin vault. The east wall of the day room comprised an open arcade with an enclosed yard to the east. The south range included, from east to west, the warming house, a north–south refectory set well to the east of centre, and a large kitchen. To the south of the kitchen, and enclosed between the west range, the refectory, and their own latrine, was the lay brothers' cloister. The construction of the east and south ranges must have been complete by 1177 when the site was first fully occupied. The refectory is unusual, being raised upon a vaulted undercroft.

In the late 1160s, a decision was taken to abandon what was almost certainly a partly built Bernardine church, and to replace it with a much larger structure in the new Gothic style, quite unlike anything the Cistercians had built in Britain before. The new church, which was aisled throughout, had a three-storey elevation, and carried wooden vaults. It seems the model for the scheme was the church begun in the 1160s at nearby Ripon under the auspices of Roger, archbishop of York (1154–81). At Byland, however, the decoration was muted by Cistercian puritanism. The short, square presbytery was retained, but here it is aisled on three sides. The shallow transepts had both eastern and western aisles, the former containing two chapels. Above the crossing was a lantern tower. Building continued until about 1195, when the west front with its rose window was finally completed. In all, Byland stood as probably the most ambitious twelfth-century Cistercian church in Europe, and certainly the largest in Britain.

Excavation in the 1920s recovered a great deal of the internal screening of the presbytery, some of which has been reset, and many of the capitals from the clustered piers that supported the arcades. These are now displayed in a museum on the site. The great glory of the Byland church, however, is its mosaic tile floors, laid in the 1230s and surviving in large areas of the south transept and presbytery.

In the first half of the thirteenth century, a new abbot's house was built to the south of the infirmary, and a new latrine block was built for the monks when the original main drain was found to be ineffective. Otherwise the late twelfth-century buildings remained virtually unaltered until the suppression. There was, however, one exception to this. In the later fourteenth century, the infirmary was demolished and was replaced by a series of two-room apartments. Others were built in the day room, blocking the open arcade in its east room, and most probably in the dormitory above. Private cells were being provided for the monks, a rare survival of a fairly

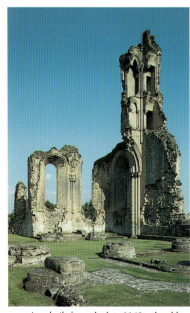

As rebuilt from the late 1160s, the abbey church at Byland was aisled throughout, with three-storey elevations and wooden vaults. An indication of the details in the elevations survives in the south transept (Malcolm Thurlby).

common practice in the later Middle Ages.

A major feature of the precinct at Byland was the creation of three great ponds when the site was first drained, which provided water to power at least two mills. Now dry, the ponds can still be traced in the earthworks that define the monastic precinct. The only building to survive outside the central core is a fragment of the inner gatehouse to the north-west of the abbey church, still spanning the road from Oldstead.

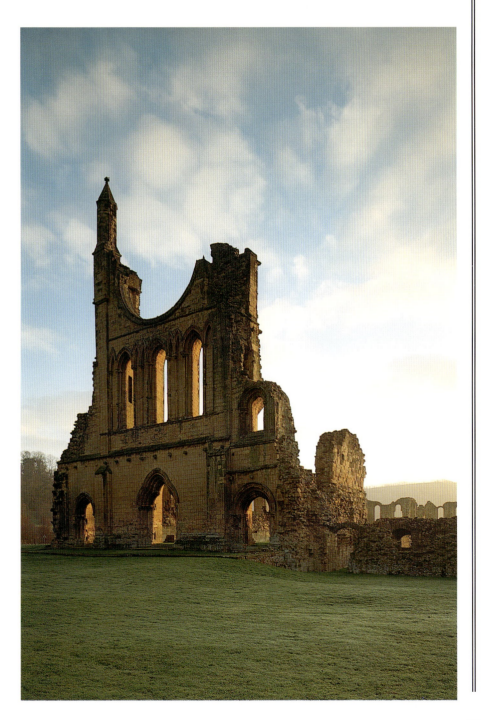

Construction of the church at Byland continued until work on the west front was completed about 1195. The great circular opening in the gable was filled with a handsome rose window.

Fergusson 1975
Fergusson 1984a, 69–90, 117–18
Harrison 1990
Harrison and Barker 1987
Knowles and St Joseph 1952, 86–89
Pevsner 1966, 94–101
Walbran 1863–64

CALDER ABBEY

1134/42–1536

Calder Abbey is situated at Calder Bridge on the A595, about 4 miles (6.5km) south-east of Egremont and about one mile (1.6km) east-north-east of Calder Bridge itself. The extensive remains are in the grounds of a late eighteenth-century private house.

Cumbria

York

NY 051064

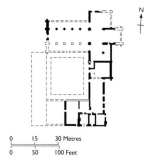

The original foundation at Calder was made in 1134 by Ranulf 'de Gernon', earl of Chester (1129–53), with Abbot Gerald as its head. It was a daughter house of Furness, which was then still within the order of Savigny. After suffering a devastating attack in 1138 by the army of King David I of Scotland and the men of Galloway, the monks returned to Furness, probably before anything more than temporary buildings had been erected. However, they were refused readmission, at least in part because Calder's abbot would not agree to resign his office, and the community had no option but to move on, first to Hood and later to Byland.

A second colonization of the site was made by Furness in 1142, under the leadership of Abbot Hardred, who also made an abortive attempt to establish his authority over the original community which was then at Hood. Calder was transferred to the Cistercian order along with Furness and the other Savigniac houses in 1147. The abbey was never a large one. In 1381 there were only four monks and three lay brethren, though the community may not by then have recovered fully from Scottish raids of 1216 and 1332. By the time of the suppression in 1536 there were nine monks, at which time the income seems to have been no more than about £50.

There are substantial upstanding remains of the church (particularly of the north side of the nave and the transepts) and of the northern end of the east claustral range. From a combination of what survives and of what has been found through excavation, it is known that the church was laid out to the common Cistercian arrangement, with a rectangular presbytery, transepts with chapels on their east side (two to each arm) and an aisled

nave, which was of five bays. One departure from early Cistercian norms was the provision for a central tower over the crossing. The earliest surviving parts of the church are the west doorway and portions of the transepts. The west doorway, which has a round arch and capitals of waterleaf type, may have been part of the work said to have been carried out for William fitz Duncan of Egremont Castle, and possibly dates to around 1175. Much of the rest of the church evidently belongs to later building operations, which could even post-date the Scottish raid of 1216. Thomas de Multon of Egremont Castle, who died in 1240, is recorded as having finished rebuilding the church and as having established a greater convent. The alternating quatrefoil and octagonal piers of the surviving north nave arcade, which carry arches of two chamfers each, would certainly be most at home in the earlier decades of the thirteenth century, though there is little obviously Cistercian in character about them.

The cloister was to the south of the church, and immediately adjacent to the south transept of the church are the remains of the chapter house, which was evidently rebuilt in the later thirteenth century. It was vaulted in three bays, and had a finely traceried window at its east end and a narrow vestibule at its west end. Towards the cloister the chapter house entrance has the characteristic arrangement of a doorway flanked by a window on each side. Unusually, however, behind the northern of the two flanking windows, and occupying over a third of the area of the vestibule, is a large book closet, above which there passes the night stair from the dormitory. This slightly awkward arrangement was presumably necessitated because there was no sacristy and library between the church and chapter house.

Of the dormitory itself, at first-floor level of the east range, there are stretches of both the east and the west walls, and these are pierced by a series of lancet windows. Returning to the ground floor, beyond the chapter house is a slype; however, it is difficult to understand the planning of the rest of the east range, and this is also true of the south range, since both are embodied in a later house. Nevertheless, it seems likely that the refectory was set out on an axis running from north to south, at right-angles to the south range itself. The west conventual range is entirely destroyed. There is a gatehouse to the precinct which is probably of fourteenth-century date.

At the dissolution, the abbey was one of those acquired by the notorious Commissioner, Thomas Leigh, and parts of it were subsequently adapted for occupation. The house which now stands over the southern side of the cloister dates largely from about 1770, though it probably incorporates work of a variety of dates.

The west doorway and parts of the transepts at Calder may date to around 1175. Much of the rest of the building is later, possibly post-dating a Scottish raid on the site in 1216 (RCHME, Crown Copyright).

Fergusson 1984a, 118
Knowles and St Joseph 1952, 76–77
Loftie 1882–88
Loftie 1892
Pevsner 1967, 84–86
VCH Cumberland 1905, 174–78

CLEEVE ABBEY

1186/98–1536

Cleeve is located at the village of Washford, some 7 miles (11.3km) south-east of Minehead, just off the A39. The remains include the well preserved south and east ranges of monastic buildings, the low foundations of the church, and the main gatehouse. The site is in the care of English Heritage and is open at all reasonable times.

Somerset
Bath and Wells

ST 046407

Sometime between 1186 and 1191, Earl William de Roumare II of Lincoln determined upon founding a Cistercian monastery near the Somerset coast. Despite protests made to the General Chapter by the abbeys of Neath and Forde that such a foundation would be to their harm, the site was eventually colonized in 1198. The first abbot, Ralph, and his twelve monks journeyed to the west country from Revesby in Lincolnshire, itself founded by Earl William's grandfather in 1143. The new abbey was named Vallis Florida, although throughout its history it has been generally known as Cleeve.

The initial endowment comprised a series of fairly compact holdings in the immediate environs of the abbey site. Additional grants were to follow from both local and greater lords. To the east, for example, Gilbert de Wolavyngton gave the community a foothold in the valley of the Parrett at Bawdrip near Bridgwater. Of greater importance, King Henry III

0   15   30 Metres

0   50   100 Feet

The main gatehouse at Cleeve was first built in the thirteenth century. It was rebuilt in the fourteenth century, and was extensively remodelled by Abbot William Dovell (1510–36) shortly before the dissolution.

granted Cleeve two-thirds of the manor of Braunton, situated more than 40 miles (64km) to the west in Bideford bay; and over the Cornish border the justiciar, Hubert de Burgh (d. 1243) — William de Roumare's father-in-law — gave the monks the manor at Poughill near Bude, and another at Treglaston, to which further lands were added in Poundstock.

The size of the abbey community during its early years is not clear, though in 1297 it was recorded that the figure of twenty-six monks was to be increased by a further two. From about 1310 to 1450, the general picture of monastic life at Cleeve is one of declining internal discipline, coupled with financial instability. Matters were later to improve, and this was reflected in several phases of renewed building activity through to the dissolution. In 1535, when the community stood at sixteen monks headed by Abbot William Dovell (1510–36), Cleeve's annual income was assessed at a little over £155. Dovell surrendered his monastery to the king's visitors on 6 September 1536. Subsequently, a good deal of the property was sold to Anthony Bustered, who also acquired a lease of twenty-one years on the abbey buildings. The church was apparently demolished soon after the suppression, though a house was established over part of the claustral complex. In due course, this was to become a farm, with the cloister serving as the farmyard. Attempts to arrest the decay began in the 1870s, and there have since been several programmes of archaeological excavation. The site has been in the care of the State since 1950–51.

The colonizing monks would almost certainly have occupied temporary buildings made ready by William de Roumare, though work on the permanent stone structures was very soon in hand. The church — of which little more than foundations survive — was under construction from about 1200. Its plan, bearing no obvious trace of later modification, was typically Cistercian and based upon the classic Bernardine model. As such, it was

distinctly conservative for the period, perhaps even deliberately so. The short, square-ended presbytery, the crossing, and both transept arms (each with solid dividing walls between the two eastern chapels) were probably all raised by 1232, the year in which Henry III granted the abbey oak to fashion its choir stalls. A change in the masonry to the west of the first bay in the nave suggests a structural break at this point. When the church was completed, around the middle years of the thirteenth century, the seven-bay nave arcades were supported on cylindrical piers set on water-holding bases. The principal elevations seem to have been of two storeys, and it is thought that the arcade arches were of two orders with chamfered mouldings. The substantial but austere remains of the south wall of the nave retain no trace of articulation.

Meanwhile, the sequence of construction had progressed to the east claustral range. The sacristy, the chapter house, the monks' day room, and the latrine block, together with the dormitory on the first floor, were all complete by around 1250. The chapter house — where the façade was again rather plain in character — was a large rectangular chamber projecting eastwards from the range. In the two western bays, the pitch of the vault ribs was kept markedly low so as to avoid interference with the floor of the dormitory above, whereas beyond the width of the range the vault rose considerably higher.

In the south range, where the initial buildings were completed in the second half of the thirteenth century, the layout was of the standard Cistercian form. A warming house was situated to the east, the kitchen to the west, and the monks' refectory projected from the centre of the range on a north–south axis. Of the early refectory, the most notable survival is a fragment of its once glorious tiled pavement, in which the heraldry depicted on the individual tiles suggests a date of between 1272 and 1300. It was probably about this time, too, that the plan of the

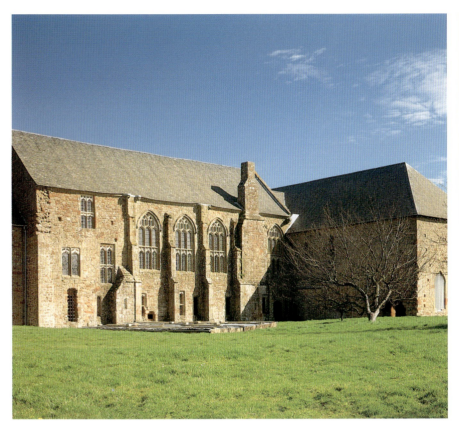

Above: *One of the carved wooden angels in the refectory roof structure at Cleeve.*

Left: *The thirteenth-century refectory at Cleeve was built in the usual Cistercian manner, at right-angles to the cloister. In the fifteenth-century, Abbot David Juyner (1435–87) rebuilt the south range, with a new east–west refectory on the first floor. The refectory hall is identified by the grand three-light windows seen in this view.*

The outstanding feature in the fifteenth-century refectory hall at Cleeve is its magnificent arch-braced timber roof.

abbey was completed with the addition of an infirmary complex in the area to the east of the dormitory range.

A little over a century and a half later, in the time of Abbot David Juyner (1435–87), a decision was taken to completely rebuild the south range, a scheme which also envisaged changes to the west cloister alley. As a whole, this phase of work at Cleeve reflects to an unusual degree those sweeping changes which had occurred in the manner of life within the vast bulk of Cistercian houses during the later Middle Ages. On the ground floor of the rebuilt refectory range, there were two sets of apartments, each with a bedchamber, a living room and a latrine, designed as accommodation for corrodians — those lay persons who for one reason or another had become the responsibility of the abbey. On the first floor, lit by a series of handsome windows in both the north and south walls, the refectory itself was now arranged on an east–west axis. The outstanding feature of this late-medieval hall is its magnificent timber roof, divided into five principal bays by richly moulded arch-braced trusses. Charmingly carved wooden angels with crowned heads project from the base of the main trusses. Until the present century, the greater part of the east wall of the refectory was covered with a wall painting of the Crucifixion.

Adjacent to the west end of the refectory, and approached via a lobby, there was a room now known as the painted chamber. The name is derived from the fact that its east wall is covered by a late fifteenth-century allegorical wall painting, the meaning of which remains unclear. A man stands on a bridge where he is flanked by a lion and a dragon. In the waters beneath the bridge, a variety of fish are shown swimming, and to the left there is the figure of St Catherine holding a diminutive wheel. The room is thought to have been used by the abbot's secretariat.

Buckle 1889
Eeles 1931
Fergusson 1984a, 119–20
Gilyard-Beer 1990
Knowles and St Joseph 1952, 142–43
MacKenzie-Walcott 1876
Simms 1950
Walcott 1875–76
Ward Perkins 1941

Beyond the central monastic complex, the precinct at Cleeve was bounded on the west side by a high wall on the bank of the Washford river. The northern and western boundaries were defined by broad wet moats, and in all an area of about 28 acres (11.3ha) was eventually enclosed. Two leats drawn from the river were used to feed fishponds and to drive mills.

The precinct was entered across a small enclosed courtyard, at the south-east corner of which there lies a handsome two-storeyed gatehouse. Originally built in the thirteenth century, the gatehouse was altered in the following century and once again extensively remodelled by Abbot William Dovell shortly before the dissolution.

COGGESHALL ABBEY

1140–1538

Coggeshall Abbey is situated at Little Coggeshall, about 2 miles (3.2km) east of Great Coggeshall on the A120. The surviving remains are in the grounds of a private house and are not normally accessible to the public.

Essex
London

TL 856223

Coggeshall was a royal abbey, founded in 1140 by King Stephen and his queen, Matilda (d. 1152), as the last of the English daughter houses of Savigny before the congregation was absorbed into the Cistercian order in 1147. The manor of Coggeshall itself was a possession which the queen had inherited from her father, Count Eustace of Boulogne. Perhaps the most important architectural fact about the abbey is that brick was used as a primary building material throughout its history. It is thus one of the earliest buildings in medieval England for which we know that bricks were being made, although there are earlier buildings elsewhere at which bricks from Roman sites were recycled for use.

The principal structural remains of the abbey are a number of buildings around the east claustral range, and a chapel which was associated with the main gateway into the precinct. Nevertheless, the basic layout of the church has been investigated, and some evidence has been found for the disposition of the claustral ranges. Coggeshall's earlier years were overshadowed by a long-running law suit between 1152 and 1160, which resulted from its attempts to remove a settlement on one of its estates — the common complaint against the Cistercians that they preferred sheep to people on their land may have

been justified in this case — and the suit eventually had to be settled at the papal court, doubtless at great expense. Despite this difficulty, however, the main building campaign was evidently nearing completion in these same years. It is possible that the setting out of the abbey on Cistercian lines had been organized by the second abbot, Simon de Toni, who is said to have returned to his original abbey of Melrose in 1168, which may indicate that he had been sent to Coggeshall to provide guidance on correct planning. The high altar of the church was ready for dedication by Gilbert Foliot, bishop of London (1163–87), in 1167.

In its final form, the church had a total length of about 210 feet (64m), with aisles along its nave and much of the chancel. The chancel, however, which was eventually over 72 feet (22m) long, was probably extended at some later stage; and another addition was a chapel dedicated to St Catherine, on the north side of the nave. The cloister was on the south side of the nave, and was evidently built as part of the first campaign, since capitals of mid-twelfth-century types have been found here. Of the surviving buildings, the earliest portions are the shell of the southern end of the dormitory undercroft, and an irregularly aligned building on the bank of the river Blackwater, to the south-east

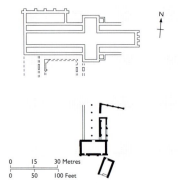

0   15   30 Metres
0   50   100 Feet

of the east range, which is thought to have been a guest house. Both of these appear to be of the late twelfth century, and it has been suggested that the guest house may be that which is mentioned in an account of a ghostly apparition in the time of Abbot Peter (1176–94). A building which is thought to have been the abbot's lodging was added at the south end of the east range, with an extension from it along the east side of that range. This seems likely to have been built in the last years of the twelfth century and the early years of the following century. The elegant gatehouse chapel, with its lancet windows, probably dates from around the 1220s. There are remains of fishponds to the east of the chapel.

In the years leading up to the Reformation the abbey passed through a disturbed period. Abbot John Sampford, who had been deposed, stirred up disaffection against his successor, William Love, who was in turn deposed in 1536 on charges of hiding valuables and supporting the power of the pope. In his place, the pliable Abbot Henry More was introduced, and, as might have been expected, he offered little resistance to the eventual dissolution of the house in 1538. The abbey was acquired by Sir Thomas Seymour, who demolished the church, but probably did little else at that time. It was resold to the Crown, and by 1581 the estates were held by the Paycocke family. Richard Benyan, the husband of Anne Paycocke, built the house which stands to the eastern side of the east range. The house incorporates part of what may have been the monastic infirmary.

Beaumont 1921
Cutts 1858
Dale 1863
Fergusson 1984a, 120–21
Gardner 1955
Knowles and St Joseph 1952, 132–33
Pevsner and Radcliffe 1965, 276–77
RCHME 1922, 165–67
Round 1894–95
Stevenson 1875
VCH Essex 1907, 125–29

COMBE ABBEY

The fifth daughter house of Waverley, Combe Abbey was founded by Richard de Camville in 1150. It was suppressed in 1539 and its cloister ranges converted into a house by John (afterwards Lord) Harington who demolished the church and used its materials for his building work. A new house was built in 1680–91, retaining much of the medieval structure, a process repeated when Eden Nesfield (d. 1888) rebuilt the house for a second time in 1860–66. Though much of Nesfield's house has been demolished, the monastic structures are still visible. The abbey and its parkland, which includes the entire monastic precinct, were bought by Coventry City Council in the 1950s to provide a public park. The abbey has recently been converted to a hotel.

Although interpretation of the remains is somewhat confused by Eden Nesfield's scholarly copying of late twelfth-century detail, it is clear that the church lay on the south side of the cloister. It was, however, largely destroyed without record when Nesfield dug out a 'moat' in 1864. The cloister itself is represented by the present

1150–1539

The site lies in Coombe Abbey Park on the north side of the A4114, 4 miles (6.4km) east of Coventry. Although the church does not survive, parts of the monastic buildings are incorporated in a Tudor and later house, recently converted to a hotel.

Warwickshire
Coventry and Lichfield

SP 405798

A detail of one of the deep twelfth-century window embrasures which flanked the chapter house doorway at Combe Abbey (University of Warwick, Richard K. Morris).

courtyard. Parts of the fifteenth-century arcade survive on the north and west sides, incorporated within the later house. It is known that the missing south side of the cloister was being rebuilt in 1509. On the east side, the arcade has been removed, but here the west wall of the east range can still be seen. The details, all of which suggest a date in the 1180s, include the fine round-headed doorway to the chapter house, together with deep twin windows on either side. To the north and south are further doorways, one to the parlour, and the other to the passage through the range. A door from the passage into the monks' day room survives.

Fergusson 1984a, 121–22
Pevsner and Wedgwood 1966, 236–38
VCH Warwick 1908, 73–75; 1951, 72–73

COMBERMERE ABBEY

1133–1538

The site lies almost 3 miles (4.8km) north-east of Whitchurch, off the A525. There are no obvious visible remains, though it is probably the east cloister range which is occupied by the private house which takes its name from the abbey.

Cheshire
Coventry and Lichfield

SJ 589441

Fergusson 1984a, 122
Hall 1896
Pevsner and Hubbard 1971, 181
VCH Chester 1980, 150–56

The abbey at Combermere was founded in 1133 by Hugh Malbank. The foundation charter was witnessed by Ranulf, earl of Chester (1129–53), whom Hugh wished to be regarded as the principal founder and protector of the new house. It was at first a daughter of Savigny, becoming Cistercian with all other houses of the congregation in 1147. Within the first century of the abbey's existence, it attracted sufficient recruits to be able to provide colonies for three daughter houses. These daughters were at Poulton (founded in 1153), Stanlaw (founded in 1172) and Hulton (founded in 1218–20).

Despite a series of successive financial crises, by 1535 the abbey's assessed income stood at £225. It was dissolved in 1538.

In August 1539, the abbey was acquired by Sir George Cotton, who adapted parts of the conventual buildings as a house for himself. An inscription records building activity in 1563. The house built at this time was extensively modified in the nineteenth century, and it would be very difficult to identify any structures of monastic origin with confidence. Even so, it seems the claustral buildings lay to the south of the church.

COUPAR ANGUS ABBEY

1161/64–1560

The abbey church is thought to have been on the site of the present parish church, on the south side of the town of Coupar Angus, and on the east side of the A923, about 15 miles (24km) north-west of Dundee. The only upstanding building, a gatehouse, is to the south-east of the church.

Perth and Kinross
Dunkeld

NO 224396

At least six of Scotland's Cistercian houses were founded either wholly or partly under the patronage of a member of the royal family: Coupar Angus was one. It is uncertain, however, who was the initiator of the foundation. Very probably it was King David I (1124–53) who had intended to found the house on his manor here, with the active encouragement of St Waldef, though it was left to his grandson, King Malcolm IV (1153–65) to carry

out his intentions. The first monks may have arrived from Melrose in 1161, though there was perhaps not a full complement until 1164. There was a dedication of the church in 1233.

The abbey evidently passed through a difficult period in the fourteenth century. In 1305 it was said that one of its granges had been burnt by King Edward I of England, while in 1351 a papal bull referred to the abbey buildings as 'exceedingly impoverished'. Nevertheless, there seems to have been a revival of its fortunes in the later Middle Ages, and there were at least twenty-four monks on the eve of the Reformation. On the basis of the Books of Assumption of thirds of benefices, started in 1561, it also seems that Coupar had become the wealthiest Cistercian house in Scotland, with an income of £5,590; for comparison, the next wealthiest house, Melrose, had £5,180 and the third wealthiest, Kinloss, had £3,480. The abbey's last years were presided over by Abbot Donald Campbell, who ensured a seemly observance of religious life, though he had gone over to the reformers by 1559, on the very eve of the Reformation. After being granted to a series of post-Reformation commendators, in 1606 the estates of the abbey were erected into a temporal lordship for James Elphinstone, the son by a second marriage of the James Elphinstone who had been granted the estates of Balmerino Abbey three years earlier. He took the title of Lord Coupar, a title which later passed to his nephew, the third Lord Balmerino.

The church is thought to have remained partly in use by the parish after the Reformation, while it is likely that some of the monastic buildings continued to house the commendator and those monks who chose to remain. However, with the eventual passing of the last of the community, and the death of Lord Coupar in 1669, it is likely the abbey buildings became little more than a source of materials, and there is plentiful evidence that the town which had grown up at the precinct gates rebuilt much of itself with the abbey's stonework.

A new church was built in 1686, probably on part of the site of the abbey church, and this in turn was largely rebuilt in 1780; the present church, on the same site, dates from 1859. As a result of all of this, the only upstanding relic of the abbey complex is a part of one of the gatehouses, to the south-east of the abbey church. A plan of 1820 in the National Library of Scotland, which claims to show the layout of the abbey, is clearly pure invention and, since excavations have so far failed to locate any evidence for the church or conventual ranges, it is sadly true that we know less about Scotland's richest Cistercian house than about any other of the order.

A fragment of one of the gatehouses is now the only upstanding feature at Coupar Angus Abbey.

Easson 1947
Hutcheson 1887–88
King 1976
O'Sullivan 1995
Rogers 1879–80

CROXDEN ABBEY

Croxden, a daughter house of the Savigniac abbey at Aulnay-sur-Odon in Normandy, was initially established at Cotton near Alton in 1176 by Bertram de Verdun. Within three years, the community moved to the present site in the valley of the Croxden brook. Though the abbey was dedicated in 1181, the construction of permanent buildings was slow. Abbot Thomas of Woodstock was responsible for raising a masonry church, parts of which can still be identified in the south transept and south nave aisle. He was buried in the partly finished chapter house in 1229. It is clear from the surviving ruins that the rebuilding of this church began about 1220, when a new presbytery with ambulatory and five radiating chapels was begun. This was consecrated in 1232. Abbot Walter of London (1242–68) completed the rebuilding of the church, which was rededicated in 1253, finished the chapter house, which he extended and vaulted, built a north–south refectory in the south range of the cloister, and began the construction of the east cloister range

1176–1538

Croxden lies 5 miles (8km) north-west of Uttoxeter on an unclassified road off the A522. The ruins of the church and cloister buildings are in the care of English Heritage and are open at any reasonable times.

Staffordshire
Coventry and Lichfield

SK 065397

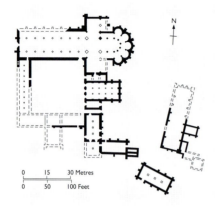

A view of Croxden looking north-west over the low foundations of the chapter house towards the south transept.

Ellis 1997

Hills 1865

Hoey 1993

Knowles and St Joseph 1952, 104–05

Lynam 1911

Pevsner 1974, 111–13

Reynolds 1964

VCH Staffordshire 1970, 226–30

and latrine building. This was completed by his successor, William de Houton who added a two-storey abbot's house at the south end of the east range before 1274.

At some time in the mid-thirteenth century, a substantial infirmary hall was built eastwards of the east range, linked by a second cloister. There was a chapel towards the centre of the east wall of the infirmary hall. The small west range, which remarkably did not house the lay brothers, was built in the 1280s and included a large guest-chamber, completing the development of the central buildings which were all roofed in shingle. It was not until 1332–34 that the cloister ranges were roofed in lead. A new abbot's house was built in 1335–36 to the south-east of the latrine block and south of the infirmary buildings. At some point in the later fourteenth century, it would appear that the abbot had taken over the infirmary as his own hall, for tables were placed along its east and west walls and it had assumed the form of a domestic hall. This almost certainly indicates that the community had broken into several 'households' centred on the principal officers of the house, a common feature of the later Middle Ages when the strict claustral life had been replaced by less formal living. The open thirteenth-century cloister arcade was replaced in the first years of the sixteenth century by a glazed cloister of elaborate design with a porch in front of the chapter house.

The church and cloister buildings lay at the centre of a rectangular precinct some 72 acres (30ha) in extent, defined today by extensive earthworks. The principal gate-house was on the north side, next to the surviving gate chapel, and both were built between 1242 and 1268 though the precinct wall was only built in the decade after 1274. The western side of the precinct contains a large mill-pond and dam and there is a larger pond to the west of the precinct, where the precinct wall is carried across the dam. At least one mill is

recorded in this area, and there was a fish-pond on the south side of the Croxden brook. The inner court lay to the north of the church, and the outer court to the east, where a substantial late medieval barn, reroofed in the late fifteenth century, remains in use among post-medieval farm buildings. In the eastern part of the precinct, to both north and south of the Croxden brook, there are extensive water meadows.

Croxden Abbey was suppressed in 1538. By 1731, when the site was drawn by the Buck brothers, the buildings appeared much as they do today. The only subsequent loss of significance was part of the west range. At some point, too, a road was driven across the site of the church, unfortunately separating the presbytery and north transept from the remainder of the ruins. Croxden was extensively recorded and excavated by Charles Lynam at the beginning of this century, and the ruins were placed in the guardianship of the Office of Works in 1936. Conservation began in 1956 and was preceded by clearance and excavation which has recovered the plan of many buildings reduced to low walling.

The west front of the abbey church at Croxden (University of Warwick, Richard K. Morris).

CULROSS ABBEY

Culross was established by Malcolm (d. 1230), earl of Fife, with monks from Kinloss in 1217–18, though he may have started planning it three years earlier. The abbey was sited above the north shore of the Forth estuary, in the place where St Serf is said to have had a community in the sixth century, and of which St Kentigern was a member before he moved on to Glasgow. Whatever the truth of such legends, cross shafts which could be as early as the eighth or ninth centuries certainly survive here. The Cistercian abbey was probably never a large one, and on the eve of the Reformation there may have been no more than about ten in the community. From 1511 the abbey was ruled by a series of commendators who, from 1531 onwards, were mainly members of the Colville family. In 1589 it was erected into a temporal lordship for James Colville of Easter Wemyss.

Despite the relatively late date of its foundation, the abbey church was laid out to the simplest of the cross-shaped plans that had been favoured by the Cistercians for nearly a century, with a rectangular presbytery, transepts with aisles for two chapels on the east side of each, and a long aisleless nave for the choirs of the monks and the lay brethren. Apart from the north and west walls of the area of the nave occupied by the lay brothers' choir, this church still survives and is perhaps the best preserved example of the early Cistercian plan type to remain in use in Britain.

The choirs of the monks and canons were separated by two stone screens, and these still survive in modified form. The western screen had a pair of doorways to each side of the nave altar, and above it at loft level was a recess for the rood altar, flanked by doors which gave access to the loft. The eastern screen had a central doorway, to allow the monks' choir stalls to

turn at right angles at the west end of the choir. By a quirk of fortune, these screens survived because in about 1500 Abbot Andrew Masoun added a bell tower, and rather than place it over the crossing, he built it above the screens. This meant that, as long as the tower was retained, so were the screens. The main changes that were made resulted from the need to thicken the walls when the tower was built, leading to the blocking of the existing doorways at both ground floor and loft levels. In their place, a reused doorway was inserted at ground-floor level, where the nave altar had been, and another door was cut to one side of the altar recess at loft level. At the same time that the tower was built, a chapel was built out to the north of it, on the side away from the cloister, though this has now gone.

The monastic buildings were to the south of the church, and had to be raised on vaulted substructures because of the steep slope of the land. These vaults suffered structural problems, and at some

1217/18–1560

Culross Abbey is on a hill above the town of the same name, on the north shore of the Firth of Forth, about 9 miles (14.5km) west of Dunfermline. The eastern parts of the church are still in use for worship, and are generally open to the public; those parts of the claustral ranges in the care of Historic Scotland are also open to the public.

Fife
Dunblane

NS 989862

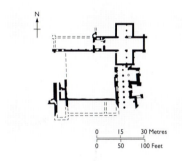

The abbey church and the ruins of the east range at Culross, seen from the south-east. The eastern parts of the church have been used for parish worship since 1633.

Part of the lay brothers' range of monastic buildings survives on the west side of the cloister at Culross.

Douglas 1925–26
Fawcett 1994a, 65–66
Gifford 1988, 146–51
MacGibbon and Ross 1896–97, **2**, 231–43.
McRoberts 1966–69
RCAHMCS 1933, 70–77

stage the rib vaults of the undercrofts were replaced by barrel vaults. The best preserved part of the monastic buildings is the central section of the range of the lay brethren, on the west side of the cloister, though the outer part is now ruined, and the part closest to the lay brothers' choir has been rebuilt as the minister's manse. On the east side of the cloister, the foundations of the undercroft have been exposed following excavation. The inner wall of the range up to the level of the cloister has also survived, because it acts as a retaining wall for what was the cloister garth. At cloister level, part of the chapter house entrance survives.

Before the Reformation the parish had its church to the west of the abbey, but in 1633 it was decided to take over the eastern parts of the monastic church for worship, which is the reason it survives so well. Nevertheless, many changes were made over the years. In 1642, for example, the north transept was adapted by Sir George Bruce of Carnock (the ancestor of the earls of Elgin), and a tomb house was constructed off its north-east corner. Within this is a magnificent tomb signed by John Mercer, with superbly carved figures of Bruce, his wife and children.

In 1823 there was a major restoration of the church by the architect William Stirling. However, while this operation gave back to the building much of the dignity it had lost by then, a great deal of architectural and historic significance was lost in the process, including the transept chapels. A more sensitive restoration, by Rowand Anderson and Paul, took place in 1905, reinstating the chapels and leaving the building much as it is now seen. Happily the church remains in use for worship, and the site of the monastic buildings has been in State care since 1913.

CWMHIR ABBEY

1176–1537

Situated about 8 miles (12.9km) north of Llandrindod Wells, and approached via minor roads off the A483, the abbey lies near the tiny village of Abbey Cwmhir. The fragmentary remains of the nave are freely accessible at all reasonable times.

Powys
St Davids

SO 055711

The secluded ruins of Cwmhir — the abbey 'of the long valley' — lie amid remote and glorious mountain scenery at the heart of central Wales. It is a site which is especially cherished among the Welsh people. Not only does it somehow still convey the Cistercian ideal, it is also the burial place of the country's most celebrated native prince, Llywelyn ap Gruffudd (d. 1282).

Cwmhir was founded in August 1176, with a colony of Whitland monks settling on land which was the gift of Cadwallon ap Madog, chief lord of the Welsh district or *cantref* of Maelienydd. Three years later, Cadwallon was killed by Roger Mortimer (d. 1214), and by the end of the century this ambitious Marcher lord had assumed patronage of the house. Mortimer's charter of 1200 — in which he referred to 'our men who died in the conquest of Maelienydd' — probably served to replace the original foundation grant. Confirmation charters of 1215 and 1232 demonstrate that land in the surrounding hills and river valleys had been given to Cwmhir by both Welsh and Anglo-Norman lords. By this time, effective control of the middle March was in the hands of Llywelyn ab Iorwerth of Gwynedd. The fact that Llywelyn retained this supremacy until his death in 1240 has very significant implications for understanding the context in which the abbey church was constructed.

Despite the importance of Marcher patronage, as well as the need to show allegiance to the English king, Cwmhir's monks were as Welsh as the land in which they dwelt. This dilemma of conflicting

Cwmhir, the abbey 'of the long valley', lies hidden in the mountainous heart of central Wales. The remains of the extraordinarily long nave, begun in the early thirteenth-century, have been recently consolidated.

This early thirteenth-century capital, with foliate decoration, is one of the many fragments of the former abbey built into later walls at Cwmhir.

loyalties was to cause many problems for the community. In 1228, for example, it was presumably the abbey's support for the native cause which led to the burning of one of its granges by royal forces. Three years later, the English army was apparently tricked into an ambush by a Cwmhir monk. In revenge, King Henry III ordered the destruction of yet another grange, and was intent on burning the monastery itself. The abbot paid a heavy fine of 300 marks (£200) to 'save the buildings, which had been erected at such very great expense and labour'.

Adding to the economic difficulties of the fourteenth century, it appears the abbey was badly damaged during the revolt of Owain Glyn Dŵr, probably in 1401–02. There is little by way of documentary or archaeological evidence to suggest recovery after this time. In the survey of 1535, although some property was overlooked, the assessed income of the then tiny community barely reached £25. Just three monks finally surrendered the abbey in March 1537. In due course, the site passed to the Fowler family, and in the Civil War of the 1640s Cwmhir was defended for the royalist cause. When taken by storm and wrecked in 1644, the Fowler house was described as 'very strong ... built with stone of the greatest thickness'.

Five bays from one of the nave arcades at Cwmhir survive in the parish church at Llanidloes. The piers (top illustration) comprise eight groups of triple shafts set around a square core. The responds, or half-piers at each end (lower illustration), feature single shafts on the side faces of the core. The capitals range from the flattish leaves (top), to more luxuriant forms (lower) with overhanging foliage (After Williams 1894–95).

Day 1911
Radford 1982
RCAHMCW 1913, 3–7
Rees 1849
Remfry 1994
Williams 1894–95

The Tudor antiquary, John Leland (d. 1552), was clearly much impressed with Cwmhir: 'No church in Wales', he said, 'is seen of such length as the foundation of walls there begun doth show'. The modern exploration of the ruins began in 1824, and the site was further investigated by Stephen Williams in 1895. The plan produced by Williams, and his account of the 'trifling excavations', still provide the main archaeological evidence on the buildings, although one or two additional details have been revealed in a recent programme of masonry consolidation. It is fortunate, too, that the remains at Cwmhir itself can be supplemented by the remarkable survival of five bays from one of the nave arcades. These now stand in the parish church at Llanidloes, some ten miles (16km) to the north-west, transported there during a phase of reconstruction of about 1540–41.

Given the foundation date of 1176, it might be expected that Cwmhir's earliest stone church followed a Bernardine layout similar to the mother house at Whitland, with construction work beginning at the east end. Unfortunately, the excavations of 1895 recovered very little evidence for the presbytery and transepts, and so it is impossible to be certain of their early form. Nevertheless, one or two fragments of recorded *ex situ* stonework can be compared with features known from the late twelfth-century transepts at the sister abbey of Strata Florida.

Regardless of the east end, the nave at Cwmhir was an astonishing conception. Even if never fully realized, the initial cash injection must have been enormous. In all, it was to be fourteen bays in length, totalling some 256 feet (78m). Everything about it betrays a patron of the very greatest ambition. The foundations of the south-west crossing pier indicate an intention to extend the work eastwards, though little more than the west walls of the transepts may have been raised.

It is suggested that each of the free-standing nave piers comprised eight groups of triple shafts set around a square core, with the central shaft in each group carrying a broad fillet. As the responds at Llanidloes show, there is some evidence of a slightly different pier form, in which single shafts were positioned on the side faces. The sculpture on the capitals ranged from somewhat crude flattish leaves and scallops, through to far more luxuriant overhanging foliage. The piers themselves are likely to have supported a characteristic two-storey Cistercian elevation, but there is no evidence for a vault over the central vessel. In the aisles, each bay was covered with a four-part vault, the ribs springing from triple wall shafts rising from low benches along the outer walls. Again, the central member of triple shafts was filleted.

All of the essential ingredients seen in this composition had been created in the west country workshops by the very early years of the thirteenth century. None the less, it is extremely difficult to assign a precise date to the Cwmhir construction programme, not least because of the complexity of the political background in the middle March at this time. Although some elements would have been rather precocious, a case could just about be made for the scheme having been initiated by Roger Mortimer, probably at the time of his 'refoundation' grant of 1200. Yet it remains more likely that the work was carried out during the period of stability in which Llywelyn ab Iorwerth controlled the region from about 1215 until his death in 1240. To underline this, several of the closest parallels for the form of the Cwmhir piers, and the mouldings of its arches, can be dated to about 1230. So close in style is the work in the choir at Pershore Abbey, and that in the Lady Chapel at St Frideswide's Priory in Oxford, it might be suggested that all three were the product of training in a single workshop.

The cloister at Cwmhir lay to the south of the church and some details of its plan were recovered in the work of the 1890s.

CYMER ABBEY

1198–1536/37

Cymer Abbey lies a mile (1.6km) north-west of Dolgellau, just off the A470. The remains of the church, and traces of the cloister layout are in the care of Cadw: Welsh Historic Monuments. The site is accessible at all reasonable times.

Gwynedd
Bangor

SH 722195

Few other sites in Britain convey the essence of the Cistercian ideal better than Cymer. Remote and tranquil, with a wonderfully majestic mountain backdrop, the abbey is located close to the point where the swirling waters of the Mawddach meet those of the Wnion. Indeed, it is the confluence of the rivers which gives rise to the full name of the site, *Kymer deu dyfyr* — the meeting of the waters.

Cymer was founded in 1198, or perhaps early in 1199, under the patronage of Maredudd ap Cynan (d. 1212), lord of Meirionydd, and it was colonized by a community of monks from Cwmhir. In a charter of 1209, Prince Llywelyn ab Iorwerth (d. 1240) confirmed the abbey's grants and privileges, 'lest what has been justly given may be taken away by unjust presumption in the future'. Much of Cymer's landed property lay in large mountainous tracts, though it also held a valuable estate at Neigwl on the Lleyn peninsula. Dairy farming was a significant element in the early economy of the house, and the brothers at sometime kept a notable stud, rendering two high-quality horses yearly to Prince Llywelyn.

The community was almost always in a state of pitiable poverty, and its buildings were never extensive or grand. The most prominent feature today is the church, dating from the first quarter of the thirteenth century, its walls raised of crude local rubble and boulders, with the main dressings cut in a buff sandstone. In the years immediately after the foundation, as a temporary measure, the monks may have worshipped in a timber oratory east of the present church. Doubtless it was intended that a formal presbytery would be constructed following the completion of the nave in stone. However, the east wall of the church is clearly not bonded to its side walls. The construction in this fashion must represent a compromise solution to an unfinished plan.

It was to remain a simple rectangular structure, measuring just 105 feet (32m) internally. For much of its length, the aisles were separated from the central vessel of the church by solid stone walls. Only the

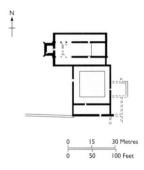

A view looking south-east along the length of the tiny Cistercian church at Cymer in north-west Wales.

A detail of one of the thirteenth-century octagonal nave piers at Cymer.

Knowles and St Joseph 1952, 112–15
Robinson 1995b
Williams 1981b

three western bays were arcaded, with heavily chamfered pointed arches set on octagonal piers. A pair of doorways, one leading from each aisle, presumably served as the upper choir entrances. Just beyond these, a single step marked the limit of the presbytery or chancel. The east wall is pierced by three lofty lancets, the taller central window having a moulded shaft around its inner splay. There was a second tier of smaller windows above. Nearby, in the south wall, are the remains of the seats used during mass by the officiating priest, his deacon and subdeacon. At the west end of the church, the tower was added in the fourteenth century. A somewhat unusual feature, its construction perhaps marks the abandonment of any hope the community may have had for completing a more conventional Cistercian church.

Cymer's thirteenth-century cloister and the surrounding monastic buildings survive as no more than foundations. To the east, traces of the chapter house were located when the abbey was first cleared for display, and to the south the refectory lay parallel to its adjacent cloister alley. On the third side of the cloister, the lay brothers' range may never have been completed in stone. The farmhouse situated to the west of the ruins probably represents the late-medieval guest house, or possibly even the abbot's private accommodation. It originally stood as a single-storey hall, and its very fine late fifteenth-century timber roof still survives.

By 1388, the size of the community had fallen to just five monks. Financial indebtedness and a marked decline in the standards of religious life already seemed to be setting the house on the brink of closure. In 1535, Cymer's annual income was assessed at a little over £51. It was to be dissolved within two years.

DEER ABBEY

1214/19–1560

The abbey is about half a mile (0.8km) west of Old Deer and 12 miles (19.3km) west of Peterhead on the A950. The extensively reconstructed footings of the church and the lower parts of the claustral ranges are in the care of Historic Scotland, and are open regularly.

Aberdeenshire
Aberdeen

NJ 968481

Right: The south range is the most prominent survival of the monastic buildings at Deer. Substructures were needed to raise the refectory to the general cloister level.

Rather like Culross, Old Deer has an unusually long history of religious life. By the twelfth century it was believed that St Columba (d. 597) himself had established a monastery here in the sixth century, with a disciple called Drostan. However, it is more likely that, if someone of that name was indeed a founder, it was the St Drostan who was a great-grandson of King Aidan mac Gabrain, and who therefore presumably lived in the seventh and eighth centuries. The early monastery is also associated with the fine ninth-century gospel book known as the *Book of Deer*, now in the university library at Cambridge. There was still a community of some sort here in the eleventh and twelfth centuries, albeit by that stage they were perhaps more likely to have been secular priests, and at least some of that community's endowments appear to have been transferred to the Cistercians.

Plans for the foundation of a Cistercian community were being made in 1214, when the site and endowments that had been offered by William Comyn (d. 1233), earl of Buchan, were under consideration by the other Scottish abbots of the order. A small core of monks may have been resident soon after 1214, and it is possible that some of those had earlier been members of the predecessor community; it was not until 1219 that the rest of the colony came from Kinloss. Very little is known of the subsequent history of the abbey, though an interesting sidelight is thrown upon it by events in the early 1530s. In 1530 King James V (1513–42) had asked the

Cistercian General Chapter to send someone to visit the Scottish houses of the order, in an attempt to introduce a stricter way of life; yet, when the abbot of Chaalis (Oise) urged reforms following his visitation, the king flew to the defence of the abbeys, urging the particular conditions of Scotland as a reason for some departures from strictness. Despite this, the abbots of Coupar Angus and Glenluce tried to introduce reforms throughout the order in Scotland, censuring those abbots regarded as guilty of derelictions of duty; however, in 1537 the community at Deer was granted relaxations, though they did promise to arrange things so that they could live 'according to the reforms of the Cistercian order'. There also seems to have been an agreement to repair buildings in a poor state.

Soon after this, in 1543, the abbey's last true abbot resigned and was replaced by a commendator, Robert Keith, a brother of the Earl Marischal, and this is unlikely to have made reforms easier to introduce. He was in turn succeeded by his fifteen-year-old nephew in 1551, about which time there were still about thirteen monks with the abbot. Keith retained his office over the Reformation period, and in 1587 the

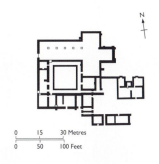

A view over the low foundations of the church at Deer, looking south towards the cloister and the south range.

MacGibbon and Ross 1896–97, 274–81
Simpson 1924–27

abbey was erected into a temporal lordship for him, when he took the title of Lord Altrie. The church and monastic buildings evidently fell into rapid decline, with the materials being carried away for other purposes. A reversal of fortunes began in 1809 when the owner, James Ferguson of Pitfour, excavated the site and laid out the ruins. This work was perhaps aimed more at emphasizing its picturesque qualities than at preserving its archaeological integrity, and much of it was undone when Admiral Ferguson built a mausoleum within the area of the church in 1854. It was only after 1930, when it was acquired by the Roman Catholic Church, and handed over to the state three years later, that the ruins again began to be more appropriately treated. Excavations in 1939 by the Ministry of Works, the predecessor of Historic Scotland, re-established the plan of the church and of the conventual buildings to its south, and there were further

excavations between 1991 and 1994.

So far as the plan of the church can now be understood, it had a short rectangular presbytery, transepts with two eastern chapels in each, and a nave probably of five bays with a single aisle on its north side which, like the single aisle at Balmerino, may be a later addition. The most complete remains of the claustral buildings are of the south range, where the slope of the land necessitated the provision of substructures to raise the refectory to the general cloister level. The dormitory does not seem to have projected further than the outer wall of the south range, though the latrine block was beyond that, and stretching eastwards from the outer angle of the latrine was an extended range which is thought to have been the abbot's residence. East of the east claustral range are the footings of a U-shaped complex of buildings which are assumed to represent the monastic infirmary.

DIEULACRES ABBEY

1158/1214–1538

The site of Dieulacres is on private land at Abbey Green, about a mile (1.6km) to the north-west of Leek, and on the east side of the A523. Slight traces of the church remain above ground.

Staffordshire
Coventry and Lichfield

SJ 983578

Klemperer 1995
Pevsner 1974, 172–73
VCH Staffordshire 1970, 230–35

The origins of Dieulacres Abbey lie in the foundation made by Robert the Butler at Poulton, on the western borders of Cheshire, about 1146–53. Following the initial plans, the site was at last occupied by monks from Combermere, probably in 1158. After more than half a century, in 1214, the community was moved to a new site in the valley of the river Churnet, to the north-west of Leek in Staffordshire, by Ranulph 'de Blundeville' (d. 1232), earl of Chester and lord of Leek. It grew to become a relatively prosperous house with an income of £227 in 1535. It was dissolved three years later. Permanent building seems to have begun before the change of site. The only visible *in situ* remains of the monastery are the bases of two southern crossing piers in the

church, and these clearly date from the first years of the thirteenth century. The northern two pier bases are more fragmentary and largely buried.

The site is now occupied by a farmhouse of 1612, together with Gothic farm buildings of about 1818, both of which contain considerable quantities of reused medieval masonry derived from the abbey. Much of the *ex situ* stonework can be dated to about 1220–60, though there is also material indicating the insertion of handsome new window tracery in the early fourteenth century. Recent survey work on the site has revealed that the below ground remains survive in good condition. There are significant earthworks defining areas of the abbey precinct.

DORE ABBEY

In his almost poetic description of Herefordshire's 'Gilden Vale', the early antiquary William Camden (d. 1623) wrote of its hills 'cloathed with woods' and of the rich and pleasant fertility of its 'fields lovely and fruitful meadows'. Amid this idyllic scene, his portrait continues, 'glides a clear and crystal river, upon which Robert Earl of Ewyas erected a beautiful monastery'. Happily, some four centuries later, the Golden Valley has lost very little of its Elizabethan rural charm. Moreover, it retains one of the best-preserved fragments of a Cistercian church to be found anywhere in Britain. All too easily overlooked in favour of the more celebrated ruins in the north of England, the early Gothic remains at Dore comprise the entire liturgical east end of the abbey church — all with roofs, and long-since serving a parochial function.

Founded in 1147, Dore's first patron was the Robert fitz Harold of Ewyas noted by Camden, its community arriving from Morimond Abbey in the Champagne region of north-eastern France. In the event, Dore was to prove the only British house directly settled by this important elder daughter of Cîteaux, although in turn it was to send out three daughter colonies of its own. To begin with, Trawscoed in Wales was founded about 1173, though it was aborted in the early years of the thirteenth century and the site was subsequently worked as a grange. Successful daughters were later established at Grace Dieu in 1226, and at Darnhall (which moved to Vale Royal) in 1274.

The monks who arrived from Morimond found themselves in Robert's border lordship of Ewyas Harold. But in due course, apart from its estates in the immediate Golden Valley area, Dore also held a number of valuable properties in Wales.

Most gifts of land were settled on the monks by the early years of the thirteenth century, and there is abundant evidence to demonstrate the subsequent consolidation of holdings through exchange, purchase, and even woodland clearance. Not everyone approved. Even allowing for his embittered outlook, Gerald of Wales (d. 1223) conveys a picture of Adam I — abbot from about 1186 to 1216 — as a grasping individual set upon extending Dore's estates by fair means or foul. The monks were, for example, quite definitely involved in extensive clearances in the royal forest of Treville at this time, and were accused by Gerald of changing 'an oak wood into a wheat field'. All in all, during the heyday of direct exploitation, the abbey's lands were centred on some seventeen granges. Nine of these were situated in the Golden Valley; four lay in what is now north Monmouthshire; and three others were in the Marcher lordship of Brecon, within the district known as *Cantref Selyf*.

For much of the first half of the fourteenth century the community was headed by Abbot Richard Straddell (d. 1346), a notable scholar and theologian who at times served as a diplomat for both the Crown and the Cistercian General Chapter. In 1321, he received a 'beautifully adorned' relic of the Holy Cross, a gift to the abbey from William de Grandisson (d. 1335). In the years after Richard's death, however, Dore's fortunes seem to have changed for the worse. Its later history was peppered by a series of financial difficulties, coupled with lapses in monastic discipline. Never a particularly cash-rich house, in 1535 its total income was assessed at just over £101. It was dissolved in the following year, when up to nine monks may still have been resident.

1147–1536

Dore is situated in the village of Abbey Dore, about a mile and a half (2.4km) off the A465, and some 10 miles (16km) south-west of Hereford. The remains comprise the crossing and the liturgical east end of the monastic church, now serving a parochial function. There are slight traces of the nave, and fragments of the claustral buildings. Both church and ruins are accessible at all reasonable times.

Herefordshire
Hereford

SO 387303

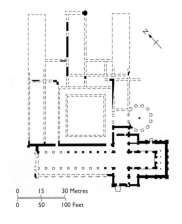

| 0 | 15 | 30 Metres |
| 0 | 50 | 100 Feet |

The late thirteenth- or early fourteenth-century vault bosses from the nave at Dore include a variety of glorious figurative scenes. In this example, a Cistercian monk (or abbot) kneels at the feet of the Virgin and Child.

The early thirteenth-century ambulatory vault at Dore was carried on delicate bundled piers of eight shafts.

Right: The early Gothic presbytery at Dore, built in two principal phases over the late twelfth and early thirteenth centuries, is one of the finest Cistercian survivals in the west of Britain. The screen dates from the restoration of the church in the early 1630s.

As the large and sometimes confusing body of literature on the subject demonstrates, the chronological sequence of the abbey buildings at Dore was complex. In beginning to unravel the detail, it seems reasonable to assume that in 1147 the founding monks were greeted by an arrangement of temporary wooden structures prepared by Robert of Ewyas. Thereafter, although the evidence is slight, there are indications that a small and austere stone monastery was laid out over the first two or three decades of the abbey's history. Within the upstanding fabric, a number of features in the north transept point to the existence of an earlier building, or at least to one designed along more primitive lines.

A distinct change in style, marked by certain elements of exotic detailing, suggests that a rebuilding of the church was initiated about 1175. In the new scheme, the liturgical east end (Dore was actually aligned on a north-west to south-east axis) was planned along typical Bernardine lines. The aisleless rectangular presbytery — apparently prepared with a stone vault in mind — was to project from a fully stressed crossing. To the north and south, there were two rib-vaulted eastern chapels opening off both transepts. In each case, the inner chapel may well have been slightly deeper than its neighbour, creating a stepped or *en echelon* plan. Although unusual among the Cistercians, stepped transept plans are known to have existed at Fountains, Rievaulx, and Melrose.

The new programme of work at Dore began with the north transept. Here, for example, there was a solid wall between the two eastern chapels, a generally early Cistercian characteristic. But in this same part of the building, the prominent bay articulation and various traits within the sculptural detail herald the arrival of the new Gothic style, with France as the ultimate source of inspiration. This said, it is far from obvious what kind of French Gothic the Dore masons knew, and they

may well have learnt their craft at a number of intermediary English buildings, not least at several projects in the west country. Indeed, the local style became more prevalent as the work progressed to the crossing and on into the south transept. Taken as a whole, the southern arm reveals many differences from its northern counterpart. The high vault, for example, was supported externally by broad angle buttresses; two large lancets pierced the principal south elevation; and the eastern chapels were left to communicate through a large chamfered arch in the later Cistercian style.

By this stage of building, some headway had presumably been made with the laying out of the nave. At the very least, the eastern bay would have been required to support the crossing and its assumed modest tower. None the less, at ten bays in length, the complete nave was an extraordinarily ambitious undertaking, and it was to be more than half a century before the community was able to bring it to a successful conclusion. Designed with cylindrical piers, not unlike those at Buildwas, the elevation was of two storeys, with the clerestory windows having steeply raking sills rising from a stringcourse set immediately above the arcade. Almost certainly, the work was begun with the intention of vaulting both the central vessel and the aisles in stone.

Soon after the ambitious Adam I became abbot in about 1186, he embarked on grandiose remodelling of Dore's barely finished Bernardine presbytery. In effect, his scheme was an interpretation of the new east end at Byland. Even if smaller in scale, it must have stretched all the available resources of the house. The existing inner transept chapels were to be sacrificed in favour of rib-vaulted aisles flanking the now extended presbytery. These single-storey aisles were continued around the end of the eastern arm as an ambulatory, where the vault was carried on delicate bundled piers of four coursed and four detached

A vault boss from Dore Abbey carved with the head of a smiling man.

Blashill 1885
Blashill 1901–02
Fergusson 1984a, 94–100, 111
Hillaby 1988–90
Malone 1984
O'Callaghan 1995
Paul 1904
Paul 1927
RCHME 1931, 1–9
Shoesmith 1979–81
Shoesmith and Richardson 1997
Sledmere 1914
Williams 1976a, 1–57

shafts, with the latter set on the cardinal points. Screen walls ran from these piers to the east wall to create five chapels. The presbytery itself was of three bays, terminating just behind the high altar in a richly moulded arcade supported centrally on two bundled piers comprised of triple shaft groups. The large lancets in the clerestory were framed by both attached and *en délit* shafting, giving the upper storey a more delicate feel. On balance, it seems likely that the high vault was of timber, and the entire programme was probably nearing completion by about 1220 at the latest.

Meanwhile, Abbot Adam had also instigated at least some of the rebuilding on the cloister ranges. Very little now survives above ground, though the plan of a large north–south refectory has been recovered. The outstanding feature of the Dore claustral complex must have been its highly impressive polygonal chapter house, the details of which have recently been reconstructed on paper. Generally dated to about 1200, and comparable to a similar scheme at Margam, it seems likely that priority should be accorded to the Welsh house. The decoration at Dore was clearly of an advanced character, as was the general form of its vestibule and entrance arches. Around the cloister garth, the mid-thirteenth-century arcade was designed with arches of unusual cinquefoil design, the bays supported on clusters of three detached shafts.

The evidence of mounting debts suggests that by the 1250s the community was struggling to bring the construction programme to an end. In 1260 the bishop of Hereford was persuaded to offer an indulgence to all those who contributed to the works at the 'sumptuous church of Dore'. At the time, although the springers had probably been in place for some decades, the nave vault was perhaps one of the main elements still requiring attention. In this context, it might be noted that the glorious figurative bosses which survive from the high vault have been habitually dated to the early years of the fourteenth century. But if, as has recently been argued, they were carved rather earlier, it was perhaps a complete abbey church that was at last consecrated during the episcopate of Thomas Cantilupe (1275–82) of Hereford.

Following the dissolution, a sale of goods was held at Dore on 1 March 1537. The chief buyer was John Scudamore (d. 1571), a local gentleman and Crown servant. In addition to almost all the household items, for £2 Scudamore acquired the roof, the slate, and the timber of the refectory; an 'old house by the wayside next to the bridge'; and the organs from the monks' choir. With two other buyers, for a further £3 3s. 0d., he also shared the spoils of the 'old infirmary', together with all the glass and iron of the windows of the dormitory, the refectory and the chapter house. By 1545, Scudamore had acquired the site of the abbey with some of the surrounding property.

The nave, together with most of the cloister buildings, were probably allowed to fall into ruin, though the east end of the church was apparently retained to serve the parish. Almost a century after the dissolution, in 1632 John (d. 1671), the first Viscount Scudamore, began the restoration and refurnishing of the building. The arches into the nave and nave aisles were blocked up, new roofs and ceilings were erected, and a tower was built over the inner chapel of the south transept. A service of reconsecration took place in March 1634. The roofs and the bellframe in the tower were the work of John Abel (d. 1675), who presumably also fashioned the handsome if rather bulky screen which now dominates the entrance to the presbytery. By the end of the nineteenth century, the church was again in need of repair. Appeals were launched in 1898 and 1901, and the work of restoration was sympathetically carried out under the direction of Roland Paul in 1901–09.

DUNDRENNAN ABBEY

Both in its setting, and in the quality of its architecture, Dundrennan Abbey is one of Scotland's most beautiful ruins. It was founded in 1142, probably with Fergus, lord of Galloway, as its principal benefactor, though some accounts indicate that King David I was also involved. The first monks almost certainly came from Rievaulx, and at least two of Dundrennan's abbots, including the first, moved on to become head of the mother house. The architectural evidence indicates that the house was in a flourishing condition for at least the first hundred years of its existence, though by the end of the thirteenth century it was already suffering in the wars with England. As early as 1299 it was said the abbey had sustained losses amounting to £8,000, and by 1328 the monks were complaining that they had been deprived of estates in Ireland through the activities of King Edward III. By 1529 it was said that some of the buildings were threatening collapse, though it is unclear if the cause of this was enemy action or failure to carry out proper maintenance.

Soon after the Reformation the abbey's income was represented as a mere £500, the lowest of any of the Scottish Cistercian houses; but it is likely that this is inaccurate and does not represent the full income, and certainly the house was still supporting about twelve monks at that time. The abbey was ruled by commendators from at least 1523, and for thirty-six years after the Reformation that office was held by members of the Maxwell family, during which time, in 1568, the abbey was the place where Mary Queen of Scots (d. 1587) passed her last night on Scottish soil. In 1598 the commendatorship was granted to John Murray, and it was for Murray, who later became earl of Annandale (1624–40), that it was erected into a temporal lordship in 1606.

Antiquarian interest in the remains of Dundrennan emerged relatively early. In 1838 there were extensive excavations by Adam Maitland, the landowner. In the following year Maitland offered to waive his claims to ownership, and in 1840 the Lord Advocate ruled that the remains were Crown property, presumably under the terms of the Act of Annexation of 1587. Further excavations followed after the abbey had been taken into State care, together with a programme of consolidation of the remains which has greatly confused the evidence, and which makes understanding of a number of features hazardous. Since then there have been a number of rather more judiciously conducted campaigns of excavation, including the clearance of the chapter house in 1913. More recently, there were excavations at the south end of the east claustral range between 1991 and 1994.

The abbey church was set out as a variant on the common Cistercian plan, with a rectangular presbytery, transepts with three chapels on the east side of each, and an aisled nave of eight bays. Only Melrose and Newbattle in Scotland were planned on a more ambitious scale. The best remains are of the transepts. Bundled piers with twelve shafts (those on the cardinal axes being keeled), and with simple chalice capitals, carry richly moulded pointed arcades on the east sides of the transepts. Above this is a middle stage which, in the south transept, has two open pointed arches in each bay, while in the north transept there are four blind pointed arches in each bay. In both transepts the single clerestory window to each bay is round headed, which has led some writers to suggest that the clerestory survives from an earlier building campaign, though on balance this seems unlikely. The keeled bundle-shaft piers, chalice capitals and three-storey

1142–1560

The remains of the abbey, of which the transepts of the church and the entrance front of the chapter house are the most complete parts, are in the village of Dundrennan, on the A711, 12 miles (19km) from Dalbeattie. It is in the care of Historic Scotland and is open on a regular basis.

Dumfries and Galloway
Galloway

NX 747475

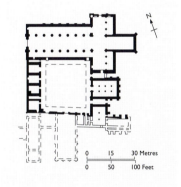

A thirteenth-century effigy of one of the abbots of Dundrennan. A dagger plunged into his heart suggests he may have been murdered.

The three-storey elevations in the transepts at Dundrennan suggest that the building was under construction around the third quarter of the twelfth century. The designer of the east end may have worked in the north of England, perhaps at Roche or Byland.

Christie 1914
Dalrymple 1899, 59–96
Fawcett 1994a, 45–47
Fergusson 1973
Gifford 1996, 285–90
Knowles and St Joseph 1952, 66–67
MacGibbon and Ross 1896–97, I, 388–98
RCAHMCS 1914, 217–28
Richardson 1994
Stringer 1980b

elevations suggest that the present building was under construction around the third quarter of the twelfth century and that the designer of its eastern parts came from northern England, from a house such as Roche or Byland. Unfortunately, there is too little remaining of the rest of the church to be certain about its architectural sources, though the pier and respond at the west end of the south nave arcade are related to the transept piers.

The chapter house, which was divided into twelve bays by two rows of three piers, each with eight filleted shafts, was evidently rebuilt around the middle of the thirteenth century. It projects well out beyond the east claustral range, and has an elegant face towards the cloister with two-light windows flanking a central doorway. The buildings on the southern side of the cloister have not been fully excavated, though it is clear that, in its final form, the refectory projected at ninety degrees to the cloister walk. Excavation in the 1990s has indicated that the east range did not extend beyond the outer line of the south range, and that the block which projected eastwards from the end of the east range was the latrine.

DUNKESWELL ABBEY

1201–1539

Dunkeswell Abbey is situated 2 miles (3.2km) from the village of Dunkeswell, and some 6 miles (9.7km) north of Honiton and the A30. Apart from fragments of the gatehouse and the west range, very little of the monastic buildings survive. Holy Trinity church was built over the nave in 1842. The site is accessible at all reasonable times.

Devon
Exeter

ST 143107

Dunkeswell Abbey was founded in 1201 by the Devon-born royal servant, William Brewer, who in a long and distinguished career had amassed lands in many parts of the country. William was already a notable monastic benefactor, but the endowments he granted to the colony of Forde monks which he settled at this remote spot on the edge of the Blackdown hills were especially lavish. In 1224, he renounced his worldly possessions and retired to Dunkeswell to take the habit. A year later, the archbishop of Canterbury and the bishop of Exeter were at the abbey, probably for a consecration ceremony. William died in 1226 and was buried before the high altar.

The lands which William Brewer and others granted to the community were chiefly located in east Devon, and included the manors of Dunkeswell, Broadhembury, and Wolford. Shortly before his death, William added the more distant manor of Lincombe, near Ilfracombe, to his earlier gifts. His son also gave the monks an important property at Buckland Brewer, located more than 35 miles (56km) away to the north-west. In a charter of 1290, the monks were granted permission to hold weekly markets and an annual fair at both Broadhembury and Buckland Brewer. By this time, Dunkeswell had come to possess a very substantial estate. At the time of the great survey of 1535, the abbey's total income was assessed at some £295. Four years later, in February 1539, the abbot and ten monks surrendered the house to the king's visitors.

Sheltered on all sides by hills, Dunkeswell is situated in the most typical of Cistercian locations. Its precinct boundary was determined to the east by the course of the Madford river, and to the north by a smaller tributary stream. To the west of the main monastic complex, in the valley of the tributary, there are well-defined earthworks of two substantial fishponds. A mill was probably located on the south side of the precinct.

Apart from a ruinous piece of the west range, together with a fragment of a later medieval gatehouse retaining some of its dressings, very little of the principal abbey buildings survives above ground. It seems, however, from limited excavations and clearance undertaken in 1841, that the church was about 185 feet (56.4m) long, and that the monastic buildings were set out around a cloister to the south. This work of investigation preceded the construction of Holy Trinity church in 1842. Partly built from medieval materials, Holy Trinity occupies much of the nave of the monastic church. Fragments of thirteenth-century tiles are set into the floor of the chancel.

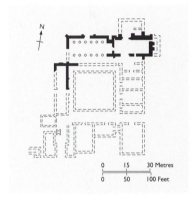

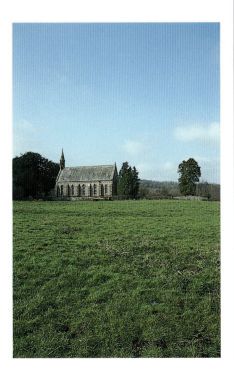

The parish church of the Holy Trinity was built over the site of the nave at Dunkeswell in 1842. The monastic buildings were arranged around a cloister to the south, the remains of which lie in the field at the foreground of this view (David Robinson).

Rowe 1878, 159–70
Sparks 1978

FLAXLEY ABBEY

1151–1536

Flaxley is situated in the Forest of Dean, about 2 miles (3.2km) off the A48, and 3 miles (4.8km) north-east of Cinderford. The remains of the abbey are incorporated within a country house, the form of which was largely determined in the seventeenth and later eighteenth centuries. The house is not open to the public, though the general layout of the site may be appreciated from St Mary's churchyard.

Gloucestershire
Worcester

SO 690154

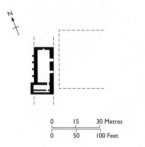

Somehow the site of Flaxley remains so very typically Cistercian. Approaching from the east, the pretty little valley in which it lies hidden away gradually becomes narrower. To the west, shelter is afforded by the wooded and steeply rising hills of the Forest of Dean. The monks who arrived here in 1151 had been sent out from Bordesley. Reputedly, the location was chosen very specifically by the founder, Earl Roger of Hereford (d. 1155), who intended that the abbey should mark the place where his father had been killed in a hunting accident.

In 1158, earlier grants to Flaxley were confirmed by King Henry II, who also gave the monks the right to take wood and other building materials from the forest. Surviving fragments of masonry, coupled with hints in documentary sources, suggest that the monastic church had been completed before the close of the twelfth century. Other building continued into the thirteenth century, with Henry III granting wood for the purpose. In 1230, for example, he gave two oaks for the 'roof of the aisle', and in 1232 there was an offer of ten more oaks for repairs to the church and to the abbot's houses. In the second half of the fourteenth century, payments made to the abbey by King Edward III may have been intended to meet building costs.

But Flaxley was never one of the wealthier Cistercian houses of Britain. In 1535 its income was assessed at £112, and a year later when the dissolution commissioners arrived they found a community of only seven monks. It seems the abbey itself was already in partial ruin, with the church damaged by fire. Indeed, the monks had gone as far as melting down the bells and selling the metal to finance repairs.

The small country house which takes the name Flaxley Abbey covers two sides of the claustral complex. In particular, to

The site of Flaxley, sometimes known as Dean Abbey, is occupied by a country house which incorporates parts of the former monastic buildings (David Robinson).

the west, five rib-vaulted bays of the late twelfth-century lay brothers' range are well preserved. The two barrel-vaulted chambers at the southern end presumably mark a latrine undercroft. In the later fourteenth century, the upper floor within this range was probably modified to provide comfortable accommodation for the abbot, with the principal space serving as his hall. To the south, a very fine room which retains its arch-braced timber roof was doubtless occupied as a solar, and may have been used on occasion for the accommodation of important guests.

On the northern side of the former cloister garth, part of the south wall of the nave was built into an early eighteenth-century orangery, as were the jambs of the processional doorway which led into the church from the east cloister alley. One of the more intriguing aspects of the Flaxley buildings, however, was discovered during landscaping work in 1788. A pencil sketch made at the time suggests that the eastern end of the chapter house may have terminated as an apse, its vault apparently supported on a single central column. A structure of this form would have been most unusual within a Cistercian context, and the possibility arises that the true plan of the Flaxley chapter house was in fact polygonal. If so, it joins the well-known examples at Dore and Margam in a distinct west country grouping.

Crawley-Boevey 1920
Crawley-Boevey 1921
Fergusson 1984a, 124–25
Middleton 1881–82
VCH Gloucester 1907, 93–96
Verey 1976, 185–87

FORDE ABBEY

1136–1539

Forde is situated about 3 miles (4.8km) south-east of Chard, close to the village of Thorncombe. The abbey church has entirely disappeared, but there are impressive remains of the monastic buildings, especially the early sixteenth-century abbot's accommodation. There was an extensive remodelling about 1649–59. Privately owned, Forde is accessible to the public at regular times through the summer months.

Dorset
Exeter

ST 359052

About 1133 Richard fitz Baldwin de Brionne (d. 1137), lord of Okehampton, decided to settle a colony of Cistercian monks at Brightley in central Devon. Sometime sheriff of the county, Richard was probably the richest landowner in the region; he was also a kinsman of the founder of Waverley, and it was to the Surrey house that he turned to provide the initial community. Although the preparations took three years, in 1136 twelve monks finally arrived with their abbot to occupy the chosen site. Alas, within a year of the settlement, the founder was dead. Thereafter it was probably difficulties with the scale of endowment, coupled with the harsh physical nature of the site, which in 1141 led the community to abandon Brightley altogether. In a later foundation narrative, it was romantically recorded that the sorry troop of monks, their possessions piled in a cart, were on their way back to Waverley when they were met near the south-eastern border of Devon by the founder's sister, Adelicia. She immediately offered them a substantial holding at Thorncombe, together with a house called Westford which would provide the necessary temporary accommodation. Permanent buildings were begun near a crossing of the river Axe, giving rise to the name Forde. Like her brother, Adelicia failed to see the foundation flourish, for she died in 1142. This time, however, the community was to survive, with the early endowments rapidly expanded by other benefactors.

Within decades, Forde established itself as the most devout religious house in the south-west. Indeed, the third abbot, Baldwin (1168–81), was to become bishop of Worcester, and from there in 1184 he was translated to the see of Canterbury. The fifth abbot, John of Forde (1191–1220), was a significant theologian and writer, his teachings steeped in the tradition of St Bernard himself. Under these two gifted men, daughter colonies were sent out to Bindon in 1171–72, and to Dunkeswell in 1201. Meanwhile the process of estate

Abbot Thomas Chard provided himself with palatial lodgings at Forde shortly before the dissolution. These survive in the later house.

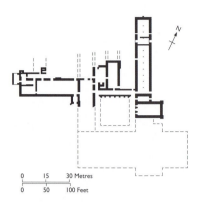

Following the dissolution, in the mid-seventeenth century the late twelfth-century chapter house at Forde was converted for use as a chapel (David Robinson).

Brakspear 1913
Clapham and Duffy 1950
Fergusson 1984a, 125
Knowles and St Joseph 1952, 144–45
RCHME 1952, 240–46
Rowe 1878, 171–92
Sherwin 1927

building had continued. Several granges had been established in the immediate Thorncombe area, and other lands were scattered further afield, in several parts of Dorset, in south and west Somerset, and as far away as the north Devon coast. By the 1530s, the abbey's property was yielding an assessed annual income of some £374.

Doubtless the first stone church and the monastic buildings at Forde were begun at the time of Abbot Robert de Penynton (1137–68), though very little survives. The church — which has entirely disappeared and has never been excavated — was situated on the higher ground to the south, with the claustral ranges set out to the north. The most prominent early survival is the fine two-bay, rib-vaulted chapter house. The ribs spring from angle shafts at the corners, and from grouped shafts recessed into the centre of the lateral walls, a feature also seen at neighbouring Bindon. The east, or dormitory range was probably completed around 1200, or soon afterwards, and extends almost 170 feet (52m) northwards from the chapter house. The almost perfectly surviving ground floor, which may have served as the monks' day room, comprises twelve rib-vaulted bays with a parlour at the southern end. The vault is carried centrally on a row of plain octagonal piers. Evidence for the original windows survives, with an impressive row of thirteen lancets still to be seen in the west face of the dormitory on the first floor. Adjacent to this range, on the north side of the cloister, the surviving fragments of the monks' refectory and the kitchen are probably of similar date.

On 19 December 1239, the abbey church was dedicated by Bishop William Briwere of Exeter (1224–44), who provided lights for the 'new' building. Such a date is too late to reflect the completion of the earliest stone church, and it is more likely to represent an eastwards extension to the initial presbytery. A century later, in the time of Abbot John Chidley (1330–54), the monastic buildings were said to be dilapidated, and the church almost in ruins. His successor, Abbot Adam (1354–73), also reported that the church needed rebuilding. In the fifteenth century, the monks' refectory — set on a north–south axis — was shortened and divided into two storeys. It is suggested that the ground floor (the servants' hall in the later house) continued to serve as a refectory. The upper floor could have been the misericord, that distinct monastic chamber where — following a papal edict of 1335 — the Cistercians were allowed to eat meat.

Under Abbot Thomas Chard (1521–39), a feverish phase of building activity was carried out on the very eve of the dissolution. The antiquary, John Leland (d. 1552), who observed the work in progress, noted that the 'abbot at incredible expense is now restoring the monastery most gloriously'. Of breathtaking richness, Chard's scheme included a palatial private lodging, joined to the north-west angle of the cloister with a hugely impressive great hall. The hall itself was entered through a three-storey towered porch, of rich Ham stone. At this same time, work began on rebuilding the cloister alleys. It is the north alley, with its four-light transomed windows which survives. A decorative frieze bears the arms and initials of Abbot Chard.

Forde was surrendered by Chard and his community of twelve monks in March 1539. The site was first leased and then sold to Richard Pollard, passing successively to Sir Amyas Paulet and William Rosewall, with the buildings at some point being converted for domestic use. Forde was eventually bought in 1649 by Sir Edmund Prideaux (d. 1659), a wealthy lawyer and parliamentarian who became Oliver Cromwell's solicitor-general. It was Prideaux who began the development and refitting of Chard's lodgings and great hall as the basis for a grand seventeenth-century mansion. Handsome plaster ceilings were introduced, the misericord became a library, and the chapter house was converted for use as a chapel. Further repairs and alterations were made in the eighteenth century.

FOUNTAINS ABBEY

There are few British monasteries more famous than the house founded in the narrow valley of the river Skell on 27 December 1132, and known from its earliest days as Fountains. It was settled by a group of dissident Benedictine monks who had failed in their attempt to reform the abbey of St Mary at York. Their frustrations had probably been brought to a head a few months earlier by the arrival in the city of a colony of Clairvaux monks on its way to occupy Rievaulx. In the event, the dissenting band found a patron and protector in Archbishop Thurstan of York (1114–40), and it was he who eventually led them to Skelldale.

With winter over, in 1133 Abbot Richard wrote on behalf of his fledgling community to Bernard of Clairvaux, seeking admission to the Cistercian order, and asking to join the family of Clairvaux. Bernard welcomed the news, and later in 1133 he sent Geoffrey d'Ainai (d. 1140) to Fountains to supervise the construction of temporary buildings and to train the monks in the Cistercian way of life. In fact, some two years earlier, Geoffrey set out the site of Rievaulx Abbey. In spite of very

1132–1539

Fountains Abbey is located at Swanley, 4 miles (6.4km) south-west of Ripon, on the south side of the B6265. The extensive and very well preserved remains are in the hands of the National Trust; they are maintained by English Heritage. There is a large visitor centre at the entrance to the site.

North Yorkshire
York

SE 274683

The west range at Fountains represents the largest and best preserved twelfth-century lay brothers' quarters in Europe (National Trust Photographic Library/Matthew Antrobus).

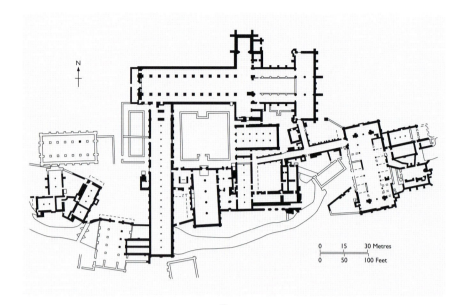

The eleven-bay nave at Fountains was built in the 1160s and survives to full height. The aisles were originally vaulted with transverse barrels, typical of the Burgundian Romanesque style.

little other early support or patronage, Fountains survived to become the richest Cistercian house in Britain with an assessed income of £1,115 in 1535. It was suppressed four years later. In 1768 the whole of the abbey site was incorporated into the parkland of Studley Royal, which ensured the survival of its buildings as a landscape feature. In State care since 1966, and owned by the National Trust since 1982, the ruins have been open to the public since the 1850s. Today, Fountains stands as one of the best-preserved White Monk abbeys in Europe.

Archaeological excavations began in the 1780s when John Martin explored the chapter house to identify the graves of abbots known to be buried there. But the buildings were only substantially cleared of fallen debris by J. R. Walbran between 1840 and 1854. William St John Hope was digging at Fountains in 1887–88, and 1904, and J. Arthur Reeve made a stone by stone record of the ruins between 1873 and 1876. Following the publication of all this research, it was believed that there was little more to be learned from the site. However, conservation of the ruins since 1966, by the Department of the Environment and later by English Heritage, required further excavation and survey,

the most significant of which took place between 1977 and 1987. This new work has substantially altered the interpretation of the site.

Excavation below the south transept of the standing church in 1980 revealed not only an earlier and unsuspected edifice, but also the temporary timber buildings built in the late summer of 1133 by Geoffrey d'Ainai. Later study of the surviving cloister ranges identified the substantial remains of an earlier cloister layout, showing that the surviving buildings are largely the remains of the third Cistercian monastery to be built on the site.

Geoffrey d'Ainai's timber buildings comprised a church aligned east to west and a two-storey domestic building aligned north to south, apparently the refectory on the ground floor with a dormitory above. Neither building was complete, and the east and west walls of the church were cut away by the foundations of later buildings. Only their postholes survived, and they themselves were partly cut away by the foundations of the south transept of a small stone church, of earlier date than that which still survives. This early church had two eastern chapels in each transept, of which the inner ones were deeper than the outer ones, a detail which was to be repeated in its successor, and one which also featured at Rievaulx and at Melrose. The earliest date for the building of this church was 1136, after a building fund was first established the year before. Completed fairly rapidly, it had painted decoration on some of its architectural detail and coloured glass in its windows, both unusual features in an early Cistercian context but typical of the initial community's Benedictine origins. The south transept of this church had been damaged by fire, and was repaired before it was finally demolished, and it is known that Fountains was partially burned in a serious fire in 1146. Cloister ranges 27 feet (8.2m) wide had been built before the fire, and the east wall of an east range was observed butted up against the south wall of the early transept.

The context for the building of permanent cloister ranges was the abbacy of Henry Murdac (1144–47), who was elected at the insistence of St Bernard, and whose role was to ensure Cistercian orthodoxy on a convent which had previously only had abbots trained in Benedictine ways. On his arrival, the only permanent building was a small church, already inadequate for a growing community. Abbot Henry's buildings, raised in less than three years, can be identified by their almost total lack of any architectural detailing, and provide the earliest surviving cloister plan of any Cistercian monastery. Substantial parts of these structures survive, particularly in the east and west cloister ranges, where they stand, in part, to roof height, incorporated in later buildings. Where excavated, the evidence is that they were plastered externally as well as inside, and were painted white. The east range, which comprised the monks' dormitory at first floor, had a chapter house contained within the range, a parlour, a day stair, and the day room on the ground floor; the south range included, from east to west, a passage through the range with a room for the abbot above, an east–west refectory, and a kitchen; and the west range housed the outer parlour, cellarage, and the lay brothers' refectory situated below their dormitory. Excavations have shown that these cloister buildings were complete before they were damaged by fire in 1146, and repaired and slightly extended after the fire. Murdac was also responsible for adding an aisled nave of nine bays to the first stone church, thereby providing a church for the lay brothers, an almost exact copy of the nave he had built at Vauclair in Picardy before he came to Fountains.

Fountains established its final daughter house in 1150, and from this date the community began to increase in size. As a result, Murdac's buildings soon proved inadequate. By this date, a new and larger church was planned, with a short square presbytery, transepts with three eastern chapels of which the inner ones were longer than the others, an unstressed crossing, and an aisleless nave. Begun by Abbot Richard (1150–70) of Clairvaux, it was certainly under construction in 1154, being built around its predecessor, and the eastern parts were completed by about 1160. At this point, the decision was taken to build an aisled nave of eleven bays and to provide a lantern tower over the crossing, an undertaking which was not completed until 1170, and which required a modification of the crossing itself. The nave and transepts of this church still survive to full height though the crossing tower has fallen.

Reconstruction of the cloister ranges began in the later 1150s and was to continue for some thirty years. Its progress can be read in the surviving ruins. First to be rebuilt was the northern half of the west range, with a cloister for the lay brothers to the west of it, and a latrine situated above the flow of the river Skell well to the south. The completion of the southern half of the west range was delayed by work elsewhere. This delay was probably the result of a more pressing need to reconstruct the east cloister range in the 1160s. Here, a large chapter house projecting four bays beyond the width of the range was finished before 1170. Because of the need to build as quickly as possible, elements of the pre-fire monastery were reused as far as possible, particularly in the east range, the blocked windows and doors being hidden by plaster. Meanwhile, guest houses were under construction in the inner court, and other programmes included a new latrine for the monks at the south end of their dormitory, an abbot's house at the east end of the latrine block, and an infirmary to the east of the chapter house. The southern half of the west range was then completed in the 1170s and the whole building vaulted. The lay brothers' infirmary and a large aisled guest hall of seven bays were also built as part of this operation. Also dating to the building

The west front at Fountains was modified with the insertion of a great traceried window by Abbot John Darnton (1479–95) in 1494. The tower was added by Abbot Marmaduke Huby (1495–1526) in the early sixteenth century.

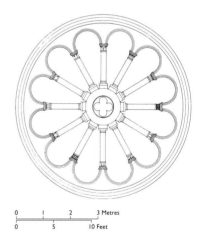

The twelfth-century west front of the abbey church at Fountains featured this simple, but rather elegant rose window of the 1160s (Stuart Harrison).

campaigns of Abbot Robert of Pipewell (1170–80) was a new cloister arcade, many fragments of which have been recovered from the site. The south range of the cloister was not reconstructed until the 1180s, when a new north–south refectory was built, with a warming house to the east and kitchen to the west, all raised in the time of Abbot William of Newminster (1180–90). As completed, the church and cloister area now stood on a scale approximately twice that of Murdac's buildings.

Fountains had become a substantial abbey with buildings of a scale that fitted its status. In the first decade of the thirteenth century, however, the community found the presbytery of the second stone church to be too dark and cramped. Thus, abbots John of York (1203–11) and John of Hessle (1211–20) were responsible for a new and spacious aisled presbytery of five bays constructed in the early Gothic style. In the 1220s, this was further extended by Abbot John of Kent (1220–47) with the construction of an eastern transept, the so-called Chapel of the Nine Altars. The whole of this new arm was covered by high rib vaults. In the meantime, the extension of the church had required the demolition of the late twelfth-century infirmary. The proximity of the Skell and the steep southern side of the valley meant that there was nowhere convenient to build a replacement infirmary, and Abbot John of Kent was obliged to raise his new building on four great tunnels which in turn carried it over the river. Though badly ruined, the infirmary hall he built, aisled on four sides, was one of the greatest aisled buildings raised in the thirteenth century in Britain. By the time of his death, John of Kent had completed the extension of his monastery.

Thereafter, the central buildings at Fountains saw little further construction work until the late fifteenth century when Abbot John Darnton (1479–95) began the repair of the abbey church which was showing serious signs of instability. He took down the high vaults of the presbytery and Chapel of the Nine Altars,

provided new east and west windows for the church, reroofed the whole structure, and replaced many of the Romanesque aisle windows with traceried lights. He also modernized the infirmary buildings and began the rebuilding of the abbot's house before his death in 1495. It was his successor, Marmaduke Huby (1495–1526), who was responsible for the final flowering of the abbey. An unstable crossing prevented Huby from raising a great tower above his church, and instead he built the massive tower of four stages, 160 feet (48.8m) tall, to the north of the north transept which still bears his name. He also completed the abbot's house, and 'left his mark on almost every part of the abbey'.

The ruins of the church and cloister buildings stand at the centre of a walled precinct of 73 acres (29.5ha), surrounded to the north, west, and south by the home granges of Swanley, Fountains Park, Haddockstanes, and Morcar. The precinct wall was built in the first quarter of the thirteenth century and remains substantially intact on the west and south sides. The late twelfth-century great or inner gatehouse, which controlled access to both the inner and outer courts, survives to the west of the church. Further west are the fragmentary remains of the gate chapel of the 1160s. The principal surviving building within the precinct is a massive watermill in the outer court. First built in the 1140s, rebuilt in the 1160s, and again in the 1220s, it is the oldest Cistercian mill to survive. Modified in the late seventeenth and mid-nineteenth centuries, it remained in use up to 1937. A second building in the outer court, now badly ruined, was the abbey's woolhouse at its north end and bakehouse at its south end, initially built in the 1160s but modified throughout the life of the monastery. A further twenty-one buried buildings are evidenced by earthworks in the outer court, as well as stock enclosures, orchards, and water collection tanks.

A detail of the trefoil-headed arcading which adorned the lower parts of the walls in the Chapel of the Nine Altars at Fountains.

Left: *Few British monasteries are more famous than the house founded in the narrow valley of the Skell in the last days of December 1132. 'Oh what a beauty and perfection of ruin', wrote the Honourable John Byng on visiting Fountains in the later eighteenth century.*

Baker 1969
Bethell 1966
Coppack 1986a
Coppack 1993
Coppack and Gilyard-Beer 1993
Fergusson 1984a, 38–48, 126
Gilyard-Beer and Coppack 1986
Hope 1900a
Knowles and St Joseph 1952, 93–97
Pevsner and Radcliffe 1967, 203–13
Reeve 1892
Walbran and Fowler 1863–1918
Wardrop 1987

FURNESS ABBEY

1124/27–1537

The site of Furness Abbey is about 2 miles (3.2km) to the north of Barrow in Furness, on the east side of the A590. The site is managed by English Heritage and is open at all reasonable times.

Cumbria

York

SD 218717

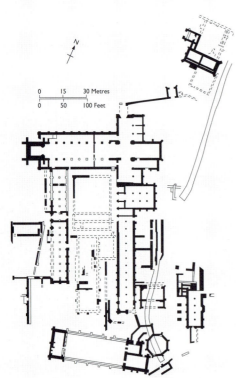

Furness Abbey was founded in 1124 by Stephen, then count of Boulogne and Mortain and later king of England (1135–54), at Tulketh near Preston in Lancashire. Three years later, Stephen moved the Savigniac brethren to a more suitable site on the Furness peninsula. After a vigorous struggle, the community was forcibly converted to the Cistercian order in 1147–48. Once converted, however, the house tried to claim primacy over Waverley, seeking to establish itself as the first Cistercian foundation in Britain. In due course, Furness grew to be one of the greatest White Monk monasteries in the north of England. In scale it challenged Fountains, and throughout the later Middle Ages the two houses were frequently to dispute landholdings in Cumbria. With an assessed income of £805 in 1535, Furness was finally suppressed in 1537. Demolition began almost immediately, though the abbot's house was reserved for a tenant. By the 1730s, when the ruins were recorded by the Buck brothers, the site looked very much as it does today. Clearance of the ruins was begun by T. J. Beck in 1840, with further work done in the early 1880s. William St John Hope was working at Furness between 1896 and 1898, and identified elements of the Savigniac church. In 1923 Lord Richard Cavendish gave the site to the Office of Works, and the ruins were conserved for public display. Today, the site is managed by English Heritage. A detailed analytical survey of the ruins was carried out in the 1980s.

Parts of the church, particularly the crossing, the south nave aisle, and the west wall of the south transept, predate the conversion of the house to the Cistercian order, and Hope identified the form of the early south transept and presbytery. The Savigniac church, which appears to have been largely completed before 1148, had a short apsidal presbytery, shallow transepts with two apsidal chapels arranged *en echelon*, and an aisled nave of ten bays. Recent examination shows that the crossing piers survive to a considerable height, and that they were raised when the church was remodelled. The Cistercian rebuilding concentrated on the transepts and presbytery which were torn down and rebuilt in the 1150s to the standard Cistercian plan. The new transepts were deeper and had three eastern chapels, and the aisleless presbytery was rebuilt with a square east end. Remodelling in the nave included the adding of responds against the aisle walls to support a ribbed vault. The rebuilding was probably completed by 1180.

Although the church remained in its essential Bernardine form throughout its life, the presbytery and transept chapels were taken down and rebuilt in the late fifteenth century, probably because the twelfth-century church had suffered from subsidence, a problem which continues to beset the ruins. It was at this time, too, that new windows were generally installed in the church. The monks' choir occupied the two eastern bays of the nave and the retrochoir the third bay. At this point, the base of a thirteenth-century rood screen divided the monks' church from that of the lay brothers. In about 1500, the west bay of the nave was taken down to make space for a new axial tower, the lowest stage of which survives.

The cloister lay to the south of the church and was originally 105 feet (32m) square. Although the buildings on its south side have been demolished to floor level or below, it is still possible to work out how they were developed from the evidence of excavation. The northern half of the west range is probably a Savigniac building, and the first refectory, which was arranged east–west, and the kitchen to its west, probably also date from before the conversion of the house. In the late 1150s, the west range was lengthened substantially to provide a refectory of nine bays for the lay brothers at ground-floor level, with a substantial dormitory above. An outer parlour was created at the north end, and an entry to the cloister provided at its centre. The south range was demolished and the cloister extended to the south, and a new kitchen and east–west refectory built for the monks. Rebuilding of their east range did not begin until the early years of the thirteenth century. The apsidal

Savigniac chapter house was replaced by a square-ended room of four bays, vaulted throughout, and entered from the cloister through a narrow vestibule between two book cupboards. Its detailing shows that it was not built before the 1220s, the last part of the range to be completed. Exceptionally, the chapter house was built against the south transept and the intervening book cupboard and sacristy were omitted. The dormitory on the first floor was a massive building, carried over the chapter house and on a vaulted undercroft of thirteen bays. At the same time, the south range was rebuilt with a large north–south refectory, and a warming house to the east. The construction of an infirmary, well to the east of the east range, completed the development of permanent Cistercian buildings. However, in the early fourteenth century, a remarkable new infirmary was raised to the south of the

Originally founded as a Savigniac monastery in 1124, Furness grew to become one of the richest Cistercian abbeys in the north of England. This view from the south-east shows the impressive scale of the surviving ruins.

cloister ranges, and the earlier infirmary was converted to a substantial abbot's house.

The whole of the precinct at Furness survives, covering some 73 acres (30 ha). It is enclosed by a wall which may be traced over most of its length. The inner court lay to the north of the church, and was entered through an outer gate and an inner gate, both of which can still be traced. On the east side of the outer gate, through which the site is still entered, is the late thirteenth-century *capella ante portas*. The north wall of this building is the early thirteenth-century precinct wall. To the south of this, at the end of a walled lane, is the great or inner gate, now reduced to its plinths but clearly a late twelfth-century building showing a typical double inner gate hall that led south to the outer court and east to the inner court. The eastern portal was later blocked.

The inner court is now largely devoid of medieval buildings, their stone being reused for a post-medieval house, and later for the Furness Abbey Hotel, parts of which survive. At its south end, however, are the substantial remains of the early fourteenth-century guest hall which has a porch against its west wall and the remains of a two-storey chamber block at its south end. Below it are traces of its late twelfth-century predecessor. Beyond the guest hall is the wall that enclosed the monks' cemetery, with a fine fourteenth-century gate. A second gatehouse, with a single gate hall, was provided in the precinct wall to the west of the cloister buildings.

The remainder of the precinct is known only from earthworks, which include a complex series of watercourses that ran down the east side of the valley and which are partly confused by the railway line that now bisects the area. A single medieval building, of unknown use, survives in the outer court, and other buildings can be traced as earthworks. At least one mill is recorded, its dam being destroyed when the railway was built. There is considerable evidence of quarrying on the west side of the precinct, and the lower ground in the valley bottom was at least partially used as water meadows.

The visitor centre at Furness contains a number of grave slabs and effigies removed from the site in the nineteenth-century clearance.

One of the corbels which supported the vault ribs in the ground floor of the east range at Furness.

Left: The chapter house at Furness was rebuilt from the 1220s, its proportions and detailing befitting the importance of this room in monastic life.

Beck 1844
Brakspear 1901a
Dickinson 1967
Dickinson 1989
Fergusson 1984a, 54–61, 126–27
Hope 1900b
Knowles and St Joseph 1952, 78–81
Pevsner 1969, 123–27

GARENDON ABBEY

Founded in 1133 by Robert 'le Bossu', earl of Leicester (1118–68), Garendon was the first of five daughter houses to be colonized by Waverley. Earl Robert's initial grants were centred around the comparatively wild landscape of Charnwood Forest, though the Garendon monks were soon to attract gifts from further afield. Eventually, they controlled an enviable group of estates, not just in Leicestershire, but also in the neighbouring counties of Derbyshire and Nottinghamshire. With the community itself expanding, five years after the foundation Garendon was in a position to dispatch a colony to settle at Bordesley in Worcestershire. In 1147, another colony was sent to Biddlesden in Buckinghamshire. At the end of the thirteenth century, even if not all was well with the abbey's economy, its annual income was assessed at a little over £168.

Following the demolition of the post-dissolution house in 1964, excavation has recovered various details of the east claustral range, including the entire plan of the

1133–1536

Garendon is located 2 miles (3.2km) west of Loughborough, and about a mile (1.6km) north of the A512. Some of the monastic buildings were incorporated within a late seventeenth-century country house known as Garendon Hall. This was demolished in 1964, leaving no significant remains of the abbey above ground.

Leicestershire
Lincoln

SK 502199

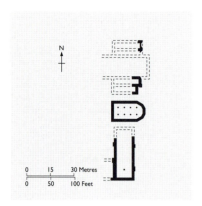

Fergusson 1984a, 127
Liddle and O'Brien 1995
VCH Leicestershire 1954, 5–7
Williams 1965
Williams 1969

chapter house, together with some traces of the east end of the abbey church. The overall layout seems comparatively small for such an important early foundation. The chapter house, none the less, was apparently rebuilt about 1360 with a polygonal east end, and with the vault supported on eight piers. Those sections of the church investigated have been interpreted as parts of the transepts, themselves situated to either side of a somewhat narrow presbytery. If this is correct, the arrangements seen in the south transept are of particular interest. The chapels may have been set out in a stepped, or so-called *en echelon* pattern, similar to that known from twelfth-century Fountains, and also at Rievaulx and Melrose. Without further investigation, however, the evidence must be treated cautiously. It is known, for example, that in 1219 the bishop of St Asaph dedicated a church at Garendon. This is too late to mark the occupation of the first stone church, and the dedication is more likely to represent the completion of a new eastern extension.

In 1535, Garendon's annual income was assessed at a little over £159. A year later, when it was dissolved, there were fourteen monks in the community and 'the large old monastery' was said to be partly ruinous. Garendon Hall, which was built over the site in 1682–83, was demolished in the1960s.

GLENLUCE ABBEY

1191/92–1560

The remains of the abbey are about one and a half miles (2.5km) north-west of the village of Glenluce, which is itself about 10 miles (16km) west-south-west of Stranraer on the A75. The site is in the care of Historic Scotland, and is open to the public.

Dumfries and Galloway
Galloway

NX 185586

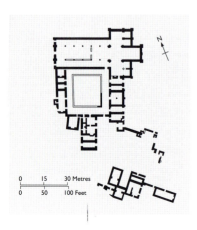

Like Dundrennan and Sweetheart, the two other Cistercian houses in the south-west corner of Scotland, Glenluce was a foundation of the family of the lords of Galloway; in this case the founder was Roland, who was grandson of the patron of Dundrennan. The date of the foundation was probably 1191 or 1192, and the first monks were brought from Dundrennan. Relatively little is known of the history of the house, though it was apparently damaged in the course of a rebellion which took place in Galloway in 1235. In the later Middle Ages there was a series of debilitating disputes over the commendatorship starting in the 1540s, which led to the abbot being expelled by the earl of Cassillis at one stage, and the invasion of the precinct by rival families soon afterwards. Nevertheless, in 1560, the year of the Reformation, there were still twelve monks when Thomas Hay was instituted as abbot, though that institution had to be carried out in the parish church since the abbey itself was still being occupied by

The chapter house at Glenluce was remodelled around the early sixteenth century.

Gordon of Lochinvar. Even as late as 1572, five monks were still living within the precinct. Eventually, in 1619, after being held by a series of commendators, the abbey was granted to the bishop of Galloway.

By the time of Grose's view of 1791, the only visible remains of the abbey were the gable of the south transept, the south wall of the presbytery, and parts of the east claustral range, which were evidently being put to agricultural use. The first recorded excavations within the precinct took place in 1898, and these were mainly within parts of the church and the chapter house. In 1933 the abbey was placed in State care, and there were clearance excavations between 1933 and 1939.

The abbey church had a short rectangular presbytery flanked by transepts with two eastern chapels, and the aisled nave was six bays long. The most telling architectural details are in the south transept, where the pier between the chapels was of octofoil form, rising from a water-holding base.

The buildings around the cloister show evidence of having been rebuilt or remodelled on a number of occasions. The refectory, which projects at right angles from the cloister, has a variety of late subdivisions at its surviving lower level; these may have been part of domestic adaptations for a post-Reformation commendator, but could equally represent changes for the monks at a time when conventual life was changing in character. The finest of the claustral buildings is the chapter house, which was remodelled around the early sixteenth century as a square chamber within the body of the east range, with four bays of vaulting carried on a central pier and two three-light windows in its outer wall. The quality of this building shows clearly that, before the peace of the abbey was disturbed by the quarrels over the commendatorship, it was still capable of high-quality building. At the south-east corner of the cloister is a reconstructed section of arcading, with a tight sequence of pointed-arched openings, which may be part of the same campaign of rebuilding as the chapter house. East and south-east of the main claustral complex are the fragmentary remains of two groups of buildings which are assumed to have served as the abbot's house and the infirmary. A particularly noteworthy feature of Glenluce is the network of interlocking clay pipes, with inspection chambers at the junctions, which carried a fresh water supply around the buildings.

A section of arcading has been reconstructed around the south-east corner of the cloister at Glenluce. The gable of the south transept appears to the rear of this view.

Cruden 1952–53
Dalrymple 1899, 197–232
Gifford 1996, 324–37
Grove 1996
Henry 1885
MacGibbon and Ross 1896–97, **3**, 132–39
RCAHMCS 1912, 102–08
Rusk 1930

GRACE DIEU ABBEY

In 1217, the General Chapter instructed the great French abbey of Morimond to send 'discreet men [to Wales] to diligently enquire' as to the provision which might be offered for the foundation of a new community by John, lord of Monmouth (d. 1248). In the event, it was not until April 1226 that a colony of monks from Dore settled at Grace Dieu, a delay probably due as much to local unrest as to the size of the benefactor's purse. In 1233, the Welsh completely burnt the newly founded abbey, and a year later they stripped the corn from its estates. It was not an auspicious start for the last of the thirteen White Monk foundations in Wales.

The initial site of the abbey may have been located on the west bank of the Trothy, on land which the Welsh claimed had been 'wrested from them' by the founder. By 1236, however, John had managed to secure the monks a new location, with King Henry III granting timber from the Forest of Dean to help in the

1226–1536

Grace Dieu lies about 4 miles (6.4km) west of Monmouth, 1 mile (1.6km) south of the B4233. The site of the permanent foundation is probably at Abbey Meadow, situated on the east bank of the river Trothy. Nothing survives above ground, and there are few indications of earthworks.

Monmouthshire
Llandaff

SO 451132 (approximately)

rebuilding process. Forty years later, Grace Dieu was in further difficulty, and Edmund of Lancaster (d. 1296), as lord of Monmouth, proposed transferring the monks yet again.

Even with some eight granges held on both sides of the Wye, Grace Dieu was from first to last crippled by financial difficulties and remained one of the poorest houses of the order in Britain. One of its most important properties lay at Stowe in the Forest of Dean, a grant from Henry III. In 1535, the net annual income of the house was given as just £19.

A small archaeological excavation in 1970–71 seems to have confirmed that the final site of the abbey lay on the east bank of the Trothy, though no convincing trace of the principal monastic buildings was recovered. Documentary sources reveal that by the later Middle Ages there was a gatehouse somewhere within the precinct complex, and the three bells recorded at the time of the suppression presumably hung in the tower of the church. When dissolved, in September 1536, there were only two monks remaining at Grace Dieu.

Williams 1970–78
Williams 1976a, 59–75

Hailes Abbey

1246–1539

Hailes Abbey is situated 2 miles (3.2km) north-east of Winchcombe, off the B4632. Low foundations mark the position of the church, and there are fragments of the cloister and the three principal ranges of monastic buildings. The site, which includes a small museum, is in the care of English Heritage and is open at all reasonable times.

Gloucestershire
Worcester

SP 050300

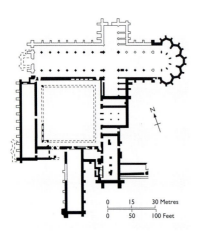

In October 1242, Earl Richard of Cornwall (d. 1272), the second son of King John and brother of King Henry III, was in danger of losing his life during a storm at sea. On his deliverance, Richard vowed that he would found a monastery by way of thanksgiving. Three years later, his brother granted him the manor of Hailes in Gloucestershire expressly to provide land for the fulfilment of this vow, and in June 1246 twenty monks and ten lay brothers arrived from Beaulieu to colonize the site. They 'set up their tents at Hailes mill', runs the picturesque narrative of the abbey's chronicler, but 'seeing the roughness of the terrain [they wondered] how from such unpromising beginnings might grow a noble monastery'.

In fact, with Earl Richard's support, the construction of the abbey church and monastic buildings was to proceed at close to breakneck speed, and by November 1251 enough progress had been made to justify a vast ceremony of dedication and celebration. The Hailes chronicler records that, 'a fine church, adequate dormitory, dignified refectory and a large spacious cloister walk with adjoining buildings'

stood complete. No fewer than thirteen bishops were involved in the solemnities, each one dedicating an altar. Mass was said at the high altar by the great Robert Grosseteste, bishop of Lincoln (1235–53), in the presence of Earl Richard and his second wife, Sanchia of Provence, together with King Henry and Queen Eleanor, most of the major barons of the realm, and over 300 knights. In all, according to the writer Matthew Paris (d. 1259), the earl had already contributed in excess of £6,600 to the total building costs.

Earl Richard intended that Hailes would serve as a mausoleum for his cadet branch of the royal family, a pattern reflecting the burial of lesser members of the French royal family at Louis IX's foundation of Royaumont (Île de France). Over the years, Richard's wife Sanchia was buried in the church in 1261; his son, Henry, was laid to rest there in 1271; and in the following year Richard himself was interred at Hailes below 'a noble pyramis' — doubtless a grand tomb. Almost three decades later his heir, Edmund of Cornwall (d. 1300), was buried at Hailes in the presence of King Edward I.

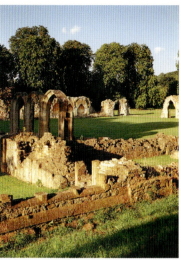

A view looking north-east over the remains of the cloister buildings at Hailes.

Left: *One of the vault bosses found at Hailes in 1899 features an exquisite depiction of Christ as a spiritual Samson rending the lion's jaw.*

From the evidence of the upstanding remains, together with the results of both Victorian and modern programmes of excavation, it appears that the initial design of the abbey church was not unduly influenced by the work at the mother house. In particular, in contrast to the apsidal arrangement seen at Beaulieu, the four-bay presbytery at Hailes terminated with a flat east end. Here, the piers consisted of bundles of four large and four smaller shafts, all with a distinctive wide fillet running down the centre. Each transept had three eastern chapels, and there was probably a low tower over the crossing. One marked similarity with Beaulieu, however, was the way in which the night stair from the monks' dormitory was accommodated within the thickness of the cloister-side wall in the south transept. To the west, the nave was eight bays in length, and — as in the presbytery — it is suggested that the principal elevations comprised three storeys, namely arcade, triforium, and clerestory.

The cloister and the monastic buildings were arranged to the south of the church in the usual manner. Today, substantial foot-

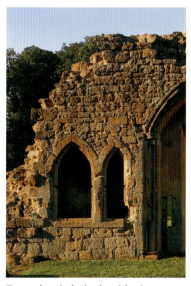

Two cupboards, both rebated for doors, can be seen to the west of the doorway in the monks' refectory at Hailes.

In the Middle Ages, the parish church at Hailes probably served as the abbey's gatehouse chapel. Inside, it houses a superb display of decorative painting dating from about 1320–30. This detail depicts St Catherine of Alexandria, with a Cistercian monk kneeling to the left of her feet.

ings of the chapter house, the dormitory undercroft, warming house, refectory, and the west range survive. The triple-arched chapter house façade is one of the most notable features. Beyond this, the moulded bases of the four central piers which supported the internal stone vault can still be seen. During the excavations of 1899, six beautifully carved vault bosses were found amongst the destruction debris covering the floor of the chapter house. Five of these carry foliate patterns, and one is an exquisite depiction of Christ as a spiritual Samson rending the lion's jaw. Across in the south range, the jambs of the entrance to the monks' refectory were richly moulded, having two detached shafts of blue lias set between three engaged shafts in contrasting cream oolite. The capitals were also of blue lias and were carved with stiff-leaf foliage. Measuring some 116 feet (35.4m) long and 30 feet (9.1m) wide, the refectory must have been an especially handsome chamber. Another notable survival at Hailes is the drain which runs through the monks' latrine block, and then under part of the south range, the cloister, and the west range. Water still flows through its stone-lined channel.

In spite of its auspicious beginnings, Hailes was soon experiencing financial difficulties. When the abbot of Beaulieu visited in 1261 he found the community in considerable debt. Fortunes were to improve when, in September 1270, Edmund of Cornwall presented his father's foundation with a phial containing the Precious Blood of Christ, authenticated under the seal of the patriarch of Jerusalem, the future Pope Urban IV. The gift was destined to make Hailes one of the most celebrated goals of pilgrimage in the country. At first, the phial may have been placed in a temporary shrine, but so precious a relic demanded an appropriate setting. A decision was taken to rebuild the east end of the church in an extended form, with an apsidal ambulatory and five radiating chapels. Indeed, the

model for the design may well have been King Henry III's rebuilding at Westminster Abbey. The new work was completed by 1277 and was dedicated in that year by Godfrey Giffard, bishop of Worcester (1268–1302). In all, the modified church stood at about 341 feet (104m) long.

According to the Hailes chronicler, a new infirmary and associated structures were begun in 1292. A little over three decades later, in 1325, the monks petitioned the bishop of Worcester in an attempt to gain the spiritual revenues of the parish church of Longborough, claiming that their abbey was in debt and bemoaning the fact that the buildings had been left incomplete by the founder and his son. After a difficult decade, there was doubtless a strong element of truth in the petition. Yet it is important to remember that the economy of the house had already been placed on a reasonable footing. Wool production, for example, generally contributed a significant element in the total income. And, apart from the acquisition of Longborough, Hailes derived spiritual revenues from a clutch of Gloucestershire churches, as well as those at Breage and Paul near Penzance in Cornwall, and at North Leigh in Oxfordshire.

Financial difficulties in the later fourteenth century led to renewed problems with the abbey buildings. In 1413, the pope accepted a petition in which it was claimed that the revenues of the house were insufficient to sustain the twenty-two monks in the community. When Hailes was visited by the abbots of Beaulieu and Waverley in 1442, the abbey was told to appoint two bursars from among the monks to take charge of financial affairs. Moreover, it was said that both internal and external repairs to the monastery should be carried out as quickly as possible. To assist with rebuilding, papal indulgences were granted in 1458, and again in 1468, to all pilgrims who made offerings at the shrine of the Precious Blood. It was probably these events which led to the rebuilding of the cloister arcades in the later fifteenth and early sixteenth centuries. It was about this time, too, that the west range was converted for use as private accommodation by the abbot.

In the great survey of 1535, the abbey's income was assessed at £357. Having survived the first round of suppressions, Abbot Stephen Sager and his community of twenty-one monks surrendered Hailes on 24 December 1539. Soon afterwards, the church, chapels, steeple, cloister, chapter house, dorter, refectory, infirmary and the prior's chamber were deemed superfluous and were dismantled. The west range (the former abbot's lodging), along with the pantry, buttery, kitchen, larder, cellars, baking and brewing houses, the gatehouse and the great barn, were all retained. By

1551, a lease on the property had been obtained by John Hodgkins, and from him it passed in marriage first to William Hoby, and later to the Tracy family. The Tracys lived at Hailes until at least 1687, and thereafter the house was gradually allowed to fall into ruin.

The abbey ruins stand amid a fairly well-preserved earthwork precinct. The parish church, near the site entrance, probably served as the *capella ante portas* (the gatehouse chapel). Although the building is essentially Romanesque, it was extensively modified in the early fourteenth century. Inside, it houses probably the finest display of decorative painting known from an English Cistercian context, dating from about 1320–30.

Bazeley 1899
Brakspear 1901b
Brakspear 1901c
Coad 1993
Knowles and St Joseph 1952, 124–25
VCH Gloucester 1907, 96–99
Winkless 1990

HOLMCULTRAM ABBEY

Holmcultram was within the area of Cumbria over which King David I (1124–53) of Scotland had claims, and it was David and his son, Earl Henry (d. 1152), who founded the abbey in 1150. Also associated with the endowment of the foundation was Allen of Allendale. Initially, the abbey was an essentially Scottish foundation, with the first monks being brought from David's own foundation of Melrose, though King Henry II was to extend his protection to it after he re-established his authority over the area in 1157. In 1193 the abbey was able to provide a colony of monks for a new foundation at Grey in Ireland, and in the later Middle Ages it had a dependent hospital dedicated to St Thomas within Holmcultram itself.

Holmcultram's situation close to the Border inevitably meant that both the abbey and its five granges were targets during the long years of warfare between England and Scotland. After an attack in 1216, Alice de Romilly gave a quarry in

Aspatria to provide stone for rebuilding. But Scottish attacks were not the only problem at this period, because Abbot Adam of Kendal (1215–23) is said to have been deposed by the abbot of Cîteaux for squandering the abbey's possessions in an attempt to gain the bishopric of Carlisle. Edward I stayed at Holmcultram in the course of his campaign against Scotland of 1299, when the royal chancery was ordered to appear at the abbey. He also stayed there in 1307, and his entrails are said to have been deposited at the abbey after his death at Burgh on the Sands on 6 July 1307, while the rest of his body was carried to Westminster for entombment.

Perhaps the greatest damage suffered by the abbey resulted from the Scottish attack of 1319, which took place despite the fact that the father of King Robert I (the Bruce) was buried there, and for a while the monks had to seek shelter in neighbouring religious houses. Later that century the abbey was reduced to bribing

1150–1538

Holmcultram Abbey is at Abbey Town, at the junction of the B5302 and B5307 about 15 miles (24km) west-north-west of Carlisle. The lowest storey of the central vessel of much of its church nave now serves as the parish church and is normally accessible to the public.

Cumbria
Carlisle

NY 177508

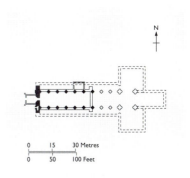

The truncated western bays of the twelfth-century abbey church at Holmcultram have been used for parish worship since the dissolution (Stuart Harrison).

Ferguson 1874

Fergusson 1984a, 127–29

Gilbanks 1899

Grainger and Collingwood 1929

Hodgson 1907

Martindale 1913

Miller 1972

Pevsner 1967, 57–58

VCH Cumberland 1905, 162–73

the earl of Douglas not to attack it in an attempt to stave off further damage. Despite this, Scottish onslaughts may have been a factor behind the state of disrepair reported in 1428, when papal indulgences were granted to those who contributed to the reparations and, even at the election of a new abbot fifty years later, orders still had to be given for the infirmary to be rebuilt. Yet, despite all of these problems, there were still twenty-four monks with the abbot at the time of the dissolution in 1538.

The chief upstanding remains are of the western bays of the nave of the abbey church. Building of the church had probably started soon after the foundation, and its design shows a number of features for which direct Burgundian inspiration seems likely; enough was complete by 1186 for Bishop Christian of Galloway, who died in October that year, to be buried within it. The plan of the eastern parts of the church are known from excavation, and it was typical of early Cistercian churches in having a short rectangular presbytery, transepts with a chapel aisle on their eastern side, and an aisled nave, which in this case was nine bays long. The total length of the church was about 265 feet (81m). The only significant addition to this plan in the course of the Middle Ages seems to have been a deep porch over the west doorway, which was added by Abbot Robert Chambers in 1507.

Engravings made before the destruction of the upper parts of the nave, of which nothing now remains, indicate that it had a three-storeyed elevation with no vertical subdivision into bays. The surviving arcade piers are of the bundled-shaft type, each with eight rounded shafts, except for the fifth piers from the west, which are of a more complex type, and which probably mark the position of the screen between the choirs of the monks and lay brethren. The arcade capitals are of waterleaf or chalice form, and they carry arches of chamfered or right-angled profile. The finest single surviving feature of the church

is the round-arched west doorway, which has four shafted orders carrying waterleaf capitals. Little is known of the details of the rest of the church, though the lower courses of a screen between the north transept and the crossing have been found through excavation. The nave of Holmcultram shows a number of detailed architectural similarities with the church at Furness, and — to a lesser extent — with that at Calder. This may indicate that some of the same masons were involved on all of these three Cistercian houses.

After the abbey was surrendered in 1538 by its last abbot, Gavin Borrodaile, the local people petitioned Thomas Cromwell for the use of the church, the nave of which had apparently been used by the parish for a considerable period. This was granted, though care of the structure seems at first to have been perfunctory, and towards the end of the sixteenth century the central tower fell. Much damage was caused by this, with further damage resulting from a fire which broke out in the course of repairs. On his visitation in 1703, Bishop William Nicholson of Carlisle expressed dismay that the church was in a shameful state; eventually, in 1724, a Trust was set up to ensure that the parts of the church still in use for worship were put into a good state.

In the course of the work then carried out, the arcade level of the six western bays of the nave was enclosed, with a roof and plaster ceiling placed above the level of the arcade arches. Walls were built between the piers, pierced by two tiers of windows, presumably in order to light galleries as well as the main level within the church. Everything which stood outside the limits of the walled-up arcades appears to have been demolished at that time as part of a general tidying up of the site. The only significant operations on the fabric since then have been a restoration in 1883, when the internal galleries were removed, and further works in 1913, when the plaster ceiling was taken down to expose the tie-beamed roof structure.

HULTON ABBEY

The abbey at Hulton was a relatively late White Monk foundation. It was established in 1218–20 by Henry de Audley (d. 1246), with monks from Combermere. The Audleys were not of the first rank of baronial families, and the endowments they were able to offer the house were somewhat less than munificent. As a result, despite late additions to the abbey's estates, it was never an especially prosperous house, with an assessed income of some £76 in 1535. There were only eight monks in addition to the abbot and prior at the time of its dissolution in 1538.

The abbey was sited in the upper reaches of the Trent valley in north Staffordshire. The buildings of the abbey have been almost entirely levelled, though their layout is known through a series of excavations carried out over the last century. Despite the late date of foundation, the church remained loyal to the common Cistercian plan type, having two chapels on the east side of each transept, flanking the short rectangular presbytery. Although much of this must have been built in the years following the foundation, evidence has been found that there was some remodelling of the north transept in the fourteenth century, possibly at a time when the abbey's financial fortunes had been placed on a rather firmer footing. The lower walls of the eastern parts of the church are now exposed and consolidated, and are to be seen within the grounds of Carmountside High School.

The plan of the rest of the church and of the monastic buildings is known from excavations carried out in 1884, with further work carried out on a number of occasions between the 1930s and 1994. From this, it is known that the aisled nave was just four bays long and

that, as was preferred, the cloister was south of the nave. The east range housed a library and sacristy immediately adjacent to the church, followed by a rectangular chapter house of three by three bays which projected eastwards from the range, a slype, and the dormitory undercroft. The refectory in the south range appears to have been set on a north–south axis, although it can only have been of slight projection; the kitchen was to its west and the warming room and day stair were to its east.

Amongst the significant finds located through excavation are several grave slabs with foliate-headed crosses. On one of these, which probably dates from the mid-fourteenth century, are depicted a mell, a rule and a set-square, the implements usually associated with a master mason, and it is tempting to suspect that this marked the burial of one of the abbey's later designers. Other finds included fragments of window glass, much of which appears to date from the fourteenth and fifteenth centuries, and a wide range of decorated floor tiles.

Following the dissolution, in 1542 the site of the abbey was acquired by Sir Edward Aston of Tixall, and it was probably during the time it was owned by his family that a large house was built, presumably using much of the abbey stonework for this purpose. Although some ruins of the abbey still remained visible into the eighteenth century, it cannot have been long after then that they almost completely disappeared. It was only when land drains were being installed at Carmountside Farm in 1884 that the wall footings were rediscovered, after which the landowner, the Reverend Walter Sneyd of Keele Hall, ordered the first of a succession of archaeological excavations to be instigated.

1218/20–1538

The site of Hulton Abbey is at Abbey Hulton, off the A5009 about 2 miles (3.2 km) north of Stoke-on-Trent. The partially excavated and consolidated remains are adjacent to Carmountside High School and are accessible to the public.

Staffordshire
Lichfield

SJ 905491

The base of a respond, or half pier, within the north aisle at Hulton (University of Warwick, Richard K. Morris).

Lynam 1885
Tomkinson 1997
VCH Staffordshire 1970, 235–37
Wise 1985

JERVAULX ABBEY

1145/56–1537

Jervaulx Abbey lies on the east side of the A6108, between Masham and Leyburn, 2 miles (3.2km) east of East Witton in Uredale. It lies in the park of the seventeenth-century Jervaulx Hall, and although privately owned it is accessible to visitors at all reasonable times.

North Yorkshire
York

SE 173856

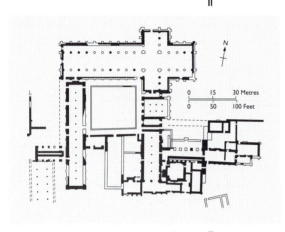

Jervaulx Abbey was originally established in 1145 at Fors in Wensleydale. It was founded by Acarius fitz Bardolph for a community of Savigniac monks, led by Peter de Quincy. It seems, however, that the foundation was made without the consent of the abbot of Savigny. Responsibility for the house was assumed by Byland Abbey before 1150, when nine Byland monks were added to the community. The site at Fors proved unsatisfactory, and in 1156 it was abandoned in favour of a new one some sixteen miles (25.8km) to the east, on the south bank of the river Ure or Jore — from which the abbey took its medieval name of Joreval. The move had almost certainly been planned from the time that Byland took over responsibility for the community, and permanent stone buildings were started before the monks actually made the transfer.

Under Abbot John of Kinstan, Jervaulx grew rapidly through the 1150s and 1160s, and the cloister ranges and church were remodelled or rebuilt towards the end of the twelfth century. The abbey was suppressed in 1537, as a direct result of Abbot Adam Sedbar's involvement in the Pilgrimage of Grace, and its demolition began early in 1539. The site was one of the first monasteries to be excavated. Clearance of the ruins was begun in 1805 by John Claridge for the earl of Ailesbury. The ruins remain very much as Claridge left them, with fallen detail stacked close to where it was found on top of ruined walls. The church and cloister became a garden in the park of the seventeenth-century Jervaulx Hall. Further excavation was carried out by William St John Hope

and Harold Brakspear in 1905–07. Since the 1980s, the ruins have been conserved for public display, but Jervaulx remains the most picturesque of any British Cistercian monastery.

Part of the south wall and south transept of the 1150s church can still be identified, incorporated in a larger building of about 1180 to 1200, a similar development to that which can still be seen at Byland. The first part of the church to be rebuilt was the nave, which was built atypically from west to east with rib-vaulted aisles and arcades supported on clustered piers, all of which have a close similarity with the contemporary work at Byland. Concentration on the nave suggests the need to provide an adequate church for the lay brothers, and meanwhile the eastern parts of the earlier church remained in use by the choir monks. The reconstruction of the eastern bays of the nave, transepts, and presbytery began in the 1190s, and here the Byland model was abandoned. The clustered piers were more developed, and the aisled presbytery of four bays terminated in a high gable wall with no external aisle. Fallen detail shows that this part of the church was built by the same masons who built the new presbytery at Fountains a decade or so later. When the church was excavated in the first decade of the nineteenth century, large areas of its early thirteenth-century mosaic tile floors were found in place, but these no longer survive.

The cloister lay on the south side of the church. The west range, the earliest building on the site, dates from the late 1150s. Only the ground floor survives, an open plan building originally divided by timber partitions and vaulted in thirteen double bays with groined vaults. The two northern bays formed the outer parlour, the next three bays provided cellarage, the sixth bay served as the cloister entry, and the remaining seven bays were used as the lay brothers' refectory. The east cloister range was initially built in the 1160s, but was extended later in the twelfth century. The west wall towards the cloister is the only surviving part of the initial building and incorporates — from north to south — doors to the library, the chapter house, the parlour, and the day stair to the dormitory (which followed the early Cistercian plan). The chapter house, however, had been rebuilt before 1180. And the dormitory, lit by large lancet windows, together with its undercroft to the south, are not much later in date. This all suggests an expansion of a smaller range to cope with growing numbers. Eastwards of the east range, a substantial latrine block was provided at the same time. The south range, also of the 1180s or 1190s, but almost totally demolished, comprised a north–south refectory, with the warming house and day stair to the east, and a small kitchen to the west. As with the east range, the cloister wall appears to have been reused from an earlier layout contemporary with the west range.

Attached to the east end of the monks' latrine block is the later thirteenth-century infirmary, an elaborate building arranged on two floors with its own latrine and a chapel on its northern side. A small yard to the north was closed by the infirmarer's lodging. To the south of the monks' latrine, and separated from the east cloister range by a small yard, was the abbot's house, an early fourteenth-century building on two floors. The abbot's chapel formed the south side of the yard, and was detached from his house. In the fifteenth century, a substantial meat kitchen was built in the enclosed yard, with fireplaces in its north, west, and south sides. It was at this period that the abbot abandoned his house in favour of more prestigious apartments in the infirmary. His old hall may have served as the misericord, a chamber in which by this time the monks were allowed to eat meat dishes.

The whole of the precinct survives as earthworks in the parkland surrounding the abbey ruins, but only two non-claustral buildings survive above ground level: a fragmentary watermill to the north of the church on the bank of the Ure, and a much altered building of thirteenth-century date (now converted to a house) well to the west of the central area. This has been described as a guest house, but this is unlikely.

The doorway at the south-west end of the nave at Jervaulx was used by the lay brothers to enter the church for services at night.

Part of the east range of monastic buildings at Jervaulx survives to a considerable height. The windows at upper floor level provided light to the monks' dormitory.

Davies 1997
Fergusson 1984a, 84, 129
Hope and Brakspear 1911
Knowles and St Joseph 1952, 90–92
Pevsner 1966, 203–05

KINGSWOOD ABBEY

1139–1538

Kingswood is on the B4060, 1 mile (1.6km) south-west of Wotton under Edge. Nothing of the abbey church or monastic buildings survives above ground, though the sixteenth-century gatehouse is in the care of English Heritage and is accessible at all reasonable times.

Gloucestershire
Worcester

ST 747920

The early sixteenth-century gatehouse is all that survives of Kingswood Abbey.

Fergusson 1984a, 129–30
Lindley 1954–56
VCH Gloucester 1907, 99–101
Verey 1976, 282

Kingswood Abbey was founded as a daughter house of Tintern by William de Berkeley in 1139. In the earliest years, the life of the community was severely disrupted as the monks were forced to move from one place to another in search of a suitable location to establish their permanent buildings. The first move took them to Hazleton, about 1149–50. Soon afterwards, they returned to Kingswood, only to move for a third time to Tetbury. Finally, about 1164–70, they returned once again to Kingswood, this time to occupy a fresh site.

In due course, Kingswood was able to exploit its position at the foot of the Cotswold scarp to become one of the more important wool-producing houses of the order in Britain. It is unfortunate that we know so little of the way in which this wealth was reflected in the abbey buildings. An isolated reference of 1242 refers to 'the work of the church', and at the same time a fraction over £18 was spent on the construction of a new hospice. In the following century, a downward trend in the economy, coupled with the effects of the Black Death, seems to have led to problems for Kingswood. By the 1360s, the church was 'in need of costly repair', and papal indulgences were offered in 1364, in 1368, and again in 1398, to all who might contribute to its upkeep.

Long since surrounded by the village of Kingswood, a sixteenth-century gatehouse is all that survives above ground. It is suggested that the church and the monastic buildings lay to the north-east, confined within a comparatively narrow strip of land between a mill leat and a small stream. The cloister may have been arranged to the north of the church. The gatehouse may very well represent one of the last pieces of monastic building in England. It is a handsome structure with a stone-vaulted passage, and with fragments of the precinct wall to either side. The lily plant formed by the mullion of the central window signifies the Annunciation of St Mary the Virgin.

In 1535, on the eve of the dissolution, Kingswood's annual income was assessed at about £239. The abbot and twelve monks eventually surrendered the house to the king's visitors in February 1538.

KINLOSS ABBEY

1150–1560

The abbey is on the edge of Kinloss village, close to Findhorn bay, on the B9089, about 3 miles (5km) north-west of Forres. The remains of the abbey are within a graveyard in the ownership of the local authority and is always accessible.

Moray
Moray

NJ 065615

Kinloss was another of King David I's benefactions for the Cistercian order, being founded in 1150 with monks brought up from Melrose. In the early thirteenth century there were as many as twenty-five monks in the community, including the abbot and prior, and there were still at least eighteen monks at the time of the Reformation. Little is known of the abbey's history in its earlier years though, rather unusually, it appears to have undergone a remarkable period of revitalization in the early sixteenth century. Under Thomas Crystall, who became abbot in 1504, determined efforts were made to re-establish the abbey's finances, while great attention was also paid to its spiritual life, and its buildings were brought back into repair. This process was continued by his successor

Robert Reid, in whose favour Crystall resigned in 1528. At the time he took up office Reid was a secular priest, but he elected to profess as a monk in the following year, thus enabling him to become a true abbot rather than a commendator, though he also became commendator of Beauly Priory in 1531, and continued as commendator of Kinloss after he became bishop of Orkney in 1541.

As a pluralist, and eventually as a commendator, it might have been expected that Reid's only interest in the religious houses under his authority would have been to draw the greater part of their incomes, but in this his behaviour was exceptional. In the 1530s he brought the Italian scholar Giovanni Ferrerio to Kinloss, where his teaching over five years made Kinloss a centre of academic excellence. Reid also built a fireproof library for the abbey's collection of books and rebuilt the abbot's lodging. In addition, he showed himself a noteworthy patron of the arts in commissioning the artist Andrew Bairhum to paint a number of altarpieces for the abbey church and to decorate some of his own rooms, though Bairhum's difficult behaviour may have led him to regret this. Reid resigned in favour of his nephew, Walter, in 1553, and

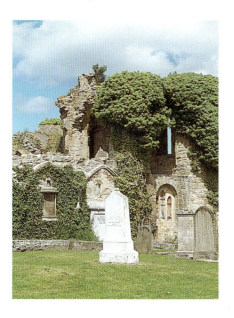

the latter may have proved more amenable to ideas of reform. After the Reformation, in 1583 Walter demitted his commendatorship in favour of Edward Bruce, for whom the abbey was erected into a temporal lordship in 1601, when Bruce took the title of Lord Kinloss, a title still held by the earls of Elgin.

The abbey church is largely destroyed, apart from its south transept, but enough of the lower parts of the walls and arcade piers of the rest is still visible amongst the memorials within the graveyard which has grown up within and around the abbey to have at least some idea of the overall plan. Unlike the great majority of Scottish Cistercian houses, the eastern limb had aisles extending down the full length of each side, though none of its arcade piers survive and it is not known if this was the original arrangement, or if the aisles were a later addition. The nave also had aisles down each side, and the fragments of clustered shaft piers which survive in places point to a date in the last decades of the twelfth century for this part of the church. The south transept has a single chapel on its east side, and south of it there is a compartment vaulted in three bays which probably served as both sacristy and library, since there appear to have been doorways from the church and the cloister. This part was converted into a family mausoleum in 1910 and was extensively remodelled at that time.

The cloister was on the south side of the church, and parts of its south and west walls survive, the former incorporating what appears to be a heavily rebuilt archway with chevron decoration and a lavatory recess. The best surviving part of the monastic buildings is the abbot's lodging, which was at the south end of the east range, and which presumably survives from the work carried out for Robert Reid in the second quarter of the sixteenth century. It is therefore a particularly interesting survival of a remarkable phase in the abbey's history, and it is unfortunate that its condition is now so precarious.

Left: Although much overgrown, the abbot's lodging is the best surviving part of the monastic buildings at Kinloss.

MacGibbon and Ross 1896–97, I, 416–21
Stuart 1872
Wilson 1839

KIRKSTALL ABBEY

1147/52–1539

Kirkstall Abbey is located on the south side of the A65, 3 miles (4.8km) north-west of Leeds city centre. The extensive ruins of the church and monastic buildings lie in a public park, and are accessible at all reasonable times.

West Yorkshire

York

SE 259362

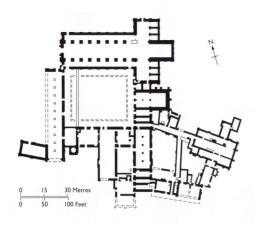

First settled at Barnoldswick in 1147 by William of Poitu and Henry de Lacy, Kirkstall Abbey was the fifth daughter house of Fountains. The site and the local population proved inhospitable, and Abbot Alexander (1147–82) sought out a new site in the valley of the Aire in 1152. Here he began the construction of a 'basilica', almost certainly the present church, and temporary buildings for the community. By 1159, the eastern parts of the church were sufficiently complete for use, and the whole church was finished by Henry de Lacy's death in 1177. Indeed, by the time of Abbot Alexander's death in 1182, all 'the buildings of Kirkstall were erected of stone and wood, that is, the church … and dormitory of the monks … and of the lay brethren, and either refectory, the cloister, and the chapter house, and other offices necessary within the abbey, and all of these covered excellently with tile'.

With an assessed income of £329 in 1535, Kirkstall was eventually suppressed in 1539. Its buildings were stripped, but not demolished. They remained surprisingly intact into the eighteenth century, until the crossing tower fell during a storm in 1779. In 1825, melting snow caused the collapse of the vault below the dormitory floor and part of the dormitory itself, and it became clear that the ruins were far from stable. The site was, however, open to the public and the earl of Cardigan employed a custodian who cleared out the ruins to make them more accessible. In 1890, the site was acquired by Leeds City Corporation and the repair of the ruins and landscaping of the precinct begun. As part of this exercise, a full analysis of the site was undertaken by

William St John Hope and John Bilson. A campaign of excavation between 1950 and 1964 by the Leeds City Museum was designed to complete Hope's interpretation of the site, and the guest hall complex was excavated by the West Yorkshire Archaeology Service between 1979 and 1984 in advance of its conservation.

The twelfth-century church at Kirkstall is the most complete Cistercian church in Britain. In plan, it is a standard Bernardine design church with a short aisleless presbytery, transepts with three square eastern chapels, and a nave of eight bays. In elevation, however, it shows a transitional design which fits conveniently between the design of the church at Fountains and the design of the church at Roche. While Kirkstall retained a two-storey elevation, it was moving from the transitional Romanesque of Fountains to a more openly Gothic design. The presbytery was intended to be roofed with a barrel vault, like those that were used in the transept chapels, but this intention was abandoned in the course of building. The inner faces of the walls were raised, and a rib vault inserted. The crossing was designed to be unstressed, but was modified to take a lantern tower. The nave aisles were vaulted with rib vaults from the first. The piers of the nave show that all but the western three bays were built in the same campaign as the transepts, and must have been completed in the early 1160s, while the clustered piers of the last three bays, and the design of the western portal, suggest the church was completed around 1170 at the latest. Throughout the church, decoration unknown on other Cistercian sites of this date is apparent, and tracery from the rose windows that originally filled its gables indicates that the design of this church must have been exceptional. Remarkably, the church was not modified until the fifteenth century when tracery was added to some of its round-headed windows, a new east window inserted, and the pitch of its main roofs lowered. In the early years of the sixteenth century, Abbot William Marshall raised the lantern tower by a full storey.

From the evidence of fragments of the surrounding arcade which have been recovered, it seems the cloister on the south side of the church was completed by the late 1160s. The first range to have been built was the lay brothers' quarters in the west range, completed in the late 1150s with an enclosed lane on its east side and a latrine block to the west. The east range was begun about 1160, and the detailing of the chapter house contained within the range at its northern end suggests completion by about 1165. To the south of the chapter house was the parlour, and next to this the day stair in its early Cistercian location. Beyond was the passage to the infirmary, and then a day room of five bays. The monks' dormitory on the upper floor extended from the south transept to the south end of the day room. The southern end of the range comprised the monks' latrines at first floor, the central drain being flanked by two small vaulted rooms. Contemporary with the building of the east range was the laying out of the south cloister range which contained a passage through the range, an east–west refectory, and the kitchen. It is apparent that this layout was abandoned in the course of construction in favour of a north–south refectory with a warming house and the day stair to the east and an enlarged kitchen to the west, the earliest use of the developed Cistercian plan recorded in Britain.

To the east of the cloister, two further buildings were raised in the early thirteenth century. The first was a small abbot's house on two storeys attached to the east side of the monks' latrines, with a chapel and kitchen to the east. The second was the infirmary, which replaced a smaller twelfth-century building. The development of the infirmary was complicated, for the infirmary hall was largely rebuilt in the fourteenth century, and was again substantially remodelled in the fifteenth century.

Although the cloister ranges were little altered throughout their lives, some significant modifications were made. In the early fourteenth century, a new chapter house was built to the east of the old one which was itself converted into a vestibule. In the later fifteenth century, a meat kitchen was built between the east range and the refectory, and the walls of the refectory were raised to enable an upper floor to be inserted. The ground floor was then converted into a misericord, a refectory where the monks were permitted to eat meat. At about this time, the lane on the west side of the cloister was removed, the space it occupied in the south range converted to a brewhouse, and the cloister alleys were rebuilt.

The rib-vaulted north nave aisle at Kirkstall (Malcolm Thurlby).

The twelfth-century church at Kirkstall seen from the south-east. The tower was raised to twice its former height during the early sixteenth century.

Barnes 1984
Fergusson 1984a, 48–51, 130
Harrison 1995
Hope and Bilson 1907
Moorhouse and Wrathmell 1987
Pevsner and Radcliffe 1967, 340–47
Thurlby 1995
Wrathmell 1987

The whole of the precinct, now bisected by the modern road, survives within a public park, though landscaping has obscured its layout. Short lengths of the precinct wall still survive on the west, north and east sides, with the Aire forming the southern boundary. Two buildings survive within the precinct, the late twelfth-century inner gatehouse, now used as a museum but converted to a house after the suppression, and a substantial guest hall that closed the west side of the inner court which lay to the west of the church and cloister buildings. The guest hall was built early in the thirteenth century and was substantially enlarged before the end of the century. It was extensively remodelled in the fifteenth century.

KIRKSTEAD ABBEY

1139/87–1537

The site lies on farmland on the south side of the B1197, 7 miles (11.3km) south-west of Horncastle. A public footpath across the earthworks of the church and cloister leads to the gate chapel.

Lincolnshire
Lincoln

SK 185620

The third daughter house of Fountains Abbey, Kirkstead was founded by Hugh Brito, lord of Tattershall, in 1139, on the east side of the Witham valley. The earliest buildings were laid out by Brother Adam, later abbot of Meaux (1150–60). But this first site proved to be too small, and was abandoned in the 1170s. Permanent building was soon in hand at the new location. The site was confirmed in 1187, by which time the church must have been largely complete. The abbey was suppressed in 1537 after the abbot and monks were implicated in the Lincolnshire Rebellion in the autumn of the previous year. Thereafter, although the roofs were stripped of lead, the buildings were temporarily left standing. By 1716, however, only the south transept of the church remained, and this is now reduced to its south-east corner. Otherwise, the abbey is represented by fine and extensive earthworks which define the church, cloister ranges, inner and outer courts. The only surviving structure is the gate chapel, converted to parochial use as the church of St Leonard.

The earthworks show that the abbey church was closely related to the plan of Roche. There was a short, square presbytery, transepts with two chapels, and an aisled nave. Kirkstead also employed a similar three-storey elevation, though here the triforium stage was open to the transept. The main vessels of the transepts were vaulted, suggesting that the church was vaulted throughout, as at Roche.

The cloister lay on the south side of the church, and though represented only by the earthworks over its buried walls, it shows the same developed plan seen at Roche, with a north–south refectory at the centre of its south range. A large infirmary hall and associated buildings can still be traced eastwards of the east range, around what appears to be an infirmary cloister. A square enclosure to the west of the west range was probably the site of the lay brothers' cloister. The inner court, with its guest accommodation, lay to the south and west of the cloister. A large walled outer court was situated in the north-west corner of the precinct. Architectural detail from the site suggests that the central buildings were completed by the late 1180s.

The gate chapel, an exquisite building of about 1230–40, is vaulted throughout with rib vaults decorated with dogtooth mouldings, and its windows and doors are enriched with stiff-leaf capitals. The decoration still shows Cistercian restraint, however, and the interior retains some of its original wall painting, a double line masonry painting in grey rather than the usual white. There was also foliate decoration, but hardly any of this has survived.

The site of Kirkstead Abbey seen from the air (Cambridge University Collection).

The only upstanding fragment of masonry to survive at Kirkstead is a corner angle of the south transept.

Fergusson 1984a, 130–31
Hartshorne 1883
Knowles and St Joseph 1952, 126–27
Pevsner and Harris 1989, 417–18
VCH Lincolnshire 1906, 135–38

LLANTARNAM ABBEY

Llantarnam was founded in 1179 by the Welsh lord of Caerleon, Hywel ab Iorwerth (d. 1211), and was colonized by monks from Strata Florida. The precise location of the initial buildings is not known, though eventually the community moved to the comparatively secluded site between the Afon Lwyd and the Dowlais brook. To begin with, and for many years, the abbey was known principally as Caerleon. In 1273, however, the general chapter decreed that *Llanterna* should be the official name. In the event, both Caerleon and Llantarnam continued to be used.

Apart from its estates in the immediate locality, from the very earliest years Llantarnam also benefited from the patronage of the native Welsh in the upland areas of eastern Glamorgan. Here, in contest with the rival house at Margam, the abbey secured lands around Pendar and Penrhys, the latter emerging in the fifteenth century as the site of the pre-eminent Welsh shrine

dedicated to the Virgin. At the end of the thirteenth century, Llantarnam's estates were focused on some ten to twelve grange centres. Although there were still twenty monks in the community in 1317, it was claimed that a generation earlier there had been sixty.

There is very little by way of visible remains or documentary sources to tell us much about the buildings at Llantarnam, though a church in the style of the Whitland family might be expected. In 1398, a papal indulgence was obtained for all who contributed to the repair of the abbey, 'the books, buildings and other ornaments of whose church have been enormously devastated by fire'. Whatever the scale of the damage, on the eve of the dissolution plans were in hand for a new programme of modifications to the church. In a will of 1532, the bequests included mention of a Lady Chapel, and provisions were set aside for 'the making of an arch at the

1179–1536

Llantarnam is situated about 3 miles (4.8km) north of Newport, and is approached off the A4042. The site of the abbey is occupied by a house which was extensively rebuilt in 1834–35. It may incorporate elements of the medieval claustral complex within its fabric. In 1946, Llantarnam was acquired by the Sisters of St Joseph, and they continue to reside there.

Torfaen
Llandaff

ST 312929

entry of the church out of the cloister', and 'the building of an arch in the body of the church'. From two years later there is a reference to the abbey's 'great gate'.

In 1535, the net annual income of the house was assessed at about £71. Llantarnam was dissolved in the summer of 1536, at which time the abbot presided over a community of six monks. The site was bought in 1554 by William Morgan, who built a house over part of the claustral complex. It was very substantially rebuilt for Reginald Blewitt in 1834–35 to a design by T. H. Wyatt. A large eleven-bay monastic barn, usually attributed to the thirteenth century, stands to the north of the house.

Williams 1976a, 77–93

LONDON ST MARY GRACES ABBEY

1350–1538/39

St Mary Graces stood just to the north-east of the Tower of London, between Tower Hill, Royal Mint Street, and East Smithfield. There are no prominent standing remains.

Greater London
London

TQ 339807

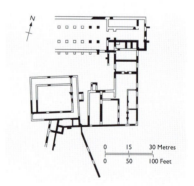

Founded by King Edward III in 1350, St Mary Graces was the last Cistercian foundation in Britain. Located on the site of a plague cemetery outside the defences of the Tower of London, it was the only house of the order in Britain established on an urban site. The small community of an abbot and six monks was drawn from the abbey of Beaulieu to serve what was essentially a new royal free chapel.

Initially, the house was not well endowed, though by the early sixteenth century it had become the third richest White Monk abbey in Britain. Building began slowly, but was largely complete by the late 1390s. There were eight monks resident in 1381, and there were eleven when the house was suppressed in 1538–39. A panorama of London, drawn about 1543, shows the church complete. It was of hall design, with a central tower and no transepts. In 1542–43, the site was granted to Sir Arthur Darcy (d. 1560), and it was he who demolished the church and converted the cloister ranges to a house. The site was sold back to the Crown, and by 1565 it had become one of the first victualling yards for the Royal Navy. Again, some monastic buildings were reused, and these were modified throughout the seventeenth and early eighteenth centuries. The

naval supply base moved to Deptford in 1748, and the buildings at Tower Hill were used as warehouses. The site was cleared in 1805 for the construction of the Royal Mint which remained here until 1975.

A large area of the site was excavated in 1986–88, and the plan of a substantial part of the monastic buildings recovered. The church, whose plan followed that of a mid-fourteenth-century friary rather than any standard Cistercian layout, had an aisled nave of at least seven bays, and initially an unaisled choir of four bays. The latter terminated in an eastern transept which appears to copy the Nine Altars chapel at Fountains. The tower was placed over the western bay of the eastern arm, and may have served the same function as the 'walking place' in a friary church. By 1442, an aisle had been added to the south side of the presbytery. In the second half of the fifteenth century, a Lady Chapel was built on the north side, effectively adding a second aisle.

The domestic ranges lay to the south of the church and did not conform, in their latest phase, to the standard Cistercian plan. The cloister was detached from the church, and separated from it by an open yard. A gallery ran from the south door of the church around the east and south sides of this yard to provide access to the cloister, with perhaps single-storey ranges of buildings to the east and south of it. Against the church was a sacristy, and to the south of this the chapter house. To the south of the chapter house, however, the regular plan was abandoned, and the remainder of the range comprised the infirmary, though there are indications that this was originally the dormitory.

On the south side of the yard, it seems there was a north–south refectory, with a small warming house to the east. By the late fifteenth century, it would appear this layout had been abandoned, and the refectory had become the dormitory, with a latrine block built on its west side. It was at this point that the detached cloister was built, with a new refectory, set in the angle to the south walk, but still maintaining a north–south alignment, kitchen, and warming house. The west side of the site remains unexcavated, but it is clear that St Mary Graces remains one of the most enigmatic Cistercian abbeys in Britain.

Clapham 1914–15
Grainger and Hawkins 1984–88
Honeybourne 1952
Mills 1984–88

LOUTH PARK ABBEY

1137/39–1536

The site lies on farmland south of Abbey House, on the east side of the village of Keddington, on an unclassified road 2 miles (3.2km) north-east of Louth. There is no public access.

Lincolnshire
Lincoln

TF 335485

The first daughter house of Fountains, the abbey of Louth Park was originally established at Haverholme near Sleaford in 1137 by Bishop Alexander of Lincoln (1123–48). The site proved to be too wet and the community was moved in 1139 to the bishop's deer park east of Louth. The community expanded rapidly in its first decade, but despite this it appears the construction of the abbey buildings proceeded slowly.

Between about 1150 and 1165, the presbytery, transepts, and the two or three easternmost bays of the nave were erected. At this point work was abandoned in favour of the construction of the cloister ranges. Work did not restart on the church until the second quarter of the thirteenth century under Abbot Roger Dunham (1227–46). Before he began work on the nave, however, he built an infirmary and kitchen, which suggests that the monks' buildings were not yet complete. Later he was responsible for the construction of the lay brothers' cloister ('from the foundations'), and he rebuilt the monks' dormitory, the warming house, chapter house and cloister. Abbot Roger also added the gate chapel and the porter's lodge adjoining the great gate. It seems that the resources for all this building were in no small part due to the wealth of William of Tournay, dean of Lincoln, who took the habit at Louth in 1239. When William died in 1258 he was buried in the Lady Chapel which he had caused to be built and dedicated.

The abbey's chronicle records that in Roger of Dunham's time there were 66 monks and 150 lay brothers. In 1535 the assessed income of the house was given as £147, and it was suppressed in 1536. In 1726, the Buck brothers recorded standing masonry, but by the mid-nineteenth century only small areas of masonry were visible. Today, the layout of the site is clear from its surviving earthworks, with the church and its southern cloister at the centre of a compact precinct. The church was partially excavated in 1873 and again in 1966. It was a substantial building, 256 feet (78m) from east to west (only a few feet shorter than Fountains) and 116 feet (35.4m) across the transepts, with a nave of ten bays. The planning of the presbytery and transepts was virtually identical to its contemporary sister houses at Kirkstall and Sawley.

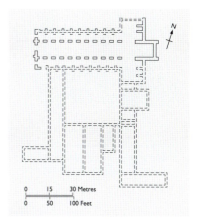

Fergusson 1984a, 131–33
Hope 1891
Pevsner and Harris 1989, 411
Trollope 1873–74
VCH Lincolnshire 1906, 138–41
Venables 1873–74

MARGAM ABBEY

1147–1536

Margam Abbey is situated a little over 3 miles (4.8km) south-east of Port Talbot, just off the A48 and close to junction 38 on the M4. Six bays of the imposing twelfth-century nave now serve as the parish church. To the east, in what is now a Country Park, will be found the remains of the presbytery and the elegant polygonal chapter house. Both church and ruins are accessible at all reasonable times.

Neath Port Talbot
Llandaff

SS 802863

A view through the early thirteenth-century doorway, which led from the cloister into the chapter house vestibule, at Margam.

Right: Despite the restoration of 1805–09, the west front at Margam still retains much of its twelfth-century character.

It was not long before his death in the autumn of 1147 that Robert, earl of Gloucester and lord of Glamorgan, finalized his plans for the foundation of a Cistercian abbey at Margam. In an impressive ceremony of endowment held at Bristol, the earl handed a deed of gift to Nivard, one of Bernard of Clairvaux's own brothers who had come to England specifically for the purpose of attending the symbolic transfer. That November, a few weeks after Robert had been laid to rest, the founding colony of monks arrived from France headed by their abbot, William of Clairvaux (1147–53). They were to be settled on a site which had been prepared for them near the west coast of the lordship of Glamorgan, at a place already rich in religious history.

Robert of Gloucester's endowments comprised almost 18,000 acres (7,287ha) of land between the Afan and Kenfig rivers, 'from the brow of the mountains to the sea'. Gradually, the Margam monks acquired by further gift, purchase, and the occasional lease, a fairly compact chain of estates across the vale and border vale of Glamorgan. By the end of the thirteenth century, their holdings were organized around some two dozen grange centres and the abbey was actively farming almost 6,500 acres (2,429ha) of arable. In all, with an annual income of nearly £256 in 1291, Margam stood as the richest monastic house in Wales.

As late as 1336, the abbot of Margam reported that his house supported thirty-eight monks and forty *conversi*, but by this time there were already clear signs of change and abandonment of early Cistercian ideals. Increasingly, the community was forced to give up the direct exploitation of its estates, moving instead towards a *rentier* economy. Adding drastically to its mounting problems, the abbey was very badly hit during the rebellion of Owain Glyn Dŵr in the early fifteenth century. In 1412, Margam was described as being utterly shattered, its abbot and monks forced to wander about like vagabonds.

In 1535, on the eve of the suppression, Margam's income was assessed at about £181. A year later, in August 1536, the convent seal was broken, the nine remaining monks dispersed, and the abbey dissolved. The site was entrusted, on the king's behalf, to Sir Rice Mansel (d. 1559) of Oxwich. With great good fortune, much of the nave of the monastic church was to be spared. Soon after the dissolution, and certainly no later than 1542, it passed into parochial use. Meanwhile, Sir Rice had quickly acquired a lease on Margam. Subsequently, between 1540 and 1557, he purchased not only the abbey buildings but also the greater share of its estates. About 1552, he began building a '*faire and sumptious house*' over much of the south and south-eastern parts of the former abbey complex. As fortune turned once more, this house was to be abandoned by Thomas Mansel Talbot (d. 1813) in the later eighteenth century. It was comprehensively swept away, and Margam was to become a pleasure garden dominated by a mighty orangery built in 1787–90. The church — described at this time as being 'in a very slovenly state' — was happily to be whole-heartedly and sympathetically restored in 1805–09. A further important renovation took place in 1872–73.

Its significance all too easily overlooked, the survival of the greater part of the twelfth-century nave at Margam is quite remarkable. Nowhere else in Britain is there more eloquent testimony of the stripped austerity of the early Cistercian architectural ideal. Though the aisles were largely rebuilt in the restoration of the

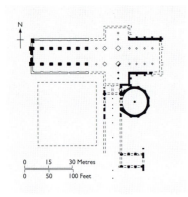

early nineteenth-century, it is the six west bays which now serve as St Mary's parish church. To judge from the stark detail, construction must have been in hand soon after the foundation and may have continued through to the 1170s. The unmoulded rectangular piers rise from low plinths, with the two-order rounded arches of the arcades springing not from true capitals, but from simple chamfered imposts. On the north side, where the later plaster has been removed, it is possible to see traces of the base and splays of the blocked clerestory windows, sitting directly over the apex of the arches to the arcade. The lack of any convincing evidence for responds or shafts suggests that the roof of the central vessel was of timber. In the aisles, however, the plaster groin vaults may reflect the pattern of the stone originals. Outside, it is very interesting to note (bearing in mind the extent of restoration) the close family resemblance between the Margam west front and that at its celebrated French sister house of Fontenay, located in the Burgundian cradle-lands of the order.

At the opposite end of the church, although the early arrangements were swept away when the presbytery and transepts were rebuilt in the early Gothic period, there are various clues on which to base a tentative reconstruction. To begin with, we can be sure that the twelfth-century nave extended a further two bays to the east. Its roof-line was probably carried through without any formal break at the crossing. Beyond this, the presbytery is likely to have been arranged in the stepped, so-called Fontenay style. The transepts, whose position is fixed by that of the east range of cloister buildings, would have opened from an assumed unsegregated crossing. There were perhaps two eastern chapels to each transept. In all, the internal measurements of the church may have been about 210 feet (64m) long and 115 feet (35m) across the transepts.

No sooner had the Margam monks grown familiar with the layout of their

first stone monastery than they began to contemplate major programmes of rebuilding. From the evidence which survives, the new work was to start with the east range of claustral buildings. Thereafter, the community would proceed to commission the scheme for the enlargement of the east end of the abbey church. In the absence of documentary sources, from the stylistic details it is very tempting to associate the inauguration of the early Gothic campaigns with the undoubtedly ambitious Abbot Gilbert (1203–13), even if construction must surely have continued under his successor, John of Goldcliff (1213–37).

The outstanding survival of the initial phase is the stunning twelve-sided chapter house. Habitually dated to about 1200, as Gilbert's work it must be considered marginally later. Nevertheless, it was almost certainly completed some few years earlier than the very similar structure at Dore. Inside, the beauty of the Margam chapter house is deeply moving. Perfectly circular, it measures about 50 feet (15.2m) from wall to wall. Each of the nine exposed faces is lit by a tall lancet window, framed internally and externally by slender detached and belted shafts. The vault, which survived until 1799, sprang from moulded capitals resting on twelve sets of triple shafts which rise from corbels set in a string-course at sill level. Centrally, the ribs were supported on a single pier of alternating round and polygonal shafts, crowned by a capital with deeply cut stiff-leaf foliage.

When complete, the new chapter house was approached by way of a vestibule contained within the body of the east range. In turn, the vestibule was given a gorgeous early Gothic composition of triple doorways opening off the east cloister alley. Apart from the detached shafts in the jambs, the heavily moulded arch of the central doorway was enriched with a band of dogtooth ornament. Above the vestibule, the monks' dormitory ran for at least 190 feet (57.9m) from its

The ribs in the chapter house vault at Margam were supported centrally on a single pier, crowned by a capital with deeply cut stiff-leaf foliage.

junction with the south transept.

With very little pause, it was decided that the Bernardine choir of the community's missionary years would have to be sacrificed to make way for a much larger and more fashionable rectangular presbytery. As part of this process, the crossing was to be regularized, and large piers were introduced to support a central tower. The transepts were remodelled, though the size of that to the south was in part restricted by the confines of the existing layout of monastic buildings. The new presbytery itself was set out in four bays, probably with the main arcades carried through at one level to a flat-ended east wall. There may have been four small chapels in the last bay. Overall, when the work was complete, the length of the church had been extended to some 262 feet (79.9m).

Again, considering the various stylistic details, Margam's thirteenth-century east end undoubtedly represents a striking departure from the propriety seen in the earlier Cistercian architecture of Britain.

The flamboyant shaft detailing to be seen around the south-east crossing pier, for example, would stand comparison with any of the finest contemporary work in the cathedrals and greater churches of the west country. It is difficult to assign a close date, but considering the plate tracery windows in the south transept and south aisle, together with the characteristics of the pier design, all may have been achieved before 1240.

After this phase, although there is a single reference, which must date from sometime before 1307, to 'a master of the works on the new church', there is little surviving evidence for later building programmes at Margam. The one feature worth highlighting is the processional doorway which would have opened from the east cloister alley into the south aisle of the church. This sits in a square-headed, moulded panel with trefoiled spandrels, and dates from the late thirteenth or early fourteenth century. It may reflect a general remodelling of the cloister arcades about this time.

The remains of the south-east crossing pier at Margam display a flamboyant arrangement of shaft detailing, typical of early Gothic work in the west country.

Adams 1984
Birch 1897
David 1929
Evans 1958
Knowles and St Joseph 1952, 120–21
Newman 1995, 424–29
Robinson 1993

MEAUX ABBEY

Meaux, the eighth and final daughter house of Fountains Abbey, was established in the last days of 1150 by William 'le Gros', count of Aumâle and earl of York (d. 1179). One of the most powerful magnates in the north of England, William had already founded the Cistercian house at Vaudey in 1147, but he was suffering from anxiety concerning a vow he had made to go to the Holy Land. It seems he was persuaded that the foundation of another White Monk abbey might prove adequate compensation. The first abbot of the new house was Adam (1151–60), the monk-architect of Fountains who had been responsible for the

earlier laying out of Woburn and Vaudey. Adam chose a site in an area the count had intended to enclose as a deer park. Lying within the flood plain of the river Hull, it required extensive drainage.

The first buildings, provided by William himself, comprised a great structure of mud and wattle occupied by the lay brothers who would begin the preparation of the rest of the site. Alongside, he built a chapel, with the monks' dormitory below. These buildings lay a little to the west of the permanent monastery and must have been built according to contemporary Cistercian custom for they were replaced on a similar plan but larger scale still with-

1150–1539

The site of Meaux Abbey lies on private land at Crown Farm on the west side of the unclassified road south of the A1035 between Routh and Wawne, about 3 miles (4.8km) to the east of Beverley.

Humberside
York

TA 091393

in the area of the later inner court by Abbot Adam as the community grew. By 1160 there were forty monks still occupying temporary buildings.

The progress of permanent building is known from the *Chronica Monasterii de Melsa*, compiled from earlier sources by Abbot Thomas Burton (1396–99) in his retirement. The chronicle records that Abbot Adam gave up his office in 1160, and the community was temporarily disbanded. It reformed the same year under its second abbot, Philip (1160–82), who began the building of a permanent church, the monks' dormitory, and the *lavatoria*, indicating that a piped water supply was provided. Adam, the founding abbot, was buried in the chapter house in 1180, which suggests that it was complete by this time. The remainder of the east range and the lavatories were finished by 1182. The next abbot, Thomas, tore down the unfinished church, because it had been arranged and 'constructed less appropriately than was proper'. He began work on a new building of more conventional Cistercian form. Before he resigned in

1197, Thomas also built the south range of the cloister, the warming house and kitchen, and laid the foundations of the lay brothers' refectory in the west range.

Alexander (1197–1210), the next abbot, completed the lay brothers' refectory and began their dormitory above it. He also erected the monks' cloister in stone, rebuilt the *lavatoria*, and was responsible for the building of the inner court, removing those temporary structures which still remained. Not content with this, Alexander 'swept away to the ground his predecessor's work [on the church] and laid with his own hands on Palm Sunday 1207 the first stone of the new church'. His successor, Hugh, completed the cloister ranges and brought the monks' church into use before 1220. Work was to continue on the church until the late 1230s, as a result of which the building of the monks' infirmary from the early 1220s was slow. Abbot William of Driffield (1249–69) added a bell-tower to the church, and also built the great granary and the infirmary for the lay brothers, as well as providing their stalls in the church. The church was not finally consecrated until 1253. Later, Abbot Roger (1286–1310) built himself an appropriate house between the infirmary and the dormitory, completing the abbey buildings.

Subsequent work was almost entirely concerned with the refitting and repair of buildings, and the Meaux chronicle paints a detailed picture of the interiors of many chambers. A chapel over the gatehouse was abandoned and the stone used to build a great brewing vat in the late 1330s. Then, in 1339–40, the monks' dormitory was roofed in lead. In the 1360s, the church was struck by lightning and its roof was damaged by fire and had to be repaired. Between 1372 and 1396, a considerable amount of work was done to improve the altars in the church, benches and bedsteads were provided for the dormitory, backs were added to the seats in the refectory, the infirmary was broken up into small, more private, chambers, a great bell called Jesus was added to Benedict which already hung in the bell-tower. Significantly, the guest chamber and the lay brothers' infirmary kitchen were demolished. Subsequently, Abbot Thomas Burton, the author of the abbey's chronicle, repaired the infirmary cloister and the

precinct wall, in addition to having three new bells cast between 1396 and 1399. Nothing is known of the later development of the abbey, and three years after the house was suppressed in 1539, its buildings were demolished to provide stone for Henry VIII's new fortifications at Hull.

The complete precinct and its home or North grange survive as exceptionally clear earthworks covering some 85 acres (34ha). The church — which was about 260 feet (79m) long with an aisled nave of nine bays — lies at the centre of the precinct. The cloister was positioned to the south, with an enclosed inner court situated to the west of the west range, and the infirmary complex to the south-east of the cloister. Excavations by G. K. Beaulah in the 1960s investigated the eastern parts of the church including the eastern bays of the nave, and part of the chapter house. Large areas of mosaic tile floor of about 1249–69 remained in place, and the planning of the three-bay eastern arm was seen to resemble the presbytery at Jervaulx, with no ambulatory but with five chapels against the east wall. The transepts had two chapels, and the clustered columns of the nave had semicircular major shafts and keeled minor shafts which suggest a date in the late 1170s or early 1180s.

Bond 1866–68
Fergusson 1983
Fergusson 1984a, 133–36
Sheppard 1926–28

MEDMENHAM ABBEY

It is perhaps unfortunate that Medmenham is now most widely remembered for its association with Sir Francis Dashwood's 'Monks of Medmenham', or 'Hell Fire Club', which sometimes met on the site in the years between 1755 and 1763. It is perhaps also true that more is known about that periodic gathering of ungodly rakes than about the Cistercian abbey.

The abbey had a rather uncertain earlier history. The manor which formed the

basis of its endowments was confirmed to the monks by the founder, Hugh de Bolebec, in 1201, though it seems that this initial grant was inadequate to maintain the community which eventually came to the site from Woburn in 1204. Consequently, the monks returned to their mother house in the same year, and it was only by about 1212 that there seems to have been a small permanent community here.

1201/04–1536

The site of Medmenham Abbey is about half a mile (0.8km) south of Medmenham Church, off the A4155, about 3 miles (4.8km) south-west of Marlow. Very little remains visible of the abbey, the site of which is occupied by the private house which takes its name from the abbey.

Buckinghamshire
Lincoln

SU 807838

The founder was so devoted to his abbey that he took their habit *ad succurrendum* as his death approached. Unfortunately, however, his children appear not to have shared his enthusiasm, and his daughter, Isabella, countess of Oxford, attempted to claim land back from the abbey, while his son went so far as to expel the monks. It was as late as 1230 that an interim settlement was reached, with final settlement in 1241.

The community seems never to have been in a thriving condition, and it was dissolved in the first onslaught on the monasteries, in 1536, when there was only one monk apart from the abbot. There are very few physical vestiges of the complex, apart from one thirteenth-century quatrefoil-shaped pier from the church and what may be part of the walling of the west range. The house now occupying the site is largely of the late nineteenth century, but has a core of about 1569, which is thought to have been built partly over the east claustral range and partly over the adjacent north transept. The cruciform church was to the south of the house.

Pevsner and Williamson 1994, 468
RCHME 1912, 255

MELROSE ABBEY

1136–1560

The abbey is on the eastern edge of the town of Melrose, on the A609, about 4 miles (6.5km) east of Galashiels. The extensive remains of the abbey church and commendator's house, together with the excavated foundations of the conventual buildings, are in the care of Historic Scotland, and are open to the public on a regular basis.

Scottish Borders
Glasgow

NT 548341

Melrose was founded in 1136 by King David I (1124–53), possibly under the influence of Ailred of Rievaulx (d. 1167), who had earlier been a close friend. The first monks came from Rievaulx, and Melrose in its turn was to be the mother house of four other Scottish abbeys, as well as of Holmcultram in northern England. David's stepson, St Waldef, after a period with Ailred became Melrose's second abbot, and his tomb in the chapter house was to become a focus of pilgrimage.

The church was sufficiently complete for a dedication in 1146. Excavation in the 1920s showed that this church was set out on a variant of the Bernardine type of plan, very like that at Rievaulx and Fountains, in which the transept chapels immediately flanking the rectangular presbytery stepped forward to create an echelon arrangement. Fragmentary remains of the extensive monastic ranges which went with this church, and of a number of the outbuildings within the wider precinct, have also been found through excavation. It is clear that there was regular expansion of those buildings to house a growing community and to meet changing needs. It can now be very difficult to understand the evidence for such changes, but excavation in 1996 has suggested, for example, that the chapter house was rebuilt at least twice in its history. The surviving lower part of its handsome entrance front probably dates from shortly before 1240, when it is known the remains of earlier abbots were reburied, and the earlier parts of an ambitious tiled pavement were probably laid about then.

Because the abbey's water supply was from the river Tweed, to the north, the monastic buildings were all on that side. A lade carried water from the river, and from this a system of drains was threaded through the buildings which required them. The abbot's hall, of which no more than foundations survive, is on the south bank of the lade. Further west is a house which replaced it, probably in the mid-fifteenth century, and which was remodelled for one of the post-Reformation commendators in 1590. That house, which was heavily restored to its presumed sixteenth-century state in 1934, now contains an important collection of carved

Right: Founded by King David I of Scotland in 1136, the abbey church at Melrose was entirely rebuilt in the later Middle Ages, with work underway by 1389. This view shows the church from the north-east corner of the cloister.

stones (including what is thought to have been part of the tomb of St Waldef), as well as pottery, tiles and other artefacts found within the abbey.

The finest element of the abbey at Melrose is the church as rebuilt in the late Middle Ages, which is still as beautiful as a ruin as it must have been when more complete, and its ruins have been a source of inspiration for both artists and writers since at least the eighteenth century. Of particular importance for the history of taste is the fact that its architecture was reflected both in Sir Walter Scott's influential Gothic revival house at Abbotsford, and in the monument erected to commemorate him in Edinburgh.

Rebuilding of the church was necessitated by the destruction caused by the armies of Richard II (1377–99) of England in 1385. Reconstruction was under way in 1389, though it seems the scale of the new

work was so great that it was never completed. Nevertheless, what was built probably represents the single most important church of the later Middle Ages in Scotland, because of what it can tell us about the changing attitudes of architectural patrons and their master masons. Although Scottish and English architecture had been closely inter-related from the early twelfth to the early fourteenth centuries, the bitter warfare between the two countries in the course of the fourteenth century had led to a breakdown in this relationship. When more buildings started to be erected in Scotland from the end of the fourteenth century onwards, a new approach to architectural design began to emerge, with inspiration being sought from further afield than England. The successive phases of

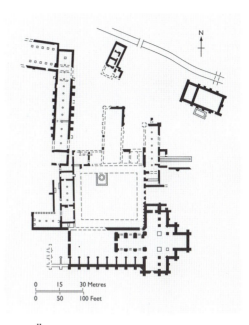

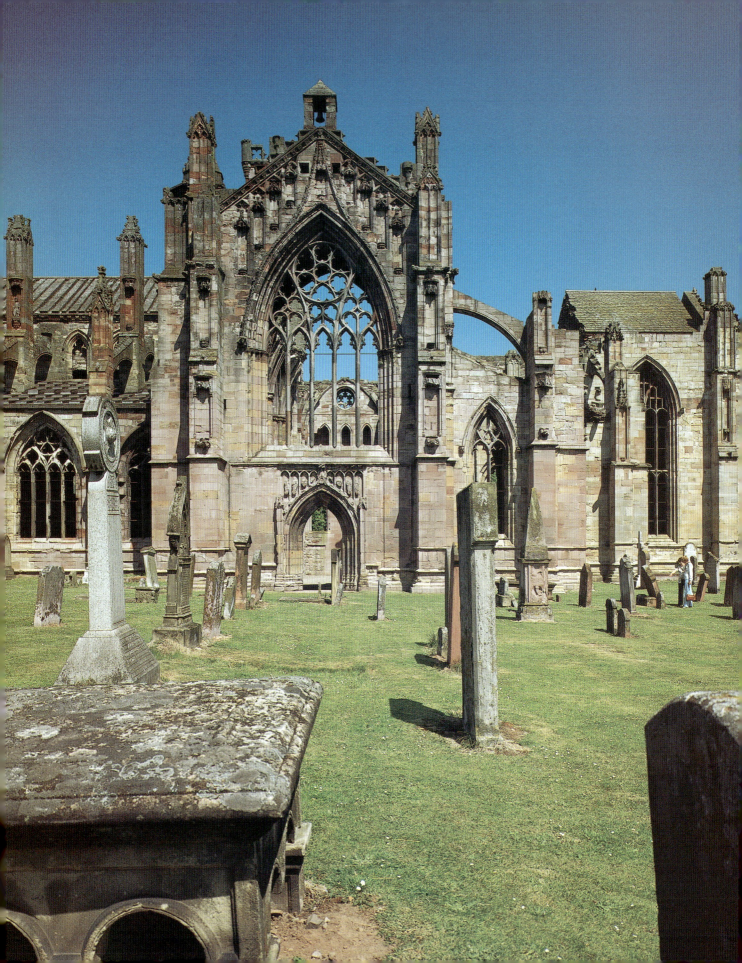

work at Melrose allow us to understand this process better than almost anywhere else.

The church is both a conservative and an advanced building. The conservatism is seen in the way the new church was laid out on a larger version of the original plan, with a rectangular presbytery flanked by an echelon arrangement of chapels. The only deviation from the original plan was the decision to add a row of chapels down the side of the nave away from the cloister, though this was in keeping with Cistercian practice elsewhere. In other respects, however, the various stages of the church were in the vanguard of taste.

The first phase of rebuilding probably saw construction of most of the presbytery, the outer walls of the transepts and the arcades of the monks' choir in the nave. These were almost certainly designed by a mason trained in England, since the windows have grid-like Perpendicular tracery of a type found nowhere other than England, and the presbytery has a form of vaulting with a net-like pattern, which is also of a type that had originated in England. But this first part of Melrose stands out as being especially English because very few other buildings of the period in Scotland were to follow current English fashions in this way.

At Melrose we can appreciate particularly well how architectural attitudes in Scotland were to change, because in the south transept and adjoining areas where the walls had been built as part of the first phase of work, tracery was installed which is very different from that in the presbytery. Instead of grid-like patterns, there are sinuously flowing forms which look more like continental than English work. The reason for this change of appearance is explained within the transept by an inscription which records that a Paris-born mason, John Morow, was at work, and that inscription also lists other places where he had worked.

Morow's work in and around the south transept shows how Scottish patrons were beginning to look to the European continent for ideas, though not only to France. Again, Melrose provides important evidence for another source of ideas. In 1441 it was said that several years earlier the abbey had ordered wooden choir stalls from Cornelius de Aeltre, the head of the carpenters' trade in Bruges (in what is now Belgium), but that they had not been delivered. It was also said that the stalls were to have been copied from those at the Cistercian abbeys of Ter Duinen and Thosan (Ter Doest), near Bruges, which suggests that the monks of Melrose had a very clear idea of what they were wanting. Eventually, Cornelius promised to come to Melrose to deliver and fit the stalls, though he sought assurances that he would not be molested.

Melrose thus demonstrates how patrons were prepared to look for ideas to France (with which there were now close political and diplomatic links) and also to the Low Countries (which had become Scotland's closest trading partner), and ideas were probably sought from other countries as well. But by the mid-fifteenth century Scottish master masons were developing greater confidence in their abilities to assimilate such fresh ideas into their own architectural vocabulary, and we find a new approach to design developing. Yet again we see this at Melrose, because work linked with Abbot Andrew Hunter (1441–71) on the evidence of heraldry shows an awareness of the wider European architectural scene without being particularly indebted to any one country.

Work probably progressed little further west than the three eastern bays of the nave, in which the monks had their choir; although the outer row of chapels was continued five bays further west down the nave, it probably went no further than that, since part of the original west front was allowed to remain in place at that point. But there is one puzzle in this. Finishing only so much of the building presented few problems for the monks, since by this stage there were almost

This effigy of the Virgin and Child, which stands in a niche on the south transept at Melrose, is perhaps the finest piece of medieval figure sculpture to survive in Scotland.

The presbytery and south transept at Melrose seen from the south-east.

Left: The superb work in and around the south transept at Melrose was designed by the Paris-born mason, John Morrow.

This corbel, depicting the reclining figure of a man bearing a scroll, is on one of the buttresses of the south transept at Melrose.

Bower 1852
Curle 1935–37
Fawcett 1994a, 33–34, 78–81
Fawcett 1994b, 28–36, 93–97
Innes 1837
Knowles and St Joseph 1952, 64–65
MacGibbon and Ross 1896–97, **2**, 344–82
Morton 1832
RCAMS 1956, **2**, 265–91
Richardson 1928-29, 293–97
Wood and Richardson 1995

1148–1538

The site of the abbey lies within a working farm on a private road on the east side of the B4116, 1 mile (1.6km) south-west of Atherstone. There is public access to the gate chapel.

Warwickshire
Coventry and Lichfield

SP 295977

Bloxham 1863–64
Dugdale 1730, 782–83
Fergusson 1984a, 136
Pevsner and Wedgwood 1966, 351
VCH Warwick 1908, 75–78

certainly no lay brethren requiring a separate choir within the western bays of the nave. However, by the later Middle Ages the layfolk of the settlement which had grown up beyond the abbey's walls were using the church for their parochial worship, though we do not know which part they were allowed to use. One possibility is the south transept, and this could be supported by the way in which a doorway was provided in the gable wall of that transept, possibly as a slight afterthought.

The idea that the south transept doorway was used by the layfolk may also be supported by later developments. In about 1621 (fifteen years after the abbey's estates had been erected into a temporal lordship for John Ramsay, Viscount Haddington), it was decided to create a parish church within the area of the monks' choir, and one entrance to it seems to have been by the south transept, over which the parish's bellcot was placed. This inserted church was an extraordinary structure, with a pointed barrel vault rising higher than the original vault had done, and supported by massive and ungainly piers in front of the original north arcade piers. The ends of this new church were enclosed to the east by a wall below the west tower arch, and to the west by a wall above the stone screen at the end of the monks' choir.

This post-Reformation church remained in use until the duke of Buccleuch, the principal heritor (landowner) of the parish, decided that a new church should be built elsewhere in the town in 1808. The end walls of the new church were then taken down, though not the vault or its supporting piers, in order to allow the beauties of the church to be seen, and successive dukes took steps to preserve the ruins. In 1919 the abbey was placed in State care and the church and monastic buildings were excavated and laid out for public access between 1921 and 1936.

MEREVALE ABBEY

Merevale Abbey was founded in 1148 by Robert de Ferrers, earl of Derby (d. 1159), as the second daughter house of Bordesley. Its site is now occupied by a working farm, but the *capella ante portas* remains in use as a church and retains some medieval window glass. According to the seventeenth-century antiquary, William Dugdale, parts of the central buildings had been converted to a house by Sir William Devereux after the suppression of the house in 1538.

The site was partly excavated from 1849 by M. H. Bloxham who recovered the partial plan of the church with an aisleless presbytery, deep transepts with three eastern chapels, and an aisled nave. A short length of the south aisle wall survives in one of the two older barns on the site and this shows no evidence of articulation. Bloxham concluded that the church had been entirely rebuilt in the fourteenth century, though it appears to have retained its twelfth-century ground plan.

The cloister lay on the south side of the church, and its south range partly survives in a second barn. This range comprised an east–west refectory with the kitchen to its west. Both refectory and kitchen doors survive and are clearly of early thirteenth-century date.

The gate chapel, now the parish church, has a two-bay aisled nave of the late thirteenth century, and a four-bay chancel of the fifteenth century. The windows contain some medieval glass.

NEATH ABBEY

Following his visit to Neath in the 1530s, the Tudor antiquary John Leland (d. 1552) described it as 'the fairest abbey of all Wales'. Long since shattered, the ruins are none the less expansive and of great interest. For many who encounter the site for the first time, Neath often comes as a great surprise.

It was in 1129 that Richard de Granville — one of the *conquistadores* of the lordship of Glamorgan — decided to grant his large but outlying fee on the west bank of the river Neath to the Norman abbey of the Holy Trinity at Savigny. Richard's gifts, which included 8,000 acres (3,240ha) of 'waste' between the Neath and Tawe rivers, were intended for the foundation of a new monastery. So it was that Savigny sent out its second colony across the English Channel, with Abbot Richard (d. 1145) and his twelve monks arriving at Neath in October 1130.

Even before the merger with the Cistercians in 1147, the fledgling community was busy building up the strength of its estates. The monks were to discover, however, that their lands were far too scattered to be managed efficiently. Such was the precarious position in which they found themselves in the 1190s, careful thought was given to transferring the entire monastery to the site of its property at Exford in Somerset. The plan was effectively scotched when, in 1198, the abbey of Cleeve was established barely 10 miles (16km) east of Exford. Thereafter, Neath began a concerted effort to consolidate its holdings closer to home. And, despite a series of bitter land disputes fought with the neighbouring house at Margam, these endeavours were eventually rewarded. At the end of the thirteenth century, Neath stood as one of the wealthier abbeys of Wales. In 1291 its annual income was assessed at about £236, and the brothers were farming more than 5,000 acres (2,224ha) of arable, with almost 5,000 sheep on their pastures.

Meanwhile, over the twelfth and thirteenth centuries, the desire if not the need for constant rebuilding had proved singularly potent. At first, the Savigniac colony which arrived in 1130 may have been accommodated in temporary wooden structures, possibly even located at the founder's nearby castle. Nevertheless, a comparatively modest stone church was probably built at the permanent site within a decade or so of the foundation. Indeed, an outline plan has been reconstructed, and it is suggested that this early church was of broadly similar proportions to the twelfth-century examples known from Waverley and Tintern.

In terms of the surviving abbey buildings at Neath, the earliest is the west range, intended as usual for the accommodation of the lay brothers. It could have been raised in the 1170s, though it also incorporates many features more likely to be of early thirteenth-century date. The range was divided into ten bays by heavy external buttressing. On the ground floor, the stone vault was supported on a row of central columns set along the length of the building. The vault ribs sprang from corbels set into the surrounding walls, and at the southern end these carried capitals attractively decorated with early Gothic scallop motifs. On the upper floor of the range, the lay brothers' dormitory was lit by narrow lancet windows in both of the side walls.

The eastern and southern ranges of monastic buildings, including the chapter house, the inner parlour, the monks' dormitory, and the refectory, were almost entirely rebuilt in the second quarter of the thirteenth century. South of the cloister, from the surviving jambs of its doorway,

1130–1539

Situated west of the river Neath, access to Neath Abbey is off the A465. The remains include much of the east and west ranges of monastic buildings, a large Gothic church of about 1280–1320, and a Tudor mansion begun in the 1540s. The site, which is in the care of Cadw: Welsh Historic Monuments, is accessible at all reasonable times.

Neath Port Talbot
Llandaff

SS 738973

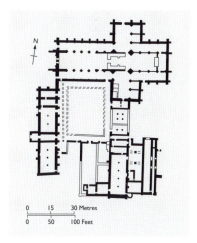

An earlier fourteenth-century roof boss, depicting Christ in Majesty, from the vault of the abbey church at Neath.

The rib-vaulted dormitory undercroft at Neath may have served as the monks' day room. It is one of the most captivating pieces of White Monk architecture in Wales.

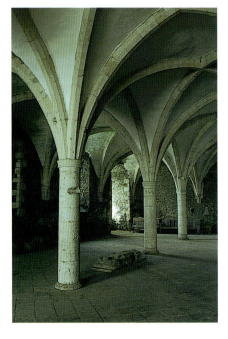

Two tall buttresses convey an impression of the scale of the west front of the church at Neath.

the entrance into the refectory was particularly fine. It was set between two recesses housing the lavers where the brothers washed before going into meals. Over in the east range, there is now little to be seen of the chapter house, but south of this lies one of the most captivating pieces of White Monk architecture to survive anywhere in Wales. The five-bay rib-vaulted dormitory undercroft is a creation of pure Cistercian austerity, and yet at the same time it manages to be one of undeniable beauty.

During the time of Abbot Adam of Carmarthen (1266–89), a decision was taken to finally replace the twelfth-century Romanesque church with a brand new Gothic construction. As at Tintern, it is assumed that building would have progressed in such a way that the community could continue to use the old church for as long as possible. Work may have begun around 1280, though the scheme was not completed until about 1320. Stylistic differences to be observed in some of the detailing of the windows may indicate at least one break in the overall programme. On a visit to Neath in 1284, King Edward I seems to have given his approval to the building scheme,

presenting the abbot with 'a very beautiful baudekyn'. This was perhaps a *baldacchino*, or canopy, intended for the high altar.

As finished, the internal length of the new church was about 203 feet (61.9m). Enough evidence survives to show that, in the nave, the elevation was of the familiar two-storey Cistercian form. The arcades were carried on clustered piers with large, half-round shafts set at the cardinal directions, and with smaller rounded shafts in the angles between them. Stone vaults covered the whole of the church, and the bosses were carved with both foliate and figurative sculpture. A splendid example bearing an image of Christ in Majesty is to be seen in the dormitory undercroft.

During the fifteenth century, Neath was beset by a catalogue of financial difficulties. But around 1500, as the house was recovering, one of its last abbots began to adapt the southern end of the dormitory and refectory ranges to provide himself with a handsome suite of private accommodation. From about 1509 until the dissolution, these new apartments were occupied by Leyshon Thomas, the most influential Cistercian abbot of late-medieval Wales. Under his leadership, and through his reputation, the abbey was to enjoy something of an Indian summer. The poet Lewis Morgannwg was particularly impressed. His eulogy in praise of Neath refers to 'crystal windows of every colour'; to the 'gold-adorned choir, the nave, the gilded tabernacle work, the pinnacles'; and to a 'vast and lofty roof ... like the sparkling heavens on high'. Even allowing for characteristic bardic exaggeration, Lewis Morgannwg's verse conveys an impression of abbey buildings which would have appeared very different from those expected by the Cistercian fathers of the early twelfth century.

With the suppression at hand, in 1535 Neath's income was assessed at little more than £130. Only on payment of the heavy fine of £150 did Abbot Leyshon manage to avoid the closure of his house along with the lesser monasteries in the following year. Dearly bought, the delay was but temporary. In February 1539, the abbot and his seven remaining monks surrendered Neath to the king's visitors. Three years later, Sir Richard Williams *alias* Cromwell (d. 1545) was allowed to purchase the site and much of the abbey's former Glamorgan estates. Parts of the monastic buildings were subsequently transformed into a splendid Tudor mansion, itself to become abandoned by the early years of the eighteenth century.

Birch 1902
Butler 1976a
Butler 1984
Newman 1995, 463–71
Robinson 1997b

NETLEY ABBEY

The foundation of Netley Abbey — the first daughter house of Beaulieu — is to be attributed to the great royal servant, Peter des Roches, bishop of Winchester (1205–38). Towards the end of his life, Peter became much enamoured with the Cistercians, and was resolved to create one new house in his native France (la Clarté-Dieu in Touraine), and another in the diocese over which he had long presided. About 1236, Bishop Peter began buying up the various estates which were to provide for the endowment of the English abbey. At the time of his death, in June

1239–1536

Netley is situated about 3 miles (4.8km) south-east of central Southampton. The extensive remains include much of the church and the east range of claustral buildings. The site is in the care of English Heritage and is open at all reasonable times.

Hampshire
Winchester

SU 453089

The original plans for the foundation of Netley were made by Bishop Peter des Roches of Winchester (1205–38), though patronage of the house was assumed by King Henry III. This aerial view shows the abbey church and cloister from the north.

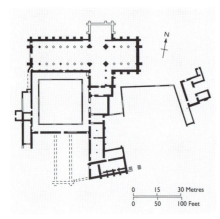

The design of the east window at Netley may have been inspired by broadly contemporary work at Westminster Abbey. It is one of the few signs in the building of Henry III's patronage.

1238, the skilful process of negotiation was sadly unfinished, and the final arrangements were left to the hands of his executors. Meanwhile, as a further mark of his devotion to the White Monks, Peter's heart was buried at Waverley, their earliest house on British shores.

The corporate existence of Bishop Peter's monastery began in July 1239, with its initial name, *Locus Sancti Edwardi* or Lieu-Saint-Edward, clearly derived from its dedication. Indeed, given King Henry III's devotion to St Edward the Confessor, it seems very likely that Peter had taken care to commend his proposals for the foundation to his sovereign. By the summer of 1241, the infant community had acquired land on the densely wooded northern shore of Southampton water, and the abbey buildings had been started at a place then known indifferently as Letley or Netley. Up until this time, although the king had made several token gifts to the house, including altar wine, chalices, and two bells, there is precious little evidence to suggest that he had made any significant contributions, either landed or financial. However, in a fascinating sequence of events, Henry gradually began to adopt the mantle of founder. The first positive signs can be traced to March 1244, when he ordered that £100 was to be supplied to the abbey of Lieu-Saint-Edward, 'whereof the king wishes to lay the first stone as founder'. Henry's foundation stone can still be seen in the footings of the north-east crossing pier, inscribed H: DI. GRA. REX ANGL (Henry, by the grace of God, king of England). From this position as a mere contributor to the foundation of the house, by 1251 Henry undoubtedly regarded himself as *the* founder, issuing three royal charters in this role. The king's motives for these actions may well have been connected with the plans of his brother, Richard of Cornwall, to establish the prestigious Cistercian house at Hailes in Gloucestershire.

In fact, almost all of Netley's annual income was derived from those lands which had been so carefully purchased by Bishop Peter and his executors. The community was to hold a comparatively compact estate, with much of its property located around Southampton water, though with other holdings scattered in several neighbouring counties, including important lands at Gomshall in Surrey, Waddon and Ashley in Dorset, Kingston Deverill in Wiltshire, and North Leigh in Oxfordshire. The one royal gift of land came in 1252–53, when Henry gave the monks a tract of some 300 acres (121ha) of uncultivated heath and scrub in the New Forest which they developed into the grange of Roydon (*le don du roi*). As a whole, it must be said, the abbey's endowments were not especially lavish, and it was certainly never one of the richer houses of southern England. In 1535, when the community numbered just seven monks, the assessed annual income was barely more than £100. Even so, Netley's buildings were described by the dissolution commissioners as 'large' and 'great', and 'in a good state of repair'.

The upstanding fabric suggests that the construction programme began with the east end of the abbey church, though the building of the east claustral range must also have been an early priority. The king's grant of thirty cartloads of lead from Derbyshire, together with timber from the forest of Bere and the New Forest, indicates a major phase of roofing work about 1251–52. Henry gave twenty more oaks for the fabric of the church in 1254, though from the stylistic details it seems the nave was not completed for several more decades. Eventually, the church was about 237 feet (72m) long, with a plan very typical of that favoured by the British Cistercians in the thirteenth-century. One unusual feature was the positioning of the high altar directly against the inner face of the east end, whereas the rectangular form of the presbytery as a whole apparently owed little to the apsidal design seen at the mother house.

The overall impression of the abbey church at Netley is of a building straddling the ideals of Cistercian austerity and rich cathedral splendour. In the principal elevations, for example, two storeys were presented in the guise of three. The upper storey was framed by a large arch, accommodating a wall-passage in the lower section, and with the clerestory windows raised in such a way that their sills avoided the level of the aisle roofs. For the most part, the surviving windows in the presbytery and in the south aisle of the nave are plain, taking the form of grouped lancets with simple chamfers. The east window, on the other hand, was far more sumptuous, and comprised a cusped oculus set over four lights. The inner splays featured detached marble shafts, and the head was elaborately moulded. Distinctly reminiscent of broadly contemporary work at Westminster Abbey, this window is perhaps one of the very few signs of Henry III's patronage in the building.

Once again, it is very largely the evidence of the window tracery which points to a later date for the final completion of the nave. In particular, the slightly higher middle light in each group of three lancets within the north aisle has cusped tracery of a late thirteenth-century type, whereas the main window in the west front could have been a work of the early fourteenth century. Thereafter, the only clear evidence of subsequent building within the church appears in the south transept. From the surviving springers, with their panelled decoration, it seems a new vault was at least planned over the main vessel of the transept towards the end of the fifteenth century.

In terms of the monastic buildings, the east range was almost certainly completed within a decade or so of the foundation. Here, adjacent to the south transept, the three attractive rib-vaulted bays were initially divided into the sacristy and book store. Next to these lies the chapter house, the façade of which was one of the more elaborate features of Netley, with the jambs of the central doorway and its flanking window openings adorned with polished marble capitals and detached shafts. Overhead, the monks' dormitory extended in the usual way along the full length of the east range. At right-angles to the southern end of the dormitory was the monks' latrine building. The four-bay vaulted chamber on the ground floor, with a large fireplace in its north wall, may have served — at least for some period of the abbey's history — as the novices' lodging. Little remains of the medieval arrangements in the south range, though the monks' refectory was undoubtedly arranged at right-angles to the southern alley of the cloister. There is also very little left of the monastic west range. East of the main complex, a detached two-storey block of thirteenth-century date is generally interpreted as the abbot's lodging. On each floor, there appears to have been a hall and a private chamber, and possibly a chapel.

Following its dissolution, in 1536 Netley was granted to Sir William Paulet (d. 1572), later marquis of Winchester, who transformed the monastery into a Tudor country house. Much of the conversion work was carried out in brick. The nave was turned into a hall and kitchen, and the presbytery was converted for use as a chapel. Paulet's private wing was built out of the south transept, with a great chamber inserted at first-floor level. The former monastic dormitory became the long gallery. The monastic refectory was levelled, and a grand entrance created with a central doorway flanked by polygonal turrets. The cloister alleys were destroyed, and the open space served as a courtyard with a fountain at the centre.

The house was occupied by Paulet's successors for much of the seventeenth century. It was sold sometime after 1676 and soon began to fall out of use. Within a century Netley had become a greatly celebrated ruin, featuring in the verse of Romantic poets, and in many illustrations in the Picturesque tradition.

The south transept and the entrance to the chapter house at Netley viewed from the south-west.

Hare 1993
Knowles and St Joseph 1952, 136–37
Meekings 1979
Thompson 1953
VCH Hampshire 1903, 146–49; 1908, 472–76

NEWBATTLE ABBEY

1140–1560

The site of Newbattle Abbey is off the B703, about 1 mile (1.6km) south of Dalkeith, and about 7 miles (11km) south-east of Edinburgh. Parts of the east claustral range are embodied within the house which takes its name from the abbey, while the plan of the church is partly marked by beds within the lawns. The abbey is not generally accessible to the public.

Midlothian
St Andrews

NT 333660

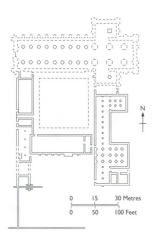

King David I (1124–53) and his son, Henry (d. 1153), were the joint founders of Newbattle in 1140, and the first monks were brought from David's earlier foundation of Melrose. Provision of temporary buildings for the new abbey was presumably started immediately, though all of the known details of the church point to a date of construction for that part starting not long before 1200. There was a dedication in 1233. As might be expected in a position so close to Edinburgh, the abbey suffered in the wars with England, being burned in King Richard II's campaign of 1385, with a further attack at the time of the 'Rough Wooing' of 1544 and another in 1548. Following the latter attack six monks were carried off to England, and by the Reformation there were only about fifteen monks, whereas there had been twenty-four with the abbot in 1528.

Following the resignation of the last abbot in 1547, a member of the powerful local family of Ker was provided as the abbey's first commendator, a family connection with the site which continued until 1957. The abbey was erected into a temporal lordship for the son of the first commendator in 1587, and by 1606 he had been created earl of Lothian. As happened at several Scottish Cistercian houses, the commendators continued to live within the abbey, adapting its buildings to meet their needs; but Newbattle is the only abbey of the order where the house remains in use, though it was adapted to serve as a college of adult education in 1957 after the twelfth marquess of Lothian donated it for this purpose.

The house of the commendators grew up over the east claustral range, and everything which lay outside the area of the house was progressively destroyed. Excavation of the site of the church in 1878 showed that it had had an aisled nave of ten bays, and transepts with two chapels on the east side of each. The eastern limb of the church was found to be one of only two in the Scottish Cistercian family in which the plan deviated from the Bernardine type, though the precise details are not entirely clear. What seems certain is that an aisle extended down the full length of each side of the short presbytery, and it also seems likely from the strong eastern piers that there was a lower row of eastern chapels, as at Byland. Queen Marie de Coucy was buried within the choir in 1241. Massive diagonal buttresses added to the transepts were perhaps necessitated by the English attacks in the fourteenth or sixteenth centuries, and may hint at more massive repairs to the superstructure.

Excavations in the claustral ranges in 1892–94 showed that the refectory had run parallel with the south cloister walk. The most complete remains of the abbey were found within the later house over the east range, where a number of vaulted undercrofts were restored following their discovery. A domestic chapel was created at the same time within what had probably been the warming house, at the east end of

A vaulted undercroft in the former east range at Newbattle Abbey.

the south range, and within this a wooden floor was laid which replicated some of the superb tile pavements found in the course of the excavations. The chapel also contains a fine font bowl which is decorated with the arms of King James V (1513–42) and the last abbot, James Haswell; this font suggests there may have been a parochial presence in the church by the early sixteenth century.

Carrick 1908
Innes 1849
MacGibbon and Ross 1896–97, **2**, 251–63
McWilliam 1978, 345–48
RCAHMCS 1929, 142–145
Richardson 1928–29, 287–92

NEWENHAM ABBEY

1247–1539

Newenham is situated about 1 mile (1.6km) south-west of Axminster, just off the A358. What little of the abbey survives lies on private ground.

Devon
Exeter

SY 287973

The initial steps in the foundation of Newenham Abbey were taken in the summer of 1246. Reginald de Mohun (d. 1257), lord of Dunster, who sometimes styled himself earl of Somerset, invited Abbot Acius of Beaulieu to decide among three possible sites for a Devon daughter house. In the event, a classic Cistercian location was chosen on a tributary of the river Axe. In the following months, all the necessary lands and endowments were put in place for the support of the new community. Finally, in January 1247, thirteen monks and four lay brothers arrived from Beaulieu to occupy the temporary buildings which had been prepared by Reginald and his brother, William.

The first five abbots followed in rapid succession, and there is no doubt that Beaulieu had to make a special effort to ensure the success of the house. By the turn of the fourteenth century, the tide was beginning to turn, with the prudent government of Abbot John of Coxwell (d. 1324) playing no small part. His successor, John of Gettington (1324–38), further strengthened the abbey's economy and also added buildings. But in 1349, when the Black Death killed twenty monks, the community at Newenham was reduced to just three. Almost two centuries later, in 1535 the abbey's income was assessed at £227. Having survived the first round of closures, it was surrendered by the abbot and nine monks in March 1539.

Very little is known about the overall form or the detail of the buildings at Newenham. An account of 1690 records that by this time there was 'hardly left standing one stone upon another'. Some excavation of the ruins was undertaken in the mid-nineteenth century and an outline plan of the church and cloister was recovered. From the details, including one of the vault bosses found in the church, it would appear that much was completed before the end of the thirteenth century. A foundation stone was laid in 1250. Four years later, in a grander ceremony, the abbot and monks processed from their temporary chapel to the site of the church and watched as the founder laid several stones. In the closing years of his life, Reginald gave the monks a hundred marks (£66) a year towards the building fund. He made them a further gift of seven hundred marks (£466) in his will. On his death in 1257, Reginald was buried near the site of the high altar. At a dedication of the church in July 1270, Bishop Walter Bronescombe (1258–80) of Exeter gave the monks six hundred marks (£400) for the provision of altars. Later, Bishop John Grandisson (1328–69) was to contribute towards the cost of a bell which the community named after him.

Only minor fragments of masonry remain at the site. A farmhouse lies over part of the west range, and part of the south wall of the nave seems to be incorporated within an outbuilding. The church may have exceeded 200 feet (61m) in length, but much of the east end now lies beneath a yard and a barn.

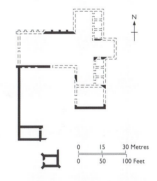

A detail of a vault boss from Newenham Abbey (After Davidson 1843).

Davidson 1843
Rowe 1878, 139–57, 193–98

NEWMINSTER ABBEY

1138–1537

Newminster Abbey is situated about a mile (1.6km) west of Morpeth, close to the junction of the A1 and B6343. The fragmentary and partly reconstructed remains are generally accessible to the public.

Northumberland
Durham

NZ 188857

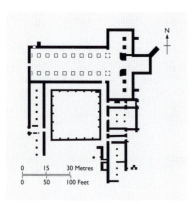

Part of the re-erected cloister arcade at Newminster (Stuart Harrison).

Newminster was one of the first daughters of Fountains, having been founded in 1138 by Ranulf de Merlay, lord of Morpeth, who had it set close to his principal castle. Its first abbot was Robert (1138–59), who had been one of the founding members of Fountains itself, and under his energetic leadership three daughter houses were established at Pipewell (in 1143), Roche (in 1147) and Sawley (also in 1147). By the later thirteenth century it also had two hospitals dependent upon it, at Mitford and Allerburn.

The abbey was endowed with vast tracts of land in Upper Coquetdale, and extending up to the Scottish Border. In addition to farming these acres, the abbey successfully exploited at least some of the mineral resources of its lands, since it is known that coal was burned as a fuel. However, the abbey suffered as a result of its position near the border with Scotland, and even in the year of its foundation it is said to have had a baptism of fire when it was attacked, though it is unlikely that any permanent structures had been completed by then.

The architectural evidence suggests that the main campaign of building was started around the 1150s, before the death of Abbot Robert in 1159, and certainly he was credited with laying out the buildings in the Cistercian manner. However, details of the transepts appear unlikely to date from before the 1180s, which may indicate that the eastern parts were rebuilt around that time; a similar date is almost certain for fragments of the cloister which were found in the 1920s and subsequently re-erected. Further building operations are suggested by the gift of a quarry at Blindwell in 1265, though it is not known what might have been built at that period. In 1429 it was said that Roger of Thornton

had covered the nave roof in lead.

In the course of excavations carried out during the 1920s and 1930s and further work in the 1960s, much of the plan of the abbey was recovered. As might be expected, the church had a short rectangular presbytery, and this was flanked by transepts with three bays of chapels on their eastern side; the aisled nave was nine bays long, and a galilee porch was added along its west front in a later campaign. The cloister was to the south of the church, and its tightly spaced arcading (with some rounded and some pointed arches) was carried on paired shafts with waterleaf capitals. The east range had a library and sacristy immediately next to the transept, with a rectangular chapter house of three by three bays next to them. The impressive round-arched doorway to the chapter house had four orders of shafts with waterleaf capitals. Between the chapter house and dormitory undercroft were a parlour and slype. Little is known of the south range apart from fragments of the day stair and warming room where the range adjoined the dormitory undercroft. Of the west range, extensive evidence for the first ten bays of the lay brethren's undercroft has been located.

Excavation has also revealed some evidence for the decoration which used to be in the church and monastic buildings. Within the chapter house it is said there were brown and white lines in imitation of masonry jointing, while fragments of later figurative paintings depicting the crucifixion and a saint were found in the north transept in 1878. The legend of the life of St Robert suggests, as might have been expected, that the dormitory was limewashed, since a monk is said to have been miraculously saved from a fall by the saint while in the process of applying wash to the walls. In addition to the painted work, fragments of window glass and of tiled floors have been found.

The abbey was dissolved in 1537, at which time there were seventeen priest monks, three junior monks and four choir boys. The income of the house had risen to over £265 on the eve of the dissolution, suggesting that, after a period of decline, its fortunes had revived. The monks resist-ed the closure of the house, and as a result only the abbot and one of his predecessors received pensions. The abbey was acquired by the Grey family, and the buildings were still habitable in the late sixteenth century, when it was in the possession of the second generation of that family. However, it was soon robbed for its building materials, leaving few upstanding fragments.

Fergusson 1984a, 136–38
Fowler 1876
Harbottle and Salway 1964
Knowles and St Joseph 1952, 74–75
Pevsner and Richmond 1992, 518

PIPEWELL ABBEY

Pipewell Abbey, the first daughter house of Newminster, was established by William Butevilain in 1143 on the site of an existing village in the valley of Harper's brook, the boundary between the parishes of Wilbarston and Rushton. Apparently, William had approached both Newminster and Garendon to supply a founding community. Only after a long argument did the Garendon monks withdraw. The abbey was suppressed in 1538, and the site granted to Sir William Parre. Before he could start demolition, the site was looted by the local populace, and a commission was appointed to inves-tigate the theft in 1540. Its report indicated that the buildings remained largely intact but for floors, roofs, and windows. Demolition must have followed soon after, and by 1720 no standing masonry was visible. The site was exam-ined by C. A. Markham in 1908 and 1909, in the second year with the assistance of Harold Brakspear.

The greater part of the precinct survives as earthworks with the church and cloister buildings at the centre. Braks-pear identified a medium sized church some 236 feet (72m) long, with a four-bay aisled presbytery, transepts with east and west aisles, a crossing with a tower, and an aisled nave. Although undated, this is probably the church which was consecrat-ed in 1311 and which is known to have been under construction at the time of Abbot Andrew (1298–1308).

The cloister lay on the south side of the church, and can still be identified as a rela-tively level area surrounded by confused earthworks. Only the chapter house in the east range has been identified, a building dedicated in 1312 and therefore either rebuilt or substantially remodelled. The cloister itself was dedicated in the same year, which suggests that the cloister ranges themselves had been modified in the late thirteenth and early fourteenth centuries. The planning of the cloister ranges cannot be recovered from their earthworks, though the east, south, and west ranges appear to extend as far south as the brook.

The precinct retains good evidence both of water management and stock enclosures. To the west of the precinct was a massive mill pond, with a dam standing 13 feet (4m) high. To the south-west of the cloister buildings are a pair of rectangular fishponds. The most notable feature of the west side of the precinct, however, is a series of quarries, some just small scoops, but others of great depth. All are probably medieval in origin, but some have contin-ued to be worked into the present century.

1143–1538

The site of the abbey lies on the south side of the village of Pipewell, to the east of Pipewell Hall. It is on an unclassified road on the west side of the A6003, 2 miles (3.2km) south-west of Corby. The site is on farm land but can be seen from the road.

Northamptonshire
Lincoln

SP 840856

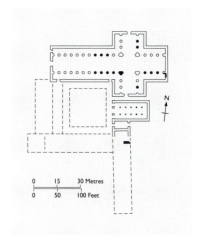

Brakspear 1909–10
Fergusson 1984a, 138
RCHME 1979, 172–74

QUARR ABBEY

1132–1536

Quarr is situated on the Isle of Wight, no more than half a mile (0.8km) from the shore of the Solent, and about 2 miles (3.2km) west of Ryde. Little remains of the abbey buildings apart from a section of the west range and a few fragments of the kitchen and refectory. The site belongs to the nearby Benedictine abbey of Quarr, and is accessible subject to permission.

Hampshire
Winchester

SZ 566927

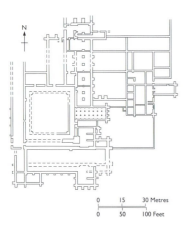

Fergusson 1984a, 138–39
Hockey 1970
Renn 1954
Stone 1891, I, 31–42, 106–12
VCH Hampshire 1903, 137–40; 1912, 152–54

It was probably in 1131 that Baldwin de Redvers (d. 1155) granted 'to the lord Geoffrey, abbot of Savigny, and to the brethren there serving God, land in the Isle of Wight for constructing a monastery'. Baldwin's gifts were to represent the first stage in the foundation of the abbey of Quarr. The small colony of missionary monks, headed by Abbot Gervase, eventually arrived sometime in 1132. They occupied a site which had been prepared for them close to the Solent shore. Baldwin's initial endowments included sizeable estates located across the island. The monks were also given the basis of important holdings at Chark on the Hampshire mainland, and at Farwood in Devon. In common with all Savigniac houses, Quarr was absorbed into the Cistercian community in 1147.

A consecration of the abbey church in 1150 by Henry of Blois, bishop of Winchester (1129–71), must represent a significant stage in the completion of the building. The following year, the strength of the Quarr community was such that it was able to send out a colony to found Stanley Abbey in Wiltshire. More than a century later, in 1278, it provided the monks who settled at Buckland in Devon. In the fourteenth century, during the English war with France, Quarr's prosperity suffered as a result of its exposed island location. In 1365, Abbot William was licensed to build stone walls to fortify the abbey and its property against invaders. There were ten monks at the house in 1535, with its annual income assessed at about £134. Quarr was dissolved in July 1536, and within four years its buildings had been comprehensively demolished and the stone used to build new coastal fortifications at East and West Cowes.

Today, the most prominent survival at Quarr is a section of the lay brothers'

Little of the abbey at Quarr survives above ground, though fragments are incorporated in the farmhouse which stands on the south-west side of the site (University of Warwick, Richard K. Morris).

range, now incorporated within a barn. There are also traces of the kitchen, with its serving hatch through to the monks' refectory. A somewhat schematic plan of the entire site was recovered during limited excavations in 1891. From this work, it is clear that the church lay south of the cloister and the monastic buildings. The plan shows a fairly typical early Cistercian church, perhaps compatible with the consecration date of 1150. It featured a short, square-ended presbytery, with three chapels to each of the transepts. The chapels flanking the north and south sides of the presbytery were probably later additions. The chapter house, which also seems later, appears to have been arranged in seven bays. Its vault was carried on twelve central columns, and on responds along the lateral walls. Beyond the main claustral complex, parts of the abbey's precinct walls survive.

REVESBY ABBEY

The fourth daughter house of Rievaulx, Revesby Abbey was founded by William de Roumare I, earl of Lincoln, on the northern edge of the Lincolnshire fen in 1143. The founding abbot was Ailred (d. 1167), who left to become head of Rievaulx in 1146. The new abbey was established on the site of an existing village which was depopulated and its existing church of St Lawrence used as a temporary church by the monks. Revesby was a moderately wealthy house, having an assessed annual income of about £287 in 1535. On the eve of its dissolution in 1538, the house was reported to be in 'great ruin and decay'. The site was subsequently granted to Charles Brandon, duke of Suffolk (1514–45).

Permanent building began on a new site about half a mile (0.8km) south of the original in the middle years of the twelfth century. The abbey church, partly excavated in 1869, had an aisled presbytery with ambulatory and eastern chapels, transepts with two eastern chapels, and an aisled nave of seven bays with piers rising from octagonal bases. What little is now visible appears to date to the later twelfth century. One of the witnesses to a charter of about 1170–98 signed himself as Master William 'of the new work', which suggests that building was still going on at this time.

Earthworks indicate a cloister on the south side of the church, and a standard late twelfth-century Cistercian layout. The lay brothers' cloister, to the west of the west range is particularly clear. The church and cloister ranges lay at the centre of an extensive precinct which is clearly defined. A series of moated enclosures on the west side of the precinct probably represents late medieval gardens (one is still called the Saffron Garth), while at the north-east corner there is a series of fishponds.

1143–1538

The site of the abbey lies on farmland half a mile (0.8km) south of the village of Revesby and the A155, on the west side of the B1183. There is no public access.

Lincolnshire
Lincoln

TF 300607

Below: *The earthworks at Revesby define not only the church and cloister, but also an extensive precinct (Cambridge University Collection).*

Barker 1869
Fergusson 1984a, 139–40
Knowles and St Joseph 1952, 128–29
Pevsner and Harris 1989, 610
VCH Lincolnshire 1906, 141–43

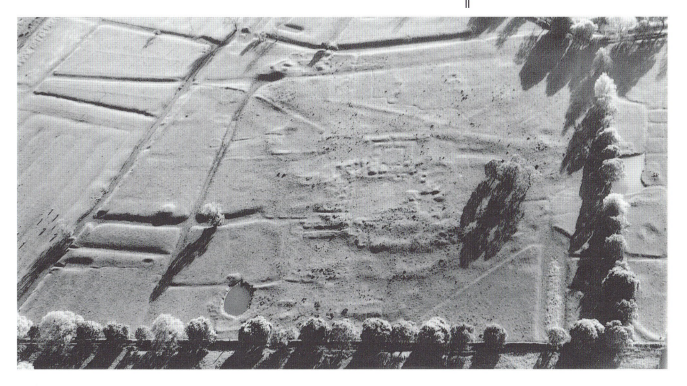

REWLEY ABBEY

1281–1536

Rewley Abbey lay on the north side of the A420, on the west side of Oxford. It is now industrial land to the east of Oxford railway station. There are no standing remains.

Oxfordshire
Lincoln

SP 596064

VCH Oxfordshire 1907, 81–83

Rewley Abbey was founded in 1281 by Edmund, earl of Cornwall (d. 1300), as a daughter house of Thame. It was initially designed to serve as a college for Cistercian monks close to the university of Oxford. The original foundation was an abbot and fourteen monks, but in 1292 it was decreed that every Cistercian abbey in the province of Canterbury should send one monk in twenty there as a student. By 1344, the General Chapter was fining houses who were reluctant to send monks to Oxford, and Rewley was criticized as too remote from the town and lacking in books. It ceased its collegiate role before 1398. In 1437 Archbishop Henry Chichele (1414–43) founded St Bernard's (now St John's) College to serve the order within the university. In 1535 Rewley's assessed income was given as £174, and it was suppressed in the following year.

The site has been partially excavated, revealing the aisled nave of the church with a cloister to its north-west which had an overshot cloister alley on its east side, together with a substantial but unidentified building at its south-west corner. Historical sources identify a chapel in the north range, and this area has been tentatively identified as the college buildings attached to the house. The main cloister was to the south of the church, though this area was badly disturbed and the layout of its buildings remains uncertain.

RIEVAULX ABBEY

1132–1538

Rievaulx Abbey is situated in the village of Rievaulx, on an unclassified road south of the B1257 between Helmsley and Stokesley, a little over 2 miles (3.2km) north-west of Helmsley. The very extensive remains of the church and monastic buildings are in the care of English Heritage and are open to the public.

North Yorkshire
York

SE 576849

Walter Espec (d. 1154), a royal justiciar and lord of Helmsley, granted the vills of Griff and Tilleston to Abbot Bernard for the founding of a Cistercian abbey in 1131. The site was colonized in March 1132 by a group of monks from Clairvaux, many of them Yorkshiremen who had joined the order in Burgundy. Rievaulx was the first Cistercian monastery to be established in the north of England and it was intended from the first to be a mission centre for the order in the colonization of the north and of Scotland. Indeed, its foundation triggered a revolt at the Benedictine abbey of St Mary's in York, which culminated in the foundation of Fountains Abbey later the same year.

Today, Rievaulx survives as substantial ruins set in a precinct of some 100 acres (40.5ha) in the deep valley of the river Rye, within the eighteenth-century landscape of Duncombe Park. Its buildings, substantially of the later twelfth and thirteenth centuries, are complex, heavily ruined in part, and of enormous scale, making their interpretation difficult. The site was taken into State care in 1917 and was substantially excavated by Charles Peers between 1919 and 1929, during which time the ruins, many exposed for the first time since their demolition in 1538–39, were conserved for public display. What is visible today are the remains of the second and third monasteries to be built on what was a difficult site in a narrow valley where the church could not be laid out east to west but had to be aligned from south to north.

The first monastery, set out by the Clairvaux monk Geoffrey d'Ainai, was of

The south transept and the east end of the abbey church at Rievaulx, seen over the foundations of the dormitory range and the infirmary cloister.

timber. Its location is unknown but is likely to have been close to the site of the later cloister laid out in the abbacy of the first abbot, William, between 1132 and 1145. The earliest permanent building appears to have been a narrow unaisled church (Rievaulx I) with shallow transepts with a single chapel in each, and a short square presbytery which has been traced by geophysical survey below the north side of the later cloister. Associated with this were temporary timber buildings which were gradually replaced by permanent ranges 27 feet (8.2m) wide, of which the surviving west range is one. The early east range, traced below the later chapter house, must also date from William's abbacy, and this indicates that the cloister was laid out as a square of 140 feet (42.7m) from the first. A large permanent church must have been intended to close the east side of this

cloister, but there is no indication that it was begun before William's death in 1145.

In 1134, Ailred, the steward of King David of Scotland, entered Rievaulx as a novice. In 1143 he was dispatched as the founding abbot of Revesby, and in 1147 he returned as abbot of Rievaulx. From then until his death in 1167 he completed the rebuilding of Abbot William's monastery on a massive scale. Construction began with a monumental church and chapter house in about 1150. The church, of which the nave and transepts remain, was an austere building with a short square-ended presbytery, transepts with three eastern chapels, the inner ones of which were extended by a full half bay to the east, an unstressed crossing, and an aisled nave of nine bays. Against

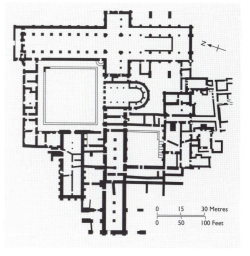

A corbel bracket from Rievaulx, carved with a triple face.

Above: *The apsidal-ended twelfth-century chapter house at Rievaulx is unique in a Cistercian context.*

Right: *A view looking along the nave, through the crossing, towards the liturgical east end of the abbey church at Rievaulx (Skyscan Balloon Photography).*

the west wall of the nave was a galilee porch. The nave was divided from its narrow aisles by an arcade of slightly pointed arches which sprang from boldly splayed piers with tall square bases and shallow imposts, or capitals. From the surviving transepts, it is clear that the elevation was only of two storeys, with small, deeply splayed round-headed windows. The arcades of the nave were continued across the aisles as pointed transverse vaults. Built of rubble for the most part, the church was plastered inside and out, white-limed, and lined out in white paint to represent neatly cut ashlar.

In comparison, the chapter house was a light and decorative Gothic structure with rib-vaulted aisles and scalloped capitals and corbels. Its plan, apsidal with an aisle carried around it, is unique in a Cistercian context, and its design resulted from Ailred's own concept of Cistercian brotherhood. The aisle, which was provided with benches on both sides, and had its own doors from the cloister, was provided to enable the lay brothers to attend chapter meetings for the abbot's sermons. Remarkably, Ailred retained Abbot William's west range which housed the lay brothers in very cramped conditions.

Only when the chapter house was completed was new accommodation provided for the choir monks. A new east range, terraced down the hillside and three storeys high at its south end, with a latrine block of three storeys at the centre of its east wall, was built to house the community which had risen to 140 brothers by the 1160s. On the ground floor at its north end was the parlour, rib vaulted to match the chapter house; to the south of this the stair to the dormitory with the treasury below, then the passage that was to lead to the infirmary and the groin-vaulted monks' day room where the brothers could work within the confines of the cloister. The south side of the cloister was closed by a refectory laid out parallel to the cloister alley, with a large kitchen at its west end. The building of this range

allowed the construction of a level terrace to the south of the church on which the cloister alleys were built and Ailred's famous cloister garden constructed. Part of Ailred's cloister arcade has been reconstructed from fallen fragments.

The completion of the cloister ranges was followed by the construction of an infirmary and infirmary cloister to the east of the dormitory range. The infirmary itself was a massive building with an aisle on its east side, divided into ten bays and with a chapel at its south-east corner. The final building, along the north side of the infirmary cloister, was the abbot's house that Ailred was licensed to build because of his illness and the need to be in close proximity to the infirmary. At his death in 1167, the central buildings of the abbey were complete.

Within a decade, however, the south range of the cloister was rebuilt to replace the refectory that ran along the cloister with a new building perpendicular to it, thereby allowing the warming house and day stair to the dormitory to be placed to its east, in the current Cistercian fashion. The style was no longer the late Romanesque favoured by Ailred, but a very restrained early Gothic. Because of the fall of the ground, the new refectory, which still dominates the site, was raised on a vaulted undercroft. This was the first building at Rievaulx to be entirely cased in ashlar. Lavers were positioned to either side of the refectory door, and the southern cloister arcade was rebuilt.

The new refectory was followed in the first years of the thirteenth century by the building of a new aisled presbytery of seven bays, the remodelling of the transepts, and the building of a crossing tower. The new presbytery was vaulted throughout, and a vault was also provided in the crossing. The reason for this appears to have been twofold: the growing campaign for the canonization of Ailred, and the rapidly growing status of the monastery. It should also be remembered that Fountains was building a new aisled

A corner of the twelfth-century cloister arcade at Rievaulx has been reconstructed to show its form.

Coppack 1986b
Coppack and Fergusson 1994
Fergusson 1984a, 31–38, 140
Fergusson and Harrison 1994
Hoey 1995
Knowles and St Joseph 1952, 82–85
Peers 1929
Pevsner 1966, 299–303
Rye 1900

1176/1250–1538

The site of Robertsbridge Abbey is off the A21 and west of Robertsbridge itself, which is almost 5 miles (8km) north of Battle. The main remains are now embodied within the private house which takes its name from the abbey and are not accessible to the public.

East Sussex
Chichester

TQ 754238

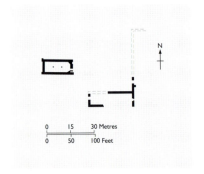

presbytery at the same time. Ailred's shrine was placed in the second bay of the new presbytery, behind the high altar, where it remained until 1536. In 1250, a shrine was built in the west wall of the chapter house for William the first abbot.

The later history of Rievaulx was marked by a steady reduction in the number of choir monks and lay brethren. The lay brothers' choir was removed from the nave in the later fourteenth century, and before this happened, chapels had begun to be set up in the aisles. The south end of their range was demolished and the kitchen reduced in size as it now served only one refectory. Most noticeable was the demolition of the southern half of the monks' dormitory. Reduction in scale, however, was not marked by a reduction in quality, for the monastery remained

wealthy. Fallen architectural detail shows that the nave was remodelled in the fourteenth and fifteenth centuries, when traceried windows with pictorial glass were inserted, and elsewhere it is apparent that accommodation continued to be improved. Larger windows were inserted in the monks' dormitory, and there is evidence that it was partitioned into private cubicles.

A late renaissance is evidenced by the conversion of the twelfth-century infirmary into a substantial abbot's house just before 1500. The old abbot's house was to become a long gallery, and a new infirmary was built to the east. The only sign that the abbey was in decline was the collapse, in 1537, of the central tower into the south transept, where its spire and bells were still lying immediately after the suppression.

ROBERTSBRIDGE ABBEY

Robertsbridge was founded in 1176 by Alured de St Martin, with monks brought from Boxley. Its first site was a short distance away at Salehurst, but this proved unsuitable because of periodic flooding, and in about 1250 it was moved to its present site on the south side of the river Rother. At the time of its suppression in 1538 there appear to have been twelve monks in the community. The abbey had a dependent hospital dedicated to St James at Seaford, though this may no longer have been active after about 1523.

Following the dissolution the site was acquired by Sir William Sidney of Penshurst, who established a forge which continued to operate until almost the end of the eighteenth century. The main physical remains of the abbey are within and to the east of the existing Abbey House, which appears to have been built on the west side of the cloister. Embodied within

the house are substantial parts of a building which must have been built soon after the move to the present site from Salehurst; it has been suggested that this was the abbot's house, despite a situation which must have been west of the west cloister range. The best surviving part of this monastic work consists of six bays of vaulted undercroft which are assumed to have underlain the hall of the residence. Of the hall at first-floor level, a roof of king-post construction and the west window survive. Nothing remains upstanding of the church, which was on the north side of the cloister, though aerial photographs indicate the usual cruciform plan with a simple rectangular eastern arm. The church is known to have been at least partly floored with mosaic patterns of tiles, of the type that has come to be particularly associated with the Medway area.

On the east side of the cloister are traces of the dormitory undercroft, while the refectory apparently ran parallel to the south cloister walk rather than at right-angles to it. There are also traces of the lay brothers' range west of the cloister.

Architectural fragments from the vicinity suggest that building programmes extended into the fourteenth century. Cropmarks indicate something of the wider configuration of the site, with a moat to the north and associated fishponds.

Cooper 1856
Fergusson 1984a, 140–41
Knowles and St Joseph 1952, 134–35
Perceval 1880
Nairn and Pevsner 1965, 589
Salzman 1934–35
VCH Sussex 1907, 71–74; 1937, 218–20

ROCHE ABBEY

1147–1538

Roche Abbey lies on an estate road, off the west side of the A634, one and a half miles (2.4km) south-east of Maltby. The site is in the care of English Heritage and is open to the public at all reasonable times.

South Yorkshire
York

SK 545898

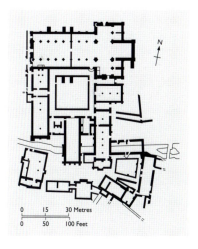

Roche Abbey, the second daughter house of Newminster and of the filiation of Fountains, was established by Richard de Buili and Richard fitz Turgis in the valley of the Maltby beck in 1147. It was to prove a moderately wealthy house with an assessed income of £224 in 1535. It was suppressed in 1538. The survival of its ruins, which have been in State guardianship since 1921, owes much to the fact that in the eighteenth century the entire walled precinct was incorporated with Lord Scarborough's residence of Sandbeck Park. The whole was landscaped by Lancelot (Capability) Brown (d. 1783) in the 1770s. Brown levelled areas of the buildings to create grass parterres, and to emphasize the surviving transept in accord with 'Poet's Feeling and Painter's Eye'. Archaeological excavation of the church and cloister buildings began in the 1870s.

The whole of the precinct can still be identified, enclosed within an early thirteenth-century wall, and entered from the north-west. The inner or great gate of about 1200 survives, of typical Cistercian form with separate gate-halls leading to the inner and outer courts, which were themselves separated by the canalized Maltby beck that bisects the enclosed area. The inner court, still buried below one of Brown's parterres, lay to the north-west of the church and west cloister range, and retains slight evidence of several buildings.

The earliest surviving buildings at Roche date to the 1170s, and must repre-sent a replacement of an earlier series of temporary structures. Both the founders provided large quantities of timber 'for the completion of their buildings', though the location of these buildings is not specified and the foundation charter provided for building on either side of the Maltby beck. It was not until stability was achieved and an estate was being consolidated that permanent buildings could be considered. When these began, however, construction moved rapidly.

The permanent church, raised in a single campaign in the 1170s, has a short, square, unaisled presbytery, transepts with two eastern chapels, and an aisled nave of eight bays. Unusually, for a twelfth-century Cistercian church, the surviving east walls of the transept and the presbytery have a triforium stage, expressed as paired blind pointed arches behind which was a wall-passage. Fallen detail from the nave also suggests that it had a three-storey elevation. The piers of the nave were clustered, with four keeled major shafts alternating with four round minor shafts. The whole of the building was constructed of fine ashlar and covered with rib vaults throughout, and had a distinctly French appearance though its detailing is English. Apart from the replacement of its east and west windows in the late fourteenth century, and perhaps the renewal of some of the windows in the nave aisles and clerestory (all evidenced by fallen architectural fragments), the church was little altered

Built over a single campaign in the 1170s, the extent to which the church at Roche is a true early Gothic building is a matter of debate. French sources may have influenced the design, though strong English elements are also evident. The remains of the north and south transepts reveal three-storey elevations, which it is thought were carried throughout the church.

throughout its life. The monks' choir occupied the two eastern bays of the nave and the crossing. In the third bay was the retro choir, divided from the lay brothers' choir to the west by a rood screen of about 1200. The base of this screen survives, and there were four chapels against its west side. With the loss of the lay brothers in the late fourteenth century, their choir in the nave was removed and the area used for

lay burials. At least one chantry chapel was built, presumably for one of the more significant benefactors. It was also at this time that a sedilia was built into the south wall of the presbytery and an Easter sepulchre added to the north wall, bringing the monks' church up to date.

The cloister lay on the south side of the church and its buildings are largely contemporary with it, adopting the layout first developed at Fountains and Kirkstall in the 1160s. Built during the time of the fifth abbot, Osmund (1184–1213), who had been the cellarer at Fountains, similarities of plan and detail if not scale are not surprising. Many elements of the cloister arcade have been recovered by excavation, showing that it was a finely detailed Gothic structure of the late 1170s and early 1180s that survived unmodified until the suppression.

The layout of the cloister buildings at Roche have for long been described as one of the best examples of a mature Cistercian plan, where the day stair to the dormitory is placed in the south range and a north–south aligned refectory was placed between the warming house and kitchen. Only the ground-floor plan can now be recovered, with two distinct periods of building. Initially, the east range and north–south refectory extended only as far as the north bank of the Maltby beck, suggesting that the accommodation they provided was modest. Certainly, the chapter house was contained within the east range and the monks' dormitory had a maximum length of 125 feet (38.1m). Between 1181 and 1213, however, both the east range and refectory were extended by bridging over the river, and the chapter house lengthened, an indication that the number of choir monks was increasing. The west range, which contained the lay brothers' quarters, was not extended at this time, possibly because their infirmary, an aisled building of three bays, lay on the south bank. The extension of the cloister ranges on to the south bank of the river was followed by the construction of an infirmary cloister and infirmary (only partially excavated) in the first decade of the thirteenth century.

In the late fourteenth or early fifteenth century, a new abbot's house was built to the west of the infirmary and south of the refectory, replacing earlier buildings that originally enclosed the south side of the infirmary cloister. To its west was a kitchen, and a bakehouse and brewhouse. More or less contemporary with this building was the conversion of the lay brothers' infirmary to a guest house. In spite of this late modification, the central buildings at Roche survived throughout their lives very much as they were originally laid out.

Aveling 1870
Fergusson 1971
Fergusson 1984a, 62–66, 141–42
Fergusson 1990a
Knowles and St Joseph 1952, 98–99
Pevsner and Radcliffe 1967, 414–17
Stacye 1883–84

RUFFORD ABBEY

Rufford, the fifth and final daughter house of Rievaulx, was founded by Gilbert de Gant, earl of Lincoln (d. 1156), in 1146. The abbey was to be located within the bounds of Sherwood Forest, and the preparations for settlement included the clearance of the villages of Rufford, Grimston, and Cratley. From documentary sources, it seems construction of permanent buildings was not underway until the 1160s, and work on the church may well have continued for almost a century. The abbey was damaged by a serious fire in the early years of the sixteenth century, though the extent of the damage is not known. In 1535 the assessed income of the house was given as £176; it was suppressed in the following year. The site of the abbey, together with its home granges of Cratley, Roumes, and South Sellars, were granted to Sir John Markham.

Within a year, Rufford had been granted to the Talbots, earls of Shrewsbury, in exchange for lands in Ireland. The family converted the west range into a house,

1146–1536

The abbey is situated within Rufford Country Park, which itself represents the monastic precinct and the medieval home grange. The park is located on the east side of the A614, one and a half miles (2.4km) south of Ollerton, and 7 miles (11.3km) north-east of Mansfield. Rufford Abbey is in the care of English Heritage and can be visited during the park opening hours.

Nottinghamshire
York

SK 645648

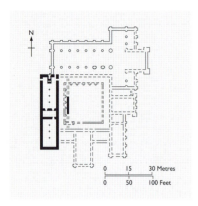

The post-dissolution house at Rufford incorporates the entire ground storey of the abbey's west monastic range, a rare example of early quarters used by lay brothers.

Fergusson 1984a, 142–43
Gilyard-Beer 1965
VCH Nottinghamshire 1910, 101–05

which was extended in the early seventeenth century. Further wings were added in the 1660s, and the house was further remodelled by Anthony Salvin (d. 1881) in the mid-nineteenth century. In 1938 Rufford was sold to Nottinghamshire County Council. During the war, the house was requisitioned by the War Ministry, and was partially demolished in 1956. At much the same time, the central area of the medieval abbey was placed in State care. Trial excavations by M. W. Thompson in 1957 defined the layout of the demolished church and the east range of cloister buildings. During further demolition of the post-suppression house, the ground storey of the west range was discovered to be intact. This fine example of an early lay brothers' range was conserved for public display. No other monastic buildings are now visible. Additional research and geophysical survey since 1993 have modified the known ground plan of the abbey.

The east end of the church was set out with a short, square-ended presbytery without aisles, and with three eastern chapels to each of the short transept arms. The aisled nave was of seven bays. Here, the piers in the south arcade had square, stepped bases, suggesting they were built before the circular piers of the northern arcade. The evidence of large circular piers at the crossing indicates a central tower.

The cloister lay on the south side of the church and adopted the mature Cistercian plan also used at nearby Roche. To the south of the south transept was the library and sacristy. South of these was an aisled chapter house of three bays, in which the eastern bay projected beyond the width of the range. Next came a narrow parlour, and then a passage which led through the range to the infirmary, which has not itself been excavated. The south end of the east range contained the four-bay monks' day room. Doubtless the upper floor comprised the monks' dormitory. The south range contained, from east to west, the day stairs to the dormitory, the warming house, a north–south refectory, and the kitchen.

The ground floor of the west range remains intact, and is essentially a building of the 1160s or 1170s, modified on at least three occasions before the suppression. As at Roche, the range is short, suggesting a limited community of lay brothers. As first built, the northernmost bay of the range served as the outer parlour and was covered with a barrel vault. There were doors in both west and east walls. The next four bays comprised cellarage, originally covered with groined vaults; and the southern five bays accommodated the lay brothers' refectory, again with a groined vault. In the early thirteenth century, the refectory was remodelled, with new piers down the centre, and a rib vault springing from corbels decorated with nailhead ornament. In the early fourteenth century, this refectory was shortened when a new outer parlour was provided at the centre of the range. The pointed barrel vault of the new chamber cut through the evidence of the earlier refectory vault. The earlier outer parlour at the north end of the range was removed, and a new day stair from the lay brothers' dormitory came to occupy the central part of the old room. In the fifteenth century, the northern half of the range was provided with a new vault supported on hexagonal pillars with moulded capitals.

It appears that the reason for this remodelling was a general conversion of the first floor to provide accommodation for the abbot. A fifteenth-century door case in the east wall of the old lay brothers' dormitory was moved to its present location in the later sixteenth century, but suggests that the upper floor of the range was being refurbished to provide accommodation of high quality.

The precinct of the abbey and its home granges survives within the bounds of the country park at Rufford, though landscaping has destroyed any evidence of layout.

SADDELL ABBEY

Patronage of the monastic orders in the Western Highlands at the turn of the twelfth and thirteenth centuries was almost entirely in the hands of the family of Somerled, lord of the Isles. It was Reginald, son of Somerled, who re-established Iona for Benedictine monks, and who probably also founded a priory there for Augustinian nuns before his death in 1207. Although one tradition says it was Somerled himself who founded the Cistercian abbey at Saddell, it seems more likely to have again been Reginald who was responsible, even if it had been planned by his father. The abbey was given a site above Carradale bay, about half way down the Kintyre peninsula and, as might be expected in the west at this period, its roots were in Ireland rather than in Lowland Scotland. The mother house was Mellifont, and the few surviving architectural details, including some chevron-decorated stones, are strongly Irish in character.

The main relics of the church are parts of the lower walls of the presbytery and of the north transept, within the graveyard at Saddell. From the way the east wall of the north transept abuts the presbytery, it seems that the church must originally have been no more than an elongated rectangle,

to which transepts were only added at a slightly later date. This would mean that the first church was the simplest of any house of the order in Scotland. The cloister was on the south side of the church, though only parts of the refectory walls survive above ground to indicate its plan; from this it can be seen that the refectory ran parallel with the cloister.

Very little is known of the history of the house. However, by about 1507, when King James IV (1488–1513) sought permission to divert the abbey's endowments to the cathedral of Argyll at Lismore, it could be said that there had been no monastic life within living memory. This request was successful, and by 1512 Bishop David Hamilton of Argyll had built himself a tower-house residence nearby. Also in 1512 there was a brief hope of a revival of the fortunes of the site, if not of the abbey, when James IV suggested that the cathedral of Argyll should be relocated to Saddell, since Lismore itself was deemed to be unsuitable because of its inaccessibility and state of decay. But nothing came of this, and the abbey continued to decay gradually until much of the stone was removed for additions to Saddell Castle in the years around 1770.

About 1207–1507

The very slight remains of Saddell Abbey are in the village of Saddell, off the B842, on the east coast of Kintyre. They are within a graveyard and are readily accessible.

Argyll and Bute
Argyll

NR 785230

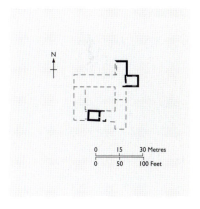

The principal remains at Saddell are parts of the lower walls of the presbytery and of the north transept.

Brown 1969
RCAHMS 1971, 140–45

SAWLEY ABBEY

1147–1536

The abbey lies in Sawley village, on the north side of the A59, a little over 3 miles (4.8km) north-east of Clitheroe. The church and cloister ranges are in the care of English Heritage and are open to the public at all reasonable times. The remainder of the site lies on private land.

Lancashire
York

SD 776464

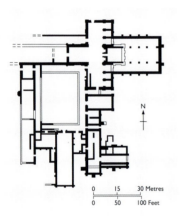

Situated on the east bank of the river Ribble in Craven, Sawley (or Salley) Abbey was founded in 1147 by William de Percy, a member of one of the most powerful northern baronial families. Established as a daughter of Newminster, Sawley was to become part of the extensive Fountains family. It appears that the site itself was purchased by Abbot Robert of Newminster (1138–59), but it was de Percy who provided the temporary wooden buildings in advance of settlement. Although the location was a good one, the initial endowments proved barely adequate, and the community's early difficulties were exacerbated by the wet climate, which it was said tended to rot the crops in the fields. In short, Sawley was on the verge of failure when, in 1189, Countess Matilda of Warwick, the daughter of William de Percy, increased the endowment. Even so, the abbey was never especially wealthy, and further difficulties arose when the monks from Stanlaw in Cheshire resettled at Whalley in 1296. Sawley complained that competition for basic commodities was driving up prices. Quite clearly, the community found difficulty in sustaining itself from its estates. The abbey was suppressed in May 1536, but monks were reinstalled by the insurgents of the Pilgrimage of Grace in October and were not finally removed until February 1537. In May 1538, the site was granted to Sir Arthur Darcy (d. 1560) who was to further develop the west range to serve as a house.

Substantial ruins survive above ground, and the site was excavated by J. R. Walbran in 1848 and again by J. E. Fattorini in the 1930s. Sawley was placed in the guardianship of the Office of Works in 1935, and further clearance work was carried out by the Ministry of Works in the 1950s. Between 1977 and 1984, the south

side of the cloister was excavated by Rich Williams for the Department of the Environment.

The development of the site bears an uncanny resemblance to the well documented history of Meaux Abbey, also within the Fountains family. At Sawley, two timber aisled buildings dating from the late 1140s have been excavated, one below the later monks' latrines, the other below the kitchen and west range of the later permanent buildings. Both these early structures had a sophisticated piped water supply, and it appears they were broadly contemporary with the first stone church to be built on the site. The church was initially laid out with a short square-ended presbytery, which was probably vaulted, transepts with three square chapels to each, and with two eastern bays of an aisleless nave. The monks' church (that is the east end) was finished by about 1160 when building paused. Work began again in the 1170s, moving towards the completion of the nave, and the building of the east claustral range together with the monks' latrines. The chapter house was a narrow building, and there is no indication of piers to support a vault. The day stair was placed within the range, to the south of the parlour, in the early Cistercian manner. Contemporary with this work was the provision of three timber buildings on the site of the later south and west claustral ranges. The first of these was a kitchen, with a central hearth below a louver. On its north side was a substantial two-storey building, the ground floor of which may have served as the refectory since it adjoined the kitchen. The upper floor was perhaps the lay brothers' dormitory. Another building adjoining it to the west, and linked to the kitchen by a corridor, is interpreted as a guest house. It was Sawley's early economic difficulties which

The low foundations of the cloister and the abbey church at Sawley seen from the south-west.

probably resulted in the cessation of building work shortly after 1180.

Matilda de Percy's refoundation of 1189 was followed by a prolonged period of construction between about 1190 and 1220. Growth of the community is suggested by the extension of the east cloister range, which, as usual, housed the monks' dormitory on the upper floor. Before the end of the twelfth century, a new abbot's house was added to the north side of the latrine block. Next came the south range of the cloister, with the north–south refectory coming first in the building sequence, followed within the same campaign by the warming house to the east and the kitchen to the west. Contemporary with the building of the kitchen was the construction of the lay brothers' quarters in the west range, and a walled lane on the west side of the cloister. The cloister alleys themselves were raised shortly afterwards, completing the development of the central buildings.

The church and cloister buildings remained little altered until the later fourteenth century. Then, in 1377, a chapel was built on the north side of the nave, but shortly after this a decision was taken to remodel the church substantially. All but the three eastern bays of the nave were demolished, thereby losing the lay brothers' choir. A new presbytery of five bays was added to the east end, and the monks'

choir stalls were moved into the former presbytery area. The inner transept chapels became entrances into the presbytery aisles, and a new *pulpitum* was built between the eastern crossing piers. By 1381 the community comprised no more than fifteen monks and two lay brothers, and clearly the old buildings no longer suited their needs. The major alteration in the cloister was the conversion of the now-redundant west range into an impressive abbot's house. A tower was raised above the old outer parlour, and a fine bay window was to light the upper end of the abbot's hall. The kitchen and warming house were remodelled, and the older abbot's house extended, perhaps for the prior.

The church and cloister lie at the centre of a walled and embanked precinct of some 40 acres (16.2ha). This was entered at its south-east corner, where traces of the gatehouse and possibly the *capella ante portas* can still be seen. The precinct is made up of walled enclosures which define the inner and outer courts. Buried buildings are apparent to the east of the east range, where the infirmary should lie, and also to the south of the south range. A perched leat runs from the Ribble southwards across the precinct , turning west to the south of the cloister buildings, and rejoining the river close to the remains of a medieval and post-medieval watermill.

The east end of the church at Sawley was first completed by about 1160, and included the south transept chapels which appear in the foreground of this view (University of Warwick, Richard K. Morris).

Bilson 1909b

Fergusson 1984a, 143–45

Knowles and St Joseph 1952, 100–01

McNulty 1939

Pevsner and Radcliffe 1967, 430–31

Walbran 1852–53

Walbran 1876

SAWTRY ABBEY

1147–1536

The site of the abbey lies 2 miles (3.2km) to the south-east of Sawtry village, off an unclassified road on the east side of the A1 road. The earthworks lie on farm land close to Abbey Farm, with no formal public access.

Cambridgeshire
Lincoln

TL 197825

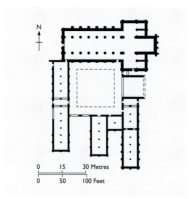

Fergusson 1984a, 144, 146
Ladds 1914
RCHME 1926, 230

Simon of Senlis, earl of Huntingdon (d. 1153), founded Sawtry Abbey as the first daughter house of Warden Abbey in 1147; the earl also provided the initial timber buildings for the community. In 1535 the assessed income of the abbey was £141 and it was dissolved in the following year. The suppression inventory describes the church, a bell tower with four bells, the gatehouse, and a 'stone house', perhaps the *capella ante portas*, or gatehouse chapel. By the early nineteenth century little was left standing, and the foundations of the buildings were being dug out for road stone. There was some excavation in the 1850s, and further work was carried out by S. I. Ladds between 1907 and 1912. Today the whole of the precinct is clearly defined by earthworks.

The church, which retained its basic twelfth-century plan through to the suppression, comprised a short aisleless presbytery, transepts with two eastern chapels divided by solid walls, and a nave

of seven aisled bays with circular piers. The superstructure of the church, however, must have been modified. It is known, for example, that Bishop Robert Grosseteste of Lincoln (1235–53) dedicated the building in 1238, and this ceremony probably marked the completion of a new programme. Moreover, Sawtry's last abbot, William Angel, claimed that he had glazed the west window and borrowed £20 for timber for 'rebuilding the church'.

The cloister lay on the south side of the church, with a north–south refectory at the centre of the southern range. The earthworks, which clearly show robbed out walls, suggest that there was an earlier east–west refectory, though this has never been examined by excavation. A substantial group of buildings lying beyond the east range probably represents the infirmary complex.

The northern side of the precinct is bounded by a canal, the Monks' Lode, which connected the abbey to the old course of the river Nene.

SIBTON ABBEY

1150–1536

A little over 4 miles (6.4km) from Saxmundham, the abbey is situated at the village of Sibton, just off the A1120. The heavily overgrown and fragmentary remains, which are on private land, include parts of the refectory and the south wall of the nave.

Suffolk
Norwich

TM 365698

Sibton was founded in 1150 by William de Chesney (d. 1174), sheriff of Norfolk and Suffolk. It was one of three daughter houses colonized from Warden, and proved the only Cistercian abbey to be established in East Anglia. From at least the 1230s, the monks had responsibility for a hospital at the precinct gate. Dedicated to St John the Baptist, it was intended for the poor and the sick, and some grants were specifically assigned to its endowment.

Based on William's generous foundation grant, the bulk of the community's extensive landholdings always lay in the immediate neighbourhood. There were, however, significant outlying estates located about 30 miles (48km) away in Norfolk, and others were situated even further afield on the borders of Suffolk and Cambridgeshire. Major land acquisitions had virtually ceased by the end of the 1180s, but the monks continued to consolidate their holdings, engaging in small purchases and exchanges right through to the middle years of the thirteenth century. Eventually, Sibton's lands were managed from about a dozen grange centres. Rents were also to feature in the abbey's economy, and by the end of the thirteenth century the community held property in up to ten parishes in the city of Norwich.

What little survives of the abbey buildings is to be found much overgrown within a wood. The overall layout can just about be interpreted with the aid of a plan prepared in the 1890s. The church was positioned on the north side of the cloister, though the only vestige is a stretch of rubble walling standing up to 15 feet (4.6m) high. Now featureless, this represents the south side of the nave, which itself extended to an overall length of about 126 feet (38.4m). Presumably there was a bell tower over the crossing, since in 1470 a legacy of £20 was left for its fabric.

On the opposite side of the cloister, the refectory walls stand quite high, and a number of its round-headed windows remain reasonably complete. The capitals feature both scalloped and early foliate

designs, suggesting a date of about 1175–80. Of greatest interest is the fact that the building was set out on an east–west axis, parallel to the south walk of the cloister. Indeed, the Sibton refectory must have been completed just as an arrangement based on a north–south axis was emerging as the commonplace Cistercian preference. In the wall facing the cloister, there is a twin-arched laver recess where the brothers washed before meals.

One or two further clues on the Sibton buildings come from documentary sources of the 1360s. Among the detailed accounts of routine maintenance there is mention, for example, of repairs to the bakehouse. More notable are the references to the construction of a new hall for the abbot, and the purchase of seven lime trees for his new chamber.

With its net income assessed at almost £251, Sibton should have avoided the first round of suppressions in 1536. At all events, whether or not they were placed under pressure, in that year the abbot and his seven remaining monks sold the house and its possessions to Thomas Howard, duke of Norfolk (d. 1554).

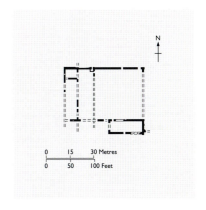

Brown 1985–88
Fergusson 1984a, 146
Hope 1894

STANLEY ABBEY

Encouraged by her chamberlain, Drogo, in 1151 the 'Empress' Matilda (d. 1167) gave the Cistercians of Quarr a site at Loxwell in Wiltshire for the foundation of a 'chief abbey'. Matilda's son, the future King Henry II, added to the endowments. Under his patronage, in 1154 the monks moved a mile and a half (2.4km) from Loxwell to Stanley. Situated on the south bank of the river Marden, the new site offered greater potential for the laying out of a monastic precinct on a generous scale. There were problems, however, over the supply of fresh drinking water. Not until

1214, when Abbot Thomas Calstone completed an aqueduct running down to Stanley from the old source at Loxwell, were the difficulties finally resolved. Meanwhile, the abbey had been growing in wealth and status, and in 1204 had provided the colony for the foundation of Graiguenamanagh in Ireland. By the early fourteenth century, Stanley held granges and other properties in many parts of Wiltshire, as well as in Somerset, Berkshire and Gloucestershire.

Work on the earliest stone buildings began as soon as the community was

1151/54–1536

Stanley is located no more than 3 miles (4.8km) east of Chippenham, and less than a mile (1.6km) off the A4. Virtually nothing survives above ground of the abbey buildings, but they are represented by a superb series of earthworks. The site is privately owned, though it is generally accessible with permission from Old Abbey Farm.

Wiltshire
Salisbury

ST 963723

firmly settled at Stanley. But in 1212 a serious fire destroyed the twelfth-century church, and may have engulfed large parts of the cloister ranges. Thereafter, the process of reconstruction proceeded slowly. Roger Poore, bishop of Salisbury (1217–28), was to offer an indulgence to all who might assist, and in 1222 Henry III gave the monks stone for the church and wood for building. In a further gift of 1246, Henry provided the oaks from which the choir stalls were made, and in the following year the community entered the east end of the new church for the first time. Some two decades later, in 1266, the king donated a tun of wine to mark the completion and dedication of the church. Elsewhere within the abbey complex, building work continued. By 1270, for example, a new refectory had been finished. Ten years later, King Edward I gave stone to construct a chamber at Stanley for his own use, and it is clear from the archaeological evidence that other

schemes were to extend into the fourteenth century. Much later, at the time of the dissolution, it was recorded that parts of the abbey were '*newe buylded*'.

In 1535, with ten monks remaining in the community, Stanley's annual income was given at a fraction over £177. The abbey was dissolved in February 1536, and a year later the site was bought by Sir Edward Baynton. Although some of the buildings were to survive into the seventeenth century, Sir Edward almost certainly began the process of destruction by salvaging materials for use in his new house at Bromham. In due course, virtually every architectural fragment was removed from above ground. Even the very foundations were extensively robbed out.

Despite this post-dissolution history, the archaeological excavations of 1905 managed to unearth some evidence for the form of Stanley's original twelfth-century church. Much more was discovered of the

Nothing of the abbey buildings survives above ground at Stanley, though the site is of particular interest because of its outstanding series of earthworks bounding the river Marden, seen here from the air (Michael Aston).

early Gothic structure which was built to replace it. As completed in 1266, this second church was to feature a somewhat larger presbytery, together with a nave of eight bays. The internal length was a comparatively modest 215 feet (65.5m). In the fourteenth century, the church was modified with the addition of chapels projecting from the south aisle of the nave.

Presumably for reasons of drainage, the monastic buildings were set out on the north side of the church. The twelfth-century west range remained unaltered throughout the abbey's history, perhaps always separated from the cloister by a wide lane or court. The east range, on the other hand, was entirely rebuilt in the years leading up to the middle of the thirteenth century. Here, the chapter house of six bays in length was doubtless the most imposing, as well as the most attractive chamber. On the third side of the cloister,

the new refectory is known to have been completed in 1270. At the centre, the cloister arcades were probably refashioned in the fourteenth century.

Today Stanley is of particular interest because of its outstanding series of archaeological earthworks extending over an area of at least 28 acres (11.3ha). These earthworks represent not just the church and cloister — located to the immediate east of Old Abbey Farm — but the entire monastic precinct, including agricultural enclosures, numerous fishponds, a mill leat, and at least one mill building. As a whole, the northern limits of the site were determined by the course of the river Marden. The three remaining sides of the precinct were determined by a more or less continuous bank and ditch. The abbey was evidently approached from the south, by way of a causeway running on top of a substantial bank.

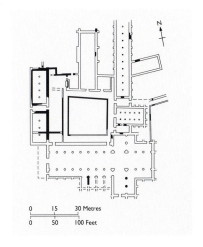

Brakspear 1906–07
Brakspear 1907–08
Fergusson 1984a, 147–48
Knowles and St Joseph 1952, 140–41
VCH Wiltshire 1956, 269–75

STONELEIGH ABBEY

Stoneleigh began its life as a community of hermits who were settled by King Stephen (1135–54) at Red Moor, or Radmore, in Staffordshire about 1141. They later agreed to the request of their patron, the 'Empress' Matilda (d. 1167), to convert to the Cistercian order, moving to a new site at Cryfield in 1154. Here, the brothers invited two monks from Bordesley to join them as they felt they needed instruction. With the support of Henry II, the community moved once again to a new site at Stoneleigh, consecrated in April 1155. Soon, work began on the construction of a church. Building was well advanced by the 1170s, though the dormitory was burned in 1241. The east end of the church was rebuilt at the time of Abbot Robert de Hockele (1310–49). The abbey was suppressed in 1536, and three years

later it was granted to Charles Brandon, duke of Suffolk (d. 1545). His descendants sold it in 1562 to Sir Thomas Leigh who built a house which incorporated the east cloister range, south transept and south nave aisle. The house was extended in 1714–26 to include the site of the west range of the cloister.

Substantial parts of the church and cloister ranges remain within the house, though the landscaping of the park has removed any clear evidence for the precinct, apart from the great gate and remains of a guest house, both originally of early fourteenth-century date. Of the church, the southern crossing piers and four bays of the south nave arcade survive, together with the south aisle wall and the entrance from the transept into the aisle. The detail of the crossing piers, and of the

1141/54–1536

The site of the abbey is in Stoneleigh Park, on the east side of the B4115, and about 2 miles (3.2km) east of Kenilworth. The sixteenth-century and later house, now the National Agricultural Centre, incorporates the south aisle and south transept of the church. The gatehouse also survives.

Warwickshire
Coventry and Lichfield

SP 318713

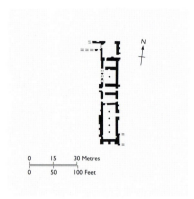

0   15   30 Metres
0   50   100 Feet

Though later modified, the great gatehouse and adjacent lodgings at Stoneleigh were built in the fourteenth century (University of Warwick, Richard K. Morris).

Fergusson 1984a, 148–49
Gresley 1854
Pevsner and Wedgwood 1966, 407–10
VCH Warwick 1908, 78–81; 1951, 231–33

eastern processional door, suggests a construction date of about 1165–70.

The present internal courtyard of the house represents the medieval cloister. The chapter house, parlour, passage, and monks' day room all survive. The chapter house vault was supported on a single central pier; the parlour and passage had barrel vaults; and the day room was rib vaulted. The scalloped capitals on the door to the chapter house suggest a date of around 1170.

STRATA FLORIDA ABBEY

1164–1539

Strata Florida Abbey is situated off the B4343, 1 mile (1.6km) from the village of Pontrhydfendigaid, and about 7 miles (11.3km) north-east of Tregaron. The ruins of the church, chapter house, and part of the cloister are in the care of Cadw: Welsh Historic Monuments, and are open at all reasonable times.

Ceredigion
St Davids

SN 746657

The earliest steps in the foundation of Strata Florida Abbey were taken by the Anglo-Norman lord, Robert fitz Stephen. In June 1164 he drew a small colony of monks from Whitland, settling them on the banks of the Fflur brook at a site known today as *yr hen fynachlog* (the old monastery). The plantation might have remained a modest one, had it not been that a year later Robert's lands were taken by Rhys ap Gruffudd (d. 1197), prince of Deheubarth. The Lord Rhys, as he is generally known, happily assumed the patronage of the infant community in the 'Vale of Flowers'. Strengthened by his munificent gifts, the monks were to move to a new site about a mile and a half (2.4km) to the north-east. Within a very few years, the abbey which Rhys was said to have especially 'loved and cherished' also held an important place in the affections of the Welsh people. It was to send out colonies to establish daughter houses at Llantarnam in 1179, and at Aberconwy in 1186.

Pastoralism was of the greatest importance to the abbey's early economy. Indeed, at the beginning of the thirteenth century, Gerald of Wales noted that Strata Florida was 'enriched far more abundantly

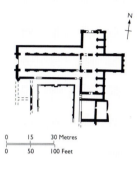

with oxen, studs of horses, herds of cattle and flocks of sheep, and the riches they produced, than all the houses of the same order throughout Wales'. The nucleus of its estates lay in the immediately surrounding landlocked uplands, where Rhys had granted vast tracts of countryside, ideally suited to large-scale sheep ranching. The need for arable cultivation also led the community to expand its holdings into nearby river valleys and the coastal plain. In all, by the end of the thirteenth century, the abbey's lands were organized around some fifteen grange centres.

Nothing now remains above ground at the *yr hen fynachlog* site, though it appears the community stayed there long enough to erect modest stone buildings. Hearsay evidence recorded in the later nineteenth century suggests that traces of a church, about 126 feet (38.4m) long, with claustral buildings on the north side, may still lie beneath the turf. In any case, developments at the new site must have been well in hand by 1184, since in the Lord Rhys's charter of that year it was stated that he had 'begun to build the venerable Abbey entitled Stratflur'.

The initial design of the church was clearly based on the model derived from the Burgundian heartlands of the order. Working in a very simple style, the masons began with the construction of the south transept, the sacristy, and with a short square-ended presbytery. As they progressed to the north transept, the sculptural detailing in the capitals and other features was to become distinctly more elaborate. Nevertheless, to this point in the programme, it seems very likely that the intention was for a church with no marked crossing, and with the presbytery joining the nave at a lower level. By Whit Sunday 1201, 'after it had been nobly and handsomely built', all was ready for the community to occupy the east end.

Subsequent progress with construction was to prove somewhat slow. Matters were certainly not helped when, having been accused of sustaining his enemies,

King John imposed a crippling fine on the abbey in 1212. Some of the delays, however, were undoubtedly the result of the various modifications introduced to the original design of the church. Of greatest significance was the decision to extend the east end by a further bay, a scheme which involved the insertion of a stone rib vault over the entire presbytery. The work was almost certainly undertaken in conjunction with a plan to formalize the crossing, probably with the intention of raising a squat stone tower or belfry above. Meanwhile, as the building of the nave was resumed, any concept there may have been for freestanding piers was abandoned. Instead, they were to sit on top of the low stone walls which separated the central vessel of the church from its aisles, thus giving a slightly squat appearance to the two-storey elevation. But perhaps the most striking feature of the church as a whole is its bold west doorway. Five of the original six orders of roll mouldings survive. All were devoid of capitals, though they were banded at regular intervals with transverse rolls terminating in crozier-like spirals around the frame. Crowned by a prominent hoodmould, it is a rich and unique work representing a west country mason of great individuality.

It is difficult to be certain just how long the building continued, though when the community purchased its 'great bell' in 1255 it was consecrated by the bishop of Bangor. The claustral ranges, which lay to the south, had almost certainly been completed by this time. The chapter house façade, for example, featured stiff-leaf capitals of about 1220–30. During a series of bitter set-backs in the later thirteenth century, in 1286 the church was struck by lightning and a disastrous fire swept through much of the building. Just over a century later, at the time of the Welsh uprising led by Owain Glyn Dŵr, English troops were billeted at Strata Florida. Nothing was spared. Even the church was said to have been 'used as a stable'. The destruction caused at the time may explain

The west doorway in the abbey church at Strata Florida is of unique design and betrays a west country mason of great individuality.

why the infirmary and the refectory were apparently already ruinous at the time of the dissolution. This said, such a picture of chronic decay cannot be entirely representative of the last century of monastic life, especially in the light of the praise lavished on some of the later abbots in the verse of native bards. It was one of these fifteenth-century abbots, for example, who was responsible for the complete rebuilding of the cloister arcades.

In the great survey of 1535, Strata Florida's income was assessed at £118.

The abbey managed to avoid suppression in the following year on payment of a large sum. It was but a brief reprieve, and the abbot and seven monks finally surrendered the house in February 1539. The greater part of its estates was acquired by Richard Devereux (d. 1547), and subsequently the lands passed to his heirs, the earls of Essex. By 1567, the site of the abbey itself had been acquired by John Stedman, whose family were to raise the house which still stands over the area to the south of the cloister.

Left: Deep in the tranquil countryside of mid-west Wales, the site of Strata Florida Abbey still conveys a great sense of the Cistercian spirit.

Knowles and St Joseph 1952, 116–17
Pierce 1950–51
Robinson and Platt 1998
Williams 1889

STRATA MARCELLA ABBEY

Strata Marcella, or Ystrad Marchell as it was known to the Welsh, was founded in 1170 at the invitation of Owain Cyfeiliog, prince of southern Powys. The initial colony of monks arrived here from Whitland, to be settled on lands given by the founder on the west bank of the river Severn. In his old age, Owain chose to take the habit of a White Monk, and on his death in 1197 he was buried in the abbey he had established. Thereafter, his son Gwenwynwyn (d. 1216) added considerably to Strata Marcella's endowments. Meanwhile, the monks made a number of purchases and small exchanges of land in an attempt to improve and consolidate their overall estate.

Today, apart from a few loose pieces of masonry, virtually no trace of the abbey is to be seen above ground. This said, areas of the church and cloister were explored with the spade in 1890, and the positions of both can be readily identified among the surviving earthworks. The results of the excavations suggest that the church was begun soon after the foundation, though from many of the architectural fragments recovered it would seem that construction continued well into the thirteenth century.

The stylistic details, particularly in features such as capitals, show that the masons who were engaged at Strata Marcella were also familiar with the building programme at the sister house of Strata Florida. This is confirmed by the fact that at least five masons' marks were common to both sites. Nevertheless, it was Strata Marcella which seems to have possessed the more fashionable and up-to-date of the two churches. Its nave piers, for example, were apparently of the fasciculated or bundled-shaft form, and might generally be considered of a slightly more advanced design. There are indications, too, that the Strata Marcella aisles were vaulted in stone, something not seen at Strata Florida.

The ground plan produced by the nineteenth-century excavators shows a church extending to an overall length of some 273 feet (83.2m), but this figure cannot be accepted without condition. Indeed, at the east end of the church, very little evidence was recovered as to the precise form and scale of the presbytery and transepts. To the west, the excavators themselves noted certain inconsistencies in the proportions of the nave bays. In short, the four western

1170–1536

Strata Marcella is situated about 2 miles (3.2km) north-east of Welshpool, beside the A483. Although earthworks denote the positions of the church and cloister, virtually nothing survives above ground in what is now a field of pasture on the west bank of the river Severn.

Powys
St Asaph

SJ 251104

The site of Strata Marcella Abbey is now marked by green pasture on the banks of the river Severn.

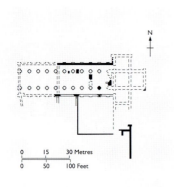

0   15   30 Metres
0   50   100 Feet

Arnold 1992
Jones and Williams 1891
Knowles and St Joseph 1952, 118–19
Thomas 1997
Williams 1976b
Williams 1892

bays may represent an ambitious attempt to extend an already sizeable church. It is now virtually impossible to say whether the work was ever completed, though such a programme may well have overstretched the resources available to the community.

Strata Marcella was one of those abbeys to suffer damage to its property during the Welsh wars of King Edward I, and in 1284 it was to receive £43 by way of compensation. But by this time its fortunes had begun to change for the worse. In the late 1320s, the then lord of Powys, John de Cherleton (d. 1353), openly opposed the community. He complained to King Edward III that there were only eight monks at the house when at one time there had been sixty. The king was prompted to write several times to the abbot of Clairvaux, requesting that the visitation rights should be transferred from Whitland to the English house at Buildwas. Most telling is the king's disclosure that unlawful assemblies were being held at the abbey 'to excite contention and hatred between the English and the Welsh'. The episode perhaps represents another example of native loyalty among the Welsh Cistercian communities, to say nothing of the simmering resentment following the English conquests of the later thirteenth century.

By the 1530s, Strata Marcella was heavily encumbered with debt, its buildings were already in a ruinous condition, and the community comprised no more than two or three monks. The abbey's income was assessed at just £64 in 1535, and it was dissolved in the following year.

STRATFORD LANGTHORNE ABBEY

1135–1538

The site of the abbey is on industrial and underground railway lands on the south side of the A11. There are no standing remains.

Greater London
London

TQ 391836

Originally founded as a Savigniac monastery by William de Montfichet in 1135, Stratford Langthorne was absorbed into the Cistercian order in 1147. The initial foundation appears to have been at Burstead, moving to its permanent site by the early 1140s. it rapidly grew to be a wealthy house, with almost a score of manors and some 1,500 acres (607ha) of demesne in West Ham alone.

Little is known of the twelfth-century buildings, but the church was being rebuilt or extended in the 1240s, when stone was brought from London with royal licence. In the late fourteenth century, flood damage led to a restoration by King Richard II. This work was continuing in 1400 when John Belhous paid for the glazing of a new west window. The abbey was suppressed in 1538 and was granted to Sir Peter Mewtas. The site was still marked by ruins in 1631, but these had gone by 1784 when Thomas Holbrook bought the site and dug out the foundations for building stone. By the early twentieth century, the site had disappeared beneath railway sidings, a sewage works and small factory buildings.

Since 1980, parts of the church, and a substantial cemetery to its north, together with the infirmary to the south-east, have all been excavated. This work has disproved an earlier suggestion that the cloister lay to the north of the church. From the evidence of architectural fragments recovered from robber trenches, it seems the aisled nave and transepts were built in the second half of the twelfth century. There were no western crossing piers, and it is unlikely there was a central tower. The early aisleless presbytery was replaced in the first half of the thirteenth century with an aisled construction, presumably the building for which stone was acquired in 1241. In the late fourteenth century, the north wall of the north transept was taken down, and the transept doubled in depth. The aisle walls of the presbytery were removed and ranges of chapels built to flank the presbytery on both sides. An eastern chapel was also added to the presbytery. The eastern parts of the church were refloored at this time, suggesting it marks the restoration programme by Richard II.

To the south-east of the church, slight evidence of the infirmary cloister was found. This lay east of the east range, and north of the main abbey drain. There was a kitchen to the east. Flanking the north side of Abbey Road, which defined the northern edge of the cemetery to the north of the church, a substantial thirteenth-century building was found. This was perhaps the guest hall, which remained in use after the dissolution, and was modified throughout the late sixteenth century.

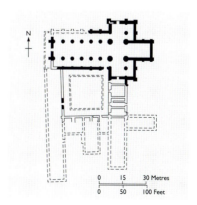

Fergusson 1984a, 149–50
Pevsner and Radcliffe 1966, 343
Powell 1973
Round 1894–95

SWEETHEART ABBEY

Sweetheart, or New Abbey, was founded by the Lady Dervorguilla of Galloway in 1273, with monks from Dundrennan, and was the last White Monk house to be founded in Scotland. It takes its name from the story that Dervorguilla took the embalmed heart of her dead husband, John Balliol (d. 1268), wherever she went, and she was eventually buried with it before the high altar of Sweetheart after her own death in 1289. The remains of a new effigy that was placed over her tomb in the later Middle Ages show her clasping a heart to her bosom. Outside Scotland, Dervorguilla is best known as the patroness of Balliol College in Oxford (which had been founded by her husband), and as the mother of the unfortunate King John Balliol (d. 1313). The latter was placed on the Scottish throne following an adjudication by King Edward I of England between rival competitors in 1292, and was deposed by Edward in 1296. The abbey was soon suffering in the wars with England. In 1299 and 1308 it was said the English had burnt the abbey's granges and destroyed its goods. There was also damage from natural causes when Sweetheart was seriously hit by lightning in 1397.

By the eve of the Reformation there was still a community of about sixteen monks, and they may have considered themselves more fortunate than members of other religious houses when Gilbert Brown, the commendator appointed in 1565, showed himself to be sympathetic to continued Catholic worship. Even as late as 1579, there was said to be still a high altar within the church, though this was removed some years later. The abbey was eventually erected into a temporal lordship for Sir Robert Spottiswoode in 1624.

The monastic buildings were arranged around a cloister to the south of the church, though relatively little has survived of them. The chief remains are of the inner wall of the south range, and the lower walls of the parts of the east range closest to the church. Within the latter can be seen a compartment originally subdivided into sacristy and library, followed by a square chapter house, a parlour and a warming house. There is also a doorway of

1273–1560

The shell of the abbey church, with the more fragmentary remains of the conventual buildings, are on the north side of the village of New Abbey, on the A710, about 6 miles (10km) south of Dumfries. It is in the care of Historic Scotland, and is open on a regular basis.

Dumfries and Galloway
Glasgow

NX 965662

the west range surviving in place, which has the arms of Douglas above it, probably in reference to Archibald 'the Grim', third earl of Douglas (d. 1400). At some distance to the north-west and north of the church is a long stretch of the wall which defined the limits of the wider precinct, and which is the greatest length of precinct wall to survive at any Scottish Cistercian abbey.

By contrast with the monastic buildings, the church has survived remarkably well, the main loss being the outer wall of the north nave aisle. This excellent state of preservation is partly because the parish church stood against the south wall of the nave from 1731 to 1877. But it is also because in 1779 a party of local benefactors raised money to preserve the ruins of the church, a notably enlightened move for that time. In 1928 the abbey was taken into State care, after which the church and monastic buildings were excavated.

Constructed of the local red sandstone, and seen against the background of the surrounding green hills, the abbey at Sweetheart is an enchanting site. The continuing preference of Scottish Cistercians for the Bernardine plan at their churches is clearly demonstrated here, since it has an aisleless rectangular presbytery flanked by transepts with a two-bay chapel aisle on the east side of each, and a six-bay aisled nave for the choirs of the monks and the lay brethren. There was a narrow galilee porch along the west front, of which only the roof corbels now remain.

The presbytery, transepts and the monastic choir in the eastern bays of the nave were presumably built soon after the foundation, so that the services of the monks could be adequately housed. Their design provides a fascinating indication of Cistercian attitudes at this time. As already said, the plan adheres to the early principles of Cistercian austerity, and this simplicity of approach is also seen in the crossing area where, although there is a tower, it barely rises above the height once

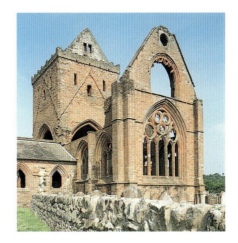

reached by the surrounding roofs. However, in contrast with the apparent austerity of the planning, little expense was spared in the design of the architectural details. The most striking element of the architectural detailing of the eastern parts is the display of bar tracery in those windows, which is the best group of the first-generation representatives of this type of tracery in Scotland. The range of tracery types used in the lower walls of the presbytery flanks is varied, and shows a close awareness of recent developments in England. But it is in the vast windows of the end walls of the presbytery and north transept that the quality of the work is best seen. The main window of the former is a fine five-light composition, with a smaller five-light window in the gable above.

The nave elevations were of a two-storeyed design. But any idea that a triforium or gallery would have been an unacceptable luxury for the Cistercians must be weighed against the fact that such designs were fashionable at this time. The same is also true of the clustered-shaft piers of the transepts and the nave arcades, which, although showing some similarities with earlier Cistercian types, also reflected current tastes. There may have been a pause in building operations after the first two bays of the nave had been completed for the monks' choir, because there is a change in the windows

A striking feature at the east end of the church at Sweetheart is the bar tracery which fills the window openings. As a whole, it is the best early group of this form of tracery in Scotland.

Left: *A relatively late Cistercian foundation, Sweetheart was established by the Lady Dervorguilla of Galloway in 1273. This view looks north-east along the length of the nave, and shows the two-storey design of the elevations.*

Chinnock 1900–05
Chinnock 1909–10
Dalrymple 1899, 1–54
Fawcett 1994a, 72–74
Gifford 1996, 456–63
Knowles and St Joseph 1952, 68–69
MacGibbon and Ross 1896–97, **2**, 334–44
RCAHMCS 1914, 200–08
Richardson 1995

on the outer face of the clerestory passage from triplets of individual windows to groups of five lancets within a semicircular containing arch. But it is unlikely that the break was a long one.

The final completion of the nave may have been interrupted by the wars with England. The vast traceried window at the west end of the nave might be more at home in the third quarter of the fourteenth century, when it is said that Earl Archibald of Douglas was doing so much for the abbey that he was regarded as its second founder and reformer. Unfortunately, much of the area of the window was later partly blocked and partly infilled with smaller windows, possibly after a strike by lightning in 1397. The last major addition to the church was probably a saddle-back roof to the tower, set behind its parapet, of which the crow-stepped gables remain.

SWINESHEAD ABBEY

1135–1536

The site of the abbey is on private land at Swineshead, just off the A52, about 5 miles (8km) south-west of Boston. Nothing survives above ground, though the site is marked by a seventeenth-century and later house.

Lincolnshire
Lincoln

SK 249408

Fergusson 1984a, 150
Pevsner and Harris 1989, 737–38
VCH Lincolnshire 1906, 145–46

Situated in the Lincolnshire fens, Swineshead Abbey was established for a community of Savigniac monks by Robert de Gresley in 1135, with the founding colony arriving from distant Furness. Along with all other houses of the Savigniac congregation, in 1147 Swineshead was absorbed into the Cistercian order. Soon afterwards, Gilbert of Hoyland (d. 1172) became abbot. He was previously a monk at Clairvaux, where he had been an intimate friend of Abbot Bernard. Doubtless Gilbert's move to Swineshead was intended to ensure the infant community followed Cistercian orthodoxy.

No trace of the abbey buildings remains above ground. However, the site is known and wall fragments have been traced in monitoring service trenches. The church was apparently substantial, with the bells and lead alone valued at some £274 at the time of suppression in 1536. The abbey site is now occupied by a house initially built for Sir John Lockton in 1607, and is situated within a landscaped park. The house incorporates stone from the monastic buildings.

THAME ABBEY

1137–1539

The site of Thame Abbey is about a mile (1.6km) south of Thame itself, off the B4012. The principal remains are embodied within the private house of Thame Park and are not accessible to the public.

Oxfordshire
Lincoln

SP 714043

Thame, a daughter house of Waverley, had rather unpromising beginnings. Its initial endowments were made by a group of local tenants, with land provided in 1137 at Otley by the small landholder Robert le Gait. Although temporary structures were evidently built, both the site and endowments soon proved inadequate. At a date between 1139 and 1142, Bishop Alexander of Lincoln (1123–48) rescued the ailing foundation by providing a new site for the community at Thame Park. Building must have started immediately, and by 1145 enough of the church was complete for a dedication to be carried out.

However, the first presbytery proved of insufficient scale, and further building was in progress by the 1230s, possibly after a structural collapse; King Henry III is known to have provided new choir stalls in 1232, and other timber in 1236. Nothing survives of the church, but a survey of about 1840 recorded fourteen bases in the nave, which suggests a structure of eight bays (seven piers on each side). The overall length of the church was said to be 230 feet (70m), with a Lady Chapel of 45 feet (13.7m) at the east end. By 1281 the community was sufficiently large for a daughter house at Rewley to be founded from it by Edmund, earl of Cornwall (d. 1300).

Little is known of Thame's history, though a visitation in 1526, by Bishop Longland of Lincoln (1521–47), presents a rather unedifying picture of the monastic life pursued within its walls towards the end of its existence. The buildings were said to be falling into ruin through neglect, and the misdemeanours of the monks included shouting and playing games in the dormitory. The abbot himself was identified as the main problem. He evidently had no interest in either the monastic rule or the liturgical requirements of his order, and was said to be excessively intimate with both boys and women. He was replaced by Robert King (d. 1557), who was then head of Bruern Abbey, and who was later to be bishop of Oxford. King presumably reformed the observance of the abbey, though his main visible memorial is the decoration of the parlour in his own residence, which was incorporated in the later house on the site. The linenfold panelling and deep plaster frieze of this room are among the best features of their date and kind to survive anywhere.

After the dissolution in 1539, at which time there were twelve monks with the abbot, the abbey was acquired by Lord Williams of Thame; twenty years later it passed to the Wenman family. The present house on the site is largely a rebuilding of about 1745 for the sixth Viscount Wenman, to the designs of William Smith of Warwick, though there are significant remains of the abbey within and around it. Apart from the parts of the abbot's lodging embodied in the south range of the house there is thirteenth- and fourteenth-century work in the kitchen wing and to the north of the house. There is also a chapel to the north-west of the house, which probably served as the *capella ante portas*, or gatehouse chapel.

Fergusson 1984a, 150–51
Lee 1888
Pewy 1888
Salter 1947–48.
Sherwood and Pevsner 1974, 809–10
VCH Oxfordshire 1907, 83–86; 1962, 168–69

TILTY ABBEY

Established as a daughter house of Warden, Tilty Abbey was founded by Maurice fitz Geoffrey in 1153, and was sited on a tributary of the river Chelmer. The first record of building comes in March 1188, suggesting that the earliest years of the house were uncertain. Ralph of Coggeshall in his *Chronicon Anglicanum* credited the second abbot, Simon (about 1188–1214), with the building of the whole monastery, transforming what had been little more than a grange into a beautiful and prosperous abbey. But on Christmas Day 1215 the abbey was sacked by soldiers of King John, and repair must have been protracted for the church was only reconsecrated five years later.

The church was partially excavated in 1901 and again in 1942, and found to be small, with an aisled nave of seven bays, shallow transepts with two eastern chapels, and a short, square presbytery, not unlike Buildwas. Only fragments of its external walls can now be seen. The

1153–1536

The surviving fragments of the abbey lie just to the north of Tilty parish church, half a mile (0.8km) to the west of the B184, and about 4 miles (6.4km) to the north-west of Great Dunmow.

Essex
London

TL 601266

Dickinson 1963
Fergusson 1984a, 151
Galpin 1928
Knowles and St Joseph 1952, 130–31
Pevsner and Radcliffe 1965, 391–92
RCHME 1916, 321–22
Steer 1949–50

1131–1536

Tintern is situated on the A466, about 5 miles (8km) north of Chepstow and the M48. The extensive remains include almost the complete later Gothic abbey church, together with large areas of the thirteenth-century monastic buildings. The site is in the care of Cadw: Welsh Historic Monuments and is open at all reasonable times.

Monmouthshire
Llandaff

ST 532998

Right: Much of Tintern's great charm rests in its setting below Wordsworth's 'steep and lofty cliffs', on the banks of his 'sylvan Wye'. The abbey was founded by Walter fitz Richard de Clare in 1131, and stood in the vanguard of Cistercian settlement in the British Isles.

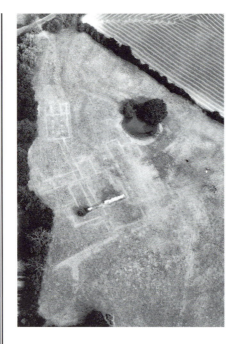

cloister lay on the north side of the church, to take advantage of the natural drainage of the site, but of the cloister buildings only the west range partly survives above ground, its east wall retaining evidence of the ground-floor vaults.

To the south of the abbey ruins, the present church of St Mary incorporates the brick-built *capella ante portas*, or gate-house chapel, first constructed in the early thirteenth century. It was originally a single cell building, and was lit by lancet windows. A chancel was added in the early fourteenth century, with traceried windows and statue niches.

In 1535 Tilty's income was assessed at £167. It was suppressed in 1536 and granted to Margaret, marchioness of Dorset, who had been resident in the abbey's guest house for some years.

TINTERN ABBEY

Close on two hundred years ago, having forced his way 'through a crowd of importunate beggars', Archdeacon William Coxe (d. 1828) stood before the recognized high point of the Wye valley tour. As the west doors of the abbey church at Tintern were thrown open, the archdeacon was filled with 'an instantaneous burst of admiration'. In his account of the experience, he was sufficiently moved to praise the picturesque beauty of the building as 'an excellent specimen of gothic architecture in its greatest purity'. Tintern has since won even greater celebrity, as much for its association with one of the finest poems in the language, as for the importance and quality of its buildings. For many people, the abbey's charm still rests in the near perfection of its natural setting, nestling below Wordsworth's 'steep and lofty cliffs' on the banks of his 'sylvan Wye'.

Tintern was founded in 1131 by Walter fitz Richard (d. 1138), the Anglo-Norman lord of Chepstow, and a member of the powerful family of Clare. Established as a daughter of the French house at l'Aumône (Loir-et-Cher), it stood in the vanguard of Cistercian settlement on these shores, preceded only by Bishop William Giffard's foundation three years earlier at Waverley in Surrey. Yet despite this early foothold in the southern March, Tintern played no further role in the White Monk colonization of Wales. Its only daughter houses were founded at Kingswood (1139), and at Tintern Parva in Ireland (1201–03).

The community was early placed on a reasonably sound economic footing with grants of land and other possessions on both sides of the river Wye. Additional benefactions were to follow through the later twelfth and on into the thirteenth century. In 1223–24, for example, William

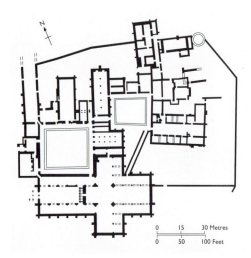

This Tintern doorway of about 1300 led from the east cloister alley into the abbey's book room.

Marshal the younger (d. 1231) proved particularly generous, adding lands near Usk to the overall estate. Wherever possible, the Tintern monks organized their holdings into typical White Monk farms or granges, and by the middle years of the thirteenth century they were operating at least twelve such properties. Moreover, in 1301–02, Earl Roger Bigod III of Norfolk (1270–1306) — who had become the abbey's patron on inheriting the lordship of Chepstow — granted the community 'all his manor of Acle'. Situated more than 200 miles (320km) away in Norfolk, it was to prove a magnificent asset, accounting for one quarter of the abbey's income by the time of the dissolution.

Work on the earliest stone monastery was set in hand within a decade or so of the 1131 foundation. The ghost of an austere Romanesque church (Tintern I), which should date from this early period, was initially proposed in 1904–08, though its outline was modified after further investigations in the 1920s. It was around 173 feet (52.7m) long, with a short, square-ended presbytery, a narrow aisleless nave, and with two diminutive eastern chapels within each of the transept arms. Other aspects of this early layout are to be gleaned from observations made during conservation works of 1901–28, and by a close examination of the fabric itself. Scattered remnants of the cloister buildings — which lay to the north side of the church — survive in part encased within later walls, or are known occasionally as foundations. The east range was about 28 feet (8.5m) wide, with the chapter house initially contained within its width; and the refectory was apparently set out on an east–west axis within the north range. The sum total of the evidence is by no means great, but it is important to bear in mind that these early structures determined much in the pattern of the subsequent building programmes.

Even before the end of the twelfth century, the expanding community necessitated the extension of the east range. However, William Marshal the younger's gifts of 1223–24 may well have been earmarked to finance the far more comprehensive programme of reconstruction which can be identified in all three claustral ranges. The most prominent indications of the extent and quality of this rebuilding can be seen, for instance, in the extended chapter house, in which the elegant rib vault was supported on eight slender piers, and also in the revised layout of the north range where the handsome new refectory was arranged on a north–south axis. From the façade and window detailing, it is tempting to attribute some of this work to Abbot Ralph (1232–45), a man 'gifted in no small way with ... splendour of wisdom'. But even for such a devout White Monk, the intoxicating beauty of the west country early Gothic style had become too much to resist. Many of the features were unashamedly elaborate when compared to the recognized propriety of Cistercian building a century earlier.

It was probably in the 1260s that attention was switched to the cloister alleys. New arcades were to be built with a design based on two rows of trefoil-headed arches, set out in a 'syncopated', or staggered, pattern of great rarity. The form of the arches appears to have varied within different sections of the four arcades, and this may reflect distinct constructional phases. Meanwhile, in much the same period, a grand infirmary hall was built on the eastern side of the complex.

With little or no pause, in 1269 the monks finally embarked on a complete rebuilding of their abbey church. Tensions must surely have arisen over the need for additional liturgical space long before this time, but all temptation to expand the twelfth-century edifice had apparently been resisted. The decision to begin at this time must have been taken by Abbot John (about 1267–77), whose Crown and

Cistercian duties are known to have taken him to Westminster, as well as providing him with opportunities to view the new building works at both Netley and Waverley.

The anonymous Tintern master mason was given the opportunity to build a Gothic great church from scratch, and in general terms the comprehensive unity of his original scheme is confirmed by an initial glance at the ruins. Nevertheless, it was not a straightforward commission since the new church had to be laid out slightly to the south and east of the original. Construction advanced in such a way that the monks were able to continue to use the old building for as long as possible. In effect, the Gothic church was to grow as an envelope, eventually surrounding its smaller and more humble predecessor. Enough progress had been made by April 1287 to permit a Mass within the new building. Eighteen months later, in October 1288, the choir monks were able to take possession of the presbytery. In due course, as the work on the western bays of the nave continued, more of the twelfth-century church would have been gradually pulled down.

At least one very distinct break seems to have occurred during the overall building programme. This is to be identified by

The north-east side of the abbey complex at Tintern does not survive to any great height, though its features are of much interest. In the foreground of this view is the infirmary hall, and in the distance lie the abbot's lodgings, close to the banks of the Wye.

Begun in 1269, the great Gothic church at Tintern took several decades to complete. It was finished under the patronage of Earl Roger Bigod III, probably in the first years of the fourteenth century. This view looks west from the presbytery along the full length of the building.

specific changes within the design details in the windows of the south nave aisle and in the south clerestory. Moving from the west, the break can be traced between bay two and bay three in the clerestory, and within bay four in the aisle. There are, too, other aspects of detailing underlining the

significance which is to be read into this structural break. The most prominent evidence is that of the greater window tracery. This progresses from the huge Geometrical oculi at the east end, and in the north and south transepts, through to the intersecting pattern with daggers and

pointed trefoils in the great seven-light window at the west front.

A transcript of a now lost chronicle records that, after thirty-two years in building, the church was finally completed by Roger Bigod in 1301. Although his patronage is not in doubt, at least during the later stages of construction, it is far more difficult to find explicit proof of Bigod's interest during the early years of the campaign. In fact, hard evidence for his support does not come until 1301–02, at which time the Tintern community was headed by the urbane Abbot Ralph, who presumably negotiated the acquisition of the manor of Acle. Indeed, Ralph is known to have moved in court circles, and doubtless had occasion to observe some of the most recent architectural trends emanating from the capital. Aided by Bigod's gifts, he may at last have pushed the long-drawn-out programme towards a successful conclusion.

The liturgical furnishing of the church is likely to have continued well into the early decades of the fourteenth century. In particular, it is now known that one of the most striking internal fittings was a magnificent five-bay *pulpitum* screen, dividing the monks' choir from the nave to the west. Almost certainly designed by the brilliant west country master, William Joy, it is to be dated to about 1325–30. In much the same period, the community also chose to commission a porch to stand at the west front of the church. Today, this is represented by little more than four fragments of masonry, assumed to have been bases which carried the piers of an arcaded construction, in turn supporting an upper chapel. The chapel was probably that which housed a revered statue of St Mary the Virgin, claimed by the monks to possess miraculous powers, and which by the early fifteenth century had led to the abbey becoming something of a place of pilgrimage.

One of the last major building schemes was begun closer to the middle years of the fourteenth century. It was at this time that one of Tintern's abbots chose to make significant improvements to his private accommodation on the north-east side of the precinct. In particular, a grand and imposing new hall was built over a cellared undercroft, and it appears to have been a work of considerable architectural prestige. There was probably direct access to and from the river, and the hall itself was designed to link with the adjacent abbot's chamber and private chapel.

By this stage, the whole complex stood in a walled precinct of some 27 acres (11ha). There was a gatehouse fronting on to the river Wye, and another on the hillside overlooking the site. Traces of the thirteenth-century gatehouse chapel still survive in a private house, and the excavated foundations of the communal guest hall and other inner court structures can be seen to the west of the abbey church.

The widespread economic changes of the fourteenth century, coupled with the decline in the lay brotherhood, eventually forced the Tintern community to abandon the ideals of grange farming. By the early sixteenth century almost the entire abbey estate had been leased out in return for regular fixed cash rents. In 1535, the annual income of the house was given at about £192, which was sufficient to make it the wealthiest monastery in Wales. But in September 1536 Abbot Richard Wyche (1521–36) and his community of twelve monks were obliged to surrender the house to the king's visitors. Within months, the buildings and border possessions were granted to Henry Somerset, earl of Worcester (d. 1549).

From the mid-eighteenth century, the wooded slopes of the Wye valley were to become a magnet for droves of 'Romantic' tourists, with Tintern acknowledged as the jewel and highlight of the tour. The appeal of the ruins continued through the nineteenth century, and in 1901 the site was finally recognized as a monument of national importance. The ruins were purchased on behalf of the State, and the long process of conservation began.

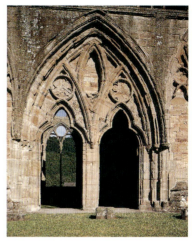

The west door in the abbey church at Tintern. The vesica, or almond-shaped niche, situated under the apex of the arch, probably housed a carved stone figure of the Virgin.

Blashill 1881–82
Harrison, Morris and Robinson 1998
Knowles and St Joseph 1952, 122–23
Potter 1847
Robinson 1995a
Robinson 1996a
Robinson 1997a
Williams 1976a, 94–146

VALE ROYAL ABBEY

1274–1538

Vale Royal Abbey lies near the village of Whitegate, a little over 2 miles (3.2km) north of Winsford and the A54. Nothing of the church remains visible, though a confected monument known as the 'Nun's Grave' marks the approximate position of the high altar. A Tudor and later house, recently converted to provide clubhouse and other facilities for a golf course, may well incorporate fabric from the south and west ranges of monastic buildings.

Cheshire
Coventry and Lichfield

SJ 639699

Had its founder's grandiose scheme been completed, Vale Royal Abbey may well have become one of the greatest works of piety ever undertaken by a medieval English king. From the outset of permanent building, the scale of the church was intended to be extraordinarily ambitious. In the event, as initial enthusiasm faded, the monastic community was left stranded in the middle of a construction programme far beyond its means. Effectively, the ground plan of the monastery was to remain a blueprint for a magnificent concept which was never fully realized.

According to one of its own monk-historians, the foundation of Vale Royal represented the fulfilment of a vow made by the future King Edward I (1272–1307) during a perilous sea voyage in the winter of 1263–64. In spite of certain difficulties, Edward was at last able to issue a foundation charter in August 1270. A site had been chosen at Darnhall in the royal forest of Delamere, and Dore had agreed to provide the colonizing community of monks. But it was to take another four years before all was ready for the beginnings of conventual life.

When the community eventually arrived at Darnhall in 1274, the site proved less than ideal. With the king's permission to move anywhere throughout 'all the kingdom of England', the monks were content to opt for a place just 4 miles (6.4km) away. Edward was to rename it Vale Royal, and on 13 August 1277 he laid one of the foundation stones on the spot which had been determined for the high altar. In 1281 the community left Darnhall, moving into the temporary accommodation which had been prepared at the Vale Royal site.

Meanwhile, the permanent works were entrusted to Master Walter of Hereford (d. 1309), one of the foremost designer-masons of his day. Building at first progressed rapidly, with the costs met by very specific financing arrangements set up by the king. Regardless of inconsistencies in the level of annual payments, huge sums were made over to the Vale Royal project in the thirteen years through to 1290. Most of the early effort appears to have gone into the church itself, though a record of 1287 reveals that the abbot contracted with two London marblers to provide columns, capitals, and bases for the cloister, all to be made in accordance with designs provided by Master Walter.

Then, for reasons which are not entirely clear, in 1290 the king announced that he had 'ceased to concern himself with the works … and henceforth will have nothing more to do with them'. The abbot had possibly incurred royal displeasure, though by this time of course Edward had enormous financial commitments arising from his castle-building programme in Wales. In any case, the community was left to manage as best it could. Four decades were to pass before, in 1330, Abbot Peter could finally lead his monks into the new abbey from the 'unsightly and ruinous' buildings they had occupied since 1281. Even at this stage, much remained to be done. In 1336, for example, the abbot noted in a report on revenues that his community had 'a very large church', but it was not completely vaulted or glazed. 'Moreover', he wrote, 'the cloister, chapter house, dormitory, refectory, and other monastic offices still remain to be built in proportion to the church'.

A new phase of patronage began with the interest shown by Edward, the Black Prince (d. 1376). In his capacity as earl of Chester, Edward decided to continue the work of his great-grandfather, and from

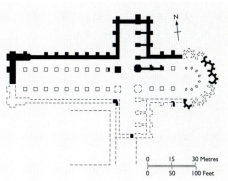

1353 money again began to flow into the abbey's construction fund. Emboldened by this new turn of fortune, the community embarked on a quite remarkable scheme to embellish the east end of the church. In 1359, Master William of Helpeston was contracted to build twelve chapels, each conforming to the height of one 'newly made by him adjoining the choir'. The whole was doubtless intended as the crowning feature of a building which had now been under construction for more than eighty years. The new work was itself expected to take at least six more years.

Yet again the community's hopes were dashed when a violent storm swept across Cheshire on 19 October 1360. The entire nave was said to have been destroyed, with the piers falling 'like trees uprooted in the wind'. After this, although Prince Edward was insistent that the chapels at the east end should be completed, there could be no chance of an entire rebuilding. In due course, Richard II (1377–99) agreed that the church should be 'reduced in height and width'.

What little survives of Vale Royal's much robbed church was first excavated in 1911–12, and the east end was further explored in 1958. It is clear from this work that Walter of Hereford's original design was for a building of at least some 380 feet (116m) in total length. The nave was to be of nine bays, and the presbytery may have featured an apsidal east end. Each of the deep transeptal arms had three eastern chapels, and — to judge from the scale of the piers — the scheme allowed for a prominent crossing tower.

It is unfortunate that so little is known of the superstructure of those important changes made to the east end of the church from about 1359 onwards, especially since the foundations reveal tantalizing evidence of radical new experiments. The excavations of 1958 confirmed that there were indeed thirteen radiating chapels, seven of which were polygonal, and six quadrangular, all opening from a wide ambulatory aisle. Such radiating schemes had appeared earlier at Croxden and Hailes, but the alternating pattern of the chapels seen at Vale Royal was most unusual. It seems almost certain that the inspiration for the design came from a European source, and it probably had very little to do with English or even continental Cistercian precedents.

The endowments which King Edward had provided for the Vale Royal community were by no means meagre, but the revenues were always to prove stretched by the demands of the building work. By the early fifteenth century the financial position of the house was further jeopardized by legal disputes, local disorder, and poor management. In 1439, Vale Royal was said to be 'so wasted by misrule that £1,000 would be required to repair its estates'. Despite this, in 1535 the annual income of the house was given at almost £519.

Vale Royal was surrendered to the king's commissioner, Thomas Holcroft, by the abbot and fourteen monks in September 1538. The following year, Holcroft wrote to Henry VIII declaring that he had 'plucked down' the church, and in 1544 he was allowed to purchase the site of the abbey together with much of the surrounding land. The evidence is perhaps not conclusive, but on the basis of tree-ring dating of the timbers in the roof trusses, Holcroft's house may have been planned around a conversion of the south and west ranges of monastic buildings. If so, the southern range had been set out on an east–west alignment. It is suggested that the late fifteenth-century refectory was located in a timber-framed upper storey. The refectory itself may have occupied a central open hall, with a small anteroom at either end. There was a kitchen on the ground floor to the west, originally open to the roof.

It is Holcroft's house, much modified in subsequent centuries, which can still be seen at Vale Royal today.

Brown, Colvin and Taylor 1963, 248–57
Denton 1992
McNeil and Turner 1987–88
Pendleton 1915
Taylor 1949
Thompson 1962
VCH Chester 1980, 156–65

VALLE CRUCIS ABBEY

1201–1536/37

Valle Crucis Abbey lies about a mile and a half (2.4km) outside Llangollen, on the A542. The extensive remains, which include the church and east range of claustral buildings, together with the foundations of the south and west ranges, are in the care of Cadw: Welsh Historic Monuments. The site is accessible at all reasonable times.

Denbighshire
St Asaph

SJ 203443

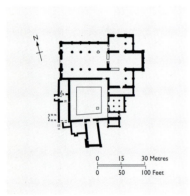

The attractive ruins of Valle Crucis lie amid a landscape of hills clad in fern and green pasture in north-east Wales.

Right: Taken as a whole, the details in the chapter house at Valle Crucis suggest a date of construction around the middle years of the fourteenth century.

Nestling in a landscape of hills clad in fern and green pasture, and neatly tucked alongside a swift-flowing little stream which finds its way into the vale of Llangollen, the abbey in the 'valley of the cross' was founded in 1201 by Madog ap Gruffudd (d. 1236), ruler of northern Powys. Its Latin name is derived from the nearby Pillar of Eliseg, a ninth-century memorial cross with an inscription recording the ancient ancestry and glories of the kings of Powys. During the Middle Ages, Valle Crucis was also known as the abbey of Llanegwestl, from the original Welsh name for its site. Indeed, before the founding colony arrived here from Strata Marcella, Madog had cleared away at least some of the settlement's inhabitants to ensure the necessary seclusion sought by a White Monk community.

From the first, the abbey's estates were centred largely around Llanegwestl itself. The monks had access to extensive grazing lands for their flocks and herds on the granges at Mwstwr and Buddugre, whereas they held arable fields, water meadows, and woodland at the more distant lowland manors of Halghton, Stansty and Wrexham. In later centuries, with the disappearance of the lay brothers, Valle Crucis leased out more and more of its lands to tenants in return for fixed rents. Of even greater significance was the revenue the abbey eventually derived from tithes, that source of income so shunned by the early Cistercians. In the 1530s, three rectories alone accounted for more than half of the community's accountable wealth.

Construction of the abbey buildings must have been set in hand very soon after the foundation, though it is clear from the surviving remains that the entire architectural history of the site was somewhat complex and is now rather difficult to unravel. Nevertheless, at a time when several of the richer Cistercian houses in both the north and south of England were beginning to rebuild their churches in new and more fashionable styles, Valle Crucis was to remain faithful to the Bernardine plan. Before the middle of the thirteenth century, the entire abbey layout had been determined.

The church, no more than about 175 feet (53.3m) in length, was to have the standard square east end, two eastern chapels in each of the transepts, a formal

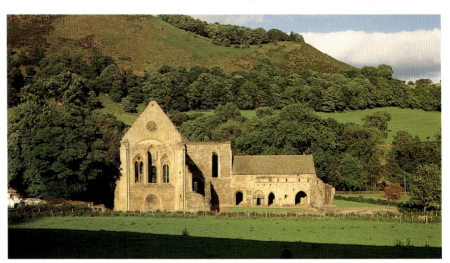

crossing with a tower, and a rather short five-bay nave in which the bundled piers were flattened along their inner face to accommodate the lay brothers' choir stalls. The transept chapels were to be vaulted in stone, and — from the evidence of the wall articulation — it appears that vaults were also intended in the presbytery, and probably in the nave aisles. As the construction of the church progressed, the monastic buildings had meanwhile been set out on the level ground to the south. Here, excavation has revealed traces of the original east range, and the lower courses of the west range and the thirteenth-century refectory have been consolidated for display. The refectory, arranged at right-angles to the cloister, retains the foot of a staircase which led to the reader's pulpit.

Before the masons were able to complete the overall scheme, a disastrous fire swept through the monastery, staining the lower courses of stonework in the church a deep, rose red colour, and leaving archaeological traces of its impact in the southern and western claustral ranges. Soon afterwards, Valle Crucis was to be hit by a further round of misfortune during the Welsh wars of King Edward I, in 1276–77 and 1282–83. The community's loyalty to the native cause meant the abbey lands were to prove a natural target for English forces. There is, moreover, every reason to suggest that the monastery itself was significantly damaged. In 1284, Valle Crucis was granted £160 by way of compensation for its losses.

It was in the wake of these episodes that the original design of the church was at first modified, and eventually finished. Among the earliest changes were those made to the west front, especially the insertion of the central doorway with its foliate capitals and richly moulded arch. The upper part of the presbytery also belongs to the second stage of building, as does the remarkable buttress arrangement on its east façade. Furthermore, it was presumably the fire which created a weakness in the south-west crossing pier and led

to the introduction of a massive supporting wall in the adjacent bay of the nave arcade.

There is greater uncertainty surrounding the chronology of the principal windows in the west front, where each of the three two-light openings was surmounted by a cusped circle (the centre one is lost), and the whole contained within an enclosing arch which appears both inside and out. Superficially, the composition might easily belong to the third quarter of the thirteenth century, though it is possible that the work followed war damage of the early 1280s. There is a suggestion that it may have been undertaken by Savoyard masons, otherwise involved with Edward I's programme of castle-building in north Wales.

Further major building was to continue at Valle Crucis well into the fourteenth century. In the church, for example, for reasons which are not entirely clear, it was necessary to rebuild the gable in the west front. The new work, which was completed in fine ashlar, stands out very clearly from the rubble construction of the lower stages. At the centre, the gable is adorned with a highly attractive eight-light rose window. Just above this, an inscription running across the stonework reads: +ADAM.ABBAS FECIT.HOC:OPVS: N.PACE/ QVIESCAT:AME (Abbot Adam carried out this work; may he rest in peace. Amen). An Adam appears in documents as abbot of Valle Crucis from about 1330 to 1344.

Of even greater significance was the almost complete rebuilding of the east range, a scheme in which the masons again made very extensive use of ashlar. In the cloister façade, the work included a flamboyant, though somewhat bizarre, screen fronting a small book cupboard, featuring mouchette or 'curving dagger' patterns in its tracery. But by far the most notable element within the rebuilt range was the handsome new chapter house, replete with wave mouldings, and with flowing tracery in its windows. Taken as a whole, the

The west doorway in the church at Valle Crucis was probably inserted into the original fabric around the middle years of the thirteenth century.

details suggest a date of around the middle years of the fourteenth century, though the evidence is far from conclusive. In fact, it is known that the abbey suffered very extensive damage during the Welsh uprising of the early fifteenth century, and that in 1419 Abbot Robert of Lancaster (1409–33) petitioned the pope claiming he had 'repaired the monastery on its destruction by fire'. It may well be reasonable to equate the rebuilding with this incident.

Later in the century, it appears that the monks' dormitory on the upper floor in the east range was completely taken over for use as a grand set of apartments for the abbot. The southern end may have been reserved for guest accommodation. The conversion can probably be attributed to the time of Abbot Dafydd ab Ieuan and Abbot Sîon Llwyd, from 1480 to about 1527. During Dafydd's period as head of the house, the poet Guto'r Glyn spent his old age at Valle Crucis. In praise, he wrote 'Of Valle Crucis Abbot good, Whose full-stocked tables ever groan'.

The last years at the house were not, however, particularly happy ones. Internal affairs were brought to a scandalous state under the penultimate abbot, Robert Salusbury, who proved little short of a desperado. At a visitation carried out by four Cistercian abbots in 1534 (headed by Leyshon Thomas of Neath), Salusbury was accused of many 'crimes and excesses'. A year later, when the king's visitors arrived, they lost no time in having Salusbury arrested for his part in highway robbery. Thereafter, although a further abbot was installed, monastic life at Valle Crucis had little time left to run. The great survey of 1535 had valued the income of the house at £188, and its final surrender by the abbot and six monks seems to have occurred in January 1537.

The abbey's estate was first granted to a Yorkshire man, Sir William Pickering. It later passed to his son, and then to Sir Edward Wootton. Although the church was soon made ruinous, by the end of the sixteenth century the east range had been further adapted to serve as a dwelling, and so it continued until perhaps 1654. A print by the brothers Samuel and Nathaniel Buck of 1742 shows the building roofless, though within a few decades it was again occupied and served as a farmhouse into the nineteenth century. Archaeological investigation of the site began in the 1850s, and in 1872 Sir Gilbert Scott (d. 1878) supervised the restoration of the west front.

Inscribed +MORVS (whose identity is unknown), this thirteenth-century stone head was found during excavations in the refectory at Valle Crucis. It may have flanked one side of the refectory pulpit (National Museum & Gallery, Cardiff).

Brock 1878
Butler 1976b
Evans 1995
Hughes 1894–95
Knowles and St Joseph 1952, 110–11
Lovegrove 1936
Price 1952

VAUDEY ABBEY

William 'le Gros', count of Aumâle and earl of York (d. 1179), settled a colony of Fountains monks close to his stronghold at Castle Bytham in south Lincolnshire in 1147. It was to prove the sixth successful daughter house established by the great Yorkshire house. Although the initial site proved unsuitable, by 1149 one of William's tenants, Geoffrey de Brachecourt, had provided the community with a fresh location in the nearby parish of Grimsthorpe. Here, the abbey was situated in a tributary valley of the river Glen and was known from this setting as Vallis Dei, or the Valley of God; in Norman French it was called Vaudey.

Brother Adam of Fountains (d. 1180) was responsible for the earliest buildings on the permanent site. These were probably of timber, and were under construction in 1149. Unfortunately, very little is known of Vaudey's later development.

1147–1536

The site of Vaudey Abbey is situated in Grimsthorpe Park, just off the A151 some 3 miles (4.8km) north-west of Bourne. Earthworks on the south side of the lake mark the position of the buildings. The park is privately owned, and the abbey site is not accessible to the public.

Lincolnshire
Lincoln

TF039217

In 1535 the abbey's income was assessed at £124 and it was suppressed in the following year. It seems the buildings were already substantially ruined when they were seen by John Leland (d. 1552) in 1543. Almost two centuries later, when the antiquary William Stukeley (d. 1765) visited Vaudey in 1736, the precinct wall remained intact, and foundations of other structures could still be traced. Today, nothing of the abbey survives above ground, though earthworks mark the position of the central monastic complex.

The church was dug into in 1831 and 1851, primarily to recover stonework for reuse. On the second occasion the materi-al was intended for the repair of Swin-stead church. No plan was made of the discoveries, though descriptions of what was uncovered have survived. It seems the nave piers, for example, were made up of clustered shafts. A larger freestand-ing pier of sixteen shafts — some 11 feet (3.4m) in diameter — was presumably one of those in the crossing. Other piers were located in the areas of the south transept and the presbytery. All of this suggests a building of perhaps the late twelfth century. The nave was apparently repaired after a collapse in the early sixteenth century, for Abbot William Style claimed 'the body of my church fell down and the rebuilding cost me £100'.

Fergusson 1984a, 152
Richardson 1851
Pevsner and Harris 1989, 346
VCH Lincolnshire 1906, 143–45
Wilde 1871

WARDEN ABBEY

1136–1537

The site of Warden Abbey is about a mile (1.6km) west-south-west of Old Warden, and about 6 miles (9.7km) south-east of Bedford, off the A600. Virtually nothing remains in identifiable form, and there is only a fragment of the house which was built on the site after the dissolution.

Bedfordshire
Lincoln

TL 122438

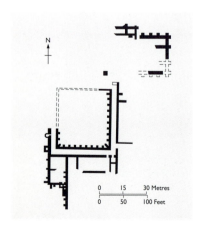

| 0 | 15 | 30 Metres |
| 0 | 50 | 100 Feet |

Warden was founded by Walter Espec (d. 1154) on his ancestral estates, as a daughter of his earlier foundation of Rievaulx. It was at Warden that St Waldef (d. 1160), the future abbot of Melrose, began his life as a Cistercian. In its turn, Warden was to be the mother house of Sawtry (founded 1147), Sibton (1150) and Tilty (1153), and by 1190 it apparently had twelve granges. In the early thirteenth century there may have been over fifty monks at the house. About 1224, as many as thirty of the community appear to have been imprisoned in Bedford Castle by Fawkes de Bréauté after an attack on the abbey, during which one monk was killed and others wounded. There was a campaign of rebuilding on the church between 1323 and 1366, which was possi-bly largely confined to the eastern limb.

In 1535 the abbey's income was assessed at £389, showing that it was still one of the wealthier British houses of the order. Warden was dissolved in 1537, at which time there were fifteen monks in addition to the abbot. Since it was evident-ly such a well-endowed house, and had been so active initially, it is particularly frustrating that little is known of its build-ings. However, a record of a visitation in 1492 suggests that all was not well at that time, and that there was then cause for concern over both the observance of the religious life and the state of the buildings.

After the dissolution the abbey was acquired by Robert Gostwick, and ruined fragments of brick extensions made by him to the monastic buildings are now the only upstanding physical remains. Much of the rest of the site was cleared of buildings as late as about 1790. Excavations in 1839, in 1960–66, and again in 1974 have revealed something of the plan of the church and cloister. Of the church itself, it is known that the presbytery was aisled and vaulted, and that the aisles later added to the presbytery extended over the site of the original inner transept chapels. Beyond this, excavation has shown something of the high quality of artistic patronage at the abbey. Apart from fragments of carved and painted stonework and stained glass, decorated tiles have been found which show affiliations with the White Monk houses at Bordesley, Boxley, Sawley, and Waverley. Perhaps the most important artefacts of any associated with the abbey are three small copper gilt and enamel roundels, which were found at Shefford and bought by the British Museum in 1853. They display the arms of the abbey and the initials WA, and on them are depicted the Virgin and Child, the Crucifixion and a shield-bearing angel.

Compton 1894.
Fergusson 1984a, 152–53
Fowler 1930
Pevsner 1968, 132
Rudd and West 1964
VCH Bedfordshire 1904, 361–66; 1912, 251–53

WAVERLEY ABBEY

Waverley Abbey was the very first Cistercian plantation in the British Isles. Founded in 1128 by Bishop William Giffard of Winchester (1107–29), it was to be sited in the valley of the river Wey, close to the episcopal manor of Farnham. The founding colony arrived in Surrey from the northern French abbey of l'Aumône (Loir-et-Cher), sometimes known as 'Le Petit-Cîteaux', and itself a daughter of the great Burgundian mother house.

The Waverley monks were to discover that the valley of the Wey was prone to periodic flooding. Consequently, they found it necessary to raise the ground level of the abbey buildings on several occasions. In archaeological terms, this has resulted in the exceptional preservation of the earliest monastic structures below the present ground surface. At the time of the

1128–1536

The site of Waverley Abbey is located south of the B3001, about 2 miles (3.2km) south-east of Farnham. Fragments of the church and monastic buildings are in the care of English Heritage and are accessible at all reasonable times.

Surrey
Winchester

SU 868453

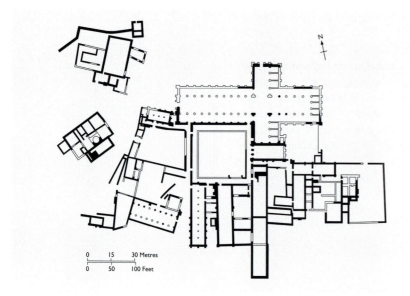

0   15   30 Metres
0   50   100 Feet

comparatively small church had a square-ended presbytery, a long aisleless nave, and the transept arms — each with a single eastern chapel — were apparently walled off from an unsegregated crossing. The cloister, which was 96 feet (29.3m) square, lay to the south of the nave. Here, in the single-storey east range, the chapter house was positioned next to the south transept, and it was contained within the limits of the range itself. Next to this was the parlour. The monks' dormitory, which was entered from the south-east corner of the cloister, lay at the southern end of the range. Although it was not excavated, it seems the south range included an east–west refectory and a kitchen. The west range was apparently of two storeys, with cellarage, the outer parlour, and the lay brothers' refectory on the ground floor. The upper floor was occupied by the lay brothers' dormitory.

In general terms, the remarkable preservation of these early structures is quite exceptional. The walls of the church stand up to 4 feet (1.2m) high, and it remains the best recorded example of one of the austere edifices of the order's pioneering years. The domestic ranges, which were 27 feet (8.2m) wide, and stand up to 6 feet (1.8m) high, are the earliest Cistercian cloister buildings yet investigated. As noted, all was buried as the community attempted to overcome the problems of flooding at the site.

As the Waverley community began to grow (with up to seventy choir monks and 120 lay brothers mentioned in 1187), it was necessary to begin rebuilding. Work began with the east and south ranges of the cloister as early as the 1160s. First, the dormitory was extended, and this was followed by the building of a new north–south refectory, a warming house and a replacement kitchen. But enlargement was by no means restricted to the monks' buildings. Indeed, a permanent infirmary was constructed for the lay brothers to the south-west of their range. As a whole, this phase of work was proba-

great survey in 1535, the assessed annual income of the house was given as £174; it was suppressed in the following year. The site was granted to Sir William fitz William (d. 1542) who built a house incorporating portions of the former monastic buildings. In 1660 the antiquarian, John Aubrey (d. 1697), recorded a precinct wall 10 feet (3m) high enclosing some 60 acres (24.3ha). Waverley was sold in 1725 to a Mr Child of Guildford, who demolished much of the abbey complex to build a new house to the north-west (outside the former precinct area). An engraving of 1737 shows the ruins much as they appear today. Waverley was excavated from 1898 to 1902, initially by William St John Hope, but from 1899 by Harold Brakspear. The ruins were taken into State care in 1964, and they have since been conserved for public display. Most of the excavated buildings have been reburied to ensure their protection, though their layout is indicated by a differential cutting of the grass.

From the evidence of Brakspear's excavations, it is clear that a church and claustral ranges were begun shortly after the 1128 foundation. Indeed, by about 1135 the layout of the earliest stone monastery may have been complete. The

bly completed before about 1180, when a new three-bay chapter house and an adjoining parlour were built in the east range. Other construction projects in hand at this time included a new infirmary situated beyond the east range, an extension to the lay brothers' infirmary, and a guest house to the west of the church.

However, it was not until 1203 that work began on a monumental new church to replace the small Romanesque structure of the original settlement. Designed by Dan William (d. 1222) of Broadwater, the Gothic edifice was raised around the early church, and it was sufficiently complete for the monks to enter their choir in 1231. But building was slow, and the nave was not completed until the third quarter of the thirteenth century. As finished, the new church had an aisled presbytery of five bays, with the aisle being carried across the east end — as at Byland — to house five chapels. The transepts each had three square eastern chapels, there was a tower at the crossing, and west of this a ten-bay aisled nave. Although the entire plan is known from excavation, very little of the superstructure of this church remains apart from the south transept.

Contemporary with the building of the new presbytery, the monks were also to embark on a further extension of the east range. As a result, the dormitory stood at more than two and a half times the length of the original structure, which suggests that the community was still continuing to grow at this time. Meanwhile, the southern part of the west range was rebuilt to provide a new refectory of eight double bays for the lay brothers. This coincided with the removal of the northern half of the range, itself occasioned by the enlargement of the cloister to suit the plans for the new nave. In short, the only space for the lay brothers' dormitory would have been over their new refectory. It would seem, therefore, that the number of *conversi* must have been falling by the middle years of the thirteenth century.

Building in the fourteenth century was largely restricted to non claustral structures. The inner court, situated to the west of the west range, saw a number of developments, and modifications to the infirmary were also undertaken. Both of these areas continued to be developed into the fifteenth century. The infirmary, for example, was divided into small, private chambers. The latest modifications noted by the excavators included the levelling up of the cloister by almost 3 feet (0.9m), and the replacement of the open arcades with a solid wall.

The east range at Waverley was extended in several phases over the later twelfth and early thirteenth centuries. Here, the early thirteenth-century gable at the southern end is shown, close to the river Wey.

Baigent 1880–82
Brakspear 1905
Fergusson 1984a, 153–54
Knowles and St Joseph 1952, 62–63
Nairn and Pevsner 1971, 502–05

WHALLEY ABBEY

1172/1296–1537

Whalley is situated some 6 miles (9.7km) north-east of Blackburn, on an unclassified road off the A59. The outer gatehouse is managed by English Heritage and is open at all reasonable times. The site of the church, cloister and abbot's house is owned by the diocese of Blackburn, and the ruins are open to the public. The west range, which remains roofed and now contains a chapel, belongs to the Catholic Church.

Lancashire
Coventry and Lichfield

SD 731359

The early fourteenth-century outer gate at Whalley included a chapel on the upper floor.

The origins of this Lancashire abbey are to be traced to the colony of Combermere monks settled at Stanlaw on the Mersey estuary by John, the constable of Chester, in 1172. Having occupied the desolate Cheshire location for more than a hundred years, all but six monks in the community abandoned the buildings in 1296, moving instead to a new site at Whalley. Their patron, Henry de Lacy (d. 1311), agreed to the transfer since Stanlaw was susceptible to flooding, and the abbey community's lands were apparently being eroded by the spring tides. The choice of the new site was not made in haste, but within twenty years the monks were considering yet a further move to Toxteth. In particular, it seems that Whalley lay too close to Sawley Abbey; the two communities were soon embroiled in a bitter dispute. There were also problems over the lack of timber for building, and even over the claim to the new site itself. All in all, it proved a difficult beginning, though the monks finally chose to stay and started work on permanent buildings.

The last abbot, John Paslew (1507–37), was implicated in the Pilgrimage of Grace in 1536. He was tried and executed as a traitor in the following March, and Whalley was seized by the Crown. It remained in royal hands until 1553 when it was sold to John Braddyll (the former abbey bailiff) and Richard Assheton. Assheton took the monastic buildings, and his family began the conversion of the infirmary and

The doorway in the chapter house façade at Whalley led into a vestibule. The chapter house itself appears to have been octagonal in plan (David Robinson).

abbot's house to a mansion. It was not until the 1660s that the church was finally demolished, in the time of Sir Ralph Assheton (d. 1680), along with the south range of the cloister. In 1923, the greater part of the site was acquired by the Church of England to establish a conference house. The first wardens, Canons J. R. Lumb and C. H. Lambert, excavated much of the abbey buildings between 1930 and 1934.

Henry de Lacy claimed to have begun the church in 1296, and a consecration in 1306 probably marks the completion of its eastern limb. All that survives of this church is the body of the south transept. Rebuilding began in 1330 and work was not completed until 1380. The first parts of the church to be erected were a new aisled presbytery of four bays, the crossing, and north transept. The crossing tower was nearing completion in 1356 when Brother Ralph of Pontefract was killed by a fall of stone from the belfry. As rebuilt, the transepts had three eastern chapels, and the new north transept had a western aisle. The monks' choir occupied the eastern two bays of the nave, where the resonance pits below their stalls remain.

The cloister lay on the south side of the church, and the east and west ranges remain substantially complete. The east range dates from the first half of the fourteenth century, and butted against the south transept retained from the earlier

church. In plan, it is typical of a later Cistercian east range, with a sacristy against the transept, a vestibule leading to a chapter house located beyond the range, a parlour, a passage through the range, and finally the monks' day room. The only departure from the norm was the planning of the chapter house, which was octagonal. The dormitory occupied all of the upper floor, with a latrine at its south-east corner that connected to the range by a short dogleg corridor on two floors. The south range comprised the day stair at its east end, followed by the warming house, an east–west refectory, and the kitchen, all built at the close of the fourteenth century. By this date, north–south refectories (designed to house large Cistercian communities during earlier centuries) were no longer required. At Whalley, as elsewhere, the more modest needs of this period meant the refectory could be fitted into the range itself. The short west range, completed in 1415, was never occupied by lay brothers. Indeed, it was built after they had ceased to be a significant element in Cistercian communities. The northern end comprised cellarage, while its two southern bays formed the outer parlour. The upper floor probably provided guest accommodation.

To the east of the east range are the somewhat confusing remains of the

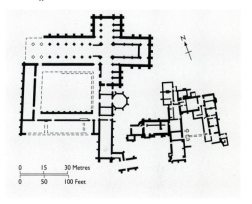

Ashmore 1996
Butler and Given-Wilson 1979, 387–88
Fergusson 1984a, 146–47
Knowles and St Joseph 1952, 102–03

1140–1539

The abbey is situated off the A40, about one and a half miles (2.4km) north-east of the village of Whitland. Very little survives by way of standing remains, though fragments of the church may be seen and its plan is marked in outline. The site is accessible at all reasonable times.

Carmarthenshire
St Davids

SN 208182

Whitland was the fount of Cistercian settlement in the heart of native Wales. The low foundations of the church, seen here from the south-east, have recently been consolidated for display.

abbot's house, built by John Paslew in the early sixteenth century, together with the site of the infirmary hall and chapel. This area lay within its own enclosure, entered through a fine late fifteenth-century gate to the north-east of the church. To the west of the central complex is the early fourteenth-century outer gate. There is a chapel on its upper floor, lit by eight three-light windows with Decorated tracery.

WHITLAND ABBEY

Whitland was one of just four abbeys in Britain directly colonized from St Bernard's Clairvaux. It was, moreover, to prove the fount of the Cistercian triumph in the heartland of medieval Wales. The house owed its origin to the initiative of Bernard, the influential Anglo-Norman bishop of St Davids (1115–48). Under his patronage, the Clairvaux monks were to arrive in Wales in 1140, and by 1144 they were probably settled at Little Trefgarn near Haverfordwest. The move to a more suitable site at Whitland took place about 1151.

In 1164, the expanding community sent out a group of monks for the foundation of Strata Florida, and the following year both houses began to attract the generous munificence of Prince Rhys ap Gruffudd (d. 1197). With his enthusiastic support, Whitland's prosperity was assured, at least for the foreseeable future. By the thirteenth century, its extensive land holdings were organized around up to seventeen grange centres, and in the years of growth further daughter colonies had been sent out to Strata Marcella (1170) and Cwmhir (1176) in Wales, and to Comber (1199) and Tracton (1224) in Ireland. Through its strength of piety, and in its deep-rooted appeal to the native people of Wales, Whitland was to inspire and enrich the religious, cultural, and even the patriotic aspirations of the country.

Sadly, considering the great importance of the foundation, very little survives of the abbey buildings. However, the church was excavated in 1926, and it was further examined in 1994–95 prior to a scheme of landscaping and display. It was a building in the classic Bernardine tradition, and must have been raised very soon after the community arrived here in 1151. A short, square-ended presbytery projected from narrow transepts, each with two eastern chapels separated by solid walls. In the nave of eight bays, the arcades were raised on rectangular piers set on low, chamfered plinths of cruciform plan. In all, Whitland's church was doubtless very similar in scale and appearance to that of twelfth-century Margam. The comparison probably extended to the fact that Whitland, too, is likely to have been designed with an unsegregated crossing, one which cannot have supported a tower of any note. Indeed, to begin with at least, the presbytery was almost certainly arranged in the stepped, so-called Fontenay style.

From the evidence of the plan alone, it would appear that the Bernardine church at Whitland was to remain largely unaltered throughout the abbey's history. This said, some of the architectural details recovered during the excavations do reveal distinct early Gothic characteristics. The jambs of a doorway, for example, which led from the crossing towards the north transept, featured water-holding bases and dogtooth ornament.

South of the church, the form of the cloister is in part preserved in a garden enclosure, and west of this can be seen traces of the lay brothers' range. In the valley to the north, there are indications of watercourses, fishponds and a large dam, all of which reflect workaday monastic landscape changes within the immediate environs of the abbey precinct.

During the second half of the thirteenth century, the Whitland community was faced with a dilemma of conflicting loyalties. In the Welsh wars of King Edward I, in particular, the monks had to choose between their allegiance to the Crown and the natural loyalty they owed their native kinsmen. In the event, havoc was wreaked across the abbey's estates, with the king eventually acknowledging the legitimacy of a claim for £260 by way of compensation. The fact that nothing was ever paid

suggests that Whitland may well have forfeited its rights as a consequence of strong partisan sympathies during the years of conflict. Thereafter, although this episode was far from the only factor, the abbey's economy never again reached the buoyant levels of the twelfth century.

In the great survey of 1535, with as few as five monks remaining in the community, Whitland's income was assessed at £135. Abbot William ap Thomas was to successfully petition against immediate closure of his house the following year, putting up the vast sum of £400 for the privilege of being spared. The short-lived respite was to last only until February 1539.

Collier 1925–26
James 1978

WOBURN ABBEY

Woburn was founded by Hugh de Bolebec in 1145, on the advice of Abbot Henry Murdac of Fountains, and it was from Fountains that the first colony came. Adam, a monk of Fountains who was to become the first abbot of Meaux in 1150, may have been involved in laying out the first buildings according to the precepts of the Cistercian order, a role he appears also to have fulfilled at the abbeys of Vaudey and Kirkstead.

In the first years of the thirteenth century Woburn was to provide a colony for Medmenham, though it seems that by 1234 the abbey's finances were in such a parlous condition that the majority of the monks and lay brethren had to be accommodated in other houses. The house's finances must have been later placed on a better footing, since in about 1535 it had an income of £391. By the dissolution in 1538 there were thirteen monks under the abbot, and three young gentlemen with a schoolmaster were said to have been boarders until recently.

The good financial state of the abbey at the dissolution is further demonstrated by the 419 ounces of gilt plate and 326 ounces of parcel gilt plate which were then removed. The abbey seems also to have been in good spiritual order, under the leadership of the scholarly Abbot Robert Hobbes. In 1534 Hobbes was persuaded to take the Oath of Supremacy, though this was clearly against his conscience, and he and several monks were later brought to trial, with the result that Hobbes and his subprior, Ralph Barnes, were executed.

Nothing survives of the abbey, which was leased by Sir Francis Bryan immediately following the dissolution. In 1547 it was granted to Lord John Russell, the ancestor of the duke of Bedford, the present owner. It has been suggested that the quadrangle around which extends the present largely eighteenth-century house could perpetuate the cloister, and if that were the case, it is possible that some of the masonry of the abbey is subsumed within the walls of the house.

1145–1538

The site of Woburn Abbey is south-east of Woburn itself on the A4012. Nothing of the medieval abbey is visible. The site is now occupied by the house of the dukes of Bedford which takes its name from the abbey, and which is open to the public on a regular basis.

Bedfordshire
Lincoln

SP 965325

Fergusson 1983
Fergusson 1984a, 154–55
Pevsner 1968, 166–67
Thomson 1933
VCH Bedfordshire 1904, 366–70; 1912, 459

BIBLIOGRAPHY

Adams 1984: D. John Adams, 'The Restoration of Margam Abbey Church in the 19th Century', *Transactions of the Port Talbot Historical Society*, **3** (1984), 60–67.

Arnold 1992: C. J. Arnold, 'Strata Marcella: The Archaeological Investigations of 1890 and the Results of a Geophysical Survey in 1990', *Montgomeryshire Collections*, **80** (1992), 88–94.

Ashmore 1996: O. Ashmore, *A Guide to Whalley Abbey*, 5th edition (Blackburn 1996).

Astill 1993: G. G. Astill, *A Medieval Industrial Complex and its Landscape: The Metalworking Watermills and Workshops of Bordesley Abbey* (Council for British Archaeology Research Report, **92**, London 1993).

Aston 1993: Michael Aston, *Monasteries* (London 1993).

Auberger 1986: J.-B. Auberger, *L'Unanimité Cistercienne Primitive: Mythe ou Réalité*, Cîteaux: Studia et Documenta, **3** (Achel 1986).

Aubert 1947: Marcel Aubert, *L'Architecture Cistercienne en France*, 2nd edition, 2 volumes (Paris 1947).

Aveling 1870: J. R. Aveling, *The History of Roche Abbey from its Foundation to its Dissolution* (Worksop 1870).

Baigent 1880–82: F. J. Baigent, 'On the Abbey and Church of the Blessed Mary at Waverley', *Surrey Archaeological Collections*, **8** (1880–82), 157–210.

Baker 1969: L. G. D. Baker, 'The Foundation of Fountains Abbey', *Northern History*, **4** (1969), 29–43.

Baker 1970: D. Baker, 'The Desert in the North', *Northern History*, **5** (1970), 1–11.

Baker 1975: D. Baker, 'Patronage in the Early Twelfth-Century Church: Walter Espec, Kirkham and Rievaulx', in B. Jaspert and R. Môhr, *Festschrift Winfried Zeller* (Marburg 1975), 92–100.

Barker 1869: T. Barker, 'Recent Excavations on the Site of Revesby Abbey', *Associated Architectural Societies' Reports and Papers*, **10** (1869), 22–26.

Barnes 1984: Guy D. Barnes, *Kirkstall Abbey, 1147–1539: An Historical Study*, Publications of the Thoresby Society, **58** (Leeds 1984).

Barrow 1953: G. W. S. Barrow, 'Scottish Rulers and the Religious Orders, 1070–1153', *Transactions of the Royal Historical Society*, series 5, **3** (1953), 77–100.

Barrow 1973: G. W. S. Barrow, *The Kingdom of the Scots* (London 1973).

Baskerville 1937: Geoffrey Baskerville, *English Monks and the Suppression of the Monasteries* (London 1937).

Bazeley 1899: W. Bazeley, 'The Abbey of St Mary, Hailes', *Transactions of the Bristol and Gloucestershire Archaeological Society*, **22** (1899), 257–71.

Beaumont 1921: G. F. Beaumont, 'The Remains of Coggeshall Abbey', *Transactions of the Essex Archaeological Society*, new series, **15** (1921), 59–76.

Beck 1844: T. J. Beck, *Annales Furnesienses: History and Antiquities of the Abbey of Furness* (London 1844).

Berman 1986: Constance Hoffman Berman, *Medieval Agriculture, the Southern French Countryside, and the Early Cistercians* (Transactions of the American Philosophical Society, **76**, Philadelphia 1986).

Berman 1992: Constance Hoffman Berman, 'The Development of Cistercian Economic Practice during the Lifetime of Bernard of Clairvaux: the Historical Perspective on Innocent II's 1132 Privilege', in Sommerfeldt 1992, 202–13.

Bethell 1966: D. Bethell, 'The Foundation of Fountains Abbey and the State of St Mary's, York, in 1132', *Journal of Ecclesiastical History*, **17** (1966), 11–27.

Bilson 1909a: John Bilson, 'The Architecture of the Cistercians, with Special Reference to Some of their Earlier Churches in England', *Archaeological Journal*, **66** (1909), 185–280.

Bilson 1909b: John Bilson, 'Salley Abbey', *Yorkshire Archaeological Journal*, **20** (1909), 454–60.

Birch 1897: Walter de Gray Birch, *A History of Margam Abbey* (London 1897).

Birch 1902: Walter de Gray Birch, *A History of Neath Abbey* (Neath 1902).

Blashill 1881–82: Thomas Blashill, 'The Architectural History of Tintern Abbey', *Transactions of the Bristol and Gloucestershire Archaeological Society*, **6** (1881–82), 88–106.

Blashill 1885: Thomas Blashill, 'The Architectural History of Dore Abbey', *Journal of the British Archaeological Association*, **41** (1885), 363–71.

Blashill 1901–02: Thomas Blashill, 'The 17th Century Restoration of Dore Abbey Church', *Transactions of the Woolhope Naturalists' Field Club*, **17** (1901–02), 184–89.

Bloxham 1863–64: M. H. Bloxham, 'Merevale Abbey', *Associated Architectural Societies' Reports and Papers*, **7** (1863–64), 324–33.

Bohs 1949: J. M. Bohs, *The Abbey of Bindon, A.D. 1172* (Dorchester 1949).

Bond 1866–68: E. A. Bond (editor), *Chronica Monasterii de Melsa*, 3 volumes (Rolls Series, **43**, London 1866–68).

Bouchard 1988: Constance Brittain Bouchard, 'Cistercian Ideals Versus Reality: 1134 Reconsidered', *Cîteaux*, **39** (1988), 217–39.

Bouchard 1991: Constance Brittain Bouchard, *Holy Entrepreneurs: Cistercians, Knights and Economic Exchange in Twelfth-Century Burgundy* (Ithaca and London 1991).

Bouton and Van Damme 1974: Jean de la Croix Bouton and Jean-Baptiste Van Damme (editors), *Les Plus Anciens Textes de Cîteaux*, Commentaria Cisterciensis, Studia et Documenta, 2nd edition (Achel 1974).

Bower 1852: J. Bower, *History and Antiquities of Melrose, Old Melrose and Dryburgh Abbey* (Melrose 1852).

Brakspear 1901a: Harold Brakspear, 'On the First Church at Furness', *Transactions of the Lancashire and Cheshire Antiquarian Society*, **18** (1901), 70–87.

Brakspear 1901b: Harold Brakspear, 'The Architecture of Hayles Abbey', *Transactions of the Bristol and Gloucestershire Archaeological Society*, **24** (1901), 126–35.

Brakspear 1901c: Harold Brakspear, 'The Church of Hayles Abbey', *Archaeological Journal*, **58** (1901), 350–57.

Brakspear 1905: Harold Brakspear, *Waverley Abbey* (Surrey Archaeological Society, Guildford 1905).

Brakspear 1906–07: Harold Brakspear, 'The Cistercian Abbey of Stanley, Wiltshire', *Archaeologia*, **60** (1906–07), 493–516.

Brakspear 1907–08: Harold Brakspear, 'Stanley Abbey', *Wiltshire Archaeological and Natural History Magazine*, **35** (1907–08), 541–81.

Brakspear 1909–10: Harold Brakspear, 'Pipewell Abbey, Northamptonshire', *Associated Architectural Societies' Reports and Papers*, **30** (1909–10), 299–313.

Brakspear 1913: Harold Brakspear, 'Forde Abbey', *Archaeological Journal*, **70** (1913), 498–99.

Brauzelius 1979: C. A. Brauzelius, 'Cistercian High Gothic: The Abbey Church of Longpont and the Architecture of the Cistercians in the Early Thirteenth Century', *Analecta Cisterciensia*, **35** (1979), 3–204.

Brock 1878: E. P. Loftus Brock, 'Valle Crucis Abbey', *Journal of the British Archaeological Association*, **34** (1878), 145–58.

Brooke 1986: C. N. L. Brooke, 'St Bernard, the Patrons and Monastic Planning', in Norton and Park 1986, 11–23.

Brooke 1989: C. N. L. Brooke, 'King David I of Scotland as a Connoisseur of the Religious Orders', in C. E. Viola (editor), *Mediaevalia Christiana* (Paris 1989), 320–34.

Brown 1969: A. L. Brown, 'The Cistercian Abbey of Saddell', *Innes Review*, **20** (1969), 130–37.

Brown 1985–88: Philippa Brown (editor), *Sibton Abbey Cartularies and Charters*, 4 volumes (Suffolk Record Society: Suffolk Charters, **7–10**, 1985–88).

Brown 1988: S. W. Brown, 'Excavations and Building Recording at Buckfast Abbey, Devon', *Proceedings of the Devon Archaeological Society*, **46** (1988), 13–89.

Brown, Colvin and Taylor 1963: R. Allen Brown, H. M Colvin and A. J. Taylor, *The History of the Kings Works*, **1**, *The Middle Ages* (London 1963).

Buckle 1889: Edmund Buckle, 'The Buildings of Cleeve Abbey', *Proceedings of the Somersetshire Archaeological and Natural History Society*, **35** (1889), 83–120.

Burton 1986: Janet Burton, 'The Foundation of the British Cistercian Houses', in Norton and Park 1986, 24–39.

Burton 1991: Janet Burton, 'The Abbeys of Byland and Jervaulx, and the Problems of the English Savigniacs, 1134–1156', in Judith Loades (editor), *Monastic Studies 2* (Bangor 1991), 119–31.

Burton 1994: Janet Burton, *Monastic and Religious Orders in Britain 1000–1300* (Cambridge 1994).

Butler 1964: L. A. S. Butler, 'An Excavation in the Vicarage Garden, Conway, 1961', *Archaeologia Cambrensis*, **113** (1964) 97–128.

Butler 1976a: L. A. S. Butler, *Neath Abbey* (HMSO, London 1976).

Butler 1976b: L. A. S. Butler, 'Valle Crucis Abbey: An Excavation in 1970', *Archaeologia Cambrensis*, **125** (1976), 80–126.

Butler 1982: Lawrence Butler, 'The Cistercians in England and Wales: A Survey of Recent Archaeological Work 1960–1980', in Meredith P. Lillich (editor), *Studies in Cistercian Art and Architecture: Volume One* (Cistercian Studies Series, **66**, Kalamazoo 1982), 88–101.

Butler 1984: Lawrence Butler, 'Neath Abbey: The Twelfth-Century Church', *Archaeologia Cambrensis*, **133** (1984), 147–51.

Butler 1994: Lawrence Butler, 'Saint Bernard of Clairvaux and the Cistercian Abbeys in Wales', *Arte Medievale*, II Serie, Anno VIII, n. 1, tomo secondo (Rome 1994), 1–11.

Butler and Evans 1980: L. A. S. Butler and D. H. Evans, 'The Cistercian Abbey of Aberconway at Maenan, Gwynedd: Excavations in 1968', *Archaeologia Cambrensis*, **129** (1980), 37–63.

Butler and Given-Wilson 1979: Lionel Butler and Chris Given-Wilson, *Medieval Monasteries of Great Britain* (London 1979).

Campbell 1899: J. Campbell, *Balmerino and its Abbey*, 2nd edition (Edinburgh and London 1899).

Canivez 1933–41: Josephus-Maria Canivez (editor), *Statuta Capitulorum Generalium Ordinis Cisterciensis ab Anno 1116 ad Annum 1786*, 8 volumes (Louvain 1933–41).

Carrick 1908: J. C. Carrick, *The Abbey of St Mary Newbottle*, 2nd edition (Selkirk 1908).

Chibnall 1969–80: M. Chibnall (editor), *The Ecclesiastical History of Orderic Vitalis*, 6 volumes (Oxford 1969–80).

Chinnock 1900–05: E. J. Chinnock, 'Edward I at Sweetheart Abbey', *Transactions of the Dumfriesshire and Galloway Natural History and Antiquarian Society*, **17** (1900–05), 172–74.

Chinnock 1909–10: E. J. Chinnock, 'Charters relating to New Abbey', *Transactions of the Dumfriesshire and Galloway Natural History and Antiquarian Society*, **22** (1909–10), 272–78.

Christie 1914: J. G. Christie, *The Abbey of Dundrennan* (Glasgow 1914).

Clapham 1914–15: A. W. Clapham, 'On the Topography of the Cistercian Abbey of Tower Hill', *Archaeologia*, **66** (1914–15), 353–64.

Clapham and Duffy 1950: Alfred Clapham and A. R. Duffy, 'Forde Abbey', *Archaeological Journal*, **107** (1950), 119–20.

Clutterbuck 1994: Robin Clutterbuck, *Buckfast Abbey: A History* (Buckfast 1994).

Coad 1993: J. G. Coad, *Hailes Abbey*, 2nd edition (English Heritage, London 1993).

Coldstream 1986: Nicola Coldstream, 'Cistercian Architecture from Beaulieu to the Dissolution', in Norton and Park 1986, 139–59.

Collier 1925–26: [E. V. Collier], 'Whitland Abbey Excavations: Interim Report', *Transactions of the Carmarthenshire Antiquarian Society*, **19** (1925–26), 63–65.

Compton 1894: C. H. Compton, 'Kirkham Priory and Warden Abbey', *Journal of the British Archaeological Association*, **50** (1894), 283–94.

Cooke 1893: Alice M. Cooke, 'The Settlement of the Cistercians in England', *English Historical Review*, **8** (1893), 625–76.

Cooper 1856: G.M. Cooper, 'Notices of the Abbey of Robertsbridge', *Sussex Archaeological Collections*, **8** (1856), 140–76.

Copeland 1953: G. W. Copeland, 'Some Problems of Buckland Abbey', *Reports and Transactions of the Devonshire Association*, **85** (1953), 41–52.

Coppack 1986a: Glyn Coppack, 'The Excavation of an Outer Court Building, Perhaps the Woolhouse, at Fountains Abbey, North Yorkshire', *Medieval Archaeology*, **30** (1986), 46–87.

Coppack 1986b: Glyn Coppack, 'Some Descriptions of Rievaulx Abbey in 1538–9: The Disposition of a Major Cistercian Precinct in the Early Sixteenth Century', *Journal of the British Archaeological Association*, **139** (1986), 100–33.

Coppack 1993: Glyn Coppack, *Fountains Abbey* (London 1993).

Coppack and Fergusson 1994: Glyn Coppack and Peter Fergusson, *Rievaulx Abbey* (English Heritage, London 1994).

Coppack and Gilyard-Beer 1993: Glyn Coppack and R. Gilyard-Beer, *Fountains Abbey* (English Heritage, London 1993).

Cowan and Easson 1976: Ian B. Cowan and D. E. Easson, *Medieval Religious Houses: Scotland*, 2nd edition (London 1976).

Cowley 1977: F. G. Cowley, *The Monastic Order in South Wales, 1066–1349* (Cardiff 1977).

Crawley-Boevey 1920: Francis Crawley-Boevey, 'Flaxley Abbey', *Archaeological Journal*, 77 (1920), 445–47.

Crawley-Boevey 1921: Francis H. Crawley-Boevey, 'Some Recent Discoveries at Flaxley Abbey', *Transactions of the Bristol and Gloucestershire Archaeological Society*, 43 (1921), 57–62.

Cross and Vickers 1995: Claire Cross and Noreen Vickers (editors), *Monks, Friars and Nuns in Sixteenth Century Yorkshire* (Yorkshire Archaeological Society Record Series, 150, 1995, for 1991 and 1992).

Cruden 1952–53: Stewart Cruden, 'Glenluce Abbey: Finds Recovered During Excavations', *Transactions of the Dumfriesshire and Galloway Natural History and Antiquarian Society*, 29 (1952), 177–94; 30 (1953), 179–80.

Curle 1935–37: J. Curle, 'Melrose: the Precinct Wall and Some Notes Upon the Abbey of Melrose', *History of the Berwickshire Naturalists' Club*, 18 (1935–37), 29–70.

Cutts 1858: E. L. Cutts, 'An Architectural Account of the Remains of Coggeshall Abbey', *Transactions of the Essex Archaeological Society*, 1 (1858), 166–85.

Dale 1863: B. Dale, *Annals of Coggeshall* (London 1863).

Dalrymple 1899: Hew H. Dalrymple, 'The Five Great Churches of Galloway', *Archaeological Collections Relating to Ayrshire and Galloway*, 10 (Edinburgh 1899).

David 1929: H. E. David, 'Margam Abbey, Glamorgan', *Archaeologia Cambrensis*, 84 (1929), 317–24.

Davidson 1843: James Davidson, *The History of Newenham Abbey* (London 1843).

Davies 1997: Stephen Davies, *Jervaulx Abbey* (Jervaulx 1997).

Day 1911: E. Hermitage Day, 'The Cistercian Abbey of Cwm Hir', *Archaeologia Cambrensis*, series 6, 11 (1911), 9–25.

Denton 1992: Jeffrey Denton, 'From the Foundation of Vale Royal Abbey to the Statute of Carlisle: Edward I and Ecclesiastical Patronage', in P. R. Coss and S. D. Lloyd (editors), *Thirteenth-Century England IV: Proceedings of the Newcastle Upon Tyne Conference, 1991* (Woodbridge 1992), 123–37.

Desmond 1971: Lawrence A. Desmond, 'The Statute of Carlisle and the Cistercians 1298–1369', in *Studies in Medieval Cistercian History presented to Jeremiah F. O'Sullivan* (Cistercian Studies, 13, Spencer 1971), 138–62.

Desmond 1975: Lawrence A. Desmond, 'The Appropriation of Churches by the Cistercians in England to 1400', *Analecta Cisterciensia*, 31 (1975), 246–66.

Dickinson 1967: J. C. Dickinson, 'Furness Abbey: An Archaeological Reconsideration', *Transactions of the Cumberland and Westmorland Antiquarian and Archaeological Society*, 67 (1967), 51–80.

Dickinson 1989: J. C. Dickinson, *Furness Abbey*, latest impression (English Heritage, London 1989).

Dickinson 1963: P. G. M. Dickinson, *Tilty Abbey and the Parish Church of St Mary* (Chelmsford 1963).

Dimier 1957: M. Anselme Dimier, 'Origine des déambulatoires à Chapelles Rayonnantes non Saillantes', *Bulletin Monumental*, 115 (1957), 23–33.

Dimier 1971: M. Anselme Dimier, *L'Art Cistercien: Hors de France* (La Pierre-qui-Vire 1971).

Dimier 1982: M. Anselme Dimier, *L'Art Cistercien: France*, 3rd edition (La Pierre-qui-Vire 1982).

Donkin 1969: R. A. Donkin, 'A Check List of Printed Works Relating to the Cistercian Order as a Whole and to the Houses of the British Isles in Particular', *Documentation Cistercienne*, 2 (Belgium: Rochefort 1969).

Donkin 1978: R. A. Donkin, *The Cistercians: Studies in the Geography of Medieval England and Wales* (Pontifical Institute of Medieval Studies: Studies and Texts, 38, Toronto 1978).

Donnelly 1949: James S. Donnelly, *The Decline of the Medieval Cistercian Laybrotherhood* (New York 1949).

Donnelly 1954: James S. Donnelly, 'Changes in the Grange Economy of English and Welsh Cistercian Abbeys, 1300–1540', *Traditio*, 10 (1954), 399–458.

Douglas 1925–26: W. Douglas, 'Culross Abbey and its Charters', *Proceedings of the Society of Antiquaries of Scotland*, 60 (1925–26), 67–94.

Dugdale 1730: W. Dugdale, *The Antiquities of Warwickshire*, 1 (London 1730).

Dunning 1985: Robert W. Dunning, 'The Last Days of Cleeve Abbey', in C. M. Barron and C. Harper-Bill (editors), *The Church in Pre-Reformation Society* (Woodbridge 1985), 58–67.

Dutton 1990: Marsha L. Dutton, 'The Conversion and Vocation of Aelred of Rievaulx: A Historical Hypothesis', in Daniel Williams (editor), *England in the Twelfth Century: Proceedings of the 1988 Harlaxton Symposium* (Woodbridge 1990), 31–49.

Easson 1947: D. E. Easson (editor), *Charters of the Abbey of Coupar Angus*, 2 volumes (Scottish History Society, 40–41, Edinburgh 1947).

Eckenrode 1973: T. R. Eckenrode, 'The English Cistercians and their Sheep during the Middle Ages', *Cîteaux*, 24 (1973), 250–66.

Eeles 1931: Francis C. Eeles, 'Cleeve Abbey: Recent Discoveries', *Proceedings of the Somersetshire Archaeological and Natural History Society*, 77 (1931), 37–47.

Ellis 1997: P. Ellis, 'Croxden Abbey, Staffordshire', *Journal of the Staffordshire Historical and Archaeological Society* (1997), 29–51.

English Heritage 1993: *Buildwas Abbey* (English Heritage, London 1993).

Esser 1953: Karl-Heinz Esser, 'Uber den Kirchenbau des Heiligen Bernhards von Clairvaux', *Archiv für Mittelrheinische Kirchengeschichte*, 5 (1953), 195–222.

Evans 1958: A. Leslie Evans, *Margam Abbey* (Port Talbot 1958).

Evans 1995: D. H. Evans, *Valle Crucis Abbey*, revised edition (Cadw, Cardiff 1995).

Fawcett 1994a: Richard Fawcett, *Scottish Abbeys and Priories* (London 1994).

Fawcett 1994b: Richard Fawcett, *Scottish Architecture from the Accession of the Stewarts to the Reformation* (Edinburgh 1994).

Ferguson 1874: C. J. Ferguson, 'St Mary's Abbey, Holme Cultram', *Transactions of the Cumberland and Westmorland Antiquarian and Archaeological Society*, 1 (1874), 263–75.

Fergusson 1970: Peter Fergusson, 'Early Cistercian Churches in Yorkshire and the Problem of the Cistercian Crossing Tower', *Journal of the Society of Architectural Historians*, 29 (1970), 211–21.

Fergusson 1971: Peter Fergusson, 'Roche Abbey: The Source and Date of the Eastern Remains', *Journal of the British Archaeological Association*, series 3, 34

(1971), 30–42.

Fergusson 1973: Peter Fergusson, 'The Late Twelfth-Century Rebuilding at Dundrennan Abbey', *Antiquaries Journal*, **53** (1973), 232–43.

Fergusson 1975: Peter Fergusson, 'The South Transept Elevation of Byland Abbey', *Journal of the British Archaeological Association*, series 3, **38** (1975), 155–76.

Fergusson 1983: Peter Fergusson, 'The First Architecture of the Cistercians in England and the Work of Abbot Adam of Meaux', *Journal of the British Archaeological Association*, **136** (1983), 74–86.

Fergusson 1984a: Peter Fergusson, *Architecture of Solitude: Cistercian Abbeys in Twelfth-Century England* (Princeton 1984).

Fergusson 1984b: Peter Fergusson, 'The Builders of Cistercian Monasteries in Twelfth Century England', in Meredith P. Lillich (editor), *Studies in Cistercian Art and Architecture: Volume Two* (Cistercian Studies Series, **69**, Kalamazoo 1984), 14–29.

Fergusson 1986: Peter Fergusson, 'The Twelfth-Century Refectories at Rievaulx and Byland Abbeys', in Norton and Park 1986, 160–80.

Fergusson 1990a: Peter Fergusson, *Roche Abbey* (English Heritage, London 1990).

Fergusson 1990b: Peter Fergusson, '"Porta Patens Esto": Notes on Early Cistercian Gatehouses in the North of England', in E. Fernie and P. Crossley (editors), *Medieval Architecture and its Intellectual Context* (London 1990), 47–59.

Fergusson and Harrison 1994: Peter Fergusson and Stuart Harrison, 'The Rievaulx Abbey Chapter House', *Antiquaries Journal*, **74** (1994), 211–55.

Fowler 1930: E. H. Fowler (editor), *Cartulary of the Abbey of Old Warden* (Bedfordshire Historical Record Society Publications, **13**, 1930).

Fowler 1876: J. T. Fowler (editor), *Chartularium Abbathiae de Novo Monasterio* (Surtees Society, **66**, Durham 1876).

France 1998: James France, *The Cistercians in Medieval Art* (Stroud 1998).

Galpin 1928: F. W. Galpin, 'The Abbey Church and Claustral Buildings of Tilty', *Transactions of the Essex Archaeological Society*, new series, **18** (1928), 85–95.

Gardner 1955: J. S. Gardner, 'Coggeshall Abbey and its Early Brickwork', *Journal of the British Archaeological Association*, series

3, **18** (1955), 19–32.

Gaskell Brown 1995: Cynthia Gaskell Brown (editor), 'Buckland Abbey, Devon: Surveys and Excavations, 1983–1995', *Proceedings of the Devon Archaeological Society*, **53** (1995), 25–82.

Gifford 1988: John Gifford, *Buildings of Scotland: Fife* (London 1988).

Gifford 1996: John Gifford, *Buildings of Scotland: Dumfries and Galloway* (London 1996).

Gilbanks 1899: G. E. Gilbanks, *Some Records of a Cistercian Abbey: Holmcultram, Cumberland* (London 1899).

Gilyard-Beer 1965: R. Gilyard-Beer, 'Rufford Abbey', *Medieval Archaeology*, **9** (1965), 161–63.

Gilyard-Beer 1990: R. Gilyard-Beer, *Cleeve Abbey*, 2nd edition (English Heritage, London 1990).

Gilyard-Beer and Coppack 1986: R. Gilyard-Beer and Glyn Coppack, 'Excavations at Fountains Abbey, North Yorkshire, 1979–80: The Early Development of the Monastery', *Archaeologia*, **108** (1986), 147–88.

Golding 1996: Brian J. Golding, 'The Cistercians and Gerald of Wales', *Reading Medieval Studies*, **21** (1996), 5–30.

Graham 1929: Rose Graham, 'The Great Schism and the English Monasteries of the Cistercian Order', *English Historical Review*, **44** (1929), 373–87.

Grainger and Collingwood 1929: F. Grainger and W. C. Collingwood, 'The Register and Records of Holmcultram', *Transactions of the Cumberland and Westmorland Antiquarian and Archaeological Society* (Record Series, **7**, 1929).

Grainger and Hawkins 1984–88: Ian Grainger and Duncan Hawkins, 'Excavations at the Royal Mint Site 1986–1988', *The London Archaeologist*, **5** (1984–88), 429–36.

Graves 1957: Coburn V. Graves, 'The Economic Activities of the Cistercians in Medieval England, 1128–1307', *Analecta Sacri Ordinis Cisterciensis*, **13** (1957), 30–60.

Greene 1992: J. Patrick Greene, *Medieval Monasteries* (Leicester 1992).

Gresley 1854: J. M. Gresley, *The Cistercian Abbey of Stoneley-in-Arden* (Ashby de la Zouche 1854).

Grove 1996: Doreen Grove, *Glenluce Abbey*, new edition (Historic Scotland, Edinburgh 1996).

Guignard 1878: P. Guignard (editor), *Les Monuments Primitifs de la Règle Cistercienne* (Dijon 1878).

Hahn 1957: Hanno Hahn, *Die Frühe Kirchenbaukunst der Zisterzienser* (Berlin 1957).

Hall 1896: J. Hall (editor), 'The Book of the Abbot of Combermere', *Record Society for Lancashire and Cheshire*, **31** (1896), 1–74.

Harbottle and Salway 1964: B. Harbottle and P. Salway, 'Excavations at Newminster Abbey, 1961–63', *Archaeologia Aeliana*, 4th series, **42** (1964), 95–171.

Hare 1993: John Hare, 'Netley Abbey: Monastery, Mansion and Ruin', *Proceedings of the Hampshire Field Club and Archaeological Society*, **49** (1993), 207–27.

Harper-Bill 1980: C. Harper-Bill, 'Cistercian Visitation in the Late Middle Ages: The Case of Hailes Abbey', *Bulletin of the Institute of Historical Research*, **53** (1980), 103–14.

Harrison 1990: Stuart A. Harrison, *Byland Abbey* (English Heritage, London 1990).

Harrison 1995: Stuart Harrison, 'Kirkstall Abbey: The 12th-Century Tracery and Rose Window', in Lawrence R. Hoey (editor), *Yorkshire Monasticism: Archaeology, Art and Architecture from the 7th to 16th Centuries* (The British Archaeological Association Conference Transactions, **16**, 1995), 73–78.

Harrison and Barker 1987: Stuart Harrison and Paul Barker, 'Byland Abbey, North Yorkshire: The West Front and Rose Window Reconstructed', *Journal of the British Archaeological Association*, **140** (1987), 134–51.

Harrison, Morris and Robinson 1998: Stuart A. Harrison, Richard K. Morris and David M. Robinson, 'A Fourteenth-Century Pulpitum Screen at Tintern Abbey, Monmouthshire', *Antiquaries Journal*, **78** (1998).

Harrison and Thurlby 1997: Stuart Harrison and Malcolm Thurlby, 'An Architectural History', in Shoesmith and Richardson 1997, 45–62.

Hartshorne 1883: S. Hartshorne, 'On Kirkstead Abbey, Lincolnshire', *Archaeological Journal*, **40** (1883), 287–88.

Hays 1963: Rhys W. Hays, *The History of the Abbey of Aberconway 1186–1537* (Cardiff 1963).

Henry 1885: David Henry, 'Glenluce Abbey', *Archaeological Collections Relating to Ayrshire and Galloway*, **5** (Edinburgh 1885),

125–88.

Hill 1968: Bennett D. Hill, *English Cistercian Monasteries and their Patrons in the Twelfth Century* (Urbana 1968).

Hill 1980: Bennett D. Hill, 'The Beginnings of the First French Foundations of the Norman Abbey of Savigny', *American Historical Review*, 31 (1980), 130–52.

Hillaby 1988–90: Joe Hillaby, '"The House of Houses": The Cistercians of Dore and the Origins of the Polygonal Chapter House', *Transactions of the Woolhope Naturalists' Field Club*, 46 (1988–90), 209–43.

Hills 1860: G. M. Hills, 'Buildwas Abbey', *Collectanea Archaeologica*, 1 (1860), 39–112.

Hills 1865: G. M. Hills, 'Croxden Abbey and its Chronicle', *Journal of the British Archaeological Association*, 21 (1865), 294–315.

Hills 1872: [Gordon M. Hills], 'Bindon Abbey', *Journal of the British Archaeological Association*, 28 (1872), 298–301.

Hinton 1977: David A. Hinton, 'Excavation at Beaulieu Abbey, 1977', *Proceedings of the Hampshire Field Club and Archaeological Society*, 34 (1977), 49–52.

Hirst, Walsh and Wright 1983: S. M. Hirst, D. A. Walsh and S. M. Wright, *Bordesley Abbey II: Second Report on Excavations at Bordesley Abbey, Redditch, Hereford–Worcestershire* (British Archaeological Reports, 111, 1983).

Hockey 1970: S. F. Hockey, *Quarr Abbey and its Lands, 1132–1631* (Leicester 1970).

Hockey 1976: Frederick Hockey, *Beaulieu: King John's Abbey* (Beaulieu 1976).

Hodgson 1907: T. H. Hodgson, 'Excavations at Holmcultram', *Transactions of the Cumberland and Westmorland Antiquarian and Archaeological Society*, new series, 7 (1907), 262–68.

Hodkinson 1905: Edward Hodkinson, 'Notes on the Architecture of Basingwerk Abbey, Flintshire', *Journal of the Chester and North Wales Architectural and Archaeological Society*, new series, 11 (1905), 169–77.

Hoey 1993: Lawrence R. Hoey, 'Croxden Abbey', in John Madison (editor), *Medieval Art and Architecture at Lichfield* (The British Archaeological Association Conference Transactions, 13, 1993), 36–49.

Hoey 1995: Lawrence R. Hoey, 'The 13th-Century Choir and Transepts of Rievaulx Abbey', in Lawrence R. Hoey (editor), *Yorkshire Monasticism: Archaeology, Art and Architecture from the 7th to 16th Centuries* (The British Archaeological Association Conference Transactions, 16, 1995), 97–116.

Holdsworth 1980: Christopher Holdsworth, 'A Cistercian Abbey and its Neighbours', *History Today*, 30 (1980), 32–37.

Holdsworth 1986a: Christopher Holdsworth, 'The Chronology and Character of Early Cistercian Legislation on Art and Architecture', in Norton and Park 1986, 40–55.

Holdsworth 1986b: Christopher Holdsworth, 'St Bernard and England', in R. Allen Brown (editor), *Anglo-Norman Studies,* 8 (Woodbridge 1986), 138–53.

Holdsworth 1989: Christopher J. Holdsworth, 'The Cistercians in Devon', in Christopher Harper-Bill, Christopher J. Holdsworth and Janet L. Nelson (editors), *Studies in Medieval History Presented to R. Allen Brown* (Woodbridge 1989), 179–91.

Holdsworth 1990: Christopher Holdsworth, *The Piper and the Tune: Medieval Patrons and Monks* (The Stenton Lecture 1990, Reading 1991).

Holdsworth 1992: Christopher Holdsworth, 'Royal Cistercians: Beaulieu, Her Daughters and Rewley', in P. R. Coss and S. D. Lloyd (editors), *Thirteenth-Century England IV* (Woodbridge 1992), 139–50.

Holdsworth 1994: Christopher Holdsworth, 'The Church', in Edmund King (editor), *The Anarchy of King Stephen's Reign* (Oxford 1994), 207–29.

Honeybourne 1952: M. B. Honeybourne, 'The Abbey of St Mary Graces, Tower Hill', *Transactions of the London and Middlesex Archaeological Society*, 11 (1952), 16–26.

Hope 1891: W. H. St John Hope, 'Notes on the Architectural History and Arrangements of Louth Park Abbey', *Lincoln Record Society*, 1 (1891), 1–85

Hope 1894: W. H. St John Hope, 'Sibton Abbey', *Proceedings of the Suffolk Institute of Archaeology and Natural History*, 8 (1894), 54–60.

Hope 1900a: W. H. St John Hope, 'Fountains Abbey', *Yorkshire Archaeological Journal*, 15 (1900), 269–402.

Hope 1900b: W. H. St John Hope, 'The Abbey of St Mary in Furness, Lancashire', *Transactions of the Cumberland and Westmorland Antiquarian and Archaeological Society*, 16 (1900), 221–302.

Hope and Bilson 1907: W. H. St John Hope and John Bilson, *Architectural Description of Kirkstall Abbey* (Thoresby Society Publications, 16, Leeds 1907).

Hope and Brakspear 1906: W. H. St John Hope and Harold Brakspear, 'The Cistercian Abbey of Beaulieu, in the County of Southampton', *Archaeological Journal*, 63 (1906), 129–86.

Hope and Brakspear 1911: W. H. St John Hope and Harold Brakspear, 'Jervaulx Abbey', *Yorkshire Archaeological Journal*, 21 (1911), 303–44.

Howlett 1884–90: R. Howlett (editor), *Chronicles of the Reigns of Stephen, Henry II, and Richard I*, 4 volumes (Rolls Series, 82, London 1884–90).

Hughes 1894–95: Harold Hughes, 'Valle Crucis Abbey', *Archaeologia Cambrensis*, series 5, 11 (1894), 169–85, 257–75; 12 (1895), 5–17.

Hughes 1895: Harold Hughes, 'The Architectural History of St. Mary's Church, Conway', *Archaeologia Cambrensis*, series 5, 12 (1895), 161–79.

Hutcheson 1887–88: A. Hutcheson, 'Notes on the Recent Discovery of Pavement and Flooring Tiles at the Abbey of Coupar Angus and the Cathedral of St Andrews', *Proceedings of the Society of Antiquaries of Scotland*, 22 (1887–88), 146–48.

Innes 1837: Cosmo Innes (editor), *Liber Sancte Marie de Melros* (London 1837).

Innes 1849: Cosmo Innes (editor), *Registrum S. Marie de Neubotle* (Edinburgh 1849).

James 1953: Bruno Scott James (translator), *The Letters of St Bernard of Clairvaux* (London 1953).

James, Brooke and Mynors 1983: M. R. James (editor), *Walter Map, 'De Nugis Curialium': Courtiers' Trifles*, revised by C. N. L. Brooke and R. A. B. Mynors (Oxford 1983).

James 1978: Terrence James, 'A Survey of the Fishponds, Watercourses and other Earthworks at the Site of Whitland Abbey and Iron Forge', *Carmarthenshire Antiquary*, 14 (1978), 71–78.

Jansen 1984: Virginia Jansen, 'Architectural Remains of King John's Abbey, Beaulieu (Hampshire)', in Meredith P. Lillich (editor), *Studies in Cistercian Art and Architecture: Volume Two* (Cistercian Studies Series, 69, Kalamazoo 1984), 76–114.

Jones and Williams 1891: M. C. Jones and Stephen W. Williams, 'Excavations on the Site of Strata Marcella Abbey', *Montgomeryshire Collections*, 25 (1891), 149–96.

Kinder 1997: Terryl N. Kinder, *L'Europe Cistercienne* (La Pierre-qui-Vire 1997).

King 1990: Edmund King, 'The Foundation of Pipewell Abbey, Northamptonshire', *Haskins Society Journal*, **2** (1990), 167–77.

King 1973: H. Peter King, 'Cistercian Financial Organization, 1335–1392', *Journal of Ecclesiastical History*, **24** (1973), 127–43.

King 1976: P. King, 'Coupar Angus and Cîteaux', *Innes Review*, **27** (1976), 46–69.

King 1991: Peter King, 'Scottish Abbeys and the Cistercian Financial System in the Fourteenth Century', *Innes Review*, **42** (1991), 68–71.

Klemperer 1995: W. D. Klemperer, 'Dieulacres Abbey', *West Midlands Archaeology*, **38** (1995), 66–72.

Knowles 1948–59: David Knowles, *The Religious Orders in England*, 3 volumes (Cambridge 1948–59).

Knowles 1963: David Knowles, *The Monastic Order in England*, 2nd edition (Cambridge 1963).

Knowles and Hadcock 1971: David Knowles and R. Neville Hadcock, *Medieval Religious Houses: England and Wales*, 2nd edition (London 1971).

Knowles and St Joseph 1952: David Knowles and J. K. S. St Joseph, *Monastic Sites from the Air* (Cambridge 1952).

Ladds 1914: S. Inskip Ladds, 'Sawtry Abbey, Huntingdonshire', *Cambridge and Huntingdonshire Archaeological Society Transactions*, **3** (1914), 295–322, 339–374.

Lawrence 1986: Anne Lawrence, 'English Cistercian Manuscripts of the Twelfth Century', in Norton and Park 1986, 284–98.

Lawrence 1960: C. H. Lawrence, 'Stephen of Lexington and Cistercian University Studies in the Thirteenth Century', *Journal of Ecclesiastical History*, **9** (1960), 164–78.

Lawrence 1989: C. H. Lawrence, *Medieval Monasticism: Forms of Religious Life in Western Europe in the Middle Ages*, 2nd edition (London 1989).

Leclercq and Casey 1970: 'Cistercians and Cluniacs: St Bernard's Apologia to Abbot William', introduced by J. Leclercq and translated by Michael Casey, in *The Works of St Bernard of Clairvaux, I, Treatises I* (Cistercian Fathers Series, **1**, Spencer 1970).

Leclercq, Talbot and Rochais 1957–77: Jean Leclercq, C. H. Talbot and H. M. Rochais (editors), *Sancti Bernardi Opera*, 8 volumes (Rome 1957–77).

Lee 1888: F. G. Lee, 'Thame Abbey', *Building News*, **30** (1888) 455.

Lekai 1977: Louis J. Lekai, *The Cistercians: Ideals and Reality* (Kent, Ohio 1977).

Liddle and O'Brien 1995: Peter Liddle and Lorna O'Brien, 'The Archaeology of the Abbeys and Priories of Leicestershire', *Transactions of the Leicestershire Archaeological and Historical Society*, **69** (1995), 1–21.

Lindley 1954–56: E. S. Lindley, 'Kingswood Abbey, its Lands and Mills', *Transactions of the Bristol and Gloucestershire Archaeological Society*, **73** (1954), 115–91; **74** (1955), 36–59; **75** (1956), 73–104.

Little 1978: Lester K. Little, *Religious Poverty and the Profit Economy in Medieval Europe* (London 1978).

Loftie 1882–88: A. G. Loftie, 'Calder Abbey', *Transactions of the Cumberland and Westmorland Antiquarian and Archaeological Society*, **6** (1882), 368–72; **8** (1886), 467–504; **9** (1888), 206–39.

Loftie 1892: A. G. Loftie, *Calder Abbey, its Ruins and History* (London 1892).

Lovegrove 1936: E. W. Lovegrove, 'Valle Crucis Abbey; its Position in Monasticism: the Men who Built it', *Archaeologia Cambrensis*, **91** (1936), 1–14.

Lynam 1885: G. Lynam, 'Recent Excavations of the Site of Hulton Abbey', *Journal of the British Archaeological Association*, **41** (1885), 65–71.

Lynam 1911: C. Lynam, *The Abbey of St Mary, Croxden, Staffordshire* (London 1911).

McCann 1972: J. McCann (editor and translator), *The Rule of St Benedict* (London 1972; frequently reprinted).

MacGibbon and Ross 1896–97: David MacGibbon and Thomas Ross, *The Ecclesiastical Architecture of Scotland*, 3 volumes (Edinburgh 1896–97).

MacKenzie-Walcott 1876: E. C. MacKenzie-Walcott, 'Old Cleeve Abbey', *Transactions of the Royal Institute of British Architects* (1876), 103–27.

McNeil and Turner 1987–88: R. McNeil and R. C. Turner, 'An Architectural and Topographical Survey of Vale Royal Abbey', *Journal of the Chester Archaeological Society*, **70** (1987–88), 51–79.

McNulty 1939: J. McNulty, 'Sallay Abbey 1148–1536', *Transactions of the Lancashire and Cheshire Antiquities Society*, **54** (1939), 194–204.

McRoberts 1966–69: David McRoberts, 'Culross in the Diocese of Dunblane', *Journal of the Society of Friends of Dunblane Cathedral*, **10** (1966–69), 91–98.

McWilliam 1978: Colin McWilliam, *Buildings of Scotland: Lothian* (Harmondsworth 1978).

Malone 1984: Carolyn Marino Malone, 'Abbey Dore: English Versus French Design', in Meredith P. Lillich (editor), *Studies in Cistercian Art and Architecture: Volume Two* (Cistercian Studies Series, **69**, Kalamazoo 1984), 50–75.

Martindale 1913: J. H. Martindale, 'The Abbey of St Mary, Holme Cultram', *Transactions of the Cumberland and Westmorland Antiquarian and Archaeological Society*, new series, **13** (1913), 244–51.

Matarasso 1993: P. Matarasso (editor and translator), *The Cistercian World: Monastic Writings of the Twelfth Century* (Harmondsworth 1993).

Mauchline, Hart-Davis and Meller 1996: Mary Mauchline, Duff Hart-Davis and Hugh Meller, *Buckland Abbey*, revised edition (National Trust, London 1996).

Meekings 1979: C. A. F. Meekings (edited by R. F. Hunnisett), 'The Early Years of Netley Abbey', *Journal of Ecclesiastical History*, **30** (1979), 1–37.

Middleton 1881–82: J. Henry Middleton, 'Flaxley Abbey: The Existing Remains', *Transactions of the Bristol and Gloucestershire Archaeological Society*, **6** (1881–82), 280–83.

Miller 1972: A. T. Miller, *Short Guide to Holm Cultram Abbey*, 2nd edition (Holm Cultram 1972).

Mills 1984–88: Peter Mills, 'The Royal Mint: First Results', *The London Archaeologist*, **5** (1984–88), 69–77.

Moorhouse and Wrathmell 1987: Stephen Moorhouse and Stuart Wrathmell, *Kirkstall Abbey Volume I: The 1950–64 Excavations — A Reassessment* (Yorkshire Archaeology, **1**, Wakefield 1987).

Morris 1997: Richard K. Morris, 'European Prodigy or Regional Eccentric?: The Rebuilding of St Augustine's Abbey Church, Bristol', in Laurence Keen (editor), *'Almost the Richest City': Bristol in the Middle Ages* (The British Archaeological Association Conference Transactions, **19**, 1997), 41–56.

Morton 1832: J. Morton, *The Monastic Annals of Teviotdale* (Edinburgh 1832).

Nairn and Pevsner 1965: Ian Nairn and Nikolaus Pevsner, *Buildings of England: Sussex* (Harmondsworth 1965).

Nairn and Pevsner 1971: Ian Nairn and Nikolaus Pevsner, *Buildings of England: Surrey*, 2nd edition revised by Bridget Cherry (Harmondsworth 1971).

Negri 1981: D. Negri, *Abbazie Cistercensi in Italia* (Pistoia 1981).

Newman 1969: John Newman, *Buildings of England: North East and East Kent* (Harmondsworth 1969).

Newman 1995: John Newman, *The Buildings of Wales: Glamorgan* (London 1995).

Newman 1996: Martha G. Newman, *The Boundaries of Charity: Cistercian Culture and Ecclesiastical Reform, 1098–1180* (Stanford 1996).

Nicholl 1964: D. Nicholl, *Thurstan, Archbishop of York 1114–1140* (York 1964).

Norton and Park 1986: Christopher Norton and David Park (editors), *Cistercian Art and Architecture in the British Isles* (Cambridge 1986).

O'Callaghan 1995: Brian O'Callaghan, 'An Analysis of the Architecture of the Cistercian Church at Abbey Dore', in David Whitehead (editor), *Medieval Art, Architecture and Archaeology at Hereford* (The British Archaeological Association Conference Transactions, **15**, 1995), 94–104.

O'Sullivan 1947: Jeremiah F. O'Sullivan, *Cistercian Settlements in Wales and Monmouthshire, 1140–1540* (New York 1947).

O'Sullivan 1995: Jerry O'Sullivan, 'Abbey, Market and Cemetery: Topographical Notes on Coupar Angus in Perthshire', *Proceedings of the Society of Antiquaries of Scotland*, **125** (1995), 1045–68.

Paul 1904: R. W. Paul, 'The Church and Monastery of Abbey Dore, Herefordshire', *Transactions of the Bristol and Gloucestershire Archaeological Society*, **27** (1904), 117–26.

Paul 1927: R. W. Paul, 'Abbey Dore Church, Herefordshire', *Archaeologia Cambrensis*, **82** (1927), 269–75.

Peers 1929: C. R. Peers, 'Rievaulx Abbey: The Shrine in the Chapter House', *Archaeological Journal*, **86** (1929), 20–28.

Pendleton 1915: Basil Pendleton, *Notes on the Cistercian Abbey of St Mary, Vale Royal, Cheshire* (Privately Printed 1915).

Pennington 1970: M. Basil Pennington (editor),

The Cistercian Spirit: A Symposium in Honour of Thomas Merton (Cistercian Studies Series, **3**, Spencer 1970).

Pennington 1977: M. Basil Pennington (editor), *Saint Bernard of Clairvaux* (Cistercian Studies, **28**, Kalamazoo 1977).

Perceval 1880: C. S. Perceval, 'Charters and Other Documents Relating to the Abbey of Robertsbridge', *Archaeologia*, **45** (1880), 427–61.

Pevsner 1966: Nikolaus Pevsner, *Buildings of England: Yorkshire, The North Riding* (Harmondsworth 1966).

Pevsner 1967: Nikolaus Pevsner, *Buildings of England: Cumberland and Westmorland* (Harmondsworth 1967).

Pevsner 1968: Nikolaus Pevsner, *Buildings of England: Bedfordshire and the County of Huntingdon and Peterborough* (Harmondsworth 1968).

Pevsner 1969: Nikolaus Pevsner, *Buildings of England: North Lancashire* (London 1969).

Pevsner 1974: Nikolaus Pevsner, *Buildings of England: Staffordshire* (Harmondsworth 1974).

Pevsner and Harris 1989: Nikolaus Pevsner and John Harris, *Buildings of England: Lincolnshire*, 2nd edition revised by Nicholas Antram (London 1989).

Pevsner and Hubbard 1971: Nikolaus Pevsner and Edward Hubbard, *Buildings of England: Cheshire* (Harmondsworth 1971).

Pevsner and Radcliffe 1965: Nikolaus Pevsner and Enid Radcliffe, *Buildings of England: Essex*, 2nd edition (Harmondsworth 1965).

Pevsner and Radcliffe 1967: Nikolaus Pevsner and Enid Radcliffe, *Buildings of England: Yorkshire, The West Riding*, 2nd edition (Harmondsworth 1967).

Pevsner and Richmond 1992: Nikolaus Pevsner and Ian A. Richmond, *Buildings of England: Northumberland*, 2nd edition revised by John Grundy, Grace McCombie, Peter Ryder and Humphrey Welfare (London 1992).

Pevsner and Wedgwood 1966: Nikolaus Pevsner and Alexandra Wedgwood, *Buildings of England: Warwickshire* (Harmondsworth 1966).

Pevsner and Williamson 1994: Nikolaus Pevsner and Elizabeth Williamson, *Buildings of England: Buckinghamshire*, 2nd edition (London 1994).

Pewy 1888: G. G. Pewy, 'The Visitation of the Monastery of Thame', *English Historical Review*, **3** (1888), 704–22.

Pierce 1950–51: T. Jones Pierce, 'Strata Florida

Abbey', *Ceredigion*, **1** (1950–51), 18–33.

Platt 1969: Colin Platt, *The Monastic Grange in Medieval England* (London 1969).

Potter 1847: Joseph Potter, *Remains of Ancient Monastic Architecture in England: Represented in a Series of Views, Plans, Elevations, Sections and Details* (London 1847).

Poulle 1994: Béatrice Poulle, 'Savigny and England', in David Bates and Anne Curry (editors), *England and Normandy in the Middle Ages* (London 1994), 159–68.

Powell 1973: W. R. Powell, 'Stratford Langthorne', in The Victoria History of the Counties of England, *Essex*, **6** (Oxford 1973), 112–15.

Powicke 1950: F. M. Powicke (editor), *The Life of Ailred of Rievaulx by Walter Daniel* (London 1950; reprinted Oxford 1978).

Pressouyre 1994: Léon Pressouyre (editor), *L'Espace Cistercien* (Paris 1994).

Pressouyre and Kinder 1992: Léon Pressouyre and Terryl N. Kinder (editors), *Saint Bernard & Le Monde Cistercien*, new edition (Paris 1992).

Price 1952: G. V. Price, *Valle Crucis Abbey* (Liverpool 1952).

Radford 1982: C. A. Ralegh Radford, 'The Cistercian Abbey of Cwmhir, Radnorshire', *Archaeologia Cambrensis*, **131** (1982), 58–76.

Rahtz and Hirst 1976: Philip Rahtz and Susan Hirst, *Bordesley Abbey, Redditch, Hereford-Worcestershire: First Report on Excavations 1969–1973* (British Archaeological Reports, **23**, Oxford 1976).

RCAHMCS 1912: Royal Commission on the Ancient and Historical Monuments and Constructions of Scotland, *Wigtown* (Edinburgh 1912).

RCAHMCS 1914: Royal Commission on the Ancient and Historical Monuments and Constructions of Scotland, *Kirkcudbright* (Edinburgh 1914).

RCAHMCS 1929: Royal Commission on the Ancient and Historical Monuments and Constructions of Scotland, *Midlothian and West Lothian* (Edinburgh 1929).

RCAHMCS 1933: Royal Commission on the Ancient and Historical Monuments and Constructions of Scotland, *Fife, Kinross, and Clackmannan* (Edinburgh 1933).

RCAHMCW 1913: Royal Commission on the Ancient and Historical Monuments and Constructions in Wales and Monmouthshire,

County of Radnor (London 1913).

RCAHMS 1971: Royal Commission on the Ancient and Historical Monuments of Scotland, *Argyll 1: Kintyre* (Edinburgh 1971).

RCAHMW 1956: Royal Commission on Ancient and Historical Monuments in Wales and Monmouthshire, *Caernarvonshire 1: East* (London 1956).

RCAMS 1956: Royal Commission on the Ancient Monuments of Scotland, *Roxburghshire,* 2 volumes (Edinburgh 1956).

RCHME 1912: Royal Commission on the Historical Monuments of England, *Buckinghamshire 1* (London 1912).

RCHME 1913: Royal Commission on the Historical Monuments of England, *Buckinghamshire 2* (London 1913).

RCHME 1916: Royal Commission on Historical Monuments England, *Essex 1, North West* (London 1916).

RCHME 1922: Royal Commission on Historical Monuments England, *Essex 3: North East* (London 1922).

RCHME 1926: Royal Commission on the Historical Monuments of England, *Huntingdonshire* (London 1926).

RCHME 1931: Royal Commission on Historical Monuments England, *Herefordshire 1: South-West* (London 1931)

RCHME 1952: Royal Commission on Historical Monuments of England, *Dorset 1: West* (London 1952).

RCHME 1970: Royal Commission on Historical Monuments of England, *Dorset 2, Part 2: South-East* (London 1970).

RCHME 1979: Royal Commission on the Historical Monuments of England, *Northampton 2: Archaeological Sites in Central Northamptonshire* (London 1979).

Rees 1849: [W. J. Rees], 'Account of Cwmhir Abbey, Radnorshire', *Archaeologia Cambrensis,* 4 (1849), 233–60.

Reeve 1892: J. Arthur Reeve, *A Monograph on the Abbey of St Mary of Fountains* (London 1892).

Remfry 1994: Paul Matin Remfry, *A Political History of Abbey Cwmhir and its Patrons, 1176 to 1282* (Malvern Link 1994).

Renn 1954: D. F. Renn, 'The *Enciente* Wall of Quarr Abbey', *Proceedings of the Isle of Wight Natural History and Archaeological Society,* 4 (1954), 350–51.

Reyerson 1988: K. L. Reyerson, 'The Way of Mary or that of Martha: Conceptions of the

Monastic Life at Savigny, 1112–1180', in A. Macleish (editor), *Medieval Studies at Minnesota,* 2 (St Cloud, Minnesota 1988), 34–42.

Reynolds 1964: P. K. Baillie Reynolds, *Croxden Abbey* (HMSO, London 1964).

Richardson 1851: E. Richardson, 'Vaudey Abbey', *Archaeological Journal,* 8 (1851), 210–11.

Richardson 1928–29: J. S. Richardson, 'A Thirteenth-Century Tile Kiln at North Berwick ... and Scottish Mediaeval Ornamented Floor Tiles', *Proceedings of the Society of Antiquaries of Scotland,* 63 (1928–29), 281–310.

Richardson 1994: J. S. Richardson, *Dundrennan Abbey,* new edition (Historic Scotland, Edinburgh 1994).

Richardson 1995: J. S. Richardson, *Sweetheart Abbey,* new edition (Historic Scotland, Edinburgh 1995).

Robinson 1993: David M. Robinson, 'Margam Abbey', in N. J. G. Pounds (editor), *The Cardiff Area* (Supplement to the *Archaeological Journal,* **150**, 1993), 54–60.

Robinson 1995a: David M. Robinson, *Tintern Abbey,* 3rd edition (Cadw, Cardiff 1995).

Robinson 1995b: David M. Robinson, *Cymer Abbey,* revised edition (Cadw, Cardiff 1995).

Robinson 1996a: David M. Robinson, 'The Twelfth-Century Church at Tintern Abbey', *Monmouthshire Antiquary,* 12 (1996), 35–39.

Robinson 1996b: David M. Robinson, *Basingwerk Abbey* (Cadw, Cardiff 1996).

Robinson 1997a: David M. Robinson, 'The Making of a Monument: The Office of Woods and its Successors at Tintern Abbey', *Monmouthshire Antiquary,* 13 (1997), 43–56.

Robinson 1997b: David M. Robinson, *Neath Abbey,* 3rd edition (Cadw, Cardiff 1997).

Robinson and Platt 1998: David M. Robinson and Colin Platt, *Strata Florida Abbey — Talley Abbey,* 2nd edition (Cadw, Cardiff 1998).

Rogers 1879–80: Charles Rogers (editor), *Rental Book of Coupar Angus with a Breviary of the Register,* 2 volumes (London 1879–80).

Round 1894–95: J. H. Round, 'The Abbeys of Coggeshall and Stratford Langthorne', *Transactions of the Essex Archaeological Society,* new series, 5 (1894–95), 139–43.

Roundell, 1858–63: H. Roundell, 'Biddlesden Abbey and its Lands', *Records of*

Buckinghamshire, 1 (1858), 275–87; 2 (1863), 33–38.

Rowe 1878: J. Brooking Rowe, *Contributions to a History of the Cistercian Houses of Devon* (Plymouth 1878).

Rowe 1884: J. Brooking Rowe, 'On Recent Excavations at Buckfast Abbey', *Transactions of the Devonshire Association,* 16 (1884), 590–94.

Rudd and West 1964: G. T. Rudd and B. B. West, 'Excavations at Warden Abbey in 1960 and 1961', *Bedford Archaeological Journal,* 2 (1964), 58–72.

Rusk 1930: J. M. Rusk, *History of the Parish and Abbey of Glenluce* (Edinburgh and London 1930).

Rye 1900: H. A. Rye, 'Rievaulx Abbey: Its Canals and Building Stones', *Archaeological Journal,* 57 (1900), 69–77.

Salter 1947–48: H. F. Salter, *The Thame Chartulary* (Oxfordshire Record Society, 25–26, 1947–48).

Salzman 1934–35: L. F. Salzman, 'Excavations at Robertsbridge Abbey', *Sussex Notes and Queries,* 5 (1934–35), 206–08.

Schaefer 1982: Jean Owens Schaefer, 'The Earliest Churches of the Cistercian Order', in Meredith Parsons Lillich (editor), *Studies in Cistercian Art and Architecture: Volume One* (Cistercian Studies Series, 66, Kalamazoo 1982), 1–12.

Scott 1988: J. G. Scott, 'The Origins of Dundrennan and Soulseat', *Transactions of the Dumfriesshire and Galloway Natural History and Antiquarian Society,* 63 (1988), 35–44.

Sheppard 1926–28: R. Sheppard, 'Meaux Abbey', *Transactions of the East Riding Antiquarian Society,* 26 (1926–28), 106–36.

Sherwin 1927: C. Sherwin, 'The History of Ford Abbey', *Reports and Transactions of the Devonshire Association,* 59 (1927), 249–64.

Sherwood and Pevsner 1974: Jennifer Sherwood and Nikolaus Pevsner, *Buildings of England: Oxfordshire* (Harmondsworth 1974).

Shoesmith 1979–81: R. Shoesmith, 'Survey Work at Dore Abbey', *Transactions of the Woolhope Naturalists' Field Club,* 43 (1979–81), 254–66.

Shoesmith and Richardson 1997: Ron Shoesmith and Ruth Richardson (editors), *A Definitive History of Dore Abbey* (Little Logaston 1997).

Simms 1950: R. S. Simms, 'Cleeve Abbey',

Archaeological Journal, **107** (1950), 118–19.

Simpson 1924–27: W. D. Simpson, 'The Celtic Monastery and Cistercian Abbey at Deer', *Transactions of the Scottish Ecclesiological Society*, **8** (1924–27), 179–86.

Sledmere 1914: E. Sledmere, *Abbey Dore, Herefordshire: Its Building and Restoration* (Hereford 1914).

Sommerfeldt 1978: John R. Sommerfeldt (editor), *Cistercian Ideals and Reality* (Cistercian Studies, 60, Kalamazoo 1978).

Sommerfeldt, 1992: John R. Sommerfeldt (editor), *Bernardus Magister: Papers Celebrating the Nonacentenary of the Birth of Saint Bernard of Clairvaux* (Cistercian Studies, 135, Spencer 1992).

Sparks 1978: J. A. Sparks, *In the Shadow of the Blackdowns: Life at the Cistercian Abbey of Dunkeswell and on its Manors and Estates 1201–1539* (Bradford on Avon 1978).

Squire 1969: A. Squire, *Aelred of Rievaulx: A Study* (London 1969).

Stacye 1883–84: J. Stacye, 'Roche Abbey', *Associated Architectural Societies' Reports and Papers*, **17** (1883–84), 39–54.

Stalley 1987: Roger Stalley, *The Cistercian Monasteries of Ireland* (London and New Haven 1987).

Steer 1949–50: F. W. Steer, 'A Short History of Tilty Abbey with an Account of Some Excavations on the Site in 1942', *Essex Review*, **58** (1949), 169–79; **59** (1950), 39–50, 95–100, 113–21.

Stéphan 1970: John Stéphan, *A History of Buckfast Abbey* (Bristol 1970).

Stevenson 1875: J. Stevenson (editor), *Radulphi de Coggeshall Chronicon Anglicanum* (Rolls Series, 66, London 1875).

Stone 1891: Percy G. Stone, *Architectural Antiquities of the Isle of Wight*, 2 volumes (London 1891).

Stringer 1980a: K. Stringer, 'A Cistercian Archive: The Earliest Charters of Sawtry Abbey', *Journal of the Society of Archivists*, **6** (1980), 325–34.

Stringer 1980b: Keith Stringer, 'Galloway and the Abbeys of Rievaulx and Dundrennan', *Transactions of the Dumfriesshire and Galloway Natural History and Antiquarian Society*, **55** (1980), 174–77.

Stuart 1872: John Stuart (editor), *Records of the Monastery of Kinloss* (Society of Antiquaries of Scotland, Edinburgh 1872).

Stubbs 1887–89: W. Stubbs (editor), *Willelmi Malmesbiriensis de Gestis Regum Anglorum*, 2 volumes (Rolls Series, **90**, London 1887–89).

Suydam 1976: Mary Suydam, 'Origins of the Savignac Order: Savigny's Role within Twelfth-Century Monastic Reform', *Revue Bénédictine*, **86** (1976), 94–108.

Swietek 1992: Francis R. Swietek, 'The Role of Bernard of Clairvaux in the Union of Savigny with Cîteaux: A Reconsideration', in Sommerfeldt 1992, 289–302.

Talbot 1967: C. H. Talbot (editor), *Letters from the English Abbots to the Chapter at Cîteaux 1442–1521* (Camden Society, series 4, **4**, 1967).

Talbot 1986: C. H. Talbot, 'The Cistercian Attitude towards Art: The Literary Evidence', in Norton and Park 1986, 56–64.

Talbot 1939: Hugh Talbot, *The Cistercian Abbeys of Scotland* (London 1939).

Taylor 1949: A. J. Taylor, 'On the Cloister of Vale Royal Abbey', *Journal of the Chester and North Wales Archaeological Society*, new series, **37** (1949), 295–97.

Tester 1973: P. J. Tester, 'Excavations at Boxley Abbey', *Archaeologia Cantiana*, **88** (1973), 129–58.

Thomas 1997: Graham C. G. Thomas (editor), *The Charters of the Abbey of Ystrad Marchell* (Aberystwyth 1997).

Thompson 1953: A. Hamilton Thompson, *Netley Abbey* (HMSO, London 1953).

Thompson 1962: F. H. Thompson, 'Excavations at the Cistercian Abbey of Vale Royal, Cheshire, 1958', *Antiquaries Journal*, **42** (1962), 183–207.

Thomson 1933: G. D. Thomson, 'Woburn Abbey and the Dissolution of the Monasteries', *Transactions of the Royal Historical Society*, series 4, **16** (1933), 129–60.

Thorpe 1994: L. Thorpe (editor and translator), *Gerald of Wales: The Journey Through Wales* (Harmondsworth 1994).

Thurlby 1993: Malcolm Thurlby, 'The Early Gothic Transepts of Lichfield Cathedral', in John Maddison (editor), *Medieval Art and Architecture at Lichfield* (The British Archaeological Association Conference Transactions, 13, 1993), 50–64.

Thurlby 1995: Malcolm Thurlby, 'Some Design Aspects of Kirkstall Abbey', in Lawrence R. Hoey (editor), *Yorkshire Monasticism: Archaeology, Art and Architecture from the 7th to 16th Centuries* (The British Archaeological Association Conference Transactions, 16, 1995), 62–72.

Tobin 1995: Stephen Tobin, *The Cistercians: Monks and Monasteries of Europe* (London 1995).

Tomkinson 1997: John L. Tomkinson, *A History of Hulton Abbey* (Staffordshire Archaeological Studies, 10, Stoke on Trent 1997).

Trollope 1873–74: Edward Trollope, 'The Architectural Remains of Louth Park Abbey', *Associated Architectural Societies' Reports and Papers*, **12** (1873–74), 22–25.

Turnbull 1841: W. B. D. D. Turnbull, *The Chartularies of Balmerino and Lindores* (Abbotsford Club, **22**, 1841).

Van der Meer 1965: Frederic Van der Meer, *Atlas de l'Ordre Cistercien* (Paris and Brussels 1965).

Van Engen 1986: J. Van Engen, 'The "Crisis of Cenobitism" Reconsidered: Benedictine Monasticism in the Years 1050–1150', *Speculum*, **61** (1986), 269–304.

VCH Bedfordshire 1904–12: *The Victoria History of the Counties of England: Bedfordshire*, **1** (London 1904); **3** (London 1912).

VCH Buckinghamshire 1905–27: *The Victoria History of the Counties of England: Buckinghamshire*, **1** (London 1905); **4** (London 1927).

VCH Chester 1980: *The Victoria History of the Counties of England: Chester*, **3** (Oxford 1980).

VCH Cumberland 1905: *The Victoria History of the Counties of England: Cumberland*, **2** (London 1905).

VCH Dorset 1908: *The Victoria History of the Counties of England: Dorset*, **2** (London 1908).

VCH Essex 1907: *The Victoria History of the Counties of England: Essex*, **2** (London 1907).

VCH Gloucester 1907: *The Victoria History of the Counties of England: Gloucester*, **2** (London 1907).

VCH Hampshire 1903–12: *The Victoria History of the Counties of England: Hampshire and the Isle of Wight*, **2** (London 1903); **3** (London 1908); **4** (London 1911); **5** (London 1912).

VCH Kent 1962: *The Victoria History of the Counties of England: Kent*, **2** (London 1962).

VCH Leicestershire 1954: *The Victoria History of the Counties of England: Leicestershire*, **2** (Oxford 1954).

VCH Lincolnshire 1906: *The Victoria History*

of the Counties of England: Lincolnshire, **2** (London 1906).

VCH Nottinghamshire 1910: *The Victoria History of the Counties of England: Nottinghamshire*, **2** (London 1910).

VCH Oxfordshire 1907–72: *The Victoria History of the Counties of England: Oxfordshire*, **2** (London 1907); **7** (London 1962); **10** (London 1972).

VCH Shropshire 1973: *The Victoria History of the Counties of England: Shropshire*, **2** (Oxford 1973).

VCH Staffordshire 1970: *The Victoria History of the Counties of England: Staffordshire*, **3** (Oxford 1970).

VCH Sussex 1907–37: *The Victoria History of the Counties of England: Sussex*, **2** (London 1907); **9** (London 1937).

VCH Warwick 1908–51: *The Victoria History of the Counties of England: Warwick*, **2** (London 1908); **6** (Oxford 1951).

VCH Wiltshire 1956: *The Victoria History of the Counties of England: Wiltshire*, **3** (Oxford 1956).

Venables 1873–74: Edmund Venables, 'Louth Park Abbey', *Associated Architectural Societies' Reports and Papers*, **12** (1873–74), 41–55.

Verey 1976: David Verey, *The Buildings of England: Gloucestershire, The Vale and the Forest of Dean*, 2nd edition (Harmondsworth 1976).

Walbran 1852–53: J. R. Walbran, 'On Recent Excavations at Sawley Abbey in Yorkshire', *Associated Architectural Societies' Reports and Papers*, **2** (1852–53), 72–89.

Walbran 1863–64: J. R. Walbran, 'Some Observations on the History and Structure of the Abbey of the Blessed Mary of Byland', *Associated Architectural Societies' Reports and Papers*, **7** (1863–64), 219–34.

Walbran 1876: J. R. Walbran, 'On the Recent Excavations at Sawley Abbey, Yorkshire', *Publications of the Surtees Society*, **67** (1876), 159–77.

Walbran and Fowler 1863–1918: J. R. Walbran and J. T. Fowler (editors), *Memorials of the Abbey of St Mary of Fountains*, 3 volumes (Surtees Society, **42, 67, 130**, 1863–1918).

Walcott 1875–76: Mackenzie E. C. Walcott, 'Old Cleeve Abbey', *Journal of the Royal Institute of British Architects*, **26** (1875–76), 103–38.

Walsh 1979: D. A. Walsh, 'A Rebuilt Cloister at Bordesley Abbey', *Journal of the British Archaeological Association*, **132** (1979), 42–49.

Walters 1923: F. A. Walters, 'The Rebuilding of Buckfast Abbey', *Architects' Journal* (1923), 258–67.

Ward Perkins 1941: J. B. Ward Perkins, 'A Late Thirteenth-Century Tile-Pavement at Cleeve Abbey', *Proceedings of the Somersetshire Archaeological and Natural History Society*, **87** (1941), 39–55.

Wardrop 1987: Joan Wardrop, *Fountains Abbey and its Benefactors 1132–1300* (Cistercian Studies, **91**, Kalamazoo 1987).

Wilde 1871: J. Wilde, *The History of Castle Bytham, Vaudey Abbey* (London 1871).

Williams 1965: B. C. J. Williams, 'Garendon Abbey', *Bulletin of the Loughborough and District Archaeological Society*, **8** (1965), 3–14.

Williams 1969: B. C. J. Williams, 'Summary of the Excavations at Garendon Abbey for 1966–7–8', *Bulletin of the Loughborough and District Archaeological Society*, **10** (1969), 9–11, 17, 26.

Williams 1970–78: David H. Williams, 'Grace Dieu Abbey: An Exploratory Excavation', *Monmouthshire Antiquary*, **3** (1970–78), 55–58.

Williams 1976a: David H. Williams, *White Monks in Gwent and the Border* (Pontypool 1976).

Williams 1976b: David H. Williams, 'The White Monks in Powys II (Strata Marcella)', *Cistercian Studies*, **11** (1976), 155–91.

Williams 1981a: David H. Williams, 'Basingwerk Abbey', *Cîteaux*, **32** (1981), 87–113.

Williams 1981b: David H. Williams, 'The Cistercians in West Wales: I. Cymer Abbey', *Archaeologia Cambrensis*, **130** (1981), 36–58.

Williams 1984: David H. Williams, *The Welsh Cistercians*, 2nd edition, 2 volumes (Caldey Island 1984).

Williams 1990: David H. Williams, *Atlas of Cistercian Lands in Wales* (Cardiff 1990).

Williams 1991: David H. Williams, 'Layfolk within Cistercian Precincts', in Judith Loades (editor), *Monastic Studies 2* (Bangor 1991), 87–117.

Williams 1998: David H. Williams, *The Cistercians in the Early Middle Ages* (Leominster 1998).

Williams 1889: Stephen W. Williams, *The Cistercian Abbey of Strata Florida* (London 1889).

Williams 1892: Stephen W. Williams, 'The Cistercian Abbey of Strata Marcella', *Archaeologia Cambrensis*, series 5, **9** (1892), 1–17.

Williams 1894–95: Stephen W. Williams, 'The Cistercian Abbey of Cwmhir, Radnorshire', *Transactions of the Honourable Society of Cymmrodorion* (1894–95), 61–98.

Wilson 1986: Christopher Wilson, 'The Cistercians as "Missionaries of Gothic" in Northern England', in Norton and Park 1986, 86–116.

Wilson 1991: Christopher Wilson, 'The Early Thirteenth-Century Architecture of Beverley Minster: Cathedral Splendours and Cistercian Austerities', in P. R. Coss and S. D. Lloyd (editors), *Thirteenth Century England III* (Woodbridge 1991), 181–95.

Wilson 1839: William D. Wilson (editor), *Ferrerii Historia Abbatum de Kynlos* (Edinburgh 1839).

Winkless 1990: Doreen Winkless, *Hailes: The Story of a Gloucestershire Abbey* (Stocksfield 1990).

Wise 1985: Philip J. Wise (editor), *Hulton Abbey: A Century of Excavations* (Staffordshire Archaeological Studies, **2**, Stoke on Trent 1985).

Wood and Richardson 1995: Marguerite Wood and J. S. Richardson, *Melrose Abbey*, new edition (Historic Scotland, Edinburgh 1995).

Woodward 1966: G. W. O. Woodward, *The Dissolution of the Monasteries* (London 1966).

Woodward 1866: J. M. Woodward, *The History of Bordesley Abbey* (London 1866).

Wrathmell 1987: Stuart Wrathmell, *Kirkstall Abbey: The Guest House*, 2nd edition (Wakefield 1987).

Forthcoming Publications

Fawcett (forthcoming): Richard Fawcett, 'Cistercian Archaeology in Scotland', in Benoit Chauvin (editor), *Proceedings of the Congrés Anselme Dimier* (forthcoming).

Fergusson, Harrison and Coppack (forthcoming): Peter Fergusson, Stuart Harrison and Glyn Coppack, *Community and Memory: An Architectural History of Rievaulx Abbey* (forthcoming).

McGee and Perkins (forthcoming): Christine McGee and Joanne Perkins, 'Rufford Abbey', in J. Alexander (editor), *Southwell and Nottinghamshire: Medieval Art, Architecture and Industry* (forthcoming).

INDEX

Page numbers in **_bold italics_** refer to illustrations

Abbreviations: (E), England;
(F), France; (G), Germany; (I), Italy;
(S), Scotland; (W), Wales